This book examines the intellectual career of St John Fisher (1469–1535), the early sixteenth-century bishop of Rochester (England) and victim of Henry VIII's Reformation, whose numerous writings included one of the most influential refutations of Martin Luther of the century. This book places his writings in the context of the contemporary movements of Renaissance and Reformation, and offers a new account of his intellectual position and achievement. It argues that he successfully combined whole-hearted receptiveness to Renaissance humanism with unshakeable commitment to the traditional teachings of the Catholic Church, and restores him to his rightful place as one of the most important English scholars of his age.

The Theology of John Fisher

The Theology
of John Fisher

RICHARD REX

Research Fellow,
St John's College, Cambridge

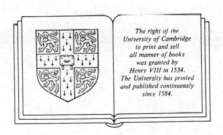

The right of the
University of Cambridge
to print and sell
all manner of books
was granted by
Henry VIII in 1534.
The University has printed
and published continuously
since 1584.

CAMBRIDGE UNIVERSITY PRESS

CAMBRIDGE

NEW YORK PORT CHESTER

MELBOURNE SYDNEY

Published by the Press Syndicate of the University of Cambridge
The Pitt Building, Trumpington Street, Cambridge CB2 1RP
40 West 20th Street, New York, NY 10011, USA
10 Stamford Road, Oakleigh, Melbourne 3166, Australia

First published 1991

Printed in Great Britain at the University Press, Cambridge

British Library cataloguing in publication data

Rex, Richard *1961–*
The theology of John Fisher.
1. Catholic Church. Fisher, John, Saint, 1469–1535
I. Title
282.092

Library of Congress cataloguing in publication data

Rex. Richard.
The theology of John Fisher / Richard Rex.
p. cm.
Revision of thesis (doctoral – University of Cambridge).
Includes bibliographical references and index.
ISBN 0 521 39177 6
1. Fisher, John, Saint, 1469–1535. 2. Catholic Church – England –
Doctrines – History – 16th century. I. Title.
BX4700.F34R29 1991
230'.2'092 – DC20 90-40259

ISBN 0 521 39177 6 hardback

BT

Contents

To Brendan Bradshaw

Acknowledgments

Among all those who have helped and encouraged me over the past four years, two people stand out above all others. First is my wife Bettina, who was not only willing to accept the risk I took in returning to academic research, but has since put up with the inevitable ups and downs, both economic and emotional, of life with a research student. Without her support I should never have embarked on research, much less brought it to the conclusion represented by this volume. I owe her more than I can say. To my erstwhile supervisor, Dr Brendan Bradshaw, are due thanks of a different kind. Without his guidance, I should never have undertaken the particular research on which this book is based. Indeed, without his encouragement I should never have taken further what might otherwise have seemed merely an idle whim for the academic life. That would have meant losing more than the opportunity to study the work of a brave, learned and holy man. It would have meant, for Bettina and me, missing years which have been the happiest and most fulfilling we have known. For that reason, this book is dedicated to him from both of us.

Many other people have also assisted me in my research. Professor Sir Geoffrey Elton and Professor Jack Scarisbrick read and criticised an earlier version of this work submitted for the doctorate of philosophy in the university of Cambridge. Their comments, suggestions and encouragement have given a great deal to this new version. Sir Geoffrey also gave me the chance to present two embryonic chapters as papers at the Cambridge Tudor History Seminar. Professor Christopher Brooke, too, has been generous with his time and goodwill, commenting on many chapters and helping to strengthen my grasp of the medieval context from which John Fisher emerged. In addition my thanks are due to him for an invitation to present another section of this work to the Church History Seminar in the Cambridge Divinity Faculty. To all the members of both seminars whose comments have helped me in too many ways to recall, much less to enumerate, I can only extend a general word of thanks. Dr Eamon Duffy has read almost all of this book at one time or another, pointing out several avenues of exploration and numerous pitfalls. Mr Colin Armstrong has read through the entire text, saving me from innumerable blunders and infelicities. Those that remain are, as the saying goes, entirely my responsibility. Dr Virginia Murphy has graciously allowed me to take advantage of her important unpublished dissertation on the controversy over Henry VIII's first divorce.

All scholars depend on the labour and goodwill of the staff of libraries and archives. I can only echo the thanks expressed by previous students to those who work in London at the British Library, the Public Record Office and the library of Lambeth Palace; at the Bodleian Library in Oxford; and in Cambridge not only at the University Library but at the libraries of Christ's, Corpus Christi, Emmanuel, Gonville and Caius, Pembroke, Peterhouse, St John's and Trinity colleges. I have benefited in particular from the assistance and advice of Mr David McKitterick, the librarian of Trinity College, and of Mr Malcolm Underwood and Mr Malcolm Pratt, respectively the archivist and the sub-librarian of St John's College.

It is a moot point which is more important to the hopeful scholar – books or money. Without books we cannot attain scholarship. Without money we cannot afford it. Like many students in the humanities, I owe my opportunity to pursue research to the British Academy, which awarded me a state studentship for the three years of my graduate studies, and to Trinity College, Cambridge, for allowing me back. The continuation of my research and the adaptation of my dissertation for publication have been made possible by the generosity of St John's College, Cambridge, in electing me to a research fellowship. I shall never forget the friendship and welcome that have been extended to me here since my arrival. It is not unfitting that someone who researched the work of St John Fisher in the college where the saint himself once studied (for Trinity absorbed his college of Michaelhouse) should afterwards be elected a fellow of the college he did more than anyone else to found – St John's. One cannot deserve such good fortune, but one can try to repay it. This book, which endeavours to recapture some of the interest and importance of John Fisher as a scholar in the intellectual and theological world of the Renaissance and the Reformation, must in the end be the only real recompense I can offer to all those individuals and institutions whose generosity has meant so much to me over the past four years.

Abbreviations

Please refer to the bibliography for full details of the books mentioned here.

Fisher's works

ALC *Assertionis Lutheranae Confutatio* (*Confutatio* in text). Cited by article and folio

CC *Convulsio Calumniarum* (*Convulsio* in text)

CSD *Confutatio Secundae Disceptationis* (*Confutatio Secundae* in text)

DCM *De Causa Matrimonii* (*De Causa* in text)

DRA *Defensio Regiae Assertionis* (*Defensio* in text)

DUM *De Unica Madgalena*. Cited by book and page

DVC *De Veritate Corporis et Sanguinis Christi in Eucharistia* (*De Veritate* in text). Cited by book, chapter, and folio

EM *Eversio Munitionis quam Iodocus Clichtoveus erigere moliebatur* (*Eversio* in text)

EW *The English Works of John Fisher*, ed. J.E.B. Mayor

OO *Opera Omnia*. Cited by column

SSD *Sacri Sacerdotii Defensio* (in text)

Others

BL British Library

BRUC *Biographical Register of the University of Cambridge*, ed. A.B. Emden

BRUO *Biographical Register of the University of Oxford*, ed. A.B. Emden

CT *Concilium Tridentinum*. Cited by volume, part and page

CUL Cambridge University Library

CWE Complete Works of Erasmus (Toronto edition)

CWTM Complete Works of Thomas More (Yale edition)

EE *Erasmi Epistolae*, ed. P.S. Allen. Cited by volume and letter number

EETS Early English Text Society

HRR *Humanism, Reform and Reformation: the career of Bishop John Fisher*, ed. B. Bradshaw and E. Duffy

LP *Letters and Papers Foreign and Domestic of the Reign of Henry VIII*. Cited

	by volume, part (where relevant) and document number
LXX	Septuagint
NT	New Testament
OT	Old Testament
PG	Migne's *Patrologia Graeca*
PL	Migne's *Patrologia Latina*
PRO	Public Record Office
SJC	Muniments of St John's College, Cambridge
SHCT	Studies in the History of Christian Thought
SMRT	Studies in Medieval and Reformation Thought
SP	State Papers (in the PRO)
STC	*Short-Title Catalogue . . . 1475–1640*
Vie	*Vie du Bienheureux Martyr Jean Fisher*, ed. F. van Ortroy
WA	*D. Martin Luthers Werke* ('Weimar Ausgabe').

Conventions

All references to *ALC, CC, DRA, DUM, DVC* and *SSD* are given both for the first editions and (in brackets) for the edition of Fisher's *Opera Omnia*. References are given in the same way for Henry VIII's *Assertio Septem Sacramentorum*, which was included in Fisher's *Opera Omnia*. In citing manuscript and printed sources, conventional scribal or typographical abbreviations have been expanded, as a matter of course and without special remark, for the convenience of the reader. The letters 'u' and 'v', and 'i' and 'j', have been interchanged where appropriate for clarity. Conjectural readings and emendations are indicated by square brackets. References to early printed books are a notorious occasion of confusion and inaccuracy. As far as possible, such books are cited according to their original foliation or pagination, be it in Arabic or Roman numerals, lower or upper case. Unfoliated and unpaginated books are cited according to their sigillation. This is often erratic, so all numerals have been converted to Arabic for ease of reference, although letters have been left in their original upper or lower case. Sigillation numbers have been supplied where necessary.

Bibliographical references to books printed before 1600 include both place and publisher where known.

Introduction

THE NAMES OF John Fisher and Thomas More, celebrated with a joint feast in the calendar of the Roman Catholic Church, will be forever linked as those of the two most illustrious opponents and victims of Henry VIII's repudiation of papal authority. Yet while the equality of honour they enjoy in the liturgy reflects their historical importance in the English Reformation, it does not reflect an equality in the treatment they have received at the hands of historians. The massive scholarly attention today lavished on More dwarfs the efforts of the few who study the career of his fellow martyr. Even the theology of Thomas More has received more extensive treatment than Fisher's, an imbalance especially hard to justify in view of the fact that the works of Fisher, a professional theologian, were more solid, enduring, original and influential than those of More. The reputation, and in consequence the study, of Fisher have suffered from his ready assimilation to the image of the hidebound conservative die-hard that is so frequently and casually applied to the early opponents of the Reformation in both England and Europe. This misleading account of Fisher originated with the Protestant opponents he faced during his life and was taken up by the royalist detractors hired to blacken his name after his death. Like so much of the work of these men, it has passed more or less uncriticised into the historiography of the English Reformation. The objectives of this study are to rescue Fisher's scholarly reputation from the oblivion into which it was cast by his English enemies and to examine the nature of his intellectual achievement, an achievement which was long held in the highest esteem in continental Catholic Europe. Its thesis is that Fisher's theology is marked by an individual and far from unsuccessful attempt to reinvigorate the old blood of the scholastics with the new blood of the humanists – not as an intermediate stage in some progress out of darkness into light, but as an interesting combination of two great, though fundamentally dissimilar, traditions. These characteristics combined with a clear perception of the fundamental issues at stake in the Reformation controversies, and with an incisive rebuttal of the theological challenges posed by the Reformers, to produce a body of work that met the contemporary need for a reliable and intellectually credible Catholic response

I

to the new doctrines, a response which avoided obscurantism on the one hand and compromise on the other.

The disproportion of the historical interest accorded to More and Fisher is nothing new. Even in 1535, when they were executed, the romantic figure of the wary and witty lawyer, cracking jokes on his way to the scaffold, attracted wider popular attention and sympathy than that of the grave and forthright bishop. The first biography of More, the memoir by his son-in-law William Roper, was in print by the end of Mary Tudor's reign. The first biography of Fisher, in contrast, was completed only under Elizabeth, and was circulated only in manuscript form until the middle of the next century. Its compilation was the work of a few members of St John's College, Cambridge (which has always been closely associated with the study of Fisher) – ecclesiastics who had been prominent in the Marian reaction before finding their freedom curtailed by house arrest or close imprisonment under Elizabeth. John Young, former vice-chancellor of Cambridge and master of Pembroke Hall, was probably the author, and he received information and advice from Thomas Watson, deprived bishop of Lincoln, Alban Langdaile and Robert Truslowe, once Fisher's chaplain.[1] The work has been described as hagiography, but it is far more like a modern life than a medieval compendium of miraculous and moralising episodes. As befitted the work of a talented humanist, it was frequently based on critical research into original documents. It makes few claims that cannot be corroborated from other evidence. Unfortunately, its first appearance in print was the work of an unscrupulous and imaginative editor, Thomas Bailey, who interpolated quantities of spurious material and palmed it off as his own.[2] The late Stuart antiquary and clergyman John Lewis stripped Bailey's fictions away, but his unsympathetic account was not published until the middle of the nineteenth century.[3] It was at this time that the serious study of John Fisher may be said to have commenced, with the publication of his English writings. His funeral sermons on Henry VII and Lady Margaret Beaufort were edited in 1840, and in 1876 there appeared what was intended as a complete edition of Fisher's English works. Both these books were the work of members of St John's College.[4] The first modern and scientific study of Fisher, which appeared in 1885, was a labour of love by another Johnian, Thomas Bridgett, a man who traced the origins of his conversion to Catholicism to a perusal of Fisher's polemical writings against the Protestants.[5] It is hardly surprising that the resurgence of interest in Fisher came when it did. The mid-nineteenth century was the heyday of Tractarianism and Ritualism in the Church of England, of pre-Raphaelitism in the arts, and of the 'second spring' of English Catholicism. Bridgett's book was occasioned in particular by Fisher's beatification, together with that of More and other English martyrs, in 1885. Even more important than Bridgett's study, though traceable to the same impulse, was the critical edition of Young's life of Fisher published by François

2

van Ortroy in the early 1890s.[6] Bridgett and van Ortroy laid the foundation for all subsequent studies of Fisher. The canonisation of Fisher and More in 1935 provoked a second wave of interest. Philip Hallett translated one of Fisher's polemical writings in anticipation of the event, and Philip Hughes edited a popular version of Young's life.[7] There were, besides, several biographies of greatly varying standard. These were all superannuated by E.E. Reynolds, whose biography of Fisher broke new ground by exploiting the evidence of his episcopal register. It remains the best English life.[8] The French account by Jean Rouschausse gave fuller weight to Fisher's polemical writings, and added a number of fresh biographical details.[9] Students of Fisher are also indebted to Rouschausse for his editions of Fisher's correspondence with Erasmus, and of his devotional writings.[10] Most recently, in the wake of the 450th anniversary of Fisher's execution, a collection of essays edited by Brendan Bradshaw and Eamon Duffy has cast new light upon several aspects of Fisher's career – his educational interests, his relationship with Erasmus, his theology, his episcopate, and his role in the opposition to Henry VIII in the early 1530s.[11] In the meantime, the study of Fisher has also been advanced by researches not primarily concerned with his career. His work as a preacher was set in its sixteenth-century context by the investigations of J.W. Blench.[12] His ecclesiology has been analysed in an appendix to Brian Gogan's comprehensive survey of Thomas More's view of the Church.[13] And his contributions to the controversy over Henry VIII's divorce have been examined in several studies of that episode.[14]

Of all the recent studies of Fisher, one must be singled out for special praise – the pioneering study by the late Edward Surtz, *The Works and Days of John Fisher* (Harvard, 1967). Surtz was the first scholar to attempt a full-scale survey of Fisher's voluminous Latin theological writings. His *Works and Days* is an indispensable handbook for any student of Fisher, presenting Fisher's views on almost every issue on which it is possible to ascertain them. If one had to criticise this important work, it would be for its length, which owes something to repetitiveness, and for its over-ready assimilation of its subject to the traditions of both Erasmian humanism and Thomist scholasticism – a pair by no means easily reconciled, from both of which Fisher in fact departed in some important respects. Surtz tends to assume an almost monolithic uniformity about the Catholic theological tradition, and this in turn gives the reader little idea of where Fisher stood in relation to the intellectual traditions he inherited, and the contemporary intellectual developments with which he was faced.[15] These problems of length, organisation and interpretation help to explain why Surtz's work has not made the impact it should have upon other scholars working in related fields, and why misconceptions about Fisher's theology still prevail among them. Nevertheless, the magnitude of Surtz's achievement should not be underestimated. To read, digest and present the essence of Fisher's works would have been valuable in itself. But Surtz added to this the fruits of monumental erudition in sixteenth-century sources, awakening the reader to Fisher's importance as a theologian on the European scene – an insight which my own study attempts to take further forward.

This book is not intended as another biography of Fisher. Nor is it intended to replace Surtz's *Works and Days* as a handbook to Fisher's theology. Its aim, rather, is to build on the foundation provided by Surtz and the biographers in order to examine the sources and character of John Fisher's theological writings, and to locate his thought in its proper intellectual tradition and in relation to the intellectual currents of his day. Specifically, this means relating his work to the Christian traditions of the early fathers and the scholastics, and to the contemporary movements of humanism and the Reformation. The writings in which Fisher engaged most directly with these various movements and traditions were works of polemical theology, and these are the main object of this study. They fall into three groups: works concerned with questions raised by the humanist criticism of scripture and ecclesiastical authority; refutations of the main propositions of Reformation theology; and examinations of the issues raised by Henry VIII's pursuit of a divorce from Catherine of Aragon. These works are of course all in Latin, and have therefore received less attention than they deserve from previous students – Surtz excepted. Fisher's sermons fall into a separate category. Written in English, they are more accessible than his polemical works, and have been treated more thoroughly in the literature. Nevertheless, they are obviously of direct relevance to a study of Fisher's theology, and for that reason receive specific attention in a chapter of this book, as well as providing illustrative material elsewhere. Fisher's other writings – mostly devotional treatises – do not bear so directly on this book's concerns. They are therefore dealt with not in their own right, but only in so far as they cast light on his general intellectual position or on his particular views of controverted matters. However, in concentrating on the less accessible sources, this study hopes to present a more accessible account of Fisher by treating the central debates of the time rather than the peripheral ones. The question of justification will thus, for example, receive the attention of a complete chapter; that of indulgences will be mentioned only in passing. The intended results of this approach are a sharper picture and sounder judgments about Fisher's intellectual and theological positions.

This book begins conventionally enough for an intellectual study with an examination of its subject's education, in so far as it can be reconstructed. In Fisher's case this means looking at the curriculum and character of late fifteenth-century Cambridge, with particular reference to the arts and theology courses. Although the evidence from this period is sadly defective, some sense can be gained of the initial impact of humanism, at least in the arts, and of the scholastic dominance of theology. Chapter 2 examines Fisher's earliest surviving theological writings, namely his sermons, most of which were delivered in the first decade of the sixteenth century. These works evince both a real interest in vernacular religious culture and a strongly Augustinian theological approach, two themes that were to come into their own later in his career. The third chapter continues to sketch the background to Fisher's polemical writings, looking at his engagement with the new currents of humanism in the sixteenth century, and in particular at his relationship with Erasmus and his attitudes to the study of the original languages of scripture. But consideration is also given to his attitude to the various medieval theological schools and to the early fathers of the Church. In the fourth chapter we come to the first of Fisher's polemical writings, three books against the French humanist Lefèvre d'Etaples on the question of whether Mary Magdalene was rightly identified by the Church with the sister of Martha and Lazarus. Although this controversy is somewhat arcane by modern standards, and even at the time was soon eclipsed in the academic world by the crisis provoked by Luther, it raised important questions about the relationship between the critical scholarship of the humanists and the doctrinal authority of the Church – a tense relationship which Fisher was reluctant to see degenerate into conflict. The position of Fisher with regard to both reveals his attitudes not only to humanism but also to what we now call popular religion. The fifth chapter provides an overview of Fisher's place in the Catholic campaign against Luther and the Reformation, outlining his own part and considering his relations with other Catholic polemicists, and assessing the importance of his contribution in the development of a standard Catholic response to Protestant teachings. It stands by way of introduction to the three chapters that follow it which in turn analyse Fisher's views on the three crucial issues of the Reformation: authority, justification, and the eucharist. On each of these issues Fisher had a distinctive and influential contribution to make. The ninth chapter turns away from the Reformation back towards humanism, exploring for the first time a controversy which briefly flared up between Fisher and Richard Pace in 1527 over the Septuagint version of the Old Testament. Once more questions of authority and criticism were at stake, and once more Fisher endeavoured to resolve the problem without prejudice to either. The last chapter moves on to the matter that was to dominate Fisher's declining years, the controversy over the validity of Henry VIII's marriage to Catherine of Aragon. His several treatises on this question reveal at once a far wider knowledge of the scholastics than we would deduce from his other writings, and a far greater facility with the original languages of scripture. They thus provide a fitting culmination to a study whose underlying thesis turns on the relationship between humanism and scholasticism in Fisher's writings.

Before we begin, though, it is worth reminding ourselves of the salient features of Fisher's career. John Fisher was born around 1469 to a moderately wealthy merchant of Beverley, Robert Fisher. John was one of several children, among them a brother named Robert who subsequently became his steward. His father died in June 1477 and his mother, Agnes, married again and bore further children, including Fisher's sister Elizabeth who became a nun at the Dominican convent of Dartford. Having presumably received his early education at the grammar school attached to the collegiate church of Beverley, Fisher was sent to Cambridge around 1483, where he appears to have studied at the college of Michaelhouse.[16] By 1491 he had become a fellow of Michaelhouse, and was ordained priest that same year in York. He was elected senior proctor of the university for the academic year (roughly October to October) 1494–5, and in this capacity he made the acquaintance of Lady Margaret Beaufort, the mother of Henry VII, while in London on university business. He proceeded to the degree of doctor of divinity on 5 June 1501, and was elected vice-chancellor of the university ten days later. In the meantime he had become confessor – in effect, spiritual director – to Lady Margaret and was the leading figure in her household. Fisher's merits were brought to the attention of the king by Richard Fox, bishop of Winchester, and he was unexpectedly appointed to the see of Rochester in 1504. At about the same time the university elected him chancellor, a post he was to hold for most of the rest of his life. In fact he resigned it in 1514 to make way for the rising Wolsey, but upon the latter's refusal of the honour he was re-elected for life, to be deprived by act of attainder only in January 1535.

Despite the extra responsibilities laid upon him by his promotion to the episcopate, Fisher remained Lady Margaret's closest adviser until her death in 1509. It was under his influence that she re-founded the Cambridge college Godshouse as Christ's College. In order to provide Fisher with a Cambridge residence from which to carry out his heavy load of business, Lady Margaret secured for him in 1505 the presidency of Queens' College (where since the death of the Queen Consort Elizabeth she had in effect wielded foundress's rights). It was around this time that Fisher obtained from Rome a dispensation releasing him from his full obligations of episcopal residence so that he could fulfil his personal obligations to his patroness.[17] He resigned the presidency of Queens' in 1508, after which he probably stayed at Christ's when he visited Cambridge. His association with Lady Margaret brought other benefits to the university, including the endowment of a lectureship in divinity and a preachership. Her greatest benefaction, though, was without doubt the foundation of St John's College, to which she was persuaded by Fisher shortly before her death. Unfortunately, her death prevented the proper completion of the arrangements and Fisher had to face two years of legal wrangles with his king (who was anxious for a share of Lady Margaret's lands), in order to vindicate the college's claim to about half of the endowment she had originally intended. The establishment and enrichment of St John's became in Fisher's own mind his chief hope for perpetuating his memory. He drafted the original statutes of the college, which were promulgated in 1516, and was engaged in almost constant revision of them until his imprisonment in 1534. Besides this he persuaded several other benefactors to add to the endowments of the college, and himself made over lands worth £500 to found a chantry chapel there with several fellowships attached for the benefit both of learning and of his immortal soul. But as chancellor, he was also interested in the wider concerns of the university. As well as those already mentioned, his services to it included the recruitment of its first two lecturers in Greek and its first lecturer in Hebrew. His fifty-year association with the university saw in addition the foundation of university lectureships in arts and mathematics and of the university preacherships, the reform of the proctorial elections, the introduction of the office of public orator, and the establishment of the first – though short-lived – Cambridge press. It has indeed rightly been said that it was under Fisher's chancellorship that Cambridge became for the first time the intellectual equal of Oxford.

Fisher was an able administrator, and he selected other talented administrators as his assistants. Much of his work for Cambridge and St John's was carried out by such men as Henry Hornby (master of Peterhouse, and also chancellor to Lady Margaret), Robert Shorton (first master of St John's and later master of Pembroke, who served in addition in the households of Wolsey and Catherine of Aragon), and Nicholas Metcalfe (third master of St John's, and Fisher's right-hand man as archdeacon of Rochester). Delegation left Fisher himself free for what he saw as his primary responsibility – the spiritual welfare of his diocese. The claim of his early biographer that he was unusually attentive to his episcopal duties has been amply borne out by recent research.[18] The evidence of his itinerary shows that he spent most of his episcopal career either in his diocese or in London on ecclesiastical business. His longest continuous absence was caused by his imprisonment in the Tower from April 1534 to his death in June 1535.[19] Anecdotal evidence remarks especially upon his zeal and skill as a preacher, and this is confirmed by his surviving sermons (mostly composed for special occasions and audiences) and by his commitment to the promotion of preaching. Fisher also took seriously his duties towards the Church on a national and international level. He played a leading part in the plans for reform in the Church of England at the convocation of 1510–11. Twice he was named as an English delegate to the Fifth Lateran Council, in 1512 and in 1515. On each occasion his preparations to depart were far advanced when political developments frustrated his plans. He remained a prominent ecclesiastical politician throughout the 1520s. His polemical writings, suffused with a high sense of his episcopal role, were his chief contribution (apart from his death) to the universal Church. His virtues recommended him as a model bishop, not only to contemporaries such as

Erasmus and Johann Fabri (bishop of Constance) but also to successors like Cardinal Borromeo.

In his private life Fisher was a man of prayer and scholarship, who might have adorned the monastery or the university with as much distinction as he did his diocese. His taste in devotion was for the fervent, personal and emotional, though he was far from undervaluing the routine of the daily office of the Church. Besides an interesting treatise on the practice of prayer, he composed a number of private prayers, some of which survive. These include some imitations of the psalms, compiled in large part by scissors-and-paste work on the Psalter, which were published perhaps as early as 1525 and remained popular for the rest of the century. By a curious irony they came to be included – without acknowledgment – in a standard work of Anglican devotion, *The King's Psalms*. These may well be the 'brief prayers' referred to in a papal dispensation of 1533 by which Fisher was absolved from the obligation to recite the daily office on condition that he said instead certain prayers of his own choosing.[20] His predilection for fervency in prayer also led him to favour the use of 'ejaculatory' prayers, short single-sentence prayers that could be repeated often and invested with considerable emotional intensity. He recommended these in his treatise on prayer and gave a few examples, all directed to 'Dulcissime Iesu'.[21] Otherwise his piety was conventional, though profoundly devout, concentrating especially on the mass. As a scholar, Fisher retained all his life the intellectual curiosity and openness of youth. Under the influence of Erasmus and Reuchlin he set himself in his forties to learn both Hebrew and Greek, embarking around the same time on an ambitious project to produce a harmony of the Gospels, and a few years later on an exposition and paraphrase of the Psalms.[22] In his fifties he branched out with striking success on a new career as polemical theologian. His opponents were, in succession, Lefèvre d'Etaples, Martin Luther, Ulrich Velenus, Johann Oecolampadius, Richard Pace, and finally Robert Wakefield together with other theological advisers of Henry VIII. The works of this period spread Fisher's scholarly reputation throughout Europe, and ensured him a place in its intellectual, as well as its political, history.

The most eventful years of Fisher's life, and those with which his biographers have traditionally been most preoccupied, were his final years, spent in opposition to Henry VIII's marital and ecclesiastical policies. This opposition began of course with the controversy over Henry's divorce. As Fisher was one of the first to see, Henry's case against the validity of his marriage to Catherine of Aragon soon bore the seeds of a revolt from the authority of the papacy. As this danger became manifest, and as Henry put increasing pressure on the English church, Fisher was in the forefront of the opposition. Indeed, without him it is hard to imagine what sort of opposition there would have been. He was by far the most able of the defenders of the marriage, and was not afraid to defend it to Henry's face. He spoke out against anti-clerical legislation in the Parliament of 1529, and appealed to Rome against its enactments in 1530 – a gesture that resulted in his first imprisonment. He led the resistance in Convocation to the submission of the clergy in 1531, and was probably the author of the saving clause 'quantum per legem Christi licet' by which the clergy qualified their acceptance of Henry as their supreme head on earth. The dozen representatives of the lower clergy who signed a protestation against the submission a few days later included several of Fisher's friends and clients. Absent through illness from the convocation of 1532, he nevertheless wrote outspokenly against the temporal invasion of the spirituality. He may even have stiffened the resolve of his old friend Archbishop Warham to make a final gesture of defiance shortly before his death that year. It is a tribute to his personal influence that so many of his friends or associates should have stood out against the divorce or the royal supremacy or both. The list includes Thomas More, Nicholas West, Cuthbert Tunstall, Nicholas Wilson, Henry Gold, Ralph Baynes, John Addison and many others. Driven to disloyalty by the attack on the church, Fisher entered into negotiations with Eustace Chapuys, the imperial ambassador, with a view to securing Henry's excommunication and deposition by the pope with the assistance of imperial arms. In 1533 he led the small dissenting minority against Convocation's declaration that marriage to a brother's widow was absolutely contrary to natural law and indispensable by the pope. The day after Convocation cleared the way for the divorce, Fisher spoke publicly in defence of the marriage, and was gaoled for his pains. Anxious to silence him, the government included him in the act of attainder against the Holy Maid of Kent, on the grounds of misprision of treason – that is, for not revealing to the king prophecies which the Holy Maid had already told the king in person. While she and her closest followers were condemned to death, he escaped with 'confiscation of body and goods'. Before he had even been brought to prison, he was presented in April 1534 with the oath to the act of succession, which he refused. He was immediately confined to the Tower.

Before long, the chain of events which would lead to Fisher's death was under way. The statutes of supremacy and treasons were enacted, despite forlorn opposition from a minority that included Fisher's brother Robert, then member of Parliament for Rochester. Under these acts, 'maliciously' denying that the king was supreme head under God of the Church of England was made high treason, punishable by death. The apparently crucial adjective 'maliciously', inserted by the opposition in a vain attempt to mitigate the severity of the legislation, ultimately proved Fisher's undoing. Thomas More's legal training warned him against putting faith in such a loophole, and in the event he could only be convicted by perjury. But Fisher was not quite so cautious. Having been informed about the inclusion of this clause by his brother, he relied upon it to protect him from the consequences of his honesty. His initial refusal of the oath around the begining of May was safe enough, and he was given six weeks to reconsider.[23] But a little later, on 7 May 1535, before a group of councillors which included Thomas Cromwell, he uttered the words 'The Kyng owre Soveraign Lord is not supreme hedd yn erthe of the Cherche of Englande.'[24] The truth of the story that Fisher was tricked by Richard Rich into denying the supremacy is difficult to assess. The chronology of the *Vie* is confused over his various interrogations, and puts Rich's stratagem at a late date in their course – which clearly cannot be true. Moreover, in the earliest version of the story Rich is not mentioned at all.[25] The subsequent introduction of his name is probably guilt by analogy with his well-known role in the entrapment of More. Yet the general outline of the story should not be dismissed out of hand.[26] The *Vie* gets the wording of the indictment right, and is surely correct in claiming that Fisher's defence rested on the 'maliciously' loophole. As it is unlikely that he would simply have blurted out a denial of the supremacy in full knowledge of the penalties, it is probable that he was manoeuvred into it. The trick described, to put him under something like confessional secrecy with regard to a conscientious scruple of the king's on which he wanted Fisher's confidential advice, has no parallel in More's story and would have been ideally suited to get through Fisher's guard. The introduction of Rich's name is something of a réd herring. But the trick itself has the ring of truth.[27] How could the honest and loyal bishop have refused such an appeal? At any rate, a few days later he was shown by his servant a letter from More to Meg Roper describing and justifying his attitude to the interrogation, namely his refusal to give any opinion on the matter whatsoever. Fisher then wrote to More asking for clarification, which he obtained. In a letter of 12 May, More described the statute to him as a 'two-edged sword', since to deny the supremacy imperilled the body, to affirm it imperilled the soul. This presumably worried Fisher, for shortly afterwards he wrote again, reminding More of the inclusion of 'maliciously' in the statute, and saying that he had thought it safe therefore to answer the questions frankly. The reply from More, written on 26 May, advised him against any further such frankness, and also urged that he should find his own words to parry further questions. Fisher did not take this sufficiently to heart. In a subsequent interrogation on 3 June, he refused to answer further questions on the supremacy, asking that his earlier answer should be allowed 'the benefite of the same statute' as it had not been malicious. However, he took up More's theme in referring to the supremacy as a 'two-edged sword', a coincidence which alerted the councillors to the possibility of collusion between the two men. They soon nosed out the story of the clandestine correspondence, and subsequent interrogations concentrated on this, presumably in the hope of finding something to incriminate More.[28] In Fisher's case the damage had already been done. In the meantime, news arrived from Rome of Fisher's inclusion among the elevations to the college of cardinals with which Paul III announced his intention to proceed with the reform of the Church.[29] This move, calculated to encourage Henry to release a man who was now a prince of the Church, achieved the opposite effect. The news seems to have reached London on 30 May.[30] Resentful of the interference, or grateful for the provocation, Henry resolved on Fisher's death. Proceedings against him began with a commission of oyer and terminer issued on 1 June. Although it was later to be claimed that the pope had caused Fisher's prosecution, this can be dismissed as exaggeration. The coincidence of dates suggests that the trial was a response to the news, but the truth would seem to be that the pope merely precipitated a course of action that had already been decided upon.[31] Fisher's 'treason' had after all been committed on 7 May, and his six weeks grace had expired. The leisurely mode of proceeding can probably be attributed to the council's hopes of implicating More in treasonable correspondence with Fisher. The Middlesex Grand Jury found a true bill against him on 5 June, and he was brought to trial on 17 June.[32] He was found guilty and condemned to death, and on Tuesday 22 June he was led to the block on Tower Hill.

Fisher's death was not the end of the story, however, for Henry's vengeance pursued him beyond his unmarked grave. A systematic campaign was launched to eradicate his memory at home and to blacken it abroad. Even before Fisher and More were brought to trial they were the target of malicious sermons in London.[33] Between the death of Fisher and the trial of More, Henry VIII ordered that the 'treasons' of the two men should be publicly declared at the assizes throughout the country.[34] Within a year, one of Fisher's sermons had been specifically banned by proclamation.[35] Possession of his writings could be dangerous or at least suspicious.[36] Fisher's various treatises against Henry VIII's divorce were passed to a committee led by Cranmer with a view to the production of a last word on the affair, but Cranmer, perhaps wisely, decided in the end against attempting a refutation.[37] On the international level, Cromwell made every effort to portray the execution of Fisher as a matter of treason, as a matter of state rather than of Church. Ambassadors were instructed to present these vague and of course unsubstantiated charges to foreign rulers.[38] The diplomatic offensive was supplemented with a propaganda drive. In one of the less creditable episodes of his chequered career, Stephen Gardiner produced an attack on Fisher and More, as did the bishop of Chichester, Richard Sampson. The process was something of an uphill struggle. Even at home, Fisher's death was widely interpreted as martyrdom.[39] A Carthusian monk named John Darlay was told in a vision that Fisher had been given the martyr's crown in heaven. Despite official attempts to suppress the story, it had reached Rome by October.[40] Another story, that Fisher's head, parboiled and stuck on a pole at London Bridge, grew miraculously rosier and healthier in appearance day by day until it was taken down because of the crowds it attracted, also achieved general currency. Richard Morison was at some pains to dismiss this miracle as a falsehood in his *Apomaxis Calumniarum*, a reply to a defence of Fisher and More published by the German polemicist Johann Cochlaeus.[41] Perhaps most petty of all was the destruction of Fisher's memory in the very college of St John's, Cambridge, that he had done so much to found. Although the college took out insurance by appealing to the patronage of Cranmer and Cromwell, it remained remarkably loyal to its fallen leader in the mid-1530s. The college sent visitors and messages of sympathy to Fisher in the Tower, and at first celebrated his obsequies after his death, as it had contracted to do in return for endowments he had made. But once his right-hand man, Nicholas Metcalfe, had been compelled to surrender the mastership, the attack was carried to his college. The college was obliged to take down the elaborate tomb Fisher had prepared for himself in the chapel, and to efface the heraldic emblems of his that were found on much of the chapel furniture.[42] Soon afterwards, the statutes of the college were revised to eliminate all mention of his name. Even the fellowships he had endowed were taken away from him and submerged in the general fellowship of the college.[43] Except for a brief revival of Fisher's statutes under Mary, he was forgotten in his own college until the time of Thomas Baker, the non-juring antiquary of the late Stuart period whose political and religious principles caused him to be ejected from the fellowship. This conclusion to the account of Fisher brings us back to where we started. The relative lack of scholarly attention given to his career in the past reflects at least to some extent the success of the 'non-personing' of Fisher by the Henrician regime. Fisher's college of St John's and his university of Cambridge have, however, long been prominent in efforts to restore him to his proper place in English and European history. It is fitting, therefore, that this account of Fisher as a theologian should begin by returning in more detail to the part played in his career by the university with which he was closely associated for all of his adult life.

I
Humanism and scholasticism in late fifteenth-century Cambridge

THE IMPORTANCE OF Cambridge in the intellectual formation of John Fisher can be readily appreciated from the outline of his brilliant career that is preserved for us in the university's records. On graduating BA in 1488 and MA in 1491 he was elected a fellow of Michaelhouse, a post which required him to be ordained priest.[1] He soon became an influential figure about the university. As senior proctor for the academic year 1494–5 he made the acquaintance of Lady Margaret Beaufort, a meeting of great consequence both for his career and for the development of the university.[2] In the years 1496–7 he was paid as an 'ordinary' lecturer, and around the turn of the century he became Lady Margaret's confessor.[3] He graduated doctor of divinity on 5 July 1501, and ten days later was elected vice-chancellor. The following year he took up the Lady Margaret readership of divinity, which he had encouraged his patroness to endow.[4] In 1504 he was appointed by Henry VII to the see of Rochester, and within a year he was elected chancellor of the university, a post to which he was re-elected every year until 1514.[5] Then, having first resigned in favour of Wolsey (who refused the honour), he accepted the university's subsequent offer of the post for life.[6]

Such a bald outline, however, tells us nothing about the nature of Cambridge's influence on Fisher. This chapter seeks to understand the place Cambridge occupied in his life and development by examining the two crucial elements in his university education – the curriculum he pursued, and the people among whom he mixed. It attempts to escape the two preconceptions that have long dominated or stifled the intellectual history of Tudor England: namely that a decadent scholasticism held sway in the universities until displaced in the early sixteenth century by the vital and innovative forces of humanism; and that (according to the flawed but enduring thesis of Frederick Seebohm) Oxford was the epicentre of an intellectual earthquake that shook the realm about the year 1500.[7] For late fifteenth-century Cambridge was on the contrary a place of considerable intellectual vitality, where renovation of the curriculum was warmly welcomed even though education remained firmly rooted in the traditions of the Middle Ages. This environment shaped a generation which was characterised by openness to educational change, concern for ecclesiastical reform, and commitment to Catholic orthodoxy; and which, as it assumed leadership first of the university and later of the Church, took the work of reform further forward. Fisher was the most prominent figure in this generation. He owed much to the formation he had received at Cambridge, and in return (as we shall see in chapter 3) the university was to owe to him much of its early sixteenth-century progress. In historiographical terms, the argument therefore follows up the task of revision that was begun by Roberto Weiss and has been continued more recently by Damian Leader. Weiss showed that the origins of humanism at Cambridge lay in the Yorkist period, but his study of humanism in fifteenth-century England retained a heavy bias towards Oxford.[8] Leader's investigation of academic reform through the collegiate and university foundations and statutes of early Tudor Cambridge found rather more enthusiasm for humanism than Weiss had allowed for.[9] This chapter takes up the same theme, exploiting evidence about the careers and concerns of Cambridge graduates selected because of their connection with Fisher in an attempt to learn something of the mentality of his circle. Little or no evidence is found of any conflict between entrenched scholasticism and insurgent humanism. The decisive break with scholasticism in English as in European universities came, if it came at all, not with the advent of humanism but with that of the Reformation. In Wittenberg it was symbolised by Luther's bonfire of 10 December 1520, when canon law texts and scholastic summas were consumed together with the papal bull of excommunication, *Exsurge Domine*.[10] In England the turning-point came in 1535, when Cromwell's injunctions to the universities swept away large tracts of the medieval curriculum. Yet in some respects this sweeping change was more apparent than real. Humanism was after all fundamentally a movement within the teaching of the arts. Here, the change from medieval to Renaissance concerns which began in the late fifteenth century proceeded swiftly and painlessly because it was popular and fashionable. To a great extent the replacement, or at least the supplementing, of scholastic texts on logic and grammar by humanist texts of rhetoric and dialectic had already been achieved by 1535, so that the Cromwellian injunctions were in effect legislating for a *fait accompli*. As for Cromwell's changes to the teaching of theology, the real crime of the scholastics and canon lawyers was not their methodology but their commitment to papal primacy. Humanist rhetoric merely put a fashionable gloss on the business. In any case, the familiarity of even late sixteenth-century Anglican theologians with the works of the scholastics, not to mention the manifest survival of those scholastics in collegiate and private libraries, casts a measure of doubt on the profundity of the changes Cromwell brought about in that sphere.[11] The humanist trend in theological studies, expressed in the return to the original text of scripture and in the increasing interest in the fathers, was already well under way when the injunctions were promulgated.

Early humanism at Cambridge was not mediated through Oxford, nor even through London, but, as in Oxford and London, was imported more or less directly from Italy. As Weiss has shown, the origins of English humanism can be traced to fifteenth-century Italian influences, such as the visit to England of Poggio Bracciolini in the 1430s and the visits to Italy of such scholars as John Gunthorpe and William Selling some years later.[12] The Cambridge which welcomed John Fisher in the 1480s was not cut off from such influences. Three Italians are known to have taught there at around this time: Gaio Auberino, Stefano Surigone and Lorenzo Traversagni. It has been suggested that the employment of Italians in late fifteenth-century Cambridge was a sign of the decadence of an institution that could not find adequate teachers from within its own ranks.[13] In fact, it was quite the vogue then for the universities of northern Europe to import talent from Italy in order to raise the standard of their Latin tuition. In following suit, Cambridge was merely keeping abreast of the times. Of the three Cambridge Italians, Auberino probably exercised the greatest influence because he stayed the longest. He was writing letters on behalf of the university as early as 1483, was elected university poet in 1486, was lecturing in 1486–7 and was still active as late as 1504.[14] Unfortunately, nothing has yet been discovered about his antecedents, not even the name of his native university. The second Italian, Stefano Surigone, is an almost equally obscure figure, but as he stayed in Cambridge only a short time he is unlikely to have made a great impact.[15] The third visitor, however, Lorenzo Guglielmo Traversagni di Savona, has left plentiful records not only of his religious and educational interests in general, but of his activities at Cambridge in particular.[16]

A brief examination of Traversagni's career and of the main characteristics of his thought offers an illuminating insight into the sort of humanist ideas which were being circulated and apparently well received in Cambridge in the latter half of the fifteenth century. This Franciscan friar from Savona, who has been aptly described as a 'tireless apostle' of humanism, had a fervent admiration for both Aristotle and the Christian fathers, and found his mission in life in fostering the effective preaching of the Word of God.[17] A much-travelled teacher, he came to Cambridge in 1476 and was a regular visitor until 1482.[18] He delivered at least three courses of lectures in those years, one on rhetoric, one on the *Nicomachean Ethics* (both in 1476) and one on Augustine's *De Civitate Dei* (in 1478). His two inaugural lectures (one for each year) still survive among numerous manuscripts of his in Savona.[19] Although we have no direct evidence with which to assess his impact on his audience, the frequency of his visits to Cambridge, and the fact that his lectures on rhetoric soon appeared in print – in response, he claimed, to popular demand – suggest that the seed he was sowing fell on fertile soil.[20] These lectures ran to three editions as the *Margarita Eloquentie Castigate*, and consisted of the staple diet of his tuition, a commentary on the *Ad Herennium,* one of the central texts of Renaissance rhetoric.[21] Traversagni placed great emphasis on the supremacy of eloquence among the liberal arts, reckoning it an indispensable accomplishment for the theologian and preacher.[22] The archetype of the Christian orator for him, as later for Erasmus, was Jerome, 'a man of outstanding erudition in both sacred and humane literature'.[23] His influence can only have been for the good on the theory and practice of rhetoric in Cambridge. Even Weiss, who described Traversagni as 'fundamentally a schoolman', conceded his 'appreciation of modern values', the 'strikingly neo-classical' flavour of his prose, and his 'association with Renaissance scholarship'.[24] That his humanism had a distinctly Christian orientation is apparent from his original compositions: spiritual treatises and dialogues in Latin verse. For, like his contemporary, Giovanni Battista Spagnuoli of Mantua, Traversagni was above all a religious poet. The religious content of his poems has not been subjected to close scrutiny, but it has been argued that their form was a conscious imitation of Petrarch.[25] In any case, the genuine humanism of Traversagni can be inferred from the manuscripts he carried with him on his travels, which included Guarino's glossary of Virgil, Bruni's *Isagogicon,* and a variety of commentaries on the *Ad Herennium.*[26] It would be tempting, though unjustifiable in view of the lack of evidence, to present Traversagni as a formative influence on late fifteenth-century Cambridge. But it is permissible to see in him a representative or symbolic figure. For the curricular changes and reforms that took place over the next thirty years reflected the concerns displayed in his life and works. There can be no doubt that his lectures were an integral part of that intellectual renovation of the university to which we must now turn.

When John Fisher came to Cambridge in the early 1480s, the official curriculum for the BA degree was in theory based on the *trivium* of grammar, logic and rhetoric. In practice it was given over almost entirely to logic and natural philosophy. The statutory requirement was to attend two years of lectures on each.[27] Logic, taught with such complexity as to give the words 'sophistry' and 'sophistication' their modern meaning, set the tone of the arts course. The basic text was the *Summulae Logicales* of Petrus Hispanus, whose infamous seventh book was the *Parva Logicalia.* Natural philosophy was based on what soon came to be called the 'old' Aristotle, a mixture of genuine and spurious texts translated in the thirteenth century and read with the aid of medieval commentaries. The three-year MA course was equally old-fashioned. In theory based on the *quadrivium* of arithmetic, music, geometry and astronomy, in practice it too consisted largely of logic and philosophy, with the statutory requirement of a year each on dialectics, Aristotle's *Posterior Analytics* and Aristotle's metaphysical works.[28] A summary of the whole seven-year course, clearly derived from conversations with Fisher, has come down to us in a letter Erasmus wrote from Rochester in August 1516: 'Thirty years ago nothing was taught in the Cambridge schools other than Alexander, the *Parva Logicalia*, those old sayings of Aristotle, and the questions of Scotus.' In the same letter he went on to outline the changes that had occurred since then: 'The intervening years have seen the arrival of *bonae literae*, mathematics, and a new or at any rate new-fangled Aristotle, as well as the knowledge of Greek, and a multitude of authors of whom they had hardly heard before.'[29] Erasmus did not attempt to conceal his distaste for the old curriculum, a distaste which his friend very probably shared. In an oration delivered at Cambridge during a royal visit of 1506–7, he painted a grim picture of the state of the university before the beneficent rays of the royal sun had brought her new life. No doubt one must be wary of taking literally a speech in which the orator, having eschewed flattery, embarked on a modest comparison of Henry VII to Moses.[30] Yet Fisher's dissatisfaction with the old regime can be detected in his exclamation to Erasmus in praise of Rudolph Agricola, whose innovative *Dialectica* he had just read: 'Would that I had had him as a teacher in my youth!'[31] It is further confirmed by his close association with the curricular reforms of this time, reforms which Erasmus frequently ascribed to Fisher's encouragement and instigation.[32]

Fisher was of the last generation to graduate under the old system. In 1488, the year of his BA, a statute was enacted establishing a new series of lectures for undergraduates: two years of 'humanities' or 'Terence'; a year of logic; and a final year of philosophy. In 1495 a further statute added attendance at these lectures to the requirements for the BA degree.[33] The real innovation was of course the humanities lecture, and we find intermittent record of Auberino as the reader of this in the 1480s and 1490s.[34] Soon afterwards the MA course was even more drastically reformed. Around 1500 a new statute dismissed the old course as 'inane, burdensome and useless', alleging that it was falling into desuetude. The new requirement was to be attendance at a year of lectures on arithmetic and music; a year on geometry and perspective; and a year on astronomy. This represented a retreat from the late medieval emphasis on logic to the original ideal of the quadrivium, and it is tempting to relate it to contemporary developments at Paris, where Lefèvre d'Etaples had recently issued a modern edition of various mathematical texts. A university lecturer in mathematics first appears in the proctorial accounts for 1501, when Fisher was vice-chancellor.[35] Since the lecturer, Roger Collingwood, was like Fisher himself a client of Richard Fox and of Lady Margaret Beaufort, his appointment was probably no coincidence. When Fisher was president of Queens' College, Collingwood, a fellow there, received leave of absence from him, and funds from Lady Margaret, to pursue his studies abroad.[36] The survival of a manuscript treatise on mathematics by Collingwood (dedicated to Fox) shows that he was well equipped for the task.[37] Fisher himself had already been connected at an earlier date with the reintroduction of mathematics to the curriculum, for he later recalled that he had been taught Euclid by William Melton, presumably as part of his MA training[38] – which tends to confirm the implication of the new statute that the old curriculum was already giving way to the new.

Another important curricular development was the arrival in Cambridge of the 'new' Aristotle, of modern translations direct from the Greek in place of the literalistic and often incomprehensible medieval versions. Although Erasmus attributed this change to Fisher's influence, it was a process rather than an event. The new Aristotle had been infiltrating Cambridge since the mid-fifteenth century and the old Aristotle was still to be found in the sixteenth. The first sign of the new Aristotle is seen at the foundation of King's College in 1450, where the original library included a copy of Leonardo Bruni's new translation of the *Ethics*.[39] Yet as late as 1518 a mildly ironic reference to John Canonicus, a favoured medieval commentator, indicates that the old Aristotle had not been put off.[40] The turning-point for the reception of the new Aristotle might be somewhat arbitrarily identified with Traversagni's lectures on the *Ethics* in 1476. Taking Bruni's version as his text, he began with a remarkable encomium of Bruni as 'limatissimi celeberrimique oratoris et vatis'.[41] From this time sightings of the new versions of Aristotle in wills and library catalogues proliferate. One such is particularly interesting, a copy of Bruni's *Ethics* which was made for William Reynoldson (a fellow of Michaelhouse). Around the modern text was copied the commentary of Thomas Aquinas, indicative perhaps of the harmonious reception of the new by the old at Cambridge.[42] John Fabe, a fellow of Godshouse who died in 1504, bequeathed a copy of the translation and exposition of the entire Aristotelian corpus recently published by the expatriate Greek John Argyropoulos.[43] This was a cornerstone of Renaissance Neo-Aristotelianism, and it is remarkable that it should have reached Cambridge so soon. In this context, it is also worth noting that a copy of Marsilio Ficino's 1491 edition of Plato was deposited as a caution at Cambridge in 1500.[44] Yet although changes can be detected in our limited evidence for the pattern of book-ownership, there was no statutory reform – after all, none would be needed in what was simply the exchange of one version of a textbook for another. And unfortunately there is no evidence at all to substantiate the plausible conjecture that this change was related to the appearance in Paris at the turn of the century of Lefèvre d'Etaples's editions and expositions of the works of Aristotle.[45]

After completing the arts course in 1491 Fisher embarked on the theology curriculum, about which the surviving evidence is distressingly sparse. It is therefore necessary to eke out the slender fare of the statutes with the limited testimony of anecdotes and booklists. What is certain is that the strongly scholastic curriculum of the Middle Ages remained dominant, although there were signs of increasing interest in the early fathers and in the original texts of scripture. Only the skeleton of the course is preserved in the statutes, which required five years study for the degree of bachelor of divinity, and a further five years for the doctorate. In pursuit of the BD, a student would perform his duties as a master lecturing in the arts schools while himself attending lectures on all four books of Peter Lombard's *Sentences* and on a considerable portion of the Bible. After five years of this he would proceed himself to lecture on the *Sentences* and on the Bible, and to fulfil certain preaching obligations in Cambridge and at St Paul's Cross in London. The other main component of the theology course besides lectures was the 'quaestio' or disputation, which in the medieval system took the place occupied by both the seminar and the examination today.[46]

All we can say about the nature of the lectures at Cambridge is that they doubtless conformed to the three models of medieval lecturing: a 'cursory' or 'ordinary' reading of the set text, that is with a minimal gloss to explain the bare sense of the author; a reading of a standard commentary on a set text, such as Duns Scotus's on the *Sentences*; or an original commentary, probably based on a comparison and evaluation of earlier commentaries. Such was the exposition of Scotus on the second book of the *Sentences* by William Chubbes, master of Jesus College, which probably dates from the last decade of the fifteenth century.[47] Chubbes deals with most of the questions raised by Scotus in that book which, though concerned in general with the creation, concentrates in particular on the nature of angels and on human nature with especial reference to sin and grace. His commentary is wholly scholastic in its approach. The only classical authorities cited are Aristotle, Euclid and Ptolemy, while the most prominent scholastic figure is the early fourteenth-century secular master, Henry of Ghent. It would be rash to presume that this unique surviving example is fully representative of late medieval Cambridge theology. But its concerns resemble those we can detect in other, less immediate sources. Scotus, as we can tell from stray remarks and from the inventories of personal and institutional libraries, was very much in fashion. Thomas Aquinas was only slightly less popular, and the theologians of the *via antiqua* were much preferred to those of the *via moderna*. Erasmus's letters, for example, refer frequently to battles with the Thomists and Scotists of Cambridge, but never to Ockhamists, Gabrielists or the *via moderna* there.[48] The tendencies of these more recent theologians were very popular in some places on the continent. At Paris, though, the *via moderna* had been officially banned in the 1480s, and Cambridge, which had close connections with Paris, may have been following their lead. The prevalence of the *via antiqua* at Cambridge is confirmed by those cases in which we know the precise subject of lecture courses in theology. One Patrick Gower was designated to lecture on Aquinas's *Summa Theologiae* in 1520, and we know of courses given in Queens' College by Ralph Songar on Aquinas's commentary on the *Sentences*, and by Humphrey Walkden on that of Scotus. King's College was paying Franciscans to lecture on Scotus in the years 1499 to 1503,[49] and the sermons of the Observant Franciscan Stephen Baron, delivered in Cambridge early in the reign of Henry VIII, assumed that the clerical audience would be familiar with such authorities as Scotus, Aquinas, Bonaventure, Francis Maro and Richard of Middleton.[50] Inventories of Cambridge libraries offer further corroboration of this. The writings of Thomas and Scotus were widely available, as was the text of the *Sentences* itself. The commentaries of Bonaventure and Francis Maro were occasionally found, as was the *Summa* of Alexander of Hales. But Ockham was rare, and there was hardly a sign of Biel and other late scholastics. Deciding which of the two predominant scholastics was the more popular is less easy. There was more of Aquinas in circulation than of Scotus, but Aquinas wrote more than Scotus and on a wider range of topics. To compare like with like, it is best to confine our attention to their major theological works: their respective *Sentences* commentaries; Scotus's *Quaestiones Quodlibetales*; and Aquinas's *Summa Theologiae*. Institutional libraries exhibit a clear preference for Aquinas, with about thirty entries against Scotus's twenty. But the evidence of personal book ownership redresses the balance, producing thirty further examples of Scotus, but only ten of Aquinas. This sort of evidence is more likely to reflect current fashion, in which case Scotus was probably the preferred authority. As we shall see in later chapters, Fisher's scholasticism followed the same pattern, giving pride of place to Scotus and Aquinas.[51]

Scriptural study was also a major component of the course, despite the subsequent Protestant propaganda about the eclipse of the Bible by scholastic works. The fact that the Bible was by far the most common book in individual and collegiate library inventories (outscoring even legal textbooks) is itself enough to demonstrate this. Statutes and anecdotes offer us no information about which books of the Bible or commentaries were used in lecturing, but inventories can help us at least on the commentaries. Prescinding from the 'Glossa Ordinaria' (or 'Common Gloss'), which was so often added to manuscript and printed Bibles as to be rarely mentioned in inventories, the most popular commentary was without doubt that of Nicholas of Lyra, followed at some distance by that ascribed to Hugh of St Cher (which was in fact the work of several authors). The latter was the classic example of the medieval fourfold interpretation of scripture, according to the literal, moral, allegorical and anagogical senses. The commentary of Lyra, a fourteenth-century Franciscan hebraist, was a literal exposition which drew heavily on rabbinical writings. It was the first scriptural commentary to be printed, and on the eve of the Reformation it was by far the most widely available in Europe – even Luther used it. While it is hard to say whether the growing popularity of Lyra was a cause or an effect of the increasing concern with the literal interpretation of scripture, it was certainly an index of it. And although the proverb 'Si Lyranus non lyrasset, Luterus non saltasset' was pure exaggeration, it was nevertheless a tribute to Lyra's wide and widely recognised influence.[52]

The popularity of Lyra suggests that Cambridge was receptive to the new academic opportunities afforded by the rise of printing. Several of the copies of Lyra recorded in inventories were certainly printed editions, and it is likely that most of them were. Richard Burton (d. 1506) bequeathed the Nuremberg four-volume Lyra of 1493 to Corpus Christi College, and Dr William Buckenham bought John Argentein's 1494 edition on the latter's death in 1509. The impact of printing can be detected in other fields. Thomas Leeke (d. 1504) left a copy of the 1498 Strasbourg edition of Horace, and Richard Nykke (bishop of Norwich, d. 1536) possessed several late fifteenth-century editions of legal, medical and theological works, doubtless acquired during his student days. The collection of John Argentein was impressive, and Thomas Rotherham's bene-factions to the University Library included a large number of printed books. The presence in Cambridge around 1500 of printed versions of Plato and Aristotle has already been noted. The significance of this trend for theology lay in the appearance of editions of the early Christian fathers. Although the effect of this process was naturally limited by the rate at which *editiones principes* were produced, evidence of the readiness with which such editions were greeted in Cambridge can be detected in the inventories around 1500. The works of Dionysius were among the possessions of Thomas Colyer (d. 1506) and Robert Mennall (d. 1503), and one suspects that the latter's copies of Lactantius's *De Divinis Institutionibus* and of Augustine's *De Trinitate* and *De Civitate Dei* were also printed.[53] One especially rich source for this trend is the inventory of the library of the Bridgettine priory of Syon, to which several Cambridge teachers retired in the early sixteenth century. Since the inventory notes which inmates donated which books, it is possible to reconstruct individual collections. Richard Reynolds, for example, took with him a wide range of classics and patristics presumably accumulated in his Cambridge days.[54] But while there were such patristic straws in the wind, the study of the fathers did not really take off until the 1510s. The dominance of the scholastics of the *via antiqua* at the end of the fifteenth century remains incontestable.

Openness to new humanist values and commitment to traditional methods, which in various ways characterised both the arts and the theology courses, helped form the outlook of the generation which passed through Cambridge at that time. Drawing together material from diverse sources it is possible to give some colour to this sketch of the education available by looking at the sort of people it produced. The picture that emerges is of a reforming circle, whose members were open to humanism, keen patrons of education, committed to orthodoxy, zealous preachers, and promoters of ecclesiastical reform. This is most obvious in the case of Fisher himself. As chancellor of the university, and as in effect co-founder with Lady Margaret Beaufort of Christ's and St John's

Colleges, his commitment to education hardly requires emphasis. His zeal in residing in his diocese and in conducting regular visitations is attested not only by his first hagiographer but by the evidence of his episcopal register.[55] And his publications are proof enough of his orthodoxy and of his performance as preacher. Yet Fisher has often been presented as an exception among his episcopal and clerical colleagues. It is therefore worth showing that he was in fact a representative, albeit an outstanding one, of a widespread reformist milieu.

Among the Cambridge contemporaries with whom Fisher had an enduring connection, the most notable and perhaps the most surprising name is that of John Colet. Appropriated exclusively for Oxford by Anthony à Wood, and apotheosised by Seebohm as an 'Oxford Reformer', Colet in fact received his original university education at Cambridge, where he took his BA in 1485 and his MA in 1489.[56] His commitment to preaching, to education and to ecclesiastical reform can certainly be paralleled in the Cambridge of the late fifteenth century. The only *caveat* which must be entered is that Colet was fiercely anti-scholastic – or at least anti-Thomist. As Colet himself had deposited a copy of Thomas's commentary on the *Sentences* as a graduation caution in 1485, and was later to refer in a marginal annotation to the 'philopompi Cantabrigienses', it is tempting to speculate that the standard of Cambridge tuition prejudiced him against this tradition.[57] However, though Colet's attitude has been taken to demonstrate that he was an outright human-ist, his distaste for Aquinas owed less to the barbarity of his style – Colet's own was hardly any better – than to his temerity in importing Aristotelian philosophy into the discussion of Christian mysteries. Moreover, it has recently been argued that Colet stood very firmly in the pre-Aristotelian scholastic tradition of Bonaventure.[58] Such a position, redolent of the 'fideism' attacked by Erasmus in the *Antibarbari*,[59] could militate as strongly against Cicero as against Aristotle. Colet's statutes for St Paul's School confirm the anti-pagan bias of his mind. Although 'Tully and Salust and Virgill and Terence' are mentioned as masters of true eloquence, the models laid down for the particular attention of scholars are 'goode auctors suche as haue the veray Romayne eliquence joyned withe wisdome specially Cristyn auctours that wrote theyre wysdom with clene and chast laten': namely, Lactantius, Prudentius, Proba, Sedulius and Iuven-cus among the fathers, and Baptista Mantuanus and Erasmus among the moderns.[60] Although his attitude to Aquinas was perhaps untypical, Colet's achievements in other fields place him in the mainstream of the reformist movement that can be discerned in late fifteenth-century Cambridge. His reputation as a preacher and a proponent of reform calls for no remark here, nor do his original efforts in scriptural exegesis. All that need be emphasised is his connection with Fisher. They shared not only a common background in Cambridge but a number of friends, including Erasmus, Thomas More and

Cuthbert Tunstall, as well as a slightly older Cambridge figure, William Melton, to whom we shall shortly turn. Besides this they shared a number of tastes – for Carthusian piety, for Greek and for the cult of the name of Jesus – which locate them in that circle of reformist devotion centred on the court and person of Lady Margaret Beaufort.[61] More reliably, a personal association between them in the cause of reform can be seen in their presence, together with another mutual friend Richard Kidderminster (abbot of Winchcombe), on the small commission for reform set up by Warham at the 1510 Convocation, where Colet delivered the sharply critical reformist sermon familiar to us from so many histories of the English Reformation.[62]

Probably the most influential figure in Fisher's own formation at Cambridge was his tutor, William Melton, who therefore deserves our close scrutiny. He first comes to our attention because of two flattering references in Fisher's *De Veritate*, where he is praised as an 'outstanding theologian' and remembered as Fisher's tutor in Euclid – a fact which connects both men with the re-introduction of mathematics to the curriculum. Fisher recalled in particular Melton's lesson that if you fail to grasp the significance of even one iota of a Euclidean proof, then you have failed to grasp the proof itself – a lesson that Fisher characteristically transferred to the exposition of scripture.[63] Melton's connection with Fisher is confirmed not only by Fisher's first hagiographer, but by two entries in the *Grace Books* for the year 1496. On Melton's graduation as doctor of divinity, John Fisher and one Ralph Collingwood stood surety to the tune of forty pounds for the fulfilment of his doctoral obligations. All three men were fellows of Michaelhouse, and soon afterwards they stood surety likewise for one John Constable on his graduation as doctor of canon law.[64] Connections between this group and John Colet persisted throughout their lives. Melton, for example, went on to become chancellor of York Minster, where both Colet and Collingwood held prebends, while Constable was master of the nearby St Leonard's Hospital.

What sort of man was this tutor whom Fisher recalled so fondly in later years? We are fortunate in being able to ascertain something about his intellectual interests, enough to cast considerable doubt on the assumption that he educated Fisher 'on a conventional, scholastic diet'.[65] Melton actually published around 1510 a short sermon, addressed to candidates for holy orders, which probably formed part of the campaign to reform the English Church that occupied the higher clergy in the opening years of Henry VIII's reign.[66] His reformist, even Christian humanist, predilections become apparent not only in his high ideal of the priesthood and in his trenchant criticisms of the contemporary clergy for falling short of it, but in his emphasis on education as a means of reform and in his use of the humanist code words 'bonae literae'.[67] He was at pains to point out that the invention of printing left no excuse for ignorance, because it brought the works of the fathers within the reach of all.[68]

In many ways Melton's sermon is reminiscent of Colet's. It is therefore neither surprising nor incongruous to find at the end of the pamphlet a short epigraph commending both the author and his message by none other than John Colet.[69] When we find in the inventory of Melton's will the revealing entry 'A little table that was Mr. Doctor Colette's', we are justified in concluding that their relationship was personal as well as professional.[70] Further light is shed on his interests by the prefaces he wrote for some Carthusian devotional treatises. These underline his concern for personal holiness and reveal that he shared with Fisher and Colet affection for the Carthusians and devotion to the Name of Jesus.[71] The last of his literary remains is a continuation of the chronicle of the archbishops of York. As a work of history it has little intrinsic merit, but it does show that he was a more conscientious chancellor than many of his predecessors. Keeping the chronicle was a statutory obligation of the chancellor – but Melton had to catch up on a backlog of 150 years. He was active too in other cancellarial duties, figuring prominently in the records of the drive against Lollardy of 1511–12.[72] His zeal for orthodoxy was also to find literary expression. According to Fisher, he wrote a tract against Luther, which unfortunately was not printed and has not survived.[73]

The most informative of Melton's scarce monuments, though, is his will, dated 20 August 1528. Attached to it is an inventory which includes a list of over a hundred books, almost all of them printed. The library has been described as 'fashionably humanist'.[74] If so, then it is emphatically Christian humanist. Its determining feature is its wealth of patristic literature. Origen, Eusebius, Athanasius, Chrysostom, Hesychius, Dionysius, John Damascene, Cyprian, Jerome, Ambrose, Augustine, Gregory, Cassiodorus and Bede – many of them in complete editions – account for a third of the volumes. There are only a dozen scholastic and medieval theologians, and about the same number of classics. The other major category of the library is contemporary literature. As well as *Utopia* and the *Novum Instrumentum*, Melton possessed two Greek grammars and several books by Valla, Pico, Lefèvre d'Etaples and Erasmus. Melton's reading list is thus markedly broader than that available in late fifteenth-century England, but very similar to what we can reconstruct for his pupil Fisher. The presence of at least three of Fisher's own polemical works in Melton's collection suggests that the two men kept up their friendship.[75] Some letters in the archives of St John's College corroborate this. John Watson, at that time a fellow of St John's, wrote to Nicholas Metcalfe (master of the college, and also Fisher's archdeacon) at Rochester in 1519 to ask for copies of the *De Unica Magdalena* to send to Melton and others of Fisher's friends in Yorkshire.[76] John Constable mentioned in a letter to Fisher that he expected to hear from Melton if Fisher was engaged in composing another book.[77] And Fisher's own knowledge of Melton's efforts against Luther confirms that their friendship was especially concerned with literary matters.

Both Fisher and Melton exhibited in their subsequent careers the intellectual tendencies characteristic of late fifteenth-century Cambridge. In this regard, it is worth noting that Melton may well have attended the lectures of Traversagni, and that he, like Traversagni, was a client of Thomas Rotherham (archbishop of York), the benefactor of the Cambridge University Library.[78] Melton's library, like Fisher's, reflected a commitment to humanism for the sake of theology rather than an interest in secular literature – only a handful of his books were classical. This common characteristic of their minds was picked up by no less a critic than Erasmus, who seems to have known Melton personally, doubtless through Fisher. He bracketed the two men together in 1525 as sound theologians who nevertheless approved of his work on scripture. Erasmus praised Melton's encouragement of the younger generation to the study of languages and letters, making specific mention of his sermon to candidates for ordination. Passing straight on to talk of Fisher, he emphasised that the latter's enthusiasm for Greek and Hebrew was directed not towards the promotion of secular literature, but to the deeper understanding of scripture.[79] And this in turn suggests a parallel with Colet who, as we have seen, had little time for secular literature and less for pagan philosophy. Perhaps the best summary possible of the attitudes of Colet, Fisher and Melton is that for them the 'Mantuan Poet' was not Publius Vergilius Maro, but Baptista Mantuanus (Giovanni Battista Spagnuoli), the fifteenth-century Italian Carmelite whose spiritual verses in classical metres enjoyed immense vogue in contemporary Europe.[80]

The names John Constable and Ralph Collingwood, which have already been mentioned, also reward investigation. Constable was a member of an influential and well-connected gentry family of the East Riding of Yorkshire. Through his mother, Agnes, he was a relative of William Melton,[81] and his family also had extensive and enduring links with that of Fisher. Indeed, Fisher may well have owed to these local magnates the patronage that gave the start to his successful career. When Fisher travelled to London as vice-chancellor in 1502, Thomas Constable, a nephew of John, accompanied him.[82] A brother of Fisher's, named Ralph, was in the service of Sir Marmaduke Constable of Flamborough, John's brother, and Sir Marmaduke himself endowed fellowships at St John's College in his will – his brother acting as executor in this matter.[83] John Constable himself was born around 1461,[84] and studied canon law at Cambridge before going on to hold a series of major benefices in the Lincoln cathedral chapter, culminating in the post of dean which he held from 1514 until his death in 1528.[85] He seems to have taken his official duties unusually seriously. The keynote of his career, in an age of absenteeism among the upper clergy, was residence. His epitaph in the cathedral proudly describes him as 'per XX annos Residentiarii'.[86] A recent study of the diocese of Lincoln has revealed that Constable was prominent in attempts to improve the record of residence of the cathedral prebendaries. Constable himself had an impressive record, and residentiary canons needed his permission for even a single night's absence. Moreover, there was a marked decline in the rate of residence after his death.[87] Given his commitment to Lincoln, he cannot have resided much at the hospital of St Leonard's York, of which he was master for nearly thirty years.[88] Yet he presumably saw that it was well-managed in his absence, because it has been recently described as 'very much alive and well', boasting 'impressive facilities'.[89] In this context it is worth remembering that the hospital offered not only shelter to the distressed, but schooling to local children, which perhaps allows us to add concern for education to concern for ecclesiastical reform among Constable's qualities, and to locate him firmly in the reforming circle we are examining.[90] Constable was certainly in sympathy with the reforming spirit of such men as Colet, Fisher and Melton, and his connection with this circle survived his departure from Cambridge. He remained a correspondent of Fisher. In one letter he declined an invitation to accompany Fisher on a projected delegation to the Fifth Lateran Council, pleading that his oath of residence prevented him. That he shared the honour of such an invitation with Erasmus is some measure of the esteem in which Fisher held him.[91] In another letter, he congratulated Fisher on his exposition of the Gospels in some recent, but unfortunately unnamed, work; confidently expected to hear from Fisher or Melton of any further books that he might produce; and mentioned a recent visit to Fisher.[92]

Ralph Collingwood, like Fisher and Melton, was a theologian and a fellow of Michaelhouse. Perhaps because his career took him away from the east of England (he ended up as dean of Lichfield), there is no evidence of continued contact between him and the others. On the other hand, some features of his career are of special interest. He refounded the song school at the church of St Thomas, Stratford-on-Avon, providing for the basic education of the choristers and ordaining that at meals they should read to the clergy from the scripture or some other approved book. At Lichfield itself he left a hundred marks towards the construction of a new cathedral library.[93] And it has been conjectured, albeit on the insubstantial basis that both were members of Doctors Commons, that he was 'Radulphus', the 'most refined philosopher', to whom Colet dedicated his exposition of Genesis.[94] Of greatest interest, though, is that Collingwood enjoyed a considerable reputation as a preacher. A manuscript he once owned contains a contemporary annotation describing him as a famous preacher,[95] and a chronicle of the cathedral written shortly afterwards records that he was the first and only dean to preach to the people every Sunday – apparently for half an hour at a time. In Collingwood and Constable we thus have two churchmen whose careers, though typical in their pluralism of the gentle born clergy, nevertheless shared in their own way the commitment to educational and ecclesiastical reform, to the interpretation of scripture and to preaching, that characterised Melton, Fisher and Colet.

Many of Fisher's friends pursued their careers almost entirely within the confines of the university. Richard Bekynsall (president of Queens'), John Fawne (first Lady Margaret preacher in the university), John Fotehed (master of Michaelhouse), Henry Hornby (master of Peterhouse) and Robert Shorton (first master of St John's), were all theologians and all in that progressive group in the university associated with the patronage of Lady Margaret Beaufort and her protégé Fisher.[96] The common factor in the careers of most of these friends of Fisher was association either with his original college of Michael-house or with St John's, the college he did so much to establish. Hornby was prominent among Lady Margaret's advisers, and composed for her an office of the Name of Jesus.[97] He also handled a great deal of business for Fisher relating to the foundation of St John's.[98] Robert Shorton (a client at first of Richard Fox, thanks to whom he became master of Pembroke) went on to become first master of St John's and receive a benefice in Fisher's diocese before moving further up the scale into the service of Wolsey and ultimately of Catherine of Aragon. He followed Fisher in defending the validity of the king's marriage to Catherine of Aragon.[99] Fotehed and Bekynsall were both col-leagues from the Michaelhouse days. Bekynsall certainly owed his preferment at Queens' to the influence of Fisher, who nominated him as his successor to the presidency there in 1508.[100] And Fotched's attitude to Fisher, as revealed in his letters, was that of client to patron even as master of Michaelhouse.[101] Closest of all to Fisher was Nicholas Metcalfe, who unites the Michaelhouse and St John's connections. A colleague of Fisher from the 1490s, Metcalfe appears to have entered his service in 1507, when a university grace dis-pensed him from his lecturing obligations because of his business with the chancellor.[102] In due course he became Fisher's right-hand man as archdeacon of Rochester and third master of St John's, apparently dividing his time between his two posts. In charge of the university's most progressive college for nearly twenty years, his wise rule there earned him a posthumous tribute from Roger Ascham as 'A man meanelie learned himselfe, but not meanely affec-tioned to set forward learning in others'.[103] He was involved in the publication of his patron's first polemical work, the De Unica Magdalena, and promoted his literary endeavours in other ways, obtaining for him a copy of Chrysostom's sermons De Iudaeis.[104] Metcalfe shared his master's zeal for orthodoxy, preaching against heresy in the wake of the scandal caused by Robert Barnes in 1525, and (with Shorton) supporting Fisher in the disputes at Convocation over Henry's divorce and the royal supremacy in the 1530s.[105] It is hardly surprising that he should have been compelled by a personal interview with Cromwell to resign his mastership in the aftermath of the Pilgrimage of Grace.[106]

The last two figures who claim our attention in this context are Nicholas West and Cuthbert Tunstall. Some proof of their friendship may be found in the fact that among only five episcopal consecrations at which Fisher is known to have assisted were those both of West to Ely (7 October 1515) and of

Tunstall to London (22 October 1522).[107] West had been a companion on the arts course with whom Fisher had practised disputation. As bishop of Ely, he was made visitor of St John's College in the original statutes of 1516, and Fisher praised his pastoral zeal in residing in his diocese and preaching the Word of God to his flock.[108] The size of West's library confirms Fisher's opinion that he was no mean scholar.[109] And he was, like Fisher, a patron both of the short-lived Cambridge printing press of John Siberch and of the man who brought Siberch to Cambridge, Richard Croke, the university's second lecturer in Greek.[110]

Tunstall's time at Cambridge, like that of Colet, is often overlooked. But an association with Fisher, who was at that time an influential figure in the university, is strongly supported by later evidence. His humanist credentials included not only the friendship of Erasmus and More, but also the study of Greek and Hebrew, and the authorship of a book on arithmetic. He was a close friend of Fisher and West, and may have kept in touch with Fisher at least during his years as almoner to Warham at Canterbury (Warham too was a friend of Fisher, who as bishop of Rochester acted as his cross-bearer on ceremonial occasions). The three men were especially close in the investigation and suppression of heresy in the 1520s. Tunstall encouraged Fisher to write against the Lutherans, and Fisher gave him and West pride of place among those to whom he submitted drafts of his writings for comment and criticism, dedicating his *Sacri Sacerdotii* to Tunstall and his *Defensio Regiae Assertionis* to West. All three men were patrons of the tireless German Catholic polemicist, Johann Cochlaeus, and their association continued into the troubled times that followed. All three were counsel to Queen Catherine in the legatine tribunal convoked to adjudge the validity of her marriage to Henry VIII, and they all wrote treatises on her behalf.[111] West joined Fisher and John Clerk (bishop of Bath and Wells) in their appeal to Rome in 1530 against the recent anti-clerical legislation, an appeal which succeeded only in getting them temporarily imprisoned; and Tunstall registered a protest against the recognition of Henry as supreme head of the Church of England.[112] Their common front in opposition to Henry's policies was dissolved only by West's timely death in 1533 and Tunstall's capitulation under pressure the following year.

It has been the intention of this chapter to go beyond the conventionally vague delineation of a subject's 'background', and to produce instead evidence from that background which casts a revealing light upon Fisher's character and development. In the course of this survey, it has become plain that Fisher was not the victim of some decadent and 'merely' medieval educational machine. He was exposed at Cambridge from an early date to the rising tide of humanism, a movement which at least in that local context supplemented rather than militated against the still dominant scholasticism. This early exposure can be reasonably assumed to have shaped his subsequent pursuit and patronage of humanists and humanist endeavours, which we shall examine in more detail in chapter 3. Even at the time, though, Fisher was closely associated with the reception of *bonae literae* and with the implementation of curricular reform, as were many of his colleagues. These men were, like him, keen (though not necessarily effective) educational and ecclesiastical reformers. They were distinguished not by the cloistered and blinkered attitudes often ascribed to the higher clergy of the late medieval Church, but by openness to change, albeit within the confines of established doctrinal orthodoxy. This is a characteristic that we will trace with increasing clarity and confidence in Fisher himself in the following chapters. In the meantime it remains to be seen whether there was any sort of common concern or underlying unity binding together the curricular changes we have investigated and explaining their attraction for the reformist circle in which Fisher was a central figure. If there was any such underlying unity, it is to be discerned in a profound concern for the preaching of the Word of God. The changes in both arts and theology, whether statutory or not, were orientated towards raising the quantity and quality of preaching. This was made explicit in the teaching of Traversagni, whose courses in rhetoric and ethics were designed to inculcate the proper style and the proper content of sermons. Rhetorical skill made a preacher's message more palatable to his audience, and knowledge of ethics clarified the virtues and the vices which he ought to commend or discourage. Commitment to the ideal of preaching was characteristic of late fifteenth-century Cambridge and can be perceived in the careers of the men it sent forth. John Alcock, founder of Jesus College in the 1490, was one of the best-known preachers of his day and had several sermons printed.[113] John Colet became a regular court preacher, chosen throughout most of the 1510s to deliver the prestigious Good Friday sermon before Henry VIII himself.[114] We have already given some attention to William Melton's extant sermon, and we have noticed the high esteem in which West and Collingwood were held as preachers. Tunstall too has left one or two sermons, and we have additional testimony to his zeal in the praise lavished on him by the visiting bishop and diplomat Johann Fabri in 1527. Fabri, who was himself a noted preacher, reformer and controversialist, ranked Tunstall with John Longland (bishop of Lincoln) and Fisher himself.[115] But it is in the career of Fisher himself that this concern with preaching the Word was best exemplified, and in the following chapter we shall see how his studies, his patronage and his personal practice were directed towards this end.

The preaching bishop

THAT PREACHING was not an invention of the Reformation is hardly an original observation. Yet it cannot be made too often. The Reformers' polemic against 'dumb dogs' and 'mass mumblers' continues to exercise a regrettable fascination over some elements of the historiographical tradition. Yet such rhetoric was in many ways little more than a continuation of an educated clerical critique of the Church which had been in circulation for more than a century before Luther came on the scene. The fact that it was to remain a common complaint of both Catholic and Protestant reformers for a further century should warn us against assuming too readily that Reformation or Counter-Reformation offered instant solutions. More importantly, the ulterior motives by which such rhetoric was often impelled should warn us against assuming too readily that the situation was as bad as enthusiastic reformers wished to make out. In fact there was considerable demand for sermons in the century preceding the Reformation, not only in England but also on the Continent. Popular revivalists such as Bernardino of Siena, Johann Geiler von Keysersberg, Olivier Maillard and Girolamo Savonarola are the most outstanding representatives of a movement whose effects are most easily measured by the printing of sermons and the spread of the pulpit in the later fifteenth century. The prerequisite of an increasing provision of sermons was a better educated clergy, and this objective was pursued from the early fifteenth century in a wave of new educational foundations, both of colleges in the universities and of grammar schools in the country at large. The role of clerical benefactors in these new foundations has long been recognised. While the education offered by grammar schools was probably too basic to make much direct contribution to the supply of preachers – although it doubtless equipped many priests to take advantage of the prepared sermons rendered more widely available by the printing press – the new collegiate foundations were often directed specifically to this end. Most such foundations gave explicit preference in their statutes to the study of theology over the study of law, and it is obvious that by the time Fisher arrived at Cambridge the provision of preachers was becoming a major aim of the university.

Even during his own lifetime John Fisher enjoyed widespread fame as a preaching bishop. Seventeen of his sermons have come down to us, more than survive from any other early sixteenth-century clergyman except John Longland.[1] Reports of his zeal in preaching to his flock come to us not merely from the hagiographic early life, but from contemporary witnesses such as Johann Fabri (bishop of Constance, who visited England in 1527) and of course Erasmus.[2] Not only was Fisher an able preacher, he was also committed to extending and improving the provision of preaching within the Church, and he entertained a high opinion of the place of preaching in the Christian life. Preaching the Word of God was the objective to which all his other intellectual and educational concerns were subordinated, as he himself made clear in his original statutes for St John's College, Cambridge (1516).[3] He embodied this principle in the requirement that a quarter of the fellows should be deputed to preach at least eight sermons a year each in the vernacular to the people anywhere they wished (other than in a benefice of theirs), and that in addition they should preach once a year in the college chapel on a Sunday or feast day. Various privileges were accorded to those undertaking these duties, and penalties were laid down for failure to fulfil their obligations.[4] Later versions of the statutes confirmed and expanded upon this requirement, allowing preachers to be chosen if necessary from outside the college, and adding to their duties that of expounding the scripture readings of the day in college every day during term.[5] Erasmus was aware of Fisher's agenda, reporting that he had founded three colleges at Cambridge to send forth theologians trained not so much for disputation as for preaching.[6] And it was for this reason also that Fisher had repeatedly urged Erasmus to compose his handbook for preachers, De Ratione Concionandi.[7] This concern reflected the milieu in which he had been immersed at Cambridge. The reformers there with whom he had been associated were mostly keen preachers or patrons of preaching themselves, and the university poured forth a stream of talented preachers in the early sixteenth century. Fisher himself was to be directly involved in several efforts to take the reform of preaching in hand. The first of his achievements in this regard was to persuade Lady Margaret Beaufort to endow at Cambridge the Lady Margaret preachership. Under the statutes of this foundation the university was to elect every year a graduate of master's or higher standing to preach six sermons at specified sites around the country. The first incumbent of this office was John Fawne.[8] A more widely felt reform was the foundation around the same time of the university preacherships. Under the terms of a papal bull granted in May 1503, the university was to select each year twelve theology students of at least MA standing who were to be free for that year to preach anywhere in the kingdom.[9] The records of the Cambridge proctors preserve for us the names of more than 150 men who held these licences between 1504 and 1523. The roll includes such names as Richard Reynolds, Thomas Cranmer, Hugh Latimer and Henry Gold, all of whom were to fall victim one way or another to Tudor religious changes.[10] The precise part that Fisher took in the establishment of these preacherships is unknown, although he was vice-chancellor when the original petition was probably made to Rome.[11]

Fisher's commitment to providing more and better preachers must be put in the context of his Pauline views on the importance of sermons in the life of the Christian and on the place of preaching in the Christian ministry. Citing Paul's statement, 'I have goten you by prechynge the holy gospel of Cryste', he observed that priests deserved to be called the fathers of the Christian people because of their role in preaching and teaching them Christian doctrine.[12] Elsewhere he warned against the laziness that might deter people from going to church 'to abyde to be at the seruyce of god, and to here holsom doctryne'. In a much later work, his *Assertionis Lutheranae Confutatio*, he criticised Luther's denial of free will on the grounds that it might give sinners an excuse not to attend the sermons that might otherwise bring about their conversion. He claimed to know several examples of sinners who had been converted by sermons. It is clear that for him the sermon was at least an occasion of grace, and preaching a primary instrument in bringing sinners to Christ.[13] His fullest statement of the Pauline theme of 'faith from hearing' was made in the sermon he delivered at the recantation of Robert Barnes in 1526, where he cited that very text in a long passage about the importance of preaching. Having cited in addition Paul's questions, 'Howe shall the people beleve/if they here nat? . . . And howe shall they here without it be preached unto them?' he went on, 'the blyndnes of our hartes can nat be put away/but by true faith: true faith can nat be gotten/but by herynge of this worde. The heryng of this worde shal nat be had/but by the meanes of preachynge: preachynge can nat be ministred without the preacher.'[14] This could almost have been a manifesto for his educational patronage.

The most important evidence we have about Fisher as a preacher is provided by his seventeen surviving sermons, and the rest of this chapter will concentrate mainly upon these in an attempt to discover how he went about his task and what he was chiefly concerned to put across to his audiences. Such conclusions as we can reach must be qualified at the start by the observation that the evidence of these sermons is limited and perhaps unrepresentative. This can be readily appreciated from a consideration of their nature. Ten of them constituted an expository cycle on the seven penitential psalms, probably delivered in 1504 to his patroness, Lady Margaret Beaufort, and her household – an unusually sophisticated audience containing a high proportion of clergy and educated laymen.[15] Their length suggests that they were not delivered in the course of mass or some other service but afterwards, as was often the case at that time. Two more were funeral sermons, one for Lady Margaret, and one for her son, Henry VII, both delivered in 1509, and both in the context of a mass for the dead, though again, on grounds of length, probably after rather than during the service. A further two sermons were delivered at St Paul's in London (in 1521 and 1526) to large and predominantly lay audiences, but their subject matter – the falsity of Lutheran doctrine – is unlikely to have been that of his everyday preaching. Their occasions were equally uncommon, the proclamation of the papal condemnation of Luther (accompanied by a burning of Lutheran books) in the first instance, and the recantation of Robert Barnes in the second. We shall postpone consideration of these sermons until a later chapter. Of the remaining three, one was a Good Friday sermon on the crucifix (clearly given at some point in, or more probably after, the service of veneration of the cross) and the other two were a pair on the text, 'except your righteousness shall exceed the righteousness of the scribes and Pharisees, ye shall in no case enter into the kingdom of heaven' (Mt 5:20). The latter formed the introduction to a longer cycle expounding the ten commandments, but the subsequent sermons were probably not published, and have certainly not survived.[16] The first of the pair contains in addition a tantalising reference to sermons Fisher had preached to the same audience in previous years. In urging his hearers to intercede with prayers and good works on behalf of the souls in Purgatory, he says 'Of the which bycause I haue spoken unto you in other yeres past, I shall nat nede now to reherce the same agayne.'[17] This leads us to the further conclusion that the cycle of sermons to which this pair formed the introduction was an annual, or at least regular, event. And it provides confirmation that Fisher preached frequently. We know besides of other lost sermons of his. He preached at a diocesan synod at Rochester in 1527, and in favour of Catherine of Aragon in June 1532.[18] Besides these, there is a reference to two sermons on prayer based on Paul's 'sine intermissione orate' (1 Thess 5:17).[19] It is in fact conceivable that one of them survives, at least in substance, in the form of Fisher's *De necessitate orandi*, a treatise on prayer cast in the tripartite structure typical of his sermons which starts with the similar text 'oportet semper orare' (Lk 18:1). Several other references to a book or sermon by Fisher in favour of papal supremacy may indicate the existence of another work, but may merely be garbled references to his first sermon against Luther.[20] In any case, it is clear that almost all the sermons which survive or of which we know were preached for special reasons or occasions, rather than in the fulfilment of ordinary pastoral duties. The only exceptions to this rule are the two sermons on justice and the one on the crucifix.

The formal structure of Fisher's sermons was traditional enough. The initial enunciation of the text ('theme') was usually followed by a general introduction to the text or to the sermon ('antitheme' and 'introduction'). Several of the sermons include at this point or later a pause for a prayer (the 'Pater Noster' or 'Ave Maria'), and it is likely that this was done even in those sermons which do not explicitly make such provision.[21] Then Fisher would outline the broad 'division' of his sermon, usually into three headings. These three headings were then taken in order (the 'dilation'). Each was subdivided, usually into three or four sections; and even these subsections were themselves sometimes further subdivided. A conclusion recapitulated the main divisions, and finished with an invocation of divine assistance. This pattern is generally known to students of medieval preaching as the 'new' style, made popular by the mendicant friars from the thirteenth century onwards.[22] The 'old' style was a less formal verse by verse exposition of a passage of scripture. It has been suggested that Fisher's sermons on the penitential psalms are examples of the 'old' style, but it would be better to say that they represent an interesting and effective blend of the two styles.[23] Their strongly tripartite divisions place them firmly in the 'new' model, yet neither interfere with nor detract from the exposition of the psalms. On the contrary, the clear structures make the exposition more memorable. In the sixteenth century the 'new' style was to give way to a more fluent and literary structure, under the growing influence of humanist canons of rhetoric, with a greater emphasis than before on the exposition of the sermon text. Fisher's sermons exhibit certain strivings in this new direction. An interest in humanist rhetoric is revealed in a passing reference to Cicero's *De Oratore*, and in the express modelling of his two funeral sermons on the pattern of classical funeral oratory.[24] Although his divisions are clearly drawn, they rarely seem excessively artificial, and transitions are handled so fluently that they are often hardly noticed as the thought is developed.

The sermons to be considered in this chapter, namely the funeral addresses, the sermons on the penitential psalms and the pair on Christian justice, were *sermones ad populum*. As such they give us some idea of what message a highly talented preacher was anxious to convey to his audience in the early sixteenth century. The relative popularity of the sermons on the psalms in particular suggests that this message found a receptive audience among the literate laity.[25] In the light of received wisdom about the prevalence of fearful and anguished consciences in the late medieval Church, we might expect the message to dwell in almost loving detail on the tortures of the damned and thus to instil fear and guilt in the minds of listeners. Yet in Fisher's sermons, hell is mentioned regularly indeed, but far from obsessively, and for the most part only in passing. Its pains are not evoked in any detail. There is no imaginative delineation of the punishments reserved for particular crimes. Instead, Fisher emphasises in rather abstract terms that the pain is intolerable and interminable. It has been unfortunate for the understanding of Fisher's preaching that one of his most striking images concerned hell. At the beginning of his exposition of Psalm 50 he portrayed man as suspended over hell like a bucket in a well, held aloft only by a thin cord, that is, by being alive, a condition dependent on God's will.[26] He emphasised that it is a 'ferefull condycyon' that people are in.[27] Yet the image itself was more concerned with the precariousness of the human condition than with the details of eternal damnation. His use of fear was not for its own sake.

He did not regard fear as a desirable thing. On the contrary, he saw it, together with sin and ignorance, as one of three varieties of 'wretchednesse' with which the human race was beset. Dividing fear into six categories – of hell, of purgatory, of pain, of death, of divine chastisement (on earth) and of sin – he offered prayer to Our Lady as a means of securing peace and comfort from such mental troubles. In his first sermon on justice, Fisher explicitly presented his audience not, as many Catholic predecessors had done and many Protestant successors were to do, with the prospect of hell, but with the prospect of purgatory to deter them from vice – an inherently far less 'negative' incentive. It has often been observed, most forcibly by C.S. Lewis, that Fisher equates the pains of purgatory in intensity with those of hell, an opinion which was of course by no means peculiar to Fisher.[28] And this topos (which occurs only twice in his sermons) has been used to present his theology as 'essentially negative', representative of a cosmology from which Christians of the sixteenth century would be only too ready to escape. This is a silly parody of a system of belief that had not only been widely accepted and practised in the three centuries preceding the Reformation, but was undergoing refinement, development and extension – largely by popular demand – until and even through the Reformation itself. Fisher's sermon is in fact more concerned with what can be done to avoid purgatory and to help other souls escape it than with the nature of their suffering. It finishes with an assurance that if his hearers follow his advice they have every chance of avoiding purgatory altogether and going straight to heaven. Like most preachers, Fisher matched his deterrent with the enticing prospect of heaven as a positive incentive to virtue. And it is worth remarking that in his surviving sermons there is more detailed consideration of the joys of heaven than of the pains of purgatory or hell.

The most striking feature of Fisher's sermons on the psalms is their strong emphasis on God's mercy and on the efficacy of penance: 'Our moost gracyous lorde almyghty god is mercyfull to them that be penytent.'[29] His message was dominated by the concepts of God, sin, penitence and mercy. These four words, and their many synonyms, run through the sermons and put other themes into the shade. Where hell and eternal damnation are mentioned about a hundred times (about as frequently as heaven), mercy and forgiveness are mentioned more than five hundred times, God and sin more frequently still. The discussion of sin is far from mere cliché. Sin (rather than hell) is presented as the enemy; and devils, when they are mentioned, as agents of temptation in this world rather than of torture in the next. Moreover, as has been properly remarked in a recent analysis of the penitential teaching of the sermons, the discussion is refreshingly free from 'the seven deadly sins'.[30] Indeed, Fisher's teaching falls instead into the pattern identified by John Bossy in which, during the fifteenth and sixteenth centuries, discussion of sin shifted from the model of the seven deadly sins to that of the ten commandments – which were the subject of the cycle to which the two sermons on justice were an introduction.[31] Fisher's concept of sin as a state is very much in the Augustinian tradition and has of course strong parallels with the concerns of Protestant Reformers. However, while sin is the most common concept, after God, in these sermons, their title itself shows that the author's primary concern is with penitence. It should be emphasised right away that it is the state or process of penitence, rather than the sacrament of penance in particular, which is uppermost in Fisher's mind. The claim that the sermons 'represent an extended meditation on the sacrament of penance in its three parts – contrition, confession, and satisfaction' is not altogether correct.[32] The sacrament of penance holds an important place in the sermons, but receives extensive consideration only in the second and to a lesser extent in the seventh. Elsewhere it is introduced in passing as the seal of the sinner's conversion. Fisher is far more concerned to awaken sinners to their state, and to stir them to conversion. His preaching is orientated more towards the change of heart. In the sermon on Henry VII, itself to a large extent a narrative of death-bed repentance, Fisher cited a text from Augustine, and in rendering it into English expanded the 'voluntatis mutatio' of his authority to a proviso that the sinner's 'wyll be clerely chaunged & tourned to god'.[33]

Even the theme of repentance is subordinated to that of the divine mercy without which repentance would be nothing more than a troubled conscience. Fisher's message is ultimately one of comfort not of terror, and his exposition of the 'Miserere', for instance, is a meditation on mercy: 'Of a trouth the mercyes of almyghty god be innumerable.'[34] As has been recently observed, 'The God of the Penitential Psalms is for Fisher above all a God of mercy and compassion.'[35] Indeed, he turns God's mercy inside out: he may 'be mercyfull vnto whome he wyll', his mercy 'is grete, and so grete that it hath all mesures of gretenes', it is deep, high, broad and long, inward and outward, countless and endless.[36] The divine mercy is the source of all spiritual good. Although, as we shall see, Fisher is far from undervaluing grace, 'mercy' is the word that springs most readily to his lips in describing God's approach to the sinner. Hope of forgiveness is rooted in remembrance of God's mercy: 'this shall soone be done, yf we call to mynde how grete the mercy is of our heuenly fader'.[37] This mercy assumes all the characteristics of the Augustinian concept of grace. 'Man hath no power of hymselfe, it lyeth not in his wyll to contynue or do ony goodnes, but onely by the mercy of god.'[38] This Augustinian theme is underlined by his citation a few lines later of the famous dictum 'Lorde graunte me to fulfyll thy commaundement, & commaunde me what thou wylte.'[39] The equation of mercy and grace is made explicit in his complaint to God, 'Truly this erth these brytell bodyes of ours wyll soone be dryed vp from doyng good werkes, without thou be mercyfull good lorde, & soone make them moyst with the due of thy grace.'[40] Moreover, without that grace it is not possible to refrain from sin – prayer for grace must therefore be incessant.[41] However, God's offer of grace could be refused, and it was not his fault if people did refuse it.[42]

Underlying the emphasis on mercy was a concern to keep sinners from the 'depe dungeon of despayre'[43] into which they might be precipitated by weighing their sins against God's justice or righteousness (he uses both terms, but tends to prefer the latter). The notion that there is some conflict between God's mercy and his justice is one that Fisher on several occasions took pains to dispel. In sermon IX he admitted that God's righteousness demands 'bothe of ryght and equyte a recompense' for sin. But he then emphasised that a perfect recompense had been made through the sacrifice of Christ on the cross: 'his moost precyous body is our sacrefyce, whiche he offred vpon a crosse for the redempcyon of all the worlde'.[44] And since this sacrifice is eternally offered by Christ to the Father in heaven, the Father is ever ready 'to forgyue as soone as we aske forgyuenes'. Because this sacrifice 'is the very strength of our penaunce wherby we may make satysfaccyon for our greuous trespasses', God's righteousness is appeased and offers no obstacle to his mercy.[45] Christ's righteousness is indeed identified with his redeeming sacrifice to the Father in words reminiscent of Luther – or to be more accurate, of Augustine. In penance, according to Fisher, the sinner 'is made clene from synne, & than veryly Iustefyed'. Having come to his confessor as a sinner, 'by the vertue of this sacrament of penaunce he gooth awaye from hym ryghtwyse, not by his owne ryghtwysnes, but by the ryghtwysnes of cryst Ihesu, whiche ryghtwysly redemed vs with his precyous blode as saynt Iohan sayth in thapocalypse, & saynt Poule sheweth. Factus est nobis iusticia.'[46] In the final sermon of the cycle, Fisher even stressed that God's righteousness is a help rather than a hindrance to the repentant sinner, 'for almyghty god of his fydelyte & Iustyce must nedes forgyue them that be confessed truly and with good wyll do penaunce for theyr synnes'.[47] He returned to the themes of mercy, promise and justice in his funeral sermons. In that on Henry VII he emphasised again that God's justice worked in favour of sinners rather than against them. This was firstly because God had promised forgiveness to the repentant sinner (and his righteousness compelled him to keep his promise), and secondly because Christ, alone of all creatures perfectly just and innocent, was the only acceptable and sufficient sacrifice for the sins of the world.[48]

This is not to say, of course, that God is somehow bound by the action of the penitent. On the contrary, God's obligation arises from his own promise and his essential truthfulness.[49] The concept of the promise, of God's 'owne worde & promyse in holy scrypture', is surprisingly prominent in Fisher's sermons – for it is a term we are more accustomed to associate with the theology and spirituality of Luther.[50] A lengthy passage of the first sermon on Psalm 50 recites various scriptural texts which offer mercy to the penitent and appeals to God as truth to keep his word, 'good lorde we knowe that thou arte true, & all that thou doost promyse is very trouth'. Fisher concludes his remarks with the prayer 'Haue in mynde the promyse thou made to euery penytent synner comynge vnto the, whiche is, thou shalte not caste them awaye, & also thou shalte refresshe them. We come therfore vnto the good lorde, caste vs not away but refresshe vs with thy grace and mercy.'[51] It is the truth of God's promises that ultimately inspires hope. Christ has taught that prayer is answered, and 'we knowe ryght well his promyse is true, why? for he is bothe true and also it selfe trouth'. Therefore, 'bycause that he made vs this good and true promyse I haue very ferme confydence and truste boldely for to aske thyn infynyte mercy'.[52] A little later Fisher returned to this theme, observing that it made no difference to God whether people were saved or not, but that since Christ had promised salvation to the repentant, God was bound by his nature to honour that promise. Returning to the subject of promise in sermon IX he paraphrased Ezechiel in the words 'Be ye turned from your synfull lyfe do penaunce for your synnes & they neuer after shall be imputed to you, ye shall neuer be dampned.'[53] To this promise he applied Psalm 129:4, 'Sustinuit anima mea in verbo eius', which he paraphrased equally generously as 'My soule is socoured from despayre by stedfast hope & truste in the promyse of almyghty god.'[54] Moreover, he invoked the traditional attributes of God, such as his omnipotence, immutability and eternity, to confirm his promise.

However, Fisher departed from the path later trodden by Luther in his insistence that the divine promise was conditional and thus in denying that the promise could give rise to absolute certainty about being in a state of grace. In his funeral sermon on Henry VII he observed, 'There is no man be he neuer so perfyte oneles he haue it by reuelacyon that knoweth certaynly wheder he be in the state of grace or no, for of an other maner be the Iugementes of god than of men.' And in his memorial sermon for Lady Margaret he repeated this more briefly, 'As for suerte veray suerte can not be had but only by the revelacyon of god almighty.'[55] Fisher was concerned that Christians might erroneously presume security of salvation on the grounds that Christ, through his passion, had won for them the inheritance of eternal life. In his second sermon on justice he pointed out that, although the inheritance was indeed theirs by virtue of Christ's passion, an individual could still lose his portion by sin, just as great magnates of a kingdom could lose their ample inheritance through treason against their sovereign. To come into their inheritance Christians had to fulfil the conditions of their own baptismal promises, to renounce the devil and all his works. The essence of this condition was that they should keep the commandments, although Fisher made it clear that this did not mean a merely pharasaical or legalistic obedience, but entailed the performance of good deeds of prayer, fasting and almsgiving.[56]

Fisher's teaching on the sacrament of penance as such was predictably mainstream in its orthodoxy. It is worth some attention despite this because it is the only area of doctrine on which we have a substantial body of evidence about his position before as well as after the impact of Luther's teaching. The division of the sacrament into its three parts of contrition, confession and satisfaction is made repeatedly in the course of the sermons on the psalms, and is explored in especial detail in the second. As we have already seen, these sermons are more concerned with the general process of conversion from sin than with the sacramental treatment of the penitent conscience, but nevertheless practical advice about penance is scattered around. All three parts of penance are presented emphatically as gifts of God.[57] Fisher pointed out the uselessness of confession and satisfaction in the absence of genuine contrition.[58] He subscribed to the scholastic commonplace that perfect contrition was itself adequate to receive God's forgiveness,[59] but reminded his listeners that an intention to confess and do satisfaction was part of such perfect contrition. Contrition itself he divided into two kinds or stages, one typified more by fear of divine punishment, the other by sorrow at having offended God. The former stage led on to the latter, and it was possible to attain a fuller sorrow for sins by praying for God's help.[60] This might be taken as an allusion to the scholastic distinction between attrition and contrition, to which he returns in his refutation of Luther twenty years later.[61] But it is important to note that Fisher never spoke in his own person of attrition, using the term only when citing or reporting the views of others. It is likely that his Augustinian views made him unhappy with the scholastic theory that attrition – that is, detestation of one's sins – was possible by man's natural powers, aided only by the 'general influence' of God.[62] He himself, as we shall see in chapter 7, gave more prominence than the scholastics to the role of prevenient grace in justification. Contrition he made dependent on grace: 'In this lyfe contrycyon may soone be had by the grace of god with a lytell sorowe.'[63] He provided a full definition of contrition in sermon IX: 'Contrycyon is a grete inwarde sorowe comynge from the very depnes of the herte with mekenes, by a profounde consyderacyon & remembraunce of our synnes ... an inwarde sorowe of the mynde set in the prevy place of the herte.'[64] This profound consideration of sins was essential, because if sinners did not remember their sins in penitence, then God would remember them in judgment. On the other hand, 'The mercy and goodnes of almyghty god shewed vpon synners is meruayllous grete whiche the more that they call vnto theyr owne mynde and expresse theyr owne trespasses, so moche the more he forgeteth & putteth them out of his mynde.'[65] This antithesis between human remembrance of sin and divine obliviousness of it was drawn almost certainly from the preaching of John Chrysostom. In the course of his *Confutatio* against Luther, Fisher was to refer explicitly to Chrysostom for a passage which included the epigram, 'If we forget our sin, God will remember it. If we are mindful of our sin, God will ignore it.'[66] The sermons contain various reminders of the customary advice for confession. Penitents should confess all their sins to an 'able priest', telling no lies, confessing only their own sins and not those of others; blaming only themselves and not fate, the stars or the devil; not confessing simply the trivial sins while concealing the graver ones; nor making excuses; and above all 'purposynge euer after to abstayne from all occasyons of synne'.[67] Finally comes the stage of satisfaction, which Fisher traditionally enough characterised as the payment of a temporal debt for sins whose debt of eternal punishment had already been met by the grace of Christ. If this temporal debt was not fully paid during one's life on earth, then it would remain to be expiated after death in purgatory.[68] Fisher equated satisfaction with the good works of prayer, fasting and almsgiving, a triad in which he awarded the first place very definitely to prayer.[69] To the 'dylygent excercysinge of good werkes . . . the grace of god is in especyall necessary, wherwith they be plentefully enfused and endewed on whom our mercyfull lorde loketh with the eyen of his mercy and grace'.[70] Zealous performance of works of satisfaction was a sign of the grace of penance, for if the penitent was negligent, he argues, then it was to be feared that 'some maner prevy gyle or faute' remains, and that therefore the contrition and confession have not been genuine.[71]

The literary style, in particular the use of metaphors and similes, of Fisher's sermons has been thoroughly investigated in previous studies.[72] But there are two common metaphors in the sermons on the psalms which cast special light on the theology they endeavour to convey. These are the images of grace as sunlight, and of devotion as a liquid. Fisher's ideal for the soul is that it should be 'full of the lycour of good deuocyon' and thus 'stronge & hardy to withstande all trybulacyons'. This condition is brought about by the word of God, the spiritual bread, which 'causeth all goodnes in the soule, it maketh it moyste and redy to sprynge in good werkes'. In the absence of that bread, 'I am blasted and smyten with dryness lyke vnto hay.' The liquor of devotion wells up in the heart, and from there irrigates the whole soul – and even, on occasion, the body. For there is a clear connection between Fisher's 'liquid' devotion and his emphasis on 'wepynge teres': 'Truly this erth these brytell bodyes of ours wyll soone be dryed vp from doyng good werkes, without thou be mercyfull good lorde, & soone make them moyst with the due of thy grace. And yf it be thy pleasure so to do, than shal the fountaynes of wepynge teres gusshe out.'[73] These tears were an outward sign and guarantee of genuine penitence and grace, because 'who soeuer calleth to mynde all his synnes with true penaunce shall scant kepe hymselfe fro wepynge',[74] and such tears proceed 'from the plenteuousnesse of thy grace'.[75] Thus the tears of Henry VII in his last Lent were an assurance of true repentance, and those of Lady Margaret evidence of her surpassing virtue.[76] In addition, they reflect the presence of the Holy Spirit, who condenses tears in the penitent as warm breath condenses on cold metal or glass.[77] The other image, of grace as sunlight, was built upon the traditional portrayal of Christ as 'lux mundi' and 'sol iustitiae', or 'sonne of ryghtwysnes'. This sun of righteousness rises upon sinners in baptism but sets upon them if they fall into mortal sin. Yet through the sacrament of penance, it 'shyneth agayne fresshe vpon them'.[78] 'From the eyen of almyghty god whiche may be called his grace shyneth forth a meruaylous bryghtnes lyke as the beme that cometh from the sonne. And that lyght of grace stereth and setteth forth the soules to brynge forth the fruyte of good werkes. Euen as the lyght of the sonne causeth herbes to growe & trees to brynge forth fruyte.'[79] Fisher was to return to this theme in his sermon against Luther of 1521, constructing an elaborate analogy on the idea that 'The bemes of almyghty god spred vpon our soules quyckeneth them & causeth this lyfe in vs and the fruyte of good workes.'[80] The light of grace striking the soul illuminates it with faith. If this grace evokes the correct response from the soul, then rays of hope are reflected back towards God and, according to Fisher's understanding of light, the beams are therefore strengthened. These beams of faith and hope are then, as it were, concentrated in one point, like the sun's rays by a magnifying glass, and enkindle the soul with the fire of charity which in turn gives rise to a harvest of good works.[81] The analogy of light is also used in the sermons on the psalms to explain how God, though in himself immutable, seems hard on sinners and kind to the penitent. According to Fisher, sin is like an infection of the eye which makes the light of the sun painful to the victim, although the same light is pleasant to those whose eyes are healthy or healed.[82] This image of Christ as the sun allowed him to expand on the idea of the Blessed Virgin Mary as the dawn in his first sermon on Psalm 37, observing that just as the dawn appears to precede the sun, but is in fact caused by it, so Mary came before Christ but owed her creation and her preservation from original sin entirely to him. Thus, 'this blyssed virgyn full of the bemes of grace was ordeyned by god as a lyght of the mornynge & afterwarde brought forth the bryght shynynge sonne with his manyfolde bemes our sauyoure Cryste'.[83]

Fisher's two funeral sermons, as we have seen, share many characteristics with the sermons on the psalms, especially in their emphasis on God's mercy and righteousness.[84] One especially interesting feature of these two sermons is their deliberate and successful fusion of the 'modern' sermon format with the classical model of the funerary panegyric. In the sermon on Henry VII, Fisher observes that the 'funerall oracyons' of 'seculer oratours' have three parts: expressing commendation of the dead person; compassion for the dead person; and finally consolation for those left behind.[85] Adopting this as the division for his sermon he then adapts it to a Christian content. Thus the commendation of Henry VII passes over his worldly achievements, which are dismissed as transient 'Fumus & umbra', and expatiates instead on his final repentance and good death – appealing to the classical authority of Solon and Seneca for the view that it is the end of one's life which really reveals its quality. In arousing compassion for the late king, Fisher dwells on his physical and spiritual agony in the face of death and judgment, reminding the audience that Henry's worldly possessions brought him no comfort in those last moments. Instead, Henry's hopes were put in God alone, on whose blessed name he called for deliverance. It is at this point, having stirred the pity of his hearers, that Fisher introduces the usual prayer, here for the rest of Henry's soul. The message of consolation which follows is most reminiscent of the sermons on the psalms, reconciling God's justice with his mercy, praising Henry's repentance and declaring him blessed to have been taken from the miseries of his world into the custody of the Lord. The sermon for Lady Margaret follows exactly the same pattern. The commendation is once again mostly of spiritual rather than worldly qualities. Although Fisher does take time to enumerate her nobility according to the various counts of birth, behaviour, character and marriage, he chiefly praises her for her self-discipline, her devotion and her charitable hospitability. The evocation of compassion relies chiefly on her agonies in death, introducing however the idea that these agonies were made less tolerable by her holy life, for the sake of which she might have expected God in his mercy and justice to mitigate her final suffering. And, as in the case of Henry, Fisher concludes this section with a prayer for her soul. The theme he takes up for consolation is that of certain hope of resurrection, adumbrating for his audience the contrast between the sinful body of this life and the risen body of the next.

These outlines, however, do not convey the skill with which in each case the discussion of the dead person is integrated with an exposition of the scriptural text from which the sermon takes its departure. The sermon on Henry VII, though divided into three parts, is at the same time a continuous exposition of the first psalm of the Dirige (Ps. 114, 'Dilexi quoniam exaudiet dominus vocem deprecationis meae'), and is thus similar in form to those on the penitential psalms.[86] The first two verses, an appeal to be heard by God, fit the final repentance for which Henry is commended. The next two verses, expressing fear of death, are woven into Fisher's evocation of compassion for the king's final agonies. And the remaining nine verses, hymning God's mercy, are admirably suited to the preacher's intention to comfort his audience. The sermon on Lady Margaret is based on a conversation between Christ and Martha during the episode of the raising of Lazarus (the gospel for the Requiem mass, Jn 11:1–45, esp. 21–7), and draws out parallels between Lady Margaret and Martha.[87] This theme offers a striking contrast to the conventional sort of discourse upon Martha, who was usually compared with her own sister Mary to the advantage of the latter as models respectively of the active and the contemplative life. Fisher puts a new twist on the traditional view of Martha by taking her as the role model for Lady Margaret in the latter's laudable choice of the active life. The comparisons of the two as noble, self-disciplined and devout are conventional enough, but the final ground for comparison, between Martha's service of Christ and Lady Margaret's of the poor, is given extra point by Fisher's reminder that the poor are the images of Christ.[88] In the second section, Martha's lament to Christ on behalf of her dead brother Lazarus is imaginatively expounded as the complaint of Lady Margaret's soul on behalf of her dead body. The final message of consolation is built around Christ's discussion with Martha about the resurrection. It is remarkable in particular for Fisher's parallel between Martha's confession of faith in Christ ('I haue beleued that thou art cryst the sone of god whiche came in to this worlde') and Margaret's profession, when presented with the blessed sacrament, 'that in the sacrament was conteyned cryst Ihesu the sone of god that dyed for wretched synners vpon the crosse, in whom holly she put her truste and confydence'.[89]

The difference between the two texts adopted as themes for the funeral sermons accounts to some extent for the differences in tone between the sermons themselves, with the emphasis for Henry on repentance and for Margaret on resurrection and hope. But the choice of texts itself reflects Fisher's different attitude towards two very different subjects. This emerges most clearly in the contrast between the total absence of information about Henry VII's life and the relatively detailed account of Margaret's. To put it another way, while he extolled Lady Margaret's life he praised only Henry's death. It is hard to evade the conclusion that Fisher was not a whole-hearted admirer of Henry VII's royal career. The comparison with Manasses, who repented 'after many grete abhomynacyons & outrages', was rather less flattering than the one he had drawn with Moses during Henry's lifetime.[90] Indeed, the way in which he praised Henry for his decision in his last days to reform his government puts this beyond doubt. Fisher's recollection of Henry's intention to reform the administration of justice, to nominate virtuous and learned men for preferment in the Church and to grant a general pardon to his people, amounts to an indictment of the whole reign.[91] His panegyric of Margaret, on the other hand, betrays not merely his closer personal knowledge of her, but also his considerably higher regard for her lifestyle. As her confessor and spiritual director,[92] he was well acquainted with her almost monastic routine of daily devotion, and doubtless had much to do with its shape.

Despite the differences in emphasis between the two sermons there are a great many points of resemblance over and above those of form and structure. The most obvious is the considerable attention lavished in each sermon on the death-bed. The explanation for this is to be found in the second sermon. There, Fisher included among the proofs of Lady Margaret's piety her diligent attendance at the death-beds of members of her household, especially of her almsfolk. Her motive, we are told, was 'to se theym departe and to lerne to deye'.[93] Fisher urged his audience to pay attention to his account of Lady Margaret's final hours, accepting her death with resignation so as 'to lerne therby to prepayre our owne bodyes' for death.[94] Thus his funeral sermons, especially in their printed form, can be taken in part at least as an 'ars moriendi'.

The death-bed scenes resemble each other closely in outline. Each draws attention to the dying person's hope, which is based on 'true beleue . . . in god, in his chirche & in the sacramentes', to their faithful and devout reception of those sacraments,[95] to their physical sufferings[96] and to their calling upon the name of Jesus.[97] In each case, all this is taken as good reason for having confidence that they have died in a state of grace and are therefore saved, but in each case there is a warning that absolute certainty on the matter is impossible without a special revelation.[98]

The *Two Fruytfull Sermons* published in 1532 were, as we have noted, a pair on the single text, 'except your righteousness shall exceed the righteousness of the scribes and Pharisees, ye shall in no case enter into the kingdom of heaven' (Mt 5:20).[99] Their precise liturgical context is unclear, though again their length suggests that they were delivered after, rather than during, a religious service. But they were apparently intended to introduce a longer series on the ten commandments. The second opens with a reminder of 'my fyrst Sermon this other day'[100] and closes with a brief indication of the content of the succeeding sermons. There, having spoken of the 'clene garment of iustyce' put on in baptism, and of its subsequent disfigurement by sin, Fisher said that it must be kept clean by a righteous life of obedience to the commandments, 'of the which my purpose is to speke at large for the tyme that I intend to be occupyed with you'.[101] Such a purpose puts into context his expostulation earlier in that sermon against lechers, bawds, blasphemers, perjurers and breakers of holy days – a list which seems to reflect thinking in terms of the commandments rather than of the seven deadly sins – as also his warning that the condition on which God offered people eternal life was that of keeping his commandments, 'if thou wilt enter into life, keep the commandments' (Mt 19:17).[102] His conclusion that it was expedient for all Christian men and women to learn, know and keep the commandments would have been nugatory if he had not meant to expound the commandments himself.[103] By this time, it was relatively common to preach a cycle of sermons on the commandments. Luther himself, for example, had done so at Wittenberg in 1518.

The role of introducing a discussion of sin and the commandments puts the fruitful sermons into their proper perspective. The first, which is cleverly designed to reflect its occasion (the feast of All Saints) as well as the preacher's wider intentions, takes as its implicit theme the communion of saints. It deals with the three states of the Church – triumphant in heaven, suffering in purgatory and militant on earth. The first section is a lengthy comparison of the true joys of heaven with the transient joys of earth (as represented by the Field of Cloth of Gold). It lays particular emphasis on the joy of seeing once more one's old friends and of meeting 'the other sayntes whiche we dyd chuse for our aduowrers and patrons here in erthe, and whom specyally we dyd worshyp in this worlde'.[104] The discussion of purgatory is oriented towards the commemoration of All Souls (2 November), and presents five reasons for remembering the dead: the general bond of common human nature; particular ties of kinship and friendship; their sorry condition, deprived of heavenly and of earthly pleasures, and experiencing bitter pain; their dependence on our help and our debt to them for benefits previously received; and finally the reward to be expected, in return for helping them, from God and from the intercession of both them and their guardian angels.[105] The final section begins by relating the doctrines of heaven and purgatory to daily life, teaching that the thought of heaven should encourage people to virtue, and the thought of purgatory discourage them from vice.[106] But having come so far with a communitarian doctrine, in which everybody helps everybody else, Fisher then proceeds in a more individualist vein, urging his audience to look to their own souls as nobody else can do it for them. You should value your soul because Christ died for it, and if you betray your low valuation by not taking proper care of it, others will value it at the same level. Other people will look after themselves first, and you should do the same.[107] Moreover, you can do more for yourself in this life than anybody can do for you after your death, for 'as all the dysputers agree, the hyghest degree of fruyte in euery mannes prayer retourneth unto hymselfe. And it is but a secondary fruyt that retourneth into other.'[108] The sermon then concludes with an exhortation to the Christian life in the traditional form, urging repentance and sacramental penance, obedience to the commandments, forgiveness for others, prayer, fasting and almsgiving. Fisher expressed a preference for 'lifetime giving' over testamentary bequests: 'Better is now one peny spent for the welth and saluacyon of thy soule whan thou mayst kepe it unto thy selfe, than a thousande after thy dethe whan thou mayst no longer haue the use therof.'[109] This might be taken as a critique of the proliferation in *post mortem* spiritual provision to which the wills of the time bear such abundant witness, in so far as it might be used as an excuse for failing to give alms during one's life. But the point was in fact a commonplace, and since Fisher himself endowed a chantry chapel for his soul in St John's College it would be a mistake to conclude that he was unhappy wth the conventional pious practice. The highly individualistic, almost 'sauve qui peut', tone of the final part of the sermon, however, deployed in conjunction with the highly communitarian doctrine of the middle section on purgatory, provides an illuminating insight into the religious condition of pre-Reformation England. For it suggests that the strength of communal ideals in one sphere of religious activity – provision for the souls of the departed – did not militate against the strength of individualism in another – provision for one's own soul in this life.

Whereas in the first of the fruitful sermons Fisher had concentrated on the ultimate end of human existence and on how to attain it, in the second he turned to the obstacles placed in the way, namely sin and its consequences, death, judgment and punishment. He began therefore with an exposition of the

Fall as a model for all sins. The three fruits of paradise (of the tree of life, of the tree of death and of other trees) represented the three kinds of earthly pleasure – good, bad and indifferent. The temptation of Adam by Eve signified the rebellion of the inferior against the superior, of the body against the soul. Adam's acceptance of the fruit Eve offered represented the assent of the will to the illicit promptings of the flesh and, as it cost him paradise, so it costs his successors heaven.[110] Against the objection that God had created all people for the inheritance of eternal life, Fisher replied that this inheritance was conditional upon keeping the commandments, and could be forfeited for disobedience.[111] The second part of the sermon expounded allegorically the barriers set before paradise to keep Adam out, namely 'Cherubims, and a flaming sword' (Gen 4:24). According to Fisher the sword represented eternal death, slaying both body and soul, preventing mortal sinners from entering heaven; the flame represented purgatory, purging souls of venial sins before they could enter heaven; and the cherubim signified the strict judgment which all had to pass before they could enter, a judgment whose outcome depended not only on freedom from actual sins, but on one's record of good works.[112] This exposition led naturally enough into the final comments on the commandments.

The final work to be considered here is *A Sermon verie fruitfull, godly, and learned,* an artful and extended exploration of the metaphor of the crucifix as a book, as a summary of 'the verye Philosophie of Christian people'.[113] Although, as has recently been observed, this conceit was by no means original, its *bravura* development into an entire sermon certainly was.[114] Fisher's creative skill emerges, rather as in the funeral sermons, in the way he interweaves this metaphor with the scriptural text he takes as his theme: 'Lamentationes, carmen, et vae' ('lamentation, songe, & woe', Ezech 2:10) – the words Ezechiel saw in a vision inscribed on a scroll.[115] The whole sermon, in fact, becomes a clever identification of the cross of Christ with the scripture, and of the ceremonial part of the Good Friday liturgy (veneration of the cross) with the scriptural readings (of which Ezechiel is of course one). This identification is particularly clear in Fisher's unmistakable allusion to Erasmus's *Paraclesis,* which urged upon Christians the reading of scripture. Where Erasmus had expressed the hope that ploughmen would sing psalms while at their work, Fisher wrote that everyone could follow the example of St Francis and say to themselves, on beholding or remembering the image of the crucifix, 'who arte thou Lord, and who am I':

A man may easily say & thinke with him selfe (beholding in his hart the Image of the Crucifixe), who arte thou, and who am I. Thus euerie person both ryche and poore, may thinke, not onely in the church here, but in euery other place, and in hys businesse where about hee goeth. Thus the poore laborer maye thinke, when he is at plough earying hys grounde, and when hee goeth to hys pastures to see hys Cattayle, or when

46

hee is sittyng at home by hys fire side, or els when he lyeth in hys bed waking and can not sleepe.[116]

Yet it be would be wrong to see this as a betrayal of Erasmus's idea, as a substitution of the image for the word. Rather, it was an assimilation of the image to the word. Erasmus himself, in his *Enchiridion Militis Christiani*, had recommended meditation on the cross as a remedy for temptation and as a fuller form of prayer than the mere emotional remembrance of the passion,[117] and had argued that it was better to have the mystery of the cross fixed in one's mind than a fragment of the true cross displayed in one's house.[118] Though Fisher certainly made more ready allowance for the uneducated than Erasmus did, their concerns are recognisably parallel. Fisher, after all, owned a copy of the *Enchiridion*.[119] The parallel is emphasised by Fisher's reference to the 'Philosophie of Christian people' in his opening words, an obvious echo of Erasmus's 'philosophia Christiana'. And Fisher's identification of the cross with the essence of scripture is illustrated by the close parallel between a comment in this sermon, 'This booke may suffice for the studie of a true christian man, all the days of his life', and his remark on his way to the scaffold, having opened his New Testament at the text 'This is eternal life, to know that you alone are God and that you have sent Jesus Christ' (Jn 17:3), 'Here is even learning ynough for me to my lives end.'[120] The essence of scripture, of Christian philosophy, as summarised by Fisher, is 'it is a thyng muche marueylous, and most wonderfull, that the sonne of God, for the loue that he had vnto the soule of man, woulde suffer hym selfe to bee crucified, and so to take vpon him that most vyllanous death vpon the Crosse'.[121]

The direct analogy of the crucifix with a book occupies most of the remainder of the 'antitheme' of the sermon following the exhortation to meditation. The two pieces of the cross are likened to the two covers of a book when it lies open, the pages are the limbs of Christ's body, written on both sides – inside with the single only begotten Word of God, and outside with the lines and letters of his various wounds.[122] The bulk of the sermon then dilates in turn on the three writings contained in the book seen by Ezechiel – lamentations, song and woe. Lamentation is divided according to four possible causes: fear, shame, sorrow and hatred. Contemplation of the crucifix should therefore cause Christians to fear the punishment of sin which Christ bore for them on the cross; to be ashamed of their own sins against Christ, who had done so much for them, and for breaching their baptismal promises; to feel sorrow at his sufferings; and to hate their own sins which had brought such suffering upon him.[123] Song was also given a fourfold division, as arising from love, hope, joy or comfort. Christ's love was manifested by his laying down his life for their sake, in return for which he above all other deserved the love of Christians. There was hope that by sharing his cross through penance they could enjoy God's mercy. And the very

47

posture of his body on the cross was a sign of the welcome he extended to repentant sinners.[124] Joy was inspired by the fact that through the cross Christ had reconciled sinners to the Father; had triumphed over devils, so that even the sign of the cross put them to flight; and had erased from the consciences of the repentant all traces of sin.[125] Comfort was to be derived from Christ's shame upon the cross, which he had undergone so that repentant sinners might 'by his shame be delivered from al shame'.[126] Finally, woe was to be seen in the many pains of Christ on the cross. For those pains were to be shared either in this life by those who repented their sins, or in the next by those who did not.[127] Fisher drew his discourse to a coherent close with the warning that if Christians were ready to lament with Christ, they would also be able to sing with him and thus, by sharing his woes in this world, would escape eternal woe in the next. Those who rejected this partnership, however, would be damned everlastingly.[128]

Interesting though his later sermons are for the light they cast on Fisher's theology and spirituality, his significance as a preacher rests on his ten sermons on the penitential psalms, which were in Surtz's estimation 'undoubtedly his literary masterpiece'.[129] They were notable not only for their popularity but for their religious message and for their method and style. The seven editions make the sermons one of the most popular works of private devotion (apart from liturgical books and lives of saints) in early sixteenth-century England. The *Golden Legend* ran to eleven editions by 1527, and Bonaventure's *Speculum Vitae Christi* to nine by 1530. But the famous *Imitation of Christ* managed only six editions by that date.[130] Moreover, Fisher's sermons were among the first to be published in English – some of John Alcock's sermons had also been printed in English, and there had been some English editions of Mirk's *Liber Festivalis*.[131] For the most part, however, even sermons presumably delivered in the vernacular were published in Latin, whether in England or elsewhere. The fact that Fisher's sermons on the psalms took what was then the relatively unusual form of a continuous exposition of scripture, with the relevant texts consistently (though loosely) translated into English, can only have added to their impact. As we shall see later, Fisher seems to have accorded a higher place to scripture and the vernacular in the Christian religion than we have been accustomed to expect of the late medieval English hierarchy.[132] In his sermon on Psalm 6 he taught, 'We in lyke wyse by ofte sayenge and redynge this psalme with a contrite herete as he [David] dyde, askynge mercy shall without doubt purchase and gete of our best and mercyfull lorde god forgyuenesse for our synnes.'[133] His sermons on the psalms cannot be claimed as typical of late medieval English piety or preaching as a whole. But they can reasonably be claimed as evidence that among the better educated clergy and the more devout laity there was a demand for a simple and scriptural style of devotion with an emphasis on the interior life in the best tradition of medieval spirituality – a style of devotion that was clearly meeting many of the needs to which Reformed religion was later to appeal. And it is evidence too that this demand could be met without recourse to heretical or destructively critical literature, and without apparent threat to the established order.

3
Fisher and the Christian humanists, 1500–1520

ACCORDING TO THE prejudices or predilections of his admirers and critics, John Fisher has been variously relegated or exalted to the intellectual categories of humanism or scholasticism. This diversity in judgments was apparent even during his own lifetime. His friend Erasmus always numbered him among the humanists, the patrons and students of *bonae literae*. His protégé Robert Wakefield praised his humanist proclivities in the early 1520s; but finding himself ranged against his former patron in the controversy over Henry VIII's marriage to Catherine of Aragon, he discovered a distasteful vein of scholastic pedantry running through Fisher's work.[1] The Lutheran Robert Barnes had no hesitation in dismissing out of hand 'my Lord of Rochester . . . and all his Duns men'.[2] As these three examples suggest, such views depend more on the vantage point of the commentator than on the position of their subject. There is more than a grain of truth in all three. It would be nugatory to doubt the sincerity of Fisher's admiration for Erasmus or the enthusiasm of his commitment to *bonae literae* and the *tres linguae* (Latin, Greek and Hebrew). His achievements as chancellor of Cambridge University and in the foundation of St John's College bear eloquent witness to this. But it would equally be short-sighted to ignore his high regard for Thomas Aquinas and Duns Scotus, or the scholastic cast of much of his theological writing. The purpose of this chapter is to ascertain how these apparently contradictory allegiances were reconciled in Fisher's mind. It will therefore explore the attitudes to various humanist and scholastic traditions revealed in his official acts, his correspondence and his polemical theology. In particular it will examine his friendship with Reuchlin and Erasmus, his encouragement of the studies of Greek and Hebrew, and his exploitation in his writings of the scholastics and the early fathers. Rather than perpetuate the slick dichotomy of humanist or scholastic, it will seek to argue that contemporaries did not always draw such sharp divisions, and that the academic culture of early sixteenth-century Europe offered a variety of middle ways between these schematised extremes. Erasmus was not the only 'role model' available, although he was the most influential. It was possible for Fisher and others to respect and admire him without being his clones. Nevertheless, any account of Fisher's leanings towards humanism must start with his friendship with Erasmus.

We do not know when Fisher and Erasmus first met. Erasmus first came to England around 1500, but since he spent his time in Oxford and London, while Fisher was either at Cambridge or else in the household of Lady Margaret Beaufort, it is unlikely that they crossed paths. However, they might have come into indirect contact in the 1490s. One of Erasmus's pupils in Paris at that time was a certain Robert Fisher (a cousin of John), for whom he wrote a treatise *De Conscribendis Epistolis*.[3] Robert was moreover an associate of another famous Dutch humanist, Jerome Busleiden, the founder of the Collegium Trilingue at Louvain.[4] Whether Robert's exalted connections had any impact on the career or development of his at this time less prominent cousin must, however, remain a matter for speculation. What is certain is that in April 1506 Erasmus stayed briefly at Queens' College, Cambridge (where Fisher was president), during a visit by Henry VII. At the same time a plan was afoot to bring Erasmus to Cambridge to lecture on Paul's Epistle to the Romans, a plan in which it is fair to conclude that Fisher played a leading role.[5] By 1511 Fisher's friendship with Erasmus was firmly established. Erasmus had come to Cambridge at Fisher's request to teach Greek, and regularly looked to him for patronage.[6] On 28 December 1512, for example, he received from him 20s for an epitaph for the tomb of Lady Margaret.[7] The correspondence which was the chief vehicle of their friendship begins at this time. Although much of it is no longer extant, the eighteen items that remain are a rich source for Fisher's activities and preoccupations.[8] They reveal a friendship that was fundamentally literary, dominated by books and scholarship of an overwhelmingly theological, yet distinctively humanist, character. They give little sign of the scholastic in Fisher, manifesting instead a clear interest in *bonae literae*, and abounding in references to such figures as Johann Reuchlin, Rudolph Agricola, Hermolao Barbaro and Giovanni Pico della Mirandola.

Much of their correspondence concerned Erasmus's researches on the scriptures, as embodied in his *Novum Instrumentum*, *Annotationes* and *Paraphrases*. It leaves no room for doubt about Fisher's commitment to the Erasmian scriptural enterprise, with which he was associated from an early stage. In 1513 Erasmus wrote to Colet that 'his Matthew' must be with either Colet or Fisher, and that he was anxious to have it back.[9] Indeed he originally intended to dedicate the *Novum Instrumentum* to Fisher, but in the event preferred Leo X, sending Fisher a presentation copy in consolation.[10] The bishop's satisfaction with this gift is evident as much in the frequent use he made of it in his writings as in his express gratitude.[11] His copy of the accompanying *Annotationes* must have been well thumbed, because it was sent to a bookbinder for repair around 1520.[12] He was equally enthusiastic about the other part of Erasmus's scriptural programme, the composition of paraphrases on the New Testament.

The genre of a prose paraphrase of scripture (as opposed to a versification or a commentary) was Erasmus's own conception, and in the period 1517–25 he produced paraphrases on all the books of the New Testament except for the Apocalypse.[13] In a letter of 1522 he remarked that Fisher had encouraged him to produce a paraphrase of John.[14] But the degree to which the paraphrase concept impressed Fisher is revealed by his own sole surviving work of scriptural exegesis, a paraphrase and exposition of the Psalms.[15] That Fisher should have made an essay in this new genre at all is a measure of his regard for it, even though Erasmus himself was not convinced that the Psalms were suitable material for paraphrase.[16] And although the strongly traditional flavour of Fisher's interpretation scarcely merits the epithet 'Erasmian', Fisher certainly wished to locate his effort in the Erasmian tradition. This becomes apparent in his exposition of Psalm 2:7, 'Dominus dixit ad me, filius meus es, ego hodie genui te.' Fisher applied this traditionally enough to the eternal generation of the Son as the Word by the Father. Yet by calling the Son 'sermo' rather than 'verbum' he implicitly declared his support for Erasmus's alternative version of the opening of John's Gospel, 'In principio erat sermo', a rendering which had attained the status of a shibboleth during the controversy over the *Novum Instrumentum*.[17]

In the debates sparked off by the *Novum Instrumentum* Fisher had already made his position clear. He had taken an especially prominent role in the dispute between Erasmus and Edward Lee which was such a severe embarrassment for the English humanist community.[18] This role has been for the most part overlooked because it can now only be detected through indirect evidence. Fisher's letters on the subject have all disappeared, whereas those of Thomas More are still extant. However, the reconstruction of Fisher's attempts at mediation in an increasingly bitter confrontation provides new evidence of his esteem for Erasmus. The episode began in about September 1517 when Lee, then at Louvain to study Greek and Hebrew, was asked by Erasmus to pass on any comments or criticisms he might have of the *Annotationes* in time for the second edition.[19] Although the invitation was presumably more polite than sincere, Lee took offence when some of his comments were greeted with scorn, and was even more wounded when he found some of them included without acknowledgment in the new edition of 1518.[20] When Erasmus returned to Louvain in October 1518 he was disturbed by rumours that Lee was preparing further, hostile annotations – rumours which Lee claimed stemmed from Erasmus himself.[21] There then followed an unedifying exchange in which Lee (despite his later claims to the contrary) withheld his comments from Erasmus, while Erasmus went to extraordinary lengths to obtain a copy of them, even trying to suborn Lee's scribe.[22] Lee proposed to put the issues in dispute before an impartial arbiter, nominating first, with Erasmus's half-hearted agreement, John Briard (the vice-chancellor of Louvain). After some time, Briard declared himself unwilling to intervene.[23] In early 1519 Lee therefore chose to submit the whole matter to Fisher, who had long been a patron of his.[24] Fisher's initial response was to urge reconciliation. Similar pleas followed from More, Pace and Colet, but to no avail.[25] In the meantime Erasmus had already published his *Apologia contra Latomum* (March 1519) which Lee felt, not without reason, contained barely veiled and far from flattering allusions to himself.[26] So Lee decided to publish his own *Annotationes* – a decision which was at first frustrated by his inability to persuade any Antwerp printer to take the book. Lee blamed even this on Erasmus, claiming that one printer had gone so far as to set the type before being intimidated by Erasmus's friends into breaking it up.[27]

Having agreed to mediate, Fisher found himself faced with an awkward dilemma. Erasmus had only consented to his appointment as an arbitrator because Fisher had previously promised to do his utmost to secure a copy of Lee's annotations for him. But Lee sent his notes to Fisher under embargo, with instructions not to show them to anybody else, with the exception of Thomas More. Fisher was thus unable to please one friend without offending the other.[28] Nevertheless, he took his role as mediator seriously, making a close study of at least one of the bones of contention. This was the upbraiding of Peter by Paul at Antioch (Gal 2:11–14). Erasmus had followed Jerome's face-saving explanation that Peter, in collusion with Paul, had played a part in order to let Paul make his point about the non-essential character of the Mosaic dietary regulations as strongly as possible. Lee (like Luther) preferred the line of Augustine, which took the incident at face value as Paul correcting Peter. Fisher's judgment on this emerged in the course of a book on another issue, written in 1519 at precisely the time when the dispute between Erasmus and Lee was coming to a head. After reviewing the text and the patristic interpretations in great detail, he concluded noncommittally that either view could be legitimately held, but that absolute certainty could not be reached on the matter.[29] We cannot tell whether this was representative of Fisher's attitude on the other disputed points. But we do know how keen he was for a peaceful solution. Even towards the end of the year he proposed a compromise to Erasmus, by which both he and Lee should publish their respective annotations in tandem, moderating their expression so as to make a contribution to knowledge rather than seek to damage each other's reputation.[30] Despite this final appeal, it was Erasmus who fired the first shot, publishing in December an open letter to Thomas Lupset which gave his version of the affair.[31] Lee's *Annotationes*, which purported to be a reply to this letter but had probably already been at press, appeared in February 1520. However, although Fisher's efforts failed to achieve the desired effect at first, his proposal for a joint publication was the method adopted later in 1520 for patching up relations between Erasmus and Lee. Their respective treatises, relieved of their more offensive remarks, were published in one volume by Froben at Basel.[32]

The surviving letters between Fisher and Erasmus tell us not only about Fisher's attitude to Erasmus's scriptural enterprise, but also about a related work by Fisher himself, of which his friend entertained a high opinion. As in the case of his role in the controversy between Lee and Erasmus, we are once more in the realm of deduction from limited evidence, for only a few tantalising traces remain of the work, a harmony of the Gospels. There is no need to emphasise how grievous is its loss. But it is at least possible to surmise something of its nature and purpose from occasional references to it, and from passages in Fisher's later writings which bear upon the problems of reconciling the evangelical accounts of Christ's life. Although an investigation of a lost work must inevitably be ambitious, it is rewarding in this case because of the light it casts on Fisher's development in a period of his life about which we already know too little. The most explicit reference to the harmony which we have occurs in a letter from Erasmus of April 1519. Commenting on Fisher's *De Unica Magdalena*, Erasmus tempered his faint praise with the wish that Fisher had published instead the harmony of the Gospels that he had once shown him.[33] The occasion Erasmus was recalling here sounds remarkably like one he had mentioned to Edward Lee a year or two before. He told how when he had last seen Fisher (on a ten-day visit to Rochester in August 1516), the bishop had been wrestling with the question of Christ's genealogy, on which he had written to consult Reuchlin.[34] Another of Fisher's friends, John Constable, may also have known of the harmony, for in an undated letter he expressed his astonishment that Fisher could find time in his busy life for the explication of the four evangelists.[35] It is even conceivable that the harmony may indeed have been published. The Paris printer Josse Bade heard a rumour in 1520 that Fisher had a commentary on Matthew in the press – though he might of course have been misinformed.[36] And an otherwise inexplicable reference by Fisher himself to 'my commentary on the Sermon on the Mount', in a context which suggests that it is publicly available, may be further testimony to the tragic disappearance of what would have been a fascinating work.[37] Some clues to the scope of the harmony can be derived from Fisher's two books against Lefèvre d'Etaples on the identity of Mary Magdalene. In one, the *De Unica Magdalena*, he collated all the scriptural references to Mary Magdalene and Mary the sister of Martha, in an effort to show that they could all be consistently taken to apply to one and the same woman.[38] And in the *Confutatio Secundae Disceptationis* he set out as one of his principles in his dispute with Lefèvre: 'Neither Luke nor any of the other evangelists invariably follows strict chronological order in his narrative.' To prove this he adduced a sheaf of narrative discrepancies: Luke mentioned John the Baptist's imprisonment before describing Christ's baptism; Matthew, Mark and Luke disagreed on the order of Christ's temptations in the desert; Matthew explicitly put the cleansing of the leper after the Sermon on the Mount (Mt 8:2–4), while Luke, without specifying its occasion, dealt with it

54

beforehand; and Matthew put the raising of Jairus's daughter before the interrogation of Christ by the Baptist's disciples, whereas Luke put them the other
way round.[39] This selection suggests strongly that the question of discrepancies
between the Gospels was one with which Fisher was already familiar.

Authors seeking to harmonise the Gospels were inevitably troubled by the
contradictory genealogies of Christ provided by Matthew and Luke. As we have
seen from Erasmus's testimony, Fisher was no exception. Work on the harmony
can be invoked with some degree of certainty to help explain other references to
the genealogical question that appear in his letters and writings. In 1515, for
example, he asked Erasmus to find out from Reuchlin the source of the
genealogy of Christ used to introduce novices to the Hebrew alphabet in the *De
Rudimentis Hebraicis*.[40] The same year he wrote to Rome in search of a
commentary on scripture by one John Anianus of Viterbo. The reply came that
no such work was known there, but that he might in fact be after a compilation
of purportedly ancient records by John Annius of Viterbo – a work which did
bear on the genealogy of Christ.[41] Three years later, having presumably
obtained a copy, he was discussing Annius with Erasmus, who expressed doubts
about the authenticity of Annius's records, and admitted his own perplexity over
the genealogical problem.[42] The concern with this problem unexpectedly
resurfaced much later in Fisher's career, during the controversy over Henry
VIII's marriage to Catherine of Aragon. In a memorandum submitted to the
legatine court in 1529, he found a providential explanation for the thoroughness
and detail of Moses's matrimonial legislation in the need to ensure that the
lineage of Christ should be clear and unstained.[43] The following year, in *De
Causa Matrimonii*, he argued at some length that Christ's ancestry included two
instances of levirate marriage. Although his polemical intention at this point
was to defend the liceity of levirate marriage, the argument amounted to an
explanation of two striking discrepancies between the Lucan and Matthaean
genealogies.[44] Since the harmony itself is no longer extant, however, the most
important result of Fisher's work on it, from our perspective, was that it brought
him to the study of Greek and Hebrew. For it seems as though he felt keenly his
technical disadvantage in working on the text of scripture without a knowledge
of its original languages. Certainly his first contacts with both Greek and
Hebrew occurred in the context of this project. His interest in Reuchlin's *De
Rudimentis* arose from his preoccupation with Christ's genealogy, and his
initiation into Greek at the hands of Erasmus took place on that same visit to
Rochester when Erasmus found him at work on the harmony of the gospels.[45]
Even so, Fisher's interest in the sacred languages was not limited to their
contribution to his immediate concerns. It soon expanded into a commitment to
the study and patronage of those languages which now demands our attention.

Fisher first emerged as a patron of the study of Greek in the early 1510s
when he induced Erasmus to teach the language at Cambridge.[46] The

introduction of Greek was a landmark in the development of Cambridge University although, according to Erasmus, pupils were few and unable to pay highly. By 1514, poor remuneration, Cambridge weather and the need to find a printer skilful enough to handle the *Novum Instrumentum* had driven Erasmus back to the continent. But Fisher's enthusiasm survived this setback. In the original statutes of St John's College, promulgated in 1516, he stipulated that some of the fellows should learn Greek as soon as possible.[47] Soon after, casting around for someone to replace Erasmus as lecturer, he chose Richard Croke, a Cambridge graduate who had left around 1510 to pursue his studies elsewhere, and who had since become professor of Greek at Leipzig.[48] In his inaugural lecture of 1518, Croke attributed his return to Fisher's influence and appealed to the chancellor's express enthusiasm for Greek in his attempt to arouse the interest of his audience.[49] He enjoyed Fisher's patronage for several years. The bishop obtained for him a sinecure post at the Strood Hospital near Rochester,[50] and made him a fellow of St John's.[51] It was for him that Fisher endowed there a lectureship in Greek on his own chantry foundation.[52] However, Croke's disinclination to perform his duties in college led to a break-down in relations with his patron. Perhaps he was more concerned to fulfil the duties of his university positions, for in 1523 he added to his professorship the new post of public orator, with precedence over all other members of the university after the vice-chancellor.[53] Letters he wrote in 1524, when he was securing his doctorate in divinity, reveal that he was already worried about the charges being brought to Fisher's attention by the president of the college, John Smith.[54] A powerful letter from Fisher to Croke, apparently written early in 1526, shows that relations were deteriorating rapidly.[55] Croke had written to Fisher accusing him of embezzling Lady Margaret Beaufort's estate, of contra-vening her intentions by unduly favouring his fellow countrymen for promotion in St John's, and of pursuing his own glory rather than hers. Fisher justified himself at length on all three counts, and retorted with information he had received about Croke's failure to give lectures in college, his absence from the common table and his holding private meals for a few favourites in his chamber. This was doubtless the substance of the stories told him by Smith a year or two before. That Croke's departure from Cambridge to become tutor to Henry, duke of Richmond, in 1526 was in part a result of this *contretemps* looks likely. But though it must have been disappointing for Fisher to lose such a talented teacher, his plans for his college were not frustrated. By the 1520s, fellows or former fellows who had some knowledge of Greek included besides Croke such men as Ralph Baynes, George Day, Henry Gold, Robert Wakefield and John Watson. The Johnian Grecians of the 1530s, including Roger Ascham, John Cheke, John Redman and Thomas Watson, became almost legendary figures.

Fisher's enthusiasm was not confined to encouraging others to study Greek. As we have seen he took up the language himself in 1516, under Erasmus's tuition, in the context of his work on the harmony of the Gospels. In the following year Erasmus was at great pains to help the bishop improve his command of the Greek tongue. Along with Thomas More, he urged William Latimer to take Fisher's tuition in hand, although the ageing Latimer could not be prevailed upon to oblige. It would be much better, he countered, if they could find some expert Italian for the task.[56] Erasmus did what he could, sending Fisher copies of his translation of Theodore of Gaza's Greek grammar, first in manuscript and then in print.[57] By 1519, when Fisher opened his career as a polemical theologian with the *De Unica Magdalena*, he was able to argue with Lefèvre d'Etaples over the interpretation of the Greek text of the New Testament.[58] He often made use of his knowledge in his later writings, drawing on Erasmus's *Novum Instrumentum*, and referring to the original Greek. But in general, like other theologians, he relied for convenience upon the Vulgate, unless there was some specific point that could be made better with the Greek, or even with the Hebrew.

Fisher's openness to new intellectual currents went beyond the study of Greek to that of Hebrew. Hebrew was first established as an academic subject in England during the reign of Henry VIII, and Fisher played a part in this that historians have tended to overlook. As a result, the story of the early reception of Hebrew in England has not yet been fully told, nor have the motives underlying it been laid bare.[59] It is therefore necessary to cover this aspect of his career more thoroughly than the relatively well-trodden ground of his promotion and study of Greek. The story begins, as does that of Greek, with Fisher's work on the harmony of the Gospels. Early in 1515 he wrote to Erasmus about Reuchlin in terms of the highest praise. Erasmus had already canvassed Fisher's support for Reuchlin in the latter's quarrel with the Dominicans over the proper attitude of the secular authorities to Hebrew books, and now Fisher asked Erasmus to send any books by the great man that he could find. In particular he asked him to obtain from Reuchlin an explanation of the genealogy of the Virgin Mary given in the *De Rudimentis Hebraicis*.[60] While Fisher can hardly have progressed beyond the alphabet at that time, and was presumably concerned primarily in the genealogy as such, the letter nevertheless testifies to a burgeoning interest in Hebrew. He avowed that, if his episcopal duties did not prevent him, he would visit Reuchlin in person. In any case, he soon established direct contact with Reuchlin, sending him a brief note of support against the Dominicans some time in 1515.[61] By 1516 he was able to tell Erasmus of what was already a flourishing correspondence, and their friendship was taken for granted by Richard Croke, who asked Reuchlin to remember him to Fisher, and urged him to dedicate his forthcoming *De Arte Cabbalistica* to the bishop.[62] Although the dedication actually went to Leo X, Reuchlin did send him a presentation copy via Erasmus.[63] Erasmus frequently played the intermediary between the two. After his ten-day stay with Fisher in

1516 he told Reuchlin how keen the bishop was to visit him, and suggested that Reuchlin send his nephew Philip Melanchthon to Rochester to study with him.[64] In the other direction, he sent Fisher various pamphlets on the Hebrew books controversy, told him of Reuchlin's perils during the sack of Stuttgart, and in 1522 conveyed the sad news of his death.[65] Fisher's admiration for Reuchlin survived even the papal condemnation of some of his ideas in 1520, for he paid tribute to him in 1523 as 'my friend John Capnion, renowned in every branch of literature', and in 1527 as 'the greatest Hebrew expert of his time'.[66]

Within a year of establishing contact with Reuchlin, Fisher had found a tutor in Hebrew – Robert Wakefield, the foremost Hebraist of Henrician England, who was throughout the ensuing decade one of the most important beneficiaries of Fisher's patronage. Wakefield himself has recorded that he taught Fisher Hebrew, and his references to other pupils give the impression that there was a veritable Hebrew seminar in progress. He specifically named a friend of Fisher's, Thomas Hurskey, the prior of Watton (near Beverley) and master general of the Gilbertine order, as a fellow pupil.[67] And elsewhere he bracketed Hurskey with several others – John Taylor (Master of the Rolls), John Stokesley (later bishop of London), James Boleyn (brother of Thomas, later earl of Wiltshire and Ormond), William Frisell (prior of the Rochester Cathedral chapter), William Tate (a contemporary of Fisher's from Cambridge) and Thomas Lovell (canon of Bath and Wells).[68] Since Stokesley had already learned Hebrew by late 1517, it seems likely that he studied it at the same time as Fisher, and one suspects that the others also learned the language then.[69] Whether or not Fisher had anything to do with Wakefield's election as a fellow of Clare Hall in 1516,[70] it is clear that he was already looking forward to recruiting him to St John's. His 1516 statutes laid down that some of the fellows should devote themselves as soon as possible to the study of Hebrew, and optimistically included Hebrew, Arabic and Aramaic, with Greek and Latin, as the only languages permitted within the college precincts.[71] Shortly afterwards Wakefield was enjoying the bishop's hospitality at Rochester on his way to and from Louvain, where he matriculated in November 1518 and graduated MA.[72] He was back in Cambridge in summer 1519, when he was incorporated MA, but later that year returned to Louvain as lecturer in Hebrew (from August to December).[73] Around 1520 Fisher made him a fellow of St John's, endowing for him there a lectureship in Hebrew on his chantry foundation.[74] Fisher continued to encourage his progress in the oriental languages, granting him a dispensation to remain in receipt of his fellowship stipend even while pursuing further study abroad.[75] Wakefield took advantage of this in 1522 when he set out for southern Germany, presumably intending to study with Reuchlin at Tübingen. However, on arrival he found himself invited to replace the recently deceased Reuchlin as lecturer, and on 1 September Erasmus told Fisher of the success of 'tuus Robertus' in the post.[76] One suspects that Fisher was not much gratified to think of his investment in Wakefield redounding to the benefit of a foreign university. At any rate, within a short time moves were afoot to reclaim him for his native land. Fisher seems to have enlisted Henry VIII's support for a proposal to establish a university lectureship in Hebrew at Cambridge, and for recalling Wakefield to fill it. Though the letters of recall are lost, we can learn something of them from the letters written by Tübingen to Fisher, and by Archduke Ferdinand (on their behalf) to Henry VIII, in an effort to defer Wakefield's departure.[77] Though Fisher is nowhere explicitly attributed with responsibility for the Hebrew lectureship, it seems probable that, as in the case of the Greek lectureship, he had the idea and picked the incumbent, while Henry put up the money. The parallels between his patronage on the one hand of Greek and Richard Croke, and on the other of Hebrew and Robert Wakefield, are indeed striking, and suggest a deliberate policy, pursued over a number of years, of establishing the two languages in the university and college curriculum.

The early sixteenth century thus witnessed a surge of interest in Hebrew among a small but influential section of English learned society led by John Fisher. In seeking an explanation for this it would be easy to invoke 'humanism' or 'the Renaissance' without casting any significant light on the motives of the people concerned. Fortunately, although only a few hints survive about the objectives of those early students, it is possible to arrange them in a coherent and convincing pattern. The key lies in the widespread fascination generated at that time by the concept of the Cabbala. The Cabbala was a system of medieval Jewish mystical lore that purported to be an oral tradition of divine wisdom going back to Moses or beyond. In 1486 this body of learning had been brought to the attention of Giovanni Pico della Mirandola. Pico had found in it not only a further source for his encyclopaedic scholarship, but one that in his eyes proved against the Jews the truth of the Christian religion they despised. Thus was born 'Christian Cabbalism', a system which, drawing on Talmudic, Rabbinical and Cabbalistic writings, promised to unlock the secrets of creation, to harmonise all branches of knowledge, and to secure at long last the conversion of the Jews. Although its practical achievements were inevitably limited, it enjoyed for a time tremendous vogue thanks to its two leading exponents, Pico and Reuchlin.[78] In England, John Fisher is the earliest figure we can associate with the fashion for the Cabbala. In a letter to Erasmus he made the revealing comment, 'his [Reuchlin's] scholarship delights me so hugely that in my reckoning no man alive comes closer to Pico'.[79] Pico, it seems, was the standard against whom even a Reuchlin was to be measured. Fisher was certainly acquainted with Pico's *De Dignitate Hominis*, which spoke with considerable enthusiasm of the Cabbala, and this may well have been the stimulus of his own interest in the subject.[80] We have already noted that Fisher received a presentation copy of Reuchlin's *De Arte Cabbalistica*, and he was also aware of Reuchlin's other major Cabbalistic work, the *De Verbo Mirifico*, the source for the Cabbalistic etymology of the name of Jesus which he cited in his manuscript commentary on the Psalms.[81] The third leading textbook of Christian Cabbalism, Petrus Galatinus's *De Arcanis*, was also known to him, for his own *Sacri Sacerdotii Defensio* contained a number of passages from rabbinical exegetes which were in fact drawn without acknowledgment from Galatinus's work.[82] Fisher's familiarity with (and probable ownership of) the three basic texts of Renaissance Cabbalism indicates more than a passing fancy, and the notion of the Cabbala as a form of traditional wisdom makes regular, though not frequent, appearances in his theological writings.[83] Other Englishmen shared his interest. His instructor, Robert Wakefield, spoke highly of Pico and of the Cabbala.[84] Among Fisher's fellow pupils, Stokesley at least shared his tastes. When in 1530 Richard Croke was busy in Italy collecting scholarly opinions against Henry VIII's marriage to Catherine, he thought it worth reporting his successful recruitment of Francesco Zorzi who, he reminded Stokesley, was the author of that curious combination of Platonic, Hermetic and Cabbalistic philosophy, the *De Harmonia Mundi*.[85] Of the views and interests of Fisher's other fellow pupils, Hurskey, Lovell, Frisell and the rest, history has preserved no trace. But the trend for the Cabbala spread beyond that immediate circle. John Fewterer, the confessor of Syon Priory, owned the *De Verbo Mirifico*, and Thomas Cranmer the *De Arte Cabbalistica*.[86] In view of the widespread fascination in England with the person and accomplishments of Pico, it is likely that an inclination to Cabbalistic and cognate studies was common to those earliest English students of Hebrew.

Even in a society as open to the concept of the supernatural as sixteenth-century England, such an inclination was characteristic of the more rather than of the less credulous. Fisher's relative credulity can be seen in his enthusiastic response to the revelations of the Holy Maid of Kent, as contrasted with the cooler reaction of Thomas More. Whereas the sceptical More treated them and their authoress with the utmost circumspection, Fisher accepted them, to his cost, too readily. And the use he made in his polemics of private revelations and of miracles confirms that for him the supernatural was almost an everyday matter. It is not enough, however, to dismiss interest in the Cabbala as *mere* credulity. Like 'mystic' philosophies and pseudo-sciences throughout the ages, the Cabbala opens a window on the mentality of its time. It is no coincidence that the Cabbala flourished in the heady atmosphere of the Renaissance. Its underlying character was an intoxication or even obsession with the power of human symbols (words, numbers and hieroglyphs), a confusion of the manipulation of those symbols with the manipulation of the reality they represented. This confusion was facilitated in the wordy culture of Renaissance humanism by the importance of the metaphor of the Word in Christian theology, and by the philosophy of language then prevalent. The Word was the ultimate expression of the divine nature and power. The eternal begetting of the Son was best described as an act of speech. Language was seen as the determining characteristic of the human race, uniting the intellectual world of thought with the material world, placing the human race between the beasts and the angels at the fulcrum of creation. Hebrew was seen as language *par excellence*, uniting the divine and the human word. It was the language in which God had spoken to his people in the Old Testament. It was the language of Adam in paradise, with which he had originally named the animal and vegetable kingdoms in a primal act of God-given dominion over creation. It was the language in which Christ had preached (in fact he preached in its near relative, Aramaic) and with which he had worked miracles. With such a complex of ideas surrounding Hebrew, it is hardly surprising that the language should have been attributed with miraculous power over the material and spiritual worlds (a view to which Origen had appealed in explaining the survival of such Hebrew words as 'amen', 'hosanna' and 'alleluia' in the Christian liturgy). The Cabbala was a blind alley, but it combined in seductive synthesis many of the noblest aspirations of the Renaissance.

Although he was a keen patron of the sacred languages, Fisher was aware of his limitations as a practitioner of them, admitting that pastoral obligations prevented him from devoting as much time to their study as he would wish. He found some consolation in associating himself in this regard with Ambrose, Hilary and Augustine, who had been prevented from pursuing the study of languages by their episcopal duties, and discouraged from it by their realisation of the confusion which a display of gratuitous erudition might engender in their simple flocks. Such studies were more suitable to Jerome, because he was no bishop and held no cure of souls.[87] One can detect in these remarks a wistful recognition of the gulf that, despite their mutual sympathy and friendship, necessarily divided Fisher the bishop from Erasmus the scholar. But they also reveal the high esteem in which Fisher held the early fathers of the Church, an esteem which is amply confirmed by his wide use of patristic citations. The vast majority of his citations from other authors come from the fathers.[88] This sets him in the mainstream of the Christian humanism of his day, which was witnessing a veritable patristic Renaissance. The stream of patristic editions produced by Erasmus, Lefèvre and their followers stimulated and supplied an unprecedented demand for such texts in England as elsewhere. Although, as we have seen, there was some interest in the fathers in the late fifteenth century, this was limited by supply. It was around 1510 that the pattern of ownership of the fathers showed a marked change. This can be seen in a comparison of the books which Richard Fox donated to Durham Cathedral in 1499 and those he gave to his own foundation of Corpus Christi, Oxford, in 1517. The former are largely medieval texts of law and scholastic theology; the latter are dominated by the fathers and the classics. Fox's statutes for Corpus, which explicitly enjoin the study of the fathers in place of the scholastics, are further testimony to this change.[89] The library of William Grocyn, who died in 1519, was packed with patristics, even though his interests were perhaps more classical than theological.[90] The trend became even more marked in the 1520s, as complete editions of many fathers became widely available. The library of William Melton, Fisher's tutor, who died in 1528, contained many such editions.[91] The strength of this fashion at Cambridge can be seen in the books taken to Syon Priory by such scholars as Richard Reynolds, William Bond, Richard Whitford and John Fewterer in the 1510s and 1520s.[92]

The writings of John Fisher show that he must take his place in this movement. Comparing his patristic citations with the printed editions then available shows that he had access, for example, to Merlin's 1512 edition of Origen; Jerome in Erasmus's edition of 1516; Rhenanus's Tertullian of 1521; Augustine's *De Civitate Dei* in Vives's edition of 1522; and Erasmus's Irenaeus of 1526. All of these except the Origen were published at Basel by John Froben. Even where particular editions cannot be identified with confidence, it is clear that Fisher's citations of Greek fathers were usually taken from modern Renaissance translations. He used Ambrogio Traversari's version of Dionysius and Matteo Palmieri's of the *Aristeas Letter*, and explicitly referred to Trapezuntius's versions of Eusebius and Chrysostom, and to other versions of Chrysostom by Bernard Brixianus and Girolamo Donato.[93] Nor was his interest in the fathers confined to meeting the exigencies of theological polemic. He was demonstrably interested in the fathers as such. In 1511 Erasmus sent him a sample of a projected translation of Basil on Isaiah.[94] Around the same time, Erasmus was working on a translation of the liturgy of John Chrysostom, of which he sent a copy to Colet. He also gave a copy to Fisher, who recalled in his *De Veritate* of 1527 that Erasmus had given this to him some sixteen years ago.[95] Fisher's correspondence reveals him to be one of the earliest recorded borrowers from the Cambridge University Library. Around 1520 he asked Nicholas Metcalfe to procure for him a copy of the volume of Chrysostom's sermons that he had previously borrowed from there.[96] Subsequently he was even to assist Erasmus in the production of his 1530 *Opera Omnia* of Chrysostom, securing for him a manuscript of Aretino's version of Chrysostom on 1 Corinthians from the University Library. In his preface Erasmus thanked the bishop for supplying him wth a text of it. In return, Fisher received a presentation copy of the edition.[97]

While Fisher made it quite clear not only by his citations but also by explicit comments that he preferred the fathers to the scholastics, he did not repudiate the scholastic tradition in the manner of Colet, Lefèvre or Erasmus. Indeed, in some respects he thought more highly of the scholastics than of the fathers, for example in their distinctions between the different types of law embodied in the

Old Testament.[98] Yet he cited their writings relatively infrequently, except in his treatises on Henry VIII's marriage. Erasmus cited Thomas Aquinas more often in his *Annotationes* than did Fisher in any of his published works.[99] Yet Fisher nowhere expressed the sort of reservations about Thomas that Erasmus did, and in fact spoke of Thomas only in terms of the highest regard, although there is little in his works to suggest that he should be thought of as a Thomist. However, he certainly preferred the scholastics of the *via antiqua* to those of the *via moderna*. He mentioned Ockham only once, in a long list of scholastic witnesses to the real presence, and cited Biel only occasionally.[100] None of the nominalists were ever cited in his published books. Even the *via antiqua*, however, played no more than a minor part in his works. Before the divorce controversy broke out, his citations from scholastic texts (excluding scriptural commentaries) were limited to Peter Lombard, Thomas, Duns Scotus and Gregory of Rimini. Lombard was cited only in order to vindicate him against misrepresentation by Oecolampadius; and Gregory only to upbraid Luther by showing that even the leading theologian of his own Augustinian order disagreed with him.[101] Thomas's *Summa Theologiae* appeared only in the writings on the divorce – and was cited, significantly enough, in Cajetan's recent edition.[102] Fisher also referred to scholastic scriptural commentaries by Thomas and Albertus Magnus in his *De Unica Magdalena* – because they were Parisian theologians and might therefore cut more ice with the audience at which he was aiming.[103] Within the *via antiqua*, Fisher was at least as much a Scotist as a Thomist. Though he named Thomas with reverence, it was Scotus 'whose acumen recommends itself most strongly to me'.[104] And he drew on Scotus in discussing the sacrament of penance[105] and in arguing that the Church did not claim to make new doctrines, but to declare that certain doctrines were articles of the faith.[106] Having said this, it must be remembered that Fisher explicitly dissociated himself from the theory of 'meritum ex congruo' which Scotus elaborated in his account of the doctrine of justification.[107] Evidence of allegiance to Scotism is also found in Fisher's 1516 statutes for St John's College, where the only scholastics laid down for study were Scotus and his pupil Francis Maro. This remained a constant feature through the revisions of 1524 and 1530.[108] But too much weight should not be put on this because it is not at all clear whether Scotus and Maro were being recommended as logicians, philosophers or theologians. Our conclusions must therefore be limited to the simple statement that Fisher was more at home with the *via antiqua* than with the *via moderna*. There just is not the evidence to locate him any more precisely in the scholastic tradition.

The best explanation of Fisher's attitude to the scholastics lies in the laudatory phrase with which he habitually referred to Thomas – 'flos theologiae', 'the flower of theology'.[109] This title, not found in the list of Thomas's usual scholastic epithets (Angelic, Common or Universal Doctor)[110] was probably coined by Pico. It was from Pico's oration *De Dignitate Hominis*, that programmatic statement of Renaissance humanism, that Fisher took the brief panegyric of Thomas, Scotus, Albert and Henry of Ghent which he cited in defence of the scholastics at the start of his *De Veritate*.[111] He seems thus to have been modelling his attitude to the scholastics on that of Pico. Later in the *De Veritate* he introduced another covert citation from Pico. In preface IV he proposed that in evaluating a Christian author three things were to be considered: erudition, piety and style, of which the least important was style. Although style was by no means to be scorned or neglected, it was no substitute for truth and holiness. This argument was derived from Pico's *Epistola ad Hermolaum Barbarum*, which defended the doctrine of the scholastics while admitting and deploring their stylistic limitations.[112] An echo of this can be heard in Fisher's 1530 statutes for St John's, where he provided that if a Hebrew lecturer could not be obtained, then the Hebrew lecture could be replaced by a course on Scotus 'if he can be turned into better Latin'.[113] This attempt to combine the subtlety of the scholastics with the style of the humanists could be taken as typical of Fisher's whole intellectual enterprise. And it looks like a deliberate reflection of Pico, who at that time commanded a large following among English scholars, especially among those close to Fisher, such as William Melton, John Colet and Thomas More.[114] Pico not only helps us to place Fisher in his domestic intellectual context, but also provides the key to understanding his personal intellectual programme. Pico was essentially a syncretist, concerned to achieve a reconciliation or harmonisation of all forms of wisdom. He aimed to reconcile Plato with Aristotle, and the Christian fathers with the classical philosophers. He sought truth in mathematics and the Pythagorean arts, in occult and hermetic philosophy, in the Jewish Cabbala and the learning of Islam. He would even reconcile the dissensions of the scholastics. It is tempting to see many of Fisher's scholarly interests as following Pico's example. His openness to *bonae literae* and the *tres linguae* might be taken on their own as indications of a pure Erasmianism. But in contrast to Erasmus he was also awake to the value of the scholastic heritage, and attracted by the arcane field of the Cabbala. Fisher's position is perhaps summed up in his letter to Erasmus about Reuchlin, in which the highest praise he could find for Reuchlin was to compare him to Pico. Although Fisher was neither as great a scholastic nor as great a humanist as Pico, it is clear that for him Pico was the model scholar, a pioneer in that attempt to harmonise the two branches of learning which characterised Fisher's writings. In the next chapter, we shall consider how this essentially harmonistic or consensual attitude coped with a humanist controversy which towards 1520 threatened to undercut not only the intellectual consensus at which Fisher aimed, but also the *consensus ecclesiae* on which he hoped it would rest.

4
The Magdalene controversy

THE PICTURE OF Fisher which emerged from the previous chapter was very much that of a Christian humanist, although neither so Erasmian as has sometimes been imagined, nor in the slightest degree intolerant of scholasticism. In the two humanist *causes célèbres* of the 1510s he adopted a position at once irenic and decidedly sympathetic to what is usually portrayed as the 'humanist' side. The man who regretted the Dominican assaults upon Reuchlin, endorsed the *Novum Instrumentum*, and unsuccessfully attempted to keep the peace between Lee and Erasmus would hardly be expected to have become entangled in protracted and rancorous theological disputes. Yet the subject of this chapter is just such an entanglement, an episode which raises serious, though not insoluble, questions about the nature and extent of Fisher's commitment to Christian humanism. For in 1519 he took an active part against the prominent French humanist Jacques Lefèvre d'Etaples in what was the third great 'humanist' controversy of the decade. Unduly neglected by historians, this controversy over the identity of the woman celebrated in the Roman calendar under the name of Mary Magdalene was potent in its own day. In some ways a 'dry run' for the Reformation debates over scripture, tradition and authority, it attracted far more attention, at least in France, than did the sparks flying in an obscure corner of Saxony over the head of a little-known Augustinian friar. The gist of the dispute is easily summarised. According to Lefèvre, the liturgical figure of Mary Magdalene was a conflation of three separate women whose careers could be disentangled through a close examination of the Gospels. The three women were: Mary Magdalene herself, the companion of Christ and the apostles, from whom seven devils had been expelled; Mary of Bethany, the sister of Martha and Lazarus; and the anonymous 'sinner in the city' whom Christ saved from stoning.[1] It is less easy for us to appreciate why his theory should have given rise to bitter dispute. But we have to realise that the composite figure of the Magdalene was a subject of popular devotion and preaching throughout Europe. The story of a woman who had been raised from the depths of prostitution and demonic possession to the ranks of Christ's closest followers and to the heights of contemplation, ending her life as a penitent ascetic near Marseilles, was an inspiring theme in the

65

heavily penitential spirituality of the later Middle Ages. The cult of the Magdalene was one of the strongest in Europe, especially in France. Lefèvre's demythologisation could thus scarcely fail to elicit a severe critical onslaught. Among the champions who entered the lists on behalf of the 'unique Magdalene', the most prominent and talented was without doubt the bishop of Rochester. He was also the most unexpected of those champions, because his decision to oppose Lefèvre struck even his contemporaries as incompatible with his previous support for Reuchlin and Erasmus. In consequence, this controversy has been taken as marking the end of a brief flirtation with humanism on his part. But such a conclusion fails to do justice to Fisher. In order to understand his motives and objectives in embarking on his defence of the Magdalene tradition, it is essential for us to pay close attention to the precise way in which he was drawn into the controversy, to the issues which he believed were at stake in it, and to the arguments with which he addressed them.

The immediate occasion of the controversy was the pilgrimage of the French Queen Mother (Louise de Savoie) over the winter of 1515–16 to the shrine of Mary Magdalene at La Sainte Baume near Marseilles. On her return she asked the former tutor of François I, one François du Moulin, to write her an account of the Magdalene's life as a souvenir.[2] While doing this, du Moulin consulted his friend Lefèvre on the scriptural niceties of the matter. Lefèvre soon came to the conclusion that 'Mary Magdalene' was more than one person, and he published his views in a pamphlet entitled De Maria Magdalena late in 1517 or early in 1518.[3] His pamphlet raised an immediate storm, albeit in modern eyes a storm in a tea-cup. Protests poured forth in sermons and pamphlets, and the question became the stuff of fashionable conversation. Marc de Grandval, a canon of St Victor and a leading light of the Paris theology faculty, produced in September the first weighty reply, the Apologia seu Defensorium. To this Lefèvre responded with a second and enlarged edition, to which he added a debunking of the legend that Anne, the mother of the Blessed Virgin Mary, had had three husbands.[4] It was to this edition that Fisher addressed his first reply, the De Unica Magdalena Libri Tres, published in Paris on 22 February 1519 by Josse Bade, one of the two leading humanist printers of the city. Since Bade had also published Grandval's book, and the other leading printer, Henri Estienne, published Lefèvre and his supporters, there may have been an element of trade rivalry in the controversy. Fisher's tract achieved instant success, soon running to a second printing,[5] and was generally regarded as conclusive.[6] In the meantime, Josse Clichtove, a long-standing collaborator of Lefèvre's, had written a loyal defence of his friend's thesis, the Disceptationis de Magdalena Defensio (Paris: Estienne, 1519).[7] Although this was not aimed at Fisher, whose book Clichtove had manifestly not read, Fisher nevertheless set to work on a refutation, the Eversio Munitionis, which was published some time that summer by another prominent humanist printer, Thierry Maartens of Louvain.[8] Around the same time, Marc de Grandval published a reply to Clichtove called *Tutamentum et Anchora* in which he paid generous tribute to Fisher's *De Unica Magdalena*.[9] While Clichtove had been defending Lefèvre's original position, however, Lefèvre himself had been rethinking it in the light of Fisher's critique. The result was a modification of his original thesis, the *De Tribus et Unica Magdalena Disceptatio* (Paris: Estienne, 1519). His new theory (which will be explained below) was no more welcome than its predecessor to Fisher, who therefore undertook a third and final refutation, the *Confutatio Secundae Disceptationis* (Paris: Bade, 1519), which appeared in September, but added almost nothing to the arguments he had developed in his two previous works.[10] The debate was by now almost over, and the last word fell to Noel Beda, also of the Paris theology faculty, whose *Scholastica Declaratio* (Paris: Bade, 1519) came out shortly afterwards.[11]

Fisher's entry into controversy with two of France's leading humanists in the company of such a dedicated opponent of humanism as Noel Beda might look like nothing more than the gut reaction of a pious conservative churchman to a dose of advanced scriptural criticism. Indeed a recent account has gone so far as to present it as an option for expediency in preference to truth.[12] But a proper consideration of Fisher's attitude to his opponents and of the way in which he was drawn into the debate shows how far from the truth such judgments are. Essential to a correct understanding of Fisher's part in the debate is the hitherto hardly noticed fact that his initial response to Lefèvre's thesis was decidedly favourable. In the dedication of *Confutatio Secundae*, which was addressed to Cardinal Campeggio, he reminded the Cardinal of a conversation that they had had 'some time ago' on the subject of the Magdalene. Campeggio had asked him for an opinion on Lefèvre's book, and Fisher had replied that he was inclined to agree that there had been two Magdalenes.[13] His sympathy with Lefèvre's thesis was accompanied by a high regard for the Frenchman's scholarship. At the start of the *De Unica Magdalena* he professed considerable respect for his opponent, and recalled his initial conviction that a man of such good character would hardly put forward such a claim without being very sure of his ground.[14] He restated his high opinion of both Lefèvre and Clichtove in the *Confutatio Secundae*, saying that although he had never met them, they were both dear to him as men of learning and righteousness.[15] Fisher was certainly acquainted with their earlier work. In the Magdalene controversy itself he drew not only on Lefèvre's edition of various medieval revelations but also on his commentaries on Paul's epistles, of which he had given a copy to St John's College in 1513.[16] And the edition of Cyril from which Fisher frequently quoted was probably that prepared by Clichtove.[17] Yet despite these good omens he was drawn into the dispute – albeit only after much persuasion. It was not until another visiting diplomat brought the matter once more to his attention that Fisher changed his mind. Stephen Poncher, bishop of Paris, who came to England in late August 1518 at the head of a French embassy, found time from his official duties to send Fisher the second edition of Lefèvre's book, along with Grandval's reply (which was dedicated to him in his capacity as chancellor of the university of Paris), asking for an opinion. When Poncher received much the same reply as Campeggio had done, he wrote again, more insistently, alleging that a dispute of this kind could seriously harm the piety of the faithful. He therefore requested Fisher to settle the question definitively. Only then did Fisher examine Lefèvre's arguments more closely and conclude that they called for refutation.[18]

The way in which Poncher secured Fisher's intervention in the controversy tells us much about Fisher's motives and spiritual priorities. Pastoral concern emerges as the driving force behind his polemical activities. Yet we must exercise caution in interpreting the nature of this pastoral concern. Fisher claimed that Poncher's letters awoke him to the threat Lefèvre's arguments posed to the piety of the simple faithful. He feared that Lefèvre's criticism of the Magdalene tradition would erode popular confidence in the cult of the saints. Fisher therefore urged his readers not to be deterred from their worship by the cavils of Lefèvre and Clichtove.[19] His overriding concern was the spiritual good of Christians. To him, the Magdalene story was a most efficacious means of ensuring that 'wretched sinners should not despair, but be stirred to repentance', and he had indeed used the Magdalene as an exemplar in his sermons on the penitential psalms.[20] This relevance for the practice of penance was the crux of the devotional issue for Fisher. Lefèvre, who did not impugn the sanctity of any of the three women into whom he divided 'Mary Magdalene', seems to have felt it incongruous that Martha's sister, who was so dear to Christ, should be supposed ever to have been a notorious sinner.[21] Fisher read this as pharasaical distaste for the sordid reality of sin, and argued that presenting Martha's sister as a repentant sinner was a tremendous incentive that offered real hope even to the most hardened of people.[22] Nevertheless, there is reason to suppose that concern for popular devotion was something of a rhetorical device. Fisher was after all writing in Latin, a medium which was hardly likely to come to the attention of the common people. And in any case, popular piety was hardly likely to be (and in the event was not) disturbed by an academic controversy of such a specific nature. Even scholarly opinion was largely unimpressed with Lefèvre's case – reformers such as Latimer and Zwingli continued to accept the traditional view of the Magdalene.[23] Fisher's rhetorical pose was carried through in his casting of himself as the champion of the maligned saint and her devotees. He professed a personal devotion to her, and felt sure that his efforts would endear him to her.[24] Although the presence of a statue of the Magdalene among the effects that he made over to St John's College in 1525 bears out his claim to some extent, the relative paucity of references to her in his writing suggest that his devotion was far from consuming.[25] Despite the bitter assaults that Protestant reformers launched on the cult of the saints, he never addressed the question in his works against them. More tellingly still, neither the Magdalene in particular nor the cult of the saints in general figures strongly in his specifically devotional writings, be they prayers or manuals of prayer. Fisher's piety, as we shall see in later chapters, was strongly Christocentric and eucharistic, and Fisher himself moved with ease in the circle of Colet and Erasmus, in which the cult of the saints was far from central and the excesses and abuses of that cult were liable to biting satire. Although the picture of Fisher as the protector of the simple faithful undoubtedly rings true to the extent that he regarded the cult of the saints as an essential part of popular devotion, the apparently limited place of that cult in his own religious life makes it implausible to see this as his primary concern in the Magdalene controversy.

Further confirmation that Fisher's position cannot be explained as blind adherence to popular tradition can be found in his attitude to Lefèvre's debunking of a similar case. In the second edition of his *De Maria Magdalena*, Lefèvre had introduced an entirely new section attacking the legend that Our Lady's mother, Anne, had been married three times and had borne to each of her husbands a daughter – Mary the mother of James and John, Mary the wife of Cleophas (and mother of James, Simon, Joseph and Jude, the 'brethren of the Lord'), and finally Our Lady herself.[26] The cult of St Anne was strong in England, France and Germany, and several of Lefèvre's opponents leapt to its defence. Peter Sutor and Noel Beda of Paris, and Konrad Wimpina of Cologne, all published vindications of Anne's three marriages.[27] On the other side, Cornelius Agrippa and Josse Clichtove defended Lefèvre's views on both Anne and the Magdalene.[28] Fisher, however, struck out an independent line by agreeing with him over Anne while still disagreeing over the Magdalene. It is in his explanation of the differences he perceived between the two cases that we can find the true motivation for his intervention in the Magdalene controversy. The story of Anne's three husbands, he argued, was not supported by weighty authorities; nor was it confirmed by miracles; nor had it been the subject of special revelations; nor had it any foundation in scripture. Moreover, it had long been controverted. Fisher remarked that he himself possessed an old and learned manuscript treatise refuting the legend, and that in his youth he had read a poem in defence of Anne's monogamy.[29] Finally, the tradition was not corroborated by the liturgy of the Roman Church.[30] The case of the Magdalene tradition was entirely different. In his view, this tradition was universally accepted among both learned and unlearned; it was confirmed by miracles and revelations; and it was not only based on scripture, but also enshrined in the liturgy.[31] The importance of Fisher's position on St Anne lies in proving that the defence of popular piety was not his primary aim. For there can be no doubt that popular devotion throughout Europe was solidly attached to the story of Anne's three husbands.[32] Luther's famous vow to enter the priesthood if he should survive a thunderstorm was made to St Anne, though later he came to entertain doubts about her legend.[33] In England, numerous guilds existed in her honour, and a fair amount of unofficial devotional literature was written for their patronal feast. Since this literature was based largely on the account in the *Legenda Aurea*, it is hardly surprising that Anne's three husbands always appear.[34] Pictorial representation of the Holy Kindred of St Anne with all her daughters and grandchildren was common in Northern Europe. For example, a tableau of this extended family was portrayed at Leadenhall in 1533 along the route of Anne Boleyn's coronation procession. One of the sons of Mary Cleophas delivered an oration on St Anne's fertility, in an obvious reference to the relevance of this saint in the Queen's case.[35] Fisher's rejection of the legend was therefore an act of dissociation from a wide and deeply-held popular tradition. To some extent, it can probably be seen as placing Fisher amid the new movement of devotion to the Holy Family of Mary, Joseph and Jesus which, it has been suggested, began to replace devotion to the Holy Kindred of Anne around 1500.[36] But in Fisher's case it was based intellectually on the existence of a contrary tradition, and on the lack of any liturgical sanction for the legend. It was thus fundamentally a question of authority.

It was not the legend of Anne but the doctrine of the Assumption of the Blessed Virgin Mary that provided Fisher with a proper analogy for the tradition about the Magdalene. That doctrine, like the Magdalene tradition, enjoyed the support of orthodox authors, of powerful reasoning, of miracles and revelations, and of the liturgy. But in addition the identification of Mary Magdalene with the sister of Martha had scriptural confirmation. Fisher found this in Christ's prophecy that the memory of the woman who anointed him would be revered wherever the Gospel was received (Mt 26:13, Mk 14:9). In his eyes, this prophecy was fulfilled in the cult of the Magdalene, and if that cult was wrong in identifying her with Martha's sister, then her memory was not revered but traduced. Besides, the Magdalene tradition was also older than that of the Assumption, as it went back beyond the time of Jerome. And Clichtove's objection that the tradition was not approved by the Church because there was no official decree defining it left it on no worse a footing than the Assumption which, though universally accepted, had not been definitively proclaimed. Since nobody could reject the Assumption without incurring the charge of heresy, nobody could deny the tradition concerning the Magdalene without risking the same charge.[37] Thus the crucial issue for Fisher was the authority of the Church. He saw no tension, however, between that authority on the one hand and truth and reason on the other. Rather, the infallible authority of the Church precluded all possibility of error on a matter where there was such striking unanimity. As he had contended in *De Unica Magdalena*, if popes, fathers, doctors and preachers should have been wrong on this matter, then he could see on reason why anyone should ever trust them again over anything.[38]

The Magdalene debate was of course a matter of authority for both sides. The question was where authority lay, and how divergent authorities were to be balanced or reconciled. But before we consider in detail the differences in interpretation between Fisher and Lefèvre, it is worth examining the evidence from scripture and tradition over which they were arguing. The primary evidence was of course scriptural, and there are a number of references in the Gospels to Mary Magdalene and to Mary the sister of Martha.[39] The most important of these were the accounts in each Gospel of the anointing of Christ by a woman at a feast. It was these four texts that gave rise to the conflation of the two figures. In only one of the accounts (Jn 12:1–7) is the woman named – as Mary the sister of Martha. Matthew (26:6–13) and Mark (14:3–9) describe the event in almost identical terms, concurring with John in locating it at Bethany, but dating it two, rather than six, days before the Passover. Luke (7:36–50) recounts a similar incident, but apparently locates it at Naim towards the beginning of Christ's public ministry, calling the woman 'a sinner in the city'. This woman came to identified with Mary Magdalene because Luke immediately went on to talk about the latter (Lk 8:3 – one must recall that there were no divisions of chapter, let alone of verse, until the thirteenth century). There were sufficient similarities and overlaps between the four narratives to cause confusion even in the patristic period. While Matthew and Mark wrote of an anointing of Christ's head, Luke and John told of a woman anointing his feet, washing them with her tears and drying them with her hair. All four agreed that the host at the feast was named Simon. But Luke called him a Pharisee, while the other three described him as a leper. Patristic interpretations of these texts varied wildly. Chrysostom believed that there were two anointings performed by two distinct women.[40] Origen divided the narratives between three occasions involving three different women: one described by Matthew and Mark; one by Luke; and one by John.[41] Yet he observed that some among his contemporaries referred the accounts to one and the same event performed by only one woman.[42] This conflation spread especially in the West, and was canonised in the writings of Gregory the Great. With his authority behind it, the identification of the Magdalene with the sister of Mary became a commonplace in the Western tradition.[43]

It is essential to appreciate that Fisher argued against Lefèvre not on the basis of tradition and authority alone, but from the scriptural texts. Indeed his refutation of Lefèvre's original position is largely based on scripture, and is absolutely conclusive. Nor is it hard to see why, as Erasmus reported, people found Fisher's first reply convincing. He triumphed because Lefèvre's initial reassessment of the Magdalene tradition was not radical enough. Lefèvre did not adopt the modern and easily defensible distinction between the woman

71

called Mary Magdalene and the woman called Mary of Bethany (the sister of Martha). On the contrary, Lefèvre at first thought that both these women, although distinct, shared the epithet 'Magdalene'; and he went on to divide the references to 'Mary Magdalene' between the healed demoniac and the sister of Martha on the basis of little more than his own prejudice.[44] Fisher's reply was masterly. Accepting without question Lefèvre's highly questionable premiss that Martha's sister was sometimes called 'Magdalene', he demonstrated what is certainly the case, namely that all the references to 'Mary Magdalene' are to one and the same woman. These premisses led inexorably to the conclusion that Martha's sister and the demoniac were one and the same. However, his victory depended crucially on Lefèvre's shaky premiss. When Lefèvre revised his case in the light of Fisher's devastating reply, he abandoned this premiss, and proposed instead the far more elegant and convincing distinction between the Mary called Magdalene and the sister of Martha who lived at Bethany. Unfortunately, Fisher did not correctly interpret Lefèvre's shift, taking as abject flight what was in fact a tactical retreat.

The differing interpretations adopted by Fisher and Lefèvre reflected different approaches to the problems of exegesis. Lefèvre held a literalistic view of scripture, whereas Fisher, as we noted in the previous chapter, took a more harmonistic view. Each approach had strengths as well as weaknesses. Lefèvre's concern for the literal accuracy of the Gospel narratives betrayed him into an absurd multiplication of individuals and events in an endeavour to save every detail. Even the slightest discrepancies between accounts suggested to him that different events were being reported. Fisher's concern for harmony led him to adopt a critical principle as important as that of literal interpretation: the recognition that minor discrepancies could mean simply that the same event was being narrated from a different point of view, with a different purpose, and thus with a different selection and perhaps arrangement of significant detail.[45] Yet this led him to an excessive readiness to tidy up the Gospels with such a slick device as the identification of the Magdalene with Mary, an identification which certainly cannot be derived from the text alone. The difference in approach can be seen in their respective treatments of the narrative concerning the morning of the Resurrection. In one account, Christ appeared to Mary Magdalene alone, forbidding her to touch him (Jn 20:14–17); in another, he appeared to her and the other women together, allowing them to embrace his feet (Mt 28:9). For Lefèvre, this meant that two different women, both called Mary Magdalene, were involved in two separate events. Fisher suggested on the other hand that the same woman might have met Christ on two separate occasions on the same morning.[46] Again, Lefèvre argued that there were two Mary Magdalenes at the Crucifixion, because one was described as standing near the cross (Jn 19:25), the other as standing some way off (Mk 15:40; Mt 27:55–56). Fisher gently observed that she might have moved.[47] However,

Fisher's exegesis remains a curious mixture of considerable acuity with in-explicable blindness. Against the multiplication of 'Magdalenes' he remarked that, though John was always most particular in differentiating individuals who shared names, he made no attempt to distinguish between any Magdalenes.[48] On the other hand, his observation that nowhere in the Gospels was there any explicit identification of Mary Magdalene with the sister of Martha failed to open his eyes to the inherent weakness of such a view.[49] His destruction of Lefèvre's original position was skilful, yet his establishment of his own was inadequate and inconclusive.

Important as scripture was in Fisher's argument, he was far from resting his case on scripture alone. On the contrary, he raised the question of the relation-ship of scripture to tradition at the very start of the *De Unica Magdalena*, claiming to detect in Lefèvre's thesis a dangerous tendency to appeal to scripture alone. And Lefèvre had indeed suggested that scripture was the only relevant authority for this dispute, although he did not in practice disdain the appeal to tradition where it suited him.[50] Fisher met this argument head on, urging that scripture was not so self-evidently clear that it could be understood properly without the aid of commentaries.[51] Recourse to the writings of popes, doctors and preachers was in his view indispensable.[52] However, Fisher's deployment of tradition in this controversy was far from impressive. His attack on the patristic testimony adduced by his opponent was especially weak. Origen and Chrysostom were dismissed on the grounds that the Greek Church was prone to error and that therefore its tradition was not to be preferred to that of the Latin Church.[53] But this cavalier disregard of the Greek fathers was not characteristic of Fisher's later works, and reads more like a debating-point. A rather better reason was that Lefèvre's authorities not only failed to agree among themselves, but failed to come anywhere near Lefèvre's own view.[54] But this too smacks more of the soap-box than the scholar's pen. Fisher's own presentation of patristic authorities, which came in the third part of *De Unica Magdalena*, was based more on dogmatic than on historical grounds. The authors he cited were presented mostly two by two, as if for Noah's ark. The classification was essentially whimsical but perhaps rhetorically inspired, based partly on an academic and partly on a dogmatic hierarchy. He began with two scholastics or 'disceptatores', Albertus Magnus and Thomas Aquinas, because of their connections with Paris University. Then he gave extracts from two simple scriptural commentators, Simon of Cassia and Ubertinus de Casale. Acknowledging that their unclassical style would hardly endear them to Lefèvre, he supported them with two more idiomatic authors, Bede and Christian Druthmar, and then with two (alleged) Parisians, Alcuin and Rabanus Maurus, and finally with two French saints, Anselm and Bernard. Augustine was cited *sui generis*, and was used to correct the mutually inconsistent Ambrose, Origen and Chrysostom. Two cardinals came next (Nicholas of Cusa and Marco Vigerio de Savona), followed by a poet (Petrarch), two popes (Leo and Gregory) and two Greeks (Theophilus and Gregory Nazianzen). Finally he adduced the evidence of revelations (Bridget of Sweden) and miracles (from the history of Vincent of Beauvais), rounding the whole book off with a poem by the Carmelite humanist, Giovanni Battista Spagnuoli.[55]

Later in the controversy Fisher's use of patristic testimony takes on a more analytical appearance, perhaps under the influence of Clichtove's *Defensio*, which took the debate about tradition onto a new level. Although Clichtove did not add materially to the arguments advanced by Lefèvre, he did clarify the exegetical and critical principles on which Lefèvre's case rested. These principles, defined by Clichtove as eight 'suppositiones', laid down that the controversy was one of history rather than of faith; that in historical controversies the original or the oldest sources should be given the most respect; that authorities who supported their views with arguments should be preferred to those who made bare assertions; and that authorities who dealt with a matter as their main subject should be preferred to those who simply mentioned it in passing.[56] In his reply, the *Eversio Munitionis*, Fisher followed Clichtove in concentrating on the methodological aspects of the controversy. He took issue with each of his opponent's eight suppositions – often, apparently, in a merely partisan spirit. First of all he objected to Clichtove's attempt to remove the issue from the realm of faith, arguing that since the scriptures were involved, the faith was necessarily at stake.[57] More tendentiously he denied that earlier evidence was intrinsically superior to later evidence. His proof for this rested on the doctrine of Our Lady's perpetual virginity, denied in the fourth century by Elvidius, which Fisher regarded as a matter of both faith and history. According to him, Elvidius had relied on scripture in constructing his argument, and Jerome, in refuting him, had been unable to adduce any evidence beyond that of Elvidius's texts: instead, he had laid out the correct interpretation of those texts in the light of the tradition of the Church.[58]

Fisher's attack on Clichtove's suppositions was followed by a test-case selected to demonstrate that they were not in fact the universally applicable propositions they purported to be. This test-case was the controversy between Jerome and Augustine over the dispute between Peter and Paul at Antioch which, as we have seen, he was probably giving close attention in the context of the contemporary controversy between Lee and Erasmus.[59] Jerome had followed the tradition of earlier commentators in arguing that when Peter sat apart from the Gentile Christians to eat with the Jewish Christians, he did so by prior arrangement with Paul, so that the latter, by publicly reproving him, could make his point against the obligation of the ceremonial law as strongly as possible. Augustine on the other hand maintained that Peter had really acted wrongly, and that Paul's reproof was therefore entirely genuine.[60] Having set out the views of the two authorities at some length, Fisher explained why it was relevant to his argument. He produced various passages from Lefèvre's commentary on Paul in which he showed that Lefèvre, despite attempting to steer a middle way between Jerome and Augustine, in fact came down on Augustine's side on the crucial issue.[61] The culmination of the argument was that Lefèvre's position in this controversy showed that he did not adhere to the critical principles Clichtove had laid down, because Augustine's position contradicted the earlier patristic consensus.[62] It is important to remember here that Fisher himself was not taking sides in the controversy, having explicitly warned that nobody should expect a definitive judgment on it from him.[63] This argument of Fisher's is of course embarrassingly full of holes. However close the association between Lefèvre and Clichtove may have been, it was not valid to argue inconsistency in the former for not adhering to the principles of the latter. But in any case, the Augustinian position in the Antiochian controversy was founded on the earliest testimony, namely that of Acts. Fisher continued his assault on Clichtove's 'suppositions' by establishing in unsubtle contrast eight rival principles which he called 'truths'. These truths were: that none of the fathers held Lefèvre's position on the Magdalene; that none of them escaped error in writing of her; that the vast majority of orthodox commentators upheld the traditional view; that the local tradition at Marseilles was clear and reliable; that the universal tradition was supported by miracles and revelations; that the Gospel too supported it; and that the general consensus of the Church was therefore correct in identifying Mary Magdalene with the sister of Martha.[64] They amounted in short to a reasoned defence of the current tradition of the Church and a rejection of arguments founded upon the contradictory testimony of the early fathers.

The Magdalene controversy does not show Fisher at his best. His thesis about the identity of the Magdalene has been almost universally rejected by modern exegetes, and the main reason for this rejection, the absence of any hint in the Gospels that Mary Magdalene was the same person as the sister of Martha, was not hidden from him. His arguments against Clichtove in particular were often weak and partisan. Nevertheless, he made a number of telling points in the course of the controversy. His destruction of Lefèvre's initial position, that there were two women in the Gospels called Mary Magdalene, was conclusive, and was probably responsible for forcing Lefèvre to shift his ground on the question. Although his deployment of tradition was partial and erratic, his marshalling of the scriptural evidence in the second part of *De Unica Magdalena* was the clearest statement of the problem in the whole of the dispute. Despite the flaws in Fisher's case, we can certainly endorse the judgment of a recent critic that in this controversy his contributions were the most interesting of those written against Lefèvre.[65] We can also reject the judgment that Fisher's role in the dispute was that of an enemy of humanism. The easy dichotomies of 'modern and medieval' and 'critical and credulous' are not applicable to this dispute, in which credulity and progress were the monopoly of neither party. Otherwise we will find ourselves at a loss to explain why the 'credulous' Fisher accepted Lefèvre's debunking of legends concerning St Anne, and why the critical Lefèvre continued to accept what Fisher rightly described as the least plausible part of the whole Magdalene story, the legend that she spent her final years as a hermit near Marseilles. Fisher himself, of course, also accepted this story, comparing it with the similar story of Joseph of Arimathea's burial at Glastonbury, on the basis of local tradition, the 'true law of history'. His point was that such evidence was hardly adequate on Lefèvre's criteria.[66] Indeed, were we to choose our ground carefully we could cast Fisher and Lefèvre in entirely opposite roles. Lefèvre always remained attached to the legend that France had been evangelised by St Denis, that is, by Dionysius the Areopagite, the convert made by Paul at Athens; and he also believed that St Denis was the author of the Dionysian treatises, which actually date from the fifth century. Fisher accepted the story of the evangelisation of France,[67] but was aware that the authorship of the Dionysian corpus was doubtful, although he remained of the opinion that the treatises were from the early Church, and regularly cited them in his polemics.[68] Again, Lefèvre believed in the spurious correspondence between Seneca and Paul, including it in his 1515 edition of the Pauline epistles.[69] But Fisher, following Erasmus – whose opinion in such a matter, he stated, he would follow against a thousand opponents – rejected that correspondence in its entirety.[70] In fact, Fisher and Lefèvre had much more in common than their appearance on opposite sides of the Magdalene controversy might at first suggest. Both were already advanced in years by the standards of the time, and they shared the experience of adjusting to the new developments in scholarship after formation in the traditional curriculum. Both men were capable of regarding the medieval heritage with a critical eye, and both were committed to the advancement of scriptural and patristic study.[71] Neither of them rejected the medieval heritage out of hand, and were rather associated with attempts to renovate it than with attempts to supersede it. And both men shared an especial regard for the attainments and example of Pico.[72] Fisher's avowed admiration for Lefèvre, his manifest use of much of Lefèvre's work and his initial sympathy even for Lefèvre's views on the Magdalene, must be given their due weight. Their disagreement over the Magdalene is no more indicative of an ideological gulf than are the disagreements between Lefèvre and Erasmus over many other points of New Testament exegesis. This is not to say that Fisher must therefore be classed with those two great Christian humanists. He was neither an Erasmian nor a 'Lefèvrite'. The main difference between him and them was without doubt that he was a bishop. His episcopal status denied him the time he would have liked to devote to scholarly pursuits, but endowed him with a deep sense of pastoral responsibility and of his duty to uphold the Church and her teaching. It was this sense of duty which impelled him to take up the pen in the Magdalene controversy, and was to draw him into a succession of further controversies over the next ten years. John Fisher's first polemical campaign shows us a scholar capable of making up his own mind and ready to commit himself in print. It also shows us a bishop determined to defend the Church's teaching against any threat, from however sympathetic and respectable a source it might derive. His relative inexperience in controversy is obvious. But the 1520s, as we shall see in the following chapters, were to give him ample opportunity to put a sharper edge on his polemical technique.

5
Fisher and the Catholic campaign against Luther

JOHN FISHER'S REPUTATION for sanctity depended in his lifetime on the assiduous fulfilment of his episcopal obligations. His academic reputation rested chiefly on the handful of polemical writings that he produced in the 1520s against the Protestant Reformers. It was left to a character assassin named Richard Morison to insinuate that there was a conflict between these two areas of endeavour. In 1535, Morison was persuaded to write in denigration of Fisher and More in an attempt to minimise the damaging publicity that followed their execution. In the course of his effort, *Apomaxis Calumniarum*, Morison charged the bishop with neglecting his pastoral duties in order to gratify a passion for self-advertisement by posturing as the Church's champion against Luther.[1] As usual, Morison's bluster was comically wide of the mark. Apart from overlooking the fact that, as Stephen Thompson has recently demonstrated, Fisher had a better record of residence than almost all his English episcopal colleagues,[2] the sneer failed to appreciate that Fisher regarded the defence of the faith against heresy as an integral part of the bishop's role. As he said himself,

I intend to confirm the weaker brethren, whose faith has for too long now been poised on the knife-edge between heresy and orthodoxy . . . It was for their sake that the order to which I belong was everlastingly established . . . if this flock should perish through our negligence, the blood shall be upon our heads.[3]

The purpose of this chapter is to explore how Fisher pursued this objective as the Church in Europe, and to a lesser extent in England, was threatened by the emergence of Protestant heresies in the 1520s. We shall examine not only his polemical writings, but also the circumstances under which he came to write them and the people who helped and encouraged him to do so. Besides this, we shall look at the other ways in which he contributed to a campaign which was waged against Luther and his followers not only in England but throughout Europe: his patronage of English and European opponents of the Reformation; and the major influence his writings exerted on an even wider circle of Catholic controversialists for many years after his death.

Fisher's first active steps against the Reformation were taken in the context of the promulgation in England of the papal condemnation of Luther, *Exsurge Domine*, and of the production of Henry VIII's famous refutation of Luther, the *Assertio Septem Sacramentorum*. The initial impact of Lutheranism in England had been limited in the extreme. John Froben exported some copies of Luther's writings to England in February 1519,[4] but the 1520 year-book of the Oxford bookseller John Dorne showed Luther's works accounting for only 15 sales out of 2000 – against at least 150 sales of Erasmus.[5] Since the earliest known English owner of a book by Luther is Thomas More, even such evidence as this should be read with caution. Erasmus's comment to Luther that the latter had highly placed supporters in England rings hollow in the absence of any names or corroborative detail.[6] And the claim that the intellectual climate in England was not antagonistic to Luther rests on an identification of Luther's interests with those of humanism and reform which should be demonstrated rather than (as too often) assumed. On the contrary, More's comment that 'Luther's attacks upon the Holy See would be piety itself' compared to a withdrawal of papal support for Erasmus's *Novum Instrumentum*, implies that Luther was not regarded favourably in England.[7] There may be a similar implication in an obscure remark of Fisher's, made in the preface to his *Confutatio Secundae Disceptationis*, which touches on the rise of new heresies 'quod futura formidatur'.[8] The anti-Lutheran activities of early 1521 were not in any sense a response to some crisis felt to be imminent within the Church of England itself. Rather, they arose from the trilateral *rapprochement* between Rome, England and the Empire. Leo X had promulgated *Exsurge Domine* on 15 June 1520, and securing political and academic support for that bull was henceforth a top priority of Roman diplomacy. To this end, Jerome Aleander was sent as papal legate to the Diet of Worms, and the pope's brother Giulio de Medici (later Clement VII) pursued the same objective in negotiations with Wolsey. The third side of the triangle was completed by Cuthbert Tunstall's mission to the Diet of Worms, and it was probably his alarming report on the success of Lutheranism in Germany, and in particular on Luther's *De Babylonica Captivitate*, that prompted Wolsey to accept de Medici's approaches.[9] Early in 1521 he forbade the importation and sale of Luther's books in England.[10] It was almost certainly Tunstall's report which also inspired Henry VIII to undertake his *Assertio Septem Sacramentorum* in refutation of the *De Babylonica Captivitate*. Henry was at work by April at the latest, as the project was known to Warham when he wrote to Wolsey on 3 April extolling the king's orthodoxy and arranging a meeting to discuss further action against Luther.[11] The result of this meeting was the convening of a number of theologians from Oxford and Cambridge to examine the bull, which was subsequently promulgated on Sunday 12 May.[12]

The promulgation of *Exsurge Domine* was conducted with great pomp and circumstance to impress not only the London crowds who turned out for the occasion, but also the foreign ambassadors who were invited to attend. The ceremony took place at Paul's Cross (the churchyard of St Paul's Cathedral) in the presence of the Lords Spiritual with Wolsey in the place of honour. Wolsey read the papal sentence, and then a bonfire of Luther's books gave it material expression.[13] It is no surprise that Fisher, the most accomplished theologian on the bench, was selected by Wolsey to preach the sermon that provided the intellectual justification for the proceedings.[14] Within a short time it had been published both in English and in a Latin translation prepared for the pope by Richard Pace.[15] It is remarkable for its penetrating account of Luther's doctrine. Rather than take up the somewhat disparate propositions specifically condemned in the bull, or resort to mere invective, it picks out three central doctrines in Luther's theology for relatively detailed refutation. These were Luther's denial of papal primacy, his assertion of justification by faith alone, and his restriction of doctrinal authority to scripture alone (all of which we shall consider more closely in the following two chapters).[16] In the course of the sermon, Fisher made – doubtless by prior arrangement – what was the first public announcement of Henry's decision to write against Luther. As he did so, Wolsey waved a copy of the book to the crowds. While all this testifies to his close involvement with the anti-Lutheran policy of the government, it remains unlikely that he had anything directly to do with the composition of Henry's *Assertio*, although it came to be widely ascribed to him later in the century.[17]

Henry's *Assertio* was intended to be but the first in a series of attacks on Luther by English theologians, and we know of several scholars who set to work on such books in 1521.[18] It is against this background that we should consider the composition of Fisher's first lengthy anti-Lutheran polemic, the *Assertionis Lutheranae Confutatio*. The close parallels between sections of the *Confutatio* and parts of his sermon suggest that he was at work on it as early as May 1521.[19] Certainly his strenuous efforts against Luther attracted comment in a letter from his chaplain, Richard Sharpe, to Nicholas Metcalfe apparently written around June that year. And the work was largely complete by the beginning of July 1522 when Sharpe reported that Fisher was on the verge of sending it to the printers.[20] From the evidence of Fisher's movements in his register, it looks as though he wrote the bulk of the *Confutatio* while residing at Halling throughout the second half of 1521.[21] The *Confutatio* was a 200,000 word refutation of Luther's *Assertio Omnium Articulorum* (Wittenberg: Lotther, 1520), which was itself a vigorous affirmation of the forty-one articles condemned in *Exsurge Domine*. Because of the scope of Luther's work, which ranged over scripture, the papacy, justification, free will, penance, the eucharist, purgatory and indulgences, Fisher's *Confutatio* was the nearest thing to a complete critique of Luther's doctrine then available. Along with Henry's *Assertio*, it was one of the most popular attacks on Luther of the decade, running to several editions in Antwerp, Cologne, Paris and Venice. However, its initial publication was delayed by the war between England and France in 1522. Making a virtue of necessity, Fisher took the opportunity to refute another Protestant polemic that had been brought to his attention the previous year by Cuthbert Tunstall. This was the *Libellus* of Ulrich Velenus, a pamphlet which sought to undermine the Petrine claims of the papacy by demonstrating that St Peter himself had never been to Rome. The *Convulsio Calumniarum Ulrichi Veleni* which Fisher produced in reply must have been composed in very short order, because its preface shows that it was begun after the completion of the *Confutatio* and the outbreak of hostilities in July, and before Tunstall's consecration as bishop of London on 19 October.[22] In the event, the two completed books must have been sent to the printers together, appearing from different Antwerp presses (Hillenius and Vorstermann) in November 1522 and January 1523. The much shorter *Convulsio* was of course printed first. John Addison, one of Fisher's chaplains, was responsible for seeing them through the press, a task in which he was assisted by Hermann Lethmaet of Utrecht.[23] It was Addison who obtained the Privy Seal warrant which conferred Henry's royal privilege on the *Confutatio* and enthusiastically commended the book and its author to the public. This warrant indicates that there was more than a hint of official encouragement behind Fisher's endeavour.[24]

The official instigation that lay behind Fisher's polemical writings against the Protestants can be readily detected in the next work he undertook, a defence of Henry VIII's *Assertio* against Luther's vitriolic reply, the *Contra Henricum Regem Angliae* (Wittenberg: Lotther, 1522.) Although his *Defensio Regiae Assertionis* was not published until 1525, we know from its dedication to Nicholas West that it had been completed two years previously.[25] It looks rather like a theologically respectable counterpart to the *Responsio ad Lutherum* written at about the same time by Thomas More under the pseudonym of Rossaeus. Before the *Defensio* was published, Fisher wrote a third attack on Luther, the *Sacri Sacerdotii Defensio*. This was a reply to Luther's *De Abroganda Missa Privata* (Wittenberg: Lotther, 1522), a work which was causing concern to the English authorities in June 1523.[26] The *Defensio* and the *Sacri Sacerdotii* were printed together, in uniform size, by Peter Quentell of Cologne in June 1525, and had clearly been revised for simultaneous publication, as each refers to the other as already written.[27] The royal coat of arms which adorns the two volumes again indicates a degree of official sanction behind their appearance. The royal hand can be seen even more clearly behind an unpublished, and indeed unfinished, work of Fisher's begun around this time. The Latin commentary on the Psalms which survives in a badly damaged manuscript was definitely undertaken at Henry VIII's instigation.[28] It can be dated with some confidence to 1525. Henry had been trying to persuade Erasmus to write a commentary on the Psalms in late 1524.[29] Erasmus had in effect refused, and it is tempting to deduce that the request was transferred to Fisher, which would help explain the

'Erasmian' character at which the commentary clearly aims. Besides, the polemical undercurrent of the commentary and the occasional explicit reference to Luther prevent us from placing it earlier than the 1520s, while the specific attack on Bugenhagen's interpretation of Psalm 23 shows beyond doubt that the work dates from after July 1524.[30] The absence of even hints at the problems surrounding Henry VIII's divorce and his attack on the liberties of the Church is strong evidence that the work dated from before 1527, after which Fisher was in any case too busy with his writings on the divorce to give time to such a large project. And the absence of polemical comments on the real presence in the eucharist means that the work probably predated his refutation of Oecolampadius. Indeed, one suspects that this latter project was what curtailed work on the commentary. He was certainly aware of Oecolampadius's ideas by early 1526, when he was called upon by Henry VIII himself to preach a second sermon against Luther at Paul's Cross, this time at the recantation of Robert Barnes on 11 February.[31] Oecolampadius had argued in a tract published in September 1525 that the body and blood of Christ were not really present in the eucharist. The sermon's mention of Oecolampadius in the context of dissensions over the eucharist within the ranks of the Reformers shows that this work had come to Fisher's attention. Indeed, he was probably busy on his refutation already, as it can hardly have taken him less than a year to complete it, and there are some close parallels between it and the sermon.[32] The work must have been well advanced by September 1526 when Fisher was in correspondence about it with the German Catholic polemicist Johann Cochlaeus.[33] It was published under the title *De Veritate Corporis et Sanguinis Christi in Eucharistia* by Quentell at Cologne in February 1527, again with the royal coat of arms prominently displayed. With the outbreak later that year of the controversy over Henry VIII's first marriage, however, Fisher found it impossible to continue his polemical offensive against the Protestants, and he informed Cochlaeus of his intention to desist from such activities.[34]

His polemical career, though, had not been an entirely solo affair. If, as we have seen, he did not enter theological controversy without encouragement from others, neither did he publish his works without exposing them to the constructively critical eyes of his friends and colleagues. His greatest debt was to Cuthbert Tunstall, who contributed in some way to at least four of Fisher's five major anti-Protestant polemics. Fisher acknowledged in the most generous terms his assistance and advice in the composition of the *Confutatio*, and we have already seen how it was Tunstall who brought the treatise of Velenus to his attention. The *Sacri Sacerdotii* was dedicated to Tunstall, who was thanked for assistance in that work also (we have seen how Tunstall tried to persuade Erasmus to refute Luther's *De Abroganda*).[35] And in the *De Veritate*, Fisher acknowledged Tunstall's loan of a Greek edition of the liturgies of Basil and Chrysostom.[36] As the real presence was later to be the subject of one of

Tunstall's own forays into theological controversy, it is possible that his contribution to this book went beyond the loan of sources. The two men co-operated in other fields as well. In 1524 Wolsey, Warham, Fisher and Tunstall were appointed to censor the book trade, and one suspects that the latter pair did more of the work.[37] At any rate, when Oxford University wrote to Warham in the wake of the Lutheran scare in Cardinal's College, they asked him to get Fisher or Tunstall to send up a list of heretical authors to be avoided.[38] Tunstall was of course active in his own right in the campaign against heresy, preaching at the burning of Tyndale's first New Testament some time in 1526.[39] But he seems to have been keener to persuade others to write against the Protestants than to do so himself. In their different ways, Henry VIII, Fisher, Erasmus and More were all inspired to write by him.

Fisher's other advisers and assistants have left fewer traces. Nicholas West was awarded the dedication of *Defensio* in return for his comments on a draft of it in 1523, and he too was active in other ways against Protestantism. After Thomas Bilney abused his licence to preach by promulgating Lutheranising doctrine in 1527, West not only withdrew his licence, but imposed an oath of orthodoxy on at least some of the clergy of his diocese. He was prominent with Tunstall and Fisher in the Protestant 'show-trials' of the 1520s and was, like them, a friend and patron of Cochlaeus.[40] There were other English scholars who commented on Fisher's works, but their names are unknown. Richard Sharpe told Metcalfe that 'diuers other well lernyd' men had read draft articles of the *Confutatio* with approval.[41] Sharpe himself was presumably among them, as doubtless was Fisher's chaplain John Addison, the doctor of divinity and former fellow of Pembroke who, as we have seen, took the *Confutatio* through the press.[42] Metcalfe himself, to whom Sharpe sent a copy of the *Confutatio*'s preface, presumably also contributed. Fisher had taken care to surround himself in his diocese with gifted academic clergy – to such an extent that his early biographer remarked 'his pallace for continencie seemed a verie monasterie and for learninge an universitie' – and it is inconceivable that he failed to avail himself of their talents.[43] But his debts were not restricted to his diocesan administrators, nor even to his episcopal colleagues. A letter to Hermann Lethmatius shows the bishop discussing and finally accepting an amendment from him even while the *Confutatio* was in press.[44] He consulted with Cochlaeus over his refutation of Oecolampadius, and it seems that John Eck, another German Catholic polemicist, had access to the *Defensio* before it appeared in 1525.[45]

The involvement of others in the production of Fisher's polemics would itself suggest what can in other ways be shown to have been the case, namely that he was but a part, albeit the most prominent part, of a much larger movement of opposition to Luther. It is especially noticeable that in England many of the opponents of Luther were personally or institutionally related to Fisher.

Cambridge University, of which he was the chancellor, witnessed a powerful backlash against heresy in the 1520s, and many of the leading figures in this were clients of the bishop in one way or another. Of the four Cambridge delegates to Wolsey's conference in London in 1521, one was a personal friend (John Watson, former fellow of St John's, and subsequently master of Christ's), while two others (Henry Bullock and Humphrey Walkden) had been elected fellows of Queens' when Fisher was president there. All three, incidentally, were also friends of Erasmus. The fourth man, Robert Ridley, cannot be directly connected with Fisher, although he was a cousin (and later secretary) of Cuthbert Tunstall and was a colleague of Fisher's among Catherine's counsel in the divorce. The colleges with which Fisher was closely connected were particularly antagonistic to Luther. It was his original college, Michaelhouse, that housed Nicholas Wilson, who published Fisher's sermon against Luther. William Melton, Fisher's friend from earlier days at Michaelhouse, even compiled a treatise against Luther.[46] Pembroke, from which he had drawn both the first master of St John's, Robert Shorton, and his chaplain, Addison, produced such other firm Catholics as John Cheesewright and Robert Cronkar. But St John's itself bears the strongest witness to Fisher's influence. Apart from Watson, the college numbered among its members numerous fellows and scholars who upheld orthodoxy. Metcalfe himself preached against Luther in 1526, and four fellows preached against Latimer in 1529: Ralph Baynes, John Rudd, Thomas Greenwood and John Brickenden.[47] The original readers in Hebrew and Greek, Robert Wakefield and Richard Croke, were both zealous opponents of heresy, as was the first Linacre lecturer, George Day. Most of these people owed their scholarly preferment directly to Fisher.[48] And the opponents of Latimer, at least, were thought to have taken up their position with the encouragement of Fisher and Watson. When we recall that the college's opposition to heresy took it into dangerous waters of resistance to the royal supremacy in the 1530s, then the leadership of Fisher by example, if not by command, becomes even more apparent. A former fellow of St John's was among the companions of the Holy Maid of Kent executed in 1534.[49] Another Johnian, John Ainsworth, was executed for denying the supremacy.[50] Ralph Baynes fled the country rather than accept the oath, and it took a personal interview with Cranmer to persuade John Rudd (who had by then moved on to a fellowship at Christ's) to abandon his opposition to the divorce and the act of succession. When Fisher was in the Tower, the college sent him a letter of sympathy, and after his execution they celebrated his exequies.[51] Most revealingly of all, the college as a whole was deemed suspect in the aftermath of the Pilgrimage of Grace, and Metcalfe was summoned to London to answer to Cromwell in person. Cromwell compelled him to resign the mastership,[52] upon which the college manifested its resentment by electing not the royal candidate, George Day (who had by then become a loyal Henrician), but Fisher's friend

Nicholas Wilson, who had only just been released from the Tower, having at last taken the oath of supremacy after three years of refusal.[53]

Fisher was also connected with a number of continental opponents of Luther. The best known of them was Erasmus, although there is no reason to pick out his relationship with Fisher from the many other motives which persuaded him to write against Luther in defence of free will. While Fisher received a presentation copy of the *De Libero Arbitrio*, so too did Henry VIII, Wolsey, Tunstall and Warham.[54] Besides him, Fisher was acquainted with Thomas Murner (one of those who translated Henry's *Assertio* into German), who visited him at Rochester in 1523;[55] and perhaps also with Johann Fabri, bishop of Constance, who spent some months in England on an embassy during 1527, and praised Fisher's pastoral zeal in one of his many polemics.[56] Fisher's connection with John Eck is rather better documented. We have already seen that Eck seems to have read the *Defensio* before its publication. Later in 1525 he came to England and met Fisher as well as Henry VIII himself, Polydore Vergil and Thomas More. In fact, he spent longer than he expected in England, and Fisher wrote on his behalf to his lord, Duke Wilhelm of Bavaria, apologising for keeping him away longer than had been planned.[57] Eck is best known for his best-selling handbook against Luther, the *Enchiridion Locorum Communum*, which was a sort of anthology of citations and arguments suitable for bringing up against Lutherans in debate. The first edition (and it was to run to more than one hundred editions) was dedicated to Henry VIII, and derived more than a fifth of its material from Henry's *Assertio* and Fisher's three anti-Lutheran books.[58] A few years later, Eck sent his nephew Severinus to study under Fisher at Rochester. When Severinus died in the 'sweat' of 1528, the bishop wrote his uncle a letter of condolence.[59] Fisher's closest continental connection, though, was with Johann Cochlaeus, who had been immensely impressed with the *Confutatio* on its appearance in 1523. He had immediately set about translating it into German, printing some of its articles that year, and would have translated the whole book had he found a publisher. By the following year, he was in direct contact with the bishop. In August he dedicated to him his reply to Luther's attack on the peasants, and they became regular correspondents.[60] Cochlaeus was at this time working with Fisher's publisher, Peter Quentell of Cologne, on a number of projects, including an edition of the works of Rupert of Deutz, a twelfth-century scriptural commentator who, it had been claimed in some quarters, was a forerunner of the Reformation. Cochlaeus kept Fisher informed on the progress of that edition, and dedicated one of its parts to him, sending it together with volumes for Henry and Wolsey in September 1526.[61] A fragment of a letter from Fisher, published in the preface to another volume, reveals that he was especially interested in Rupert's comments on the Gospel and Revelations of St John.[62] We have already noted that the two men were in correspondence over the eucharistic heresies of

Oecolampadius, and it is possible that Cochlaeus in fact persuaded Fisher to undertake a refutation of them. At any rate, he reported to the Lutheran Bilibald Pirckheimer that Fisher was busy with a reply to Oecolampadius, and sent Fisher a copy of Pirckheimer's similar effort. He later told Pirckheimer that Fisher thought it good 'in so far as it is Catholic'.[63] Cochlaeus himself received two very favourable mentions in the *De Veritate*, and went on to translate its five lengthy prefaces into German.[64] In 1528 he pressed Fisher to refute the heresies of the Anabaptists, and as late as 1531 was urging him to enter the lists against Melanchthon.[65] But these efforts were in vain, as Fisher had already informed him of his intention to desist from such polemic – a decision which probably owed much to his increasing preoccupation with the domestic controversy over Henry's marriage to Catherine of Aragon. The degree of Cochlaeus's esteem for Fisher is further confirmed by the fact that three of his publications were dedicated to him.[66] These dedications testify to a regular correspondence, most of which has unfortunately not survived. After the execution of Fisher and More in 1535, Cochlaeus published two pamphlets in defence of their reputation, and in fierce assault upon Henry's ecclesiastical and marital policies, which he had no hesitation in denouncing as tyranny.[67]

Fisher thus had a considerable personal role in the European campaign against Luther. He had a far wider influence through his polemical publications. Although his holy life and heroic death set a seal of moral authority on his writings, it was the writings themselves that chiefly spread his fame. Some general impression of the effect his writings had on his contemporaries and successors can be gathered from the conclusion to Surtz's study, where the author accumulates a somewhat haphazard collection of references to Fisher found in sixteenth-century sources.[68] While a final assessment of Fisher's influence could be attempted only in the context of a full account of the Catholic polemical effort that culminated in the Council of Trent, it is possible to provide a more systematic analysis of the theological issues in which, and the theologians on whom, Fisher's influence was most conspicuous. The first step is to assess, as far as possible, the dissemination of his books and the nature of their readership. The extent of that readership can be appreciated to a limited degree from the frequency with which his major works were reprinted. Reprinting was by no means an assured fate for the majority of polemical publications. Yet even the least popular of Fisher's four main anti-Protestant polemics, the *Defensio Regiae Assertionis*, ran to three editions, while the *Sacri Sacerdotii* ran to seven and the weighty *De Veritate* to six. In pride of place, however, stands the *Confutatio*, which appeared in more than twenty editions in the sixteenth century – twice as many as, for example, Thomas More's *Utopia*. This total was exceeded in its genre by only a handful of works. Most notable was of course Eck's *Enchiridion*, which ran to more than a hundred editions. Alphonsus de Castro's *Adversus Omnes Haereses* reached twenty-five editions, and the Polish theologian Stanislav Hosius equalled the *Confutatio*'s numbers with three books. A few other books, such as Henry's *Assertio* and Erasmus's *De Libero Arbitrio*, ran the *Confutatio* close.[69] Yet even allowing for the inevitable deficiencies of the data, the *Confutatio* must figure in any 'top ten' Catholic polemics of the period. This goes some way towards explaining and substantiating the claim of Ruard Tapper, the dean of the university of Louvain and a leading expert at the Council of Trent, that Fisher's works were in everyone's hands.[70]

Tapper's claim receives further support from a perusal of a range of Counter-Reformation polemic. Almost all the major Catholic controversialists of the century expressed great respect for Fisher's work, and made copious use of it. Eck's *Enchiridion* owed much to Fisher. Eck placed him third in a list of those from whom he had garnered his material, and as much as a seventh of the original edition may have been derived from Fisher.[71] A similar tendency can be seen in another 'best-seller', Alphonsus de Castro's *Adversus Omnes Haereses*, which contains twice as many references to Fisher as to any other sixteenth-century Catholic polemicist (Clichtove came second). The same is true of Tapper's *Explicatio Articulorum* (although Tapper did make as many references to Cajetan's commentary on Thomas as to Fisher), as also of Andreas de Vega's *De Vera Iustificatione*.[72] The contributions of the Jesuit Alfonso Salmeron to the Council of Trent hardly mention any modern theologian other than Fisher,[73] and the writings of Cochlaeus abound with his praises.[74] Impressive though such evidence is, to rely on explicit citations could still leave us with an unduly restricted view of Fisher's influence, for he could have been widely used in sermons or university disputations of which no record survives. There is one recorded instance of this. In the mid-1520s Alexander Alesius was 'refuting Luther out of Fisher' at St Andrews with the approval of the theology faculty there (although his subsequent apostasy perhaps illustrates the danger of making heretical works accessible through detailed refutations).[75] We may therefore conjecture that, at least in Cambridge, other theologians drew on Fisher's work in such ways. At any rate, it is certain that the list of those who drew on him is a lengthy one, including both great and humble names: in England, Gardiner, More, Peryn, Smyth, Stapleton, Tunstall and Villasancta; and in Europe, Bellarmine, Cochlaeus, Dungersheim, Erasmus, Fabri, Guidiccio, Lippomano, Murner, Nausea, Noguera, Witzel and Zanettini. The readership of Fisher's works must have been wider still. At Cambridge alone it included Barnes, Cecil, Cranmer and Shaxton among the Protestants; Perne in a class of his own; and John Bateman, Henry Bullock, John Cheesewright, George Day, William Gockman, John Parkyn and Robert Ridley among the Catholics.[76]

It is clear that Fisher's audience was numerous. But what aspects of his work did his readers find useful? In fact, he made significant contributions to the polemic against the Reformation in most of the fields with which he dealt. His analysis of Luther's doctrine in the *Confutatio* was of critical importance. Although this lengthy, humourless and repetitious work shared the characteristic limitations of its genre, its undeniable success was a result of its penetrating and comprehensive account of Luther's teaching. For it was the first major assault on Luther to identify and grapple with his fundamental doctrines, the authority of scripture alone, and salvation by faith alone. Following up the analysis he had adumbrated in his sermon of 1521, Fisher dealt with 'sola scriptura' and 'sola fides' before anything else, in the preface and first article respectively, even though neither of these doctrines had figured among the forty-one articles condemned by *Exsurge Domine*. The *Confutatio* thus became the first of many works that were to begin their critique of Lutheranism with the questions of authority and justification. This approach can be seen in Eck's *Enchiridion*, and also in the proceedings of the Council of Trent, which took these as the first doctrinal issues to be debated. Indeed, Fisher's derivation of all Luther's teachings from the single root of justification by faith alone was perhaps the first attempt to systematise that prince among unsystematic theologians.

Besides helping to shape the Catholic approach to Luther's doctrine, Fisher contributed a large number of particular arguments to the common fund to Counter-Reformation polemic. His attack on Luther's scripture principle attracted especial attention. Fisher was the first to adduce the testimony of Tertullian to the role of tradition of defining doctrine, and from him this topos passed via Eck's *Enchiridion* into the mainstream of Catholic controversy.[77] His appeal to the example given by Jerome's controversy with Elvidius was subsequently taken up by More, Dietenberger, Eck and even Erasmus.[78] And his casual remark in the *Confutatio* that the truths of revelation were passed down partly in scripture and partly in tradition came very close to being enshrined in the Tridentine decree on the subject.[79] His defence of the papacy also made a deep impression. Thomas More referred his readers to the relevant article of the *Confutatio* rather than deal with it himself, and Castro, comparing it with the efforts of other Catholic theologians, observed 'Fisher handles the matter best'.[80] The bishop of Ross read out extracts from article 25 to the fathers at Trent, taking pains to emphasise that this powerful attack on Luther was not his own work but Fisher's.[81]

Fisher's work on justification, however, was far more influential. He bequeathed to posterity not only a perception of the importance of 'sola fides' in Luther's thought, but a picture of Luther's thinking on faith. The account of Luther's doctrine in Vega's *De Vera Iustificatione* is almost entirely dependent on article 1 of the *Confutatio*, following Fisher even to the extent of citing the same texts, and reproducing his complaint about Luther's wilful ambiguity on the subject.[82] A stray reference by Vega to Luther's *Sermo de Eucharistia* 'referente Roffense' confirms what one would suspect from his other citations of Luther, namely that they are drawn not from the original, but from the *Confutatio*.[83] Elsewhere he relied on Fisher in attributing to Luther the view that all sins are mortal sins.[84] Another writer on justification, John Redman, likewise drew on the *Confutatio* (albeit without acknowledgment), citing the same scriptural text as Fisher to demonstrate the value of good works, and even giving the same single word in Greek.[85] At Trent, Fisher was one of the few contemporary theologians to be cited in the debates on justification.[86] If his importance in this area has gone unremarked, this is because recent interest in immediately pre-Tridentine Catholic theology has concentrated more on the 'irenicists' than on the polemicists. Yet the gap between the theological positions of the two groups was probably not as great as the simplistic terminology suggests. For example, the 'irenical' *Diatriba De Libero Arbitrio* of Erasmus is not markedly different in tone from the polemical article 36 of the *Confutatio*. And while it is going too far to claim that the *Diatriba* drew heavily on the *Confutatio* for its scriptural and patristic material,[87] the fact remains that the most thorough study of Erasmus's work finds a 'profound resemblance' between the views of its author and those of Fisher, and concludes that Erasmus wrote with a copy of the *Confutatio* to hand.[88] Whatever the extent of its influence on Erasmus, Fisher's treatment of free will commended itself to several other leading Catholic controversialists. Ruard Tapper thought it done 'copiose atque catholice', and referred his readers to it for a refutation of Luther, confining his own efforts to the opinions of Melanchthon and Calvin.[89] A veritable 'apostolic succession' of writers on free will can be detected in the following chain of cross-references: Cochlaeus's *De Libero Arbitrio* drew heavily, though without acknowledgment, on Fisher; Eck's *Enchiridion* made use of both Cochlaeus and Fisher; Castro drew on all three; and Vega listed Fisher, Cochlaeus, Eck, Driedo and Castro among his authorities.[90]

Fisher's writings on the eucharist, which we shall examine in more detail in chapter 8, were if anything even more influential than his analysis of Luther. Although his *De Veritate*, his most important work on the eucharist, was not reprinted for seventy years after its initial four editions of 1527,[91] it occupied a major place in mainstream Catholic theology, both in England and on the continent. In England, where the real presence was to become the central issue of the Reformation, it set the agenda for the Catholic side in the debate. His arguments and proof-texts recur continually in the writings of English defenders of Catholic doctrine, and their opponents were well aware of their dependence of Fisher. Cranmer, for example, observed caustically that Gardiner's attribution of a realist text to Theophilus of Alexandria rather than to its genuine author (Theophylact) arose from an edition of the *De Veritate* – of which Cranmer of course possessed a copy, heavily annotated.[92] When John Redman finally abandoned the doctrine of transubstantiation during Edward's reign, he did so after a thorough examination of the relevant texts of Tertullian and Irenaeus – texts which lay at the heart of the debate between Fisher and Oecolampadius.[93] Fisher's characteristic arguments for the real presence appear throughout the works of William Peryn and Richard Smyth on the eucharist. Peryn in particular was dependent on the *De Veritate*, of which his *Thre Sermons* is often little more than a direct translation. His first sermon summarises book I, and his second sermon book II, of the *De Veritate*, while his third sermon translates most of the prefaces to books II, III, IV and V.[94] Since Peryn never so much as mentions Fisher's name, and presents the bishop's arguments as though they were his own, it is hard to acquit him of plagiarism, even by sixteenth-century standards. Smyth, an altogether better-equipped theologian than Peryn, made less obvious and less wholesale use of Fisher's ideas. Yet he too reproduced without acknowledgment, though not uncritically, the bulk of the preface to book IV of the *De Veritate*, as well as many other arguments too numerous to recount here.[95] That neither Smyth nor Peryn mentioned Fisher's name probably reflects the suspicion that was still attached to it in the latter years of Henry's reign, for it is in marked contrast to the habits of the continental polemicists. Yet this apparently did not deter William Cecil from donating a copy of the *De Veritate* to the university library of Cambridge in 1544 with a hearty dedication.[96] A similar diffidence about even literary association with a convicted traitor may account for the absence of tributes to Fisher in Alban Langdaile's *Catholica Confutatio* and Cuthbert Tunstall's *De Veritate Corporis Domini*, both of which were composed under Edward VI though not published until the reign of Mary. Langdaile in fact made one parenthetical reference to Fisher, comparing him with Nicholas Ridley (against whom he was writing) to the latter's disadvantage, but this was probably a late addition to the text.[97] But his discursus on the many names of the eucharist was manifestly based upon the preface to book II of the *De Veritate*.[98] And Tunstall's work echoed Fisher's not only in its title, but in its profoundly patristic approach to the problem.[99]

The *De Veritate* was equally popular on the continent, where opinions of Fisher were extremely high. Castro, after reciting the patristic and scholastic witnesses to the real presence, noted that Fisher had written at greater length and with greater acumen than any of them in his refutation of Oecolampadius. He referred his readers to it for a comprehensive and conclusive treatment of the subject.[100] Ioannes Fabri upbraided Oecolampadius with Fisher's exposure of his distortion of patristic texts.[101] Ruard Tapper drew especially heavily on Fisher's 'divine work against Oecolampadius' in his *Explicatio Articulorum*, and was also aware of the contributions to the eucharistic debate by Gardiner, Langdaile and Tunstall.[102] And the Spanish theologian, Francisco Mendoza, cardinal bishop of Burgos, followed up Fisher's treatment of sacramental union with Christ in his *De Naturali cum Christo Unitate*, written in the 1560s.[103] But it was at the Council of Trent that Fisher's work came into its own.[104] Half the references made to him in the records of the Council are to his eucharistic writings, and the *De Veritate* seems to have been a sort of reference-book for the debates on the real presence. One of the most interesting relics of these debates is a document drawn up by the Jesuits Alfonso Salmeron and Diego Lainez, which is so full of implicit and explicit borrowings from the *De Veritate's* five prefaces that it is practically a summary of them.[105] The arguments against a figurative interpretation of 'hoc est corpus meum' and for the application of chapter 6 of John's Gospel to the eucharist were strongly reminiscent of Fisher's, while the supplementary proofs of the real presence were clearly drawn from the *De Veritate* even though only one was explicitly acknowledged. The most obvious debts were to the distinctive argument from the many names of the sacrament in preface II, and to the catena of patristic texts in preface IV.[106] If the summary does indeed reflect the general character of the debate, and not simply the predilections of its compilers, then Fisher was the single most important influence on the Council's discussion of the issue, a conclusion which gains support from the many other delegates to the Council who cited his writings. Sigismund Diruta referred to his 'catalogue' of patristic authorities, and Francisco de Villalba relied on him for arguments about John 6.[107] In addition, the debate on the administration of communion saw references to Fisher's defence of lay communion under only one kind by Salmeron, Ferdinando de Bellosillo and Petrus Ciumel.[108] His defence of the sacrifice of the mass was even more widely used. The 'periti' or theologians who adduced his testimony included the influential Dominicans Melchior Cano and Bartolomeo Carranza, as well as Alfonso de Contreras,[109] and the bishops numbered Petrus Tagliavia (archbishop of Palermo), Juan Salazar ('Lancianensis'), Georg Flach of Salona, Juan Bernardo Diaz ('Calagurritanus'), Pietro di Capua of Otranto and Juan Suarez of Coimbra.[110] A recent study has shown that the committee of bishops played a major role in ensuring that the Tridentine decree upheld the essential unity and identity of Christ's sacrifice on the cross with the sacrifice of the mass and since, as we shall see, this was one of Fisher's most emphatic points, it is likely that his writings, with which the bishops seem to have been well acquainted, had a considerable effect on the final shape of the decree.[111]

Fisher's influence at Trent was not confined to the debates on the eucharist. At least one Tridentine delegate admitted that he had no direct knowledge of Luther's teachings, and had come across them only in Fisher's refutation. Another delegate knew *Exsurge Domine* only through the *Confutatio*.[112] As we have seen, Vega's knowledge of Luther's teaching on justification was derived from Fisher's account, and we are therefore left to speculate, on the basis of this perhaps slight evidence, that Fisher may have been just as important in informing the delegates about Luther's views as he was in informing their response. A full account of the role played by his writings is hampered not only by the sheer bulk of surviving evidence, but also by its variable level of detail, and of course by the habitually casual attitude of sixteenth-century scholars to the acknowledgment of intellectual debts. Nevertheless there are plentiful references to Fisher in the course of the published records. He was cited on, for example, scripture and tradition; on justification by Juan Fonseca; on penance by Richard Cenomanus OFM; on indulgences by Antonio Ricci O. Carm; on holy orders by Diego Lainez SJ; and on purgatory by Juan Salazar.[113] In short, he was familiar to theologians of all orders and to bishops of all countries. His authority at the Council was, of course, enhanced by his martyrdom and by his reputation for sanctity. 'Gloriosissimus martyr','athleta et martyr', and 'sanctissimus praesul' are just a few of the laudatory epithets applied to him during the debates. This spontaneous canonisation was accorded him by most of those – outside England – who had cause to draw upon his writings.

The theology which we are to consider in the following chapters, then, was to play a major part in the development of the Catholic response to the German and Swiss Reformers. It not only indicated lines of attack against the new doctrines, but illustrated ways of pursuing them. Fisher refused to concede to his opponents the humanist ground on which they boasted of standing. Even though the Church was to abandon certain ideological aspects of Christian humanism, the technical advances in Hebraic, classical and patristic scholarship were not to be lost. Fisher's own use of Greek and Hebrew was inevitably limited, but he pointed the way for linguists better than himself. And his employment of patristic sources – allowing for his dependence on translations rather than originals for the Greeks – was, as we shall see, wide and sophisticated. In the following three chapters we shall examine Fisher's views on authority, justification and the eucharist, the three central issues of the Reformation debates. The discussion will be thematic rather than chronological, drawing on each of Fisher's four major polemical writings as necessary, and illustrating the argument where relevant from his other publications and from his unpublished manuscripts.

6
Authority

OF ALL THE theological divisions of the Reformation, the easiest to describe is that over authority in Christian life and belief. Unlike the debates over justification and the eucharist, it raises no profound problems of metaphysics. It can be summarised briefly. In settling controversies about faith and morals, Catholics were accustomed to appeal not only to scripture, but also to tradition as embodied in the writings and decrees of the fathers, doctors, bishops and councils of the Church. When a definitive statement was required, it could be provided either by the pope or by a general council of the Church. But this apparatus of tradition and hierarchy was regarded by the Reformers as the substitution of human for divine authority. Led by Luther, they insisted that scripture alone, in its literal sense, could be taken as sufficient authority in matters of faith and morals – although the testimony of the fathers remained a powerful polemical weapon in those areas in which it could be plausibly invoked. This simple proposition has remained, despite its arguable epistemological naivety, one of the most beguiling features of Reformed religion ever since. Its attraction has been so great that in the countries where the Reformed religion struck root it has come to seem, even to non-Christians, the self-evident method for ascertaining the content of Christian doctrine. In those countries this has led to a failure to appreciate the theological position of those who argued against the Reformers. Thus Fisher has been reproached for begging the question by determining on an appeal to tradition as well as to scripture in his polemics.[1] Liberal scholars of a later, but now passing, age have further obscured the issue by contrasting the 'private judgment' of the Reformers (somewhat whimsically identified with humanism and the appeal to reason) with the 'authoritarian' approach of scholastic Catholics. In fact it cannot be emphasised too strongly that almost all theologians of the sixteenth century argued from authority. Their differences were explained by where they located that authority, and how, if they located it in more than one place, they reconciled its various expressions.

The systematic study of authority in Church and doctrine was a product of the high and later Middle Ages. Serious reflection on the sources of Christian doctrine had begun only with Thomas Aquinas in the thirteenth century, and in many respects it made little progress between then and the Reformation. The nascent subject raised many questions but supplied few answers and was therefore in a state of some confusion. Rival theories of doctrinal authority and Church government flourished. There was a widespread consensus that all the truths necessary for salvation were contained in scripture – a statement which was far from logically equivalent to the sole sufficiency of scripture as a means of ascertaining and communicating all such truths.[2] Yet there was little attempt to distinguish those 'necessary' truths from others, or to identify their origins. Besides, tradition was allocated an important place in theory as well as in practice. Some held that tradition was merely the authentic interpretation of scripture, others that there were certain truths of revelation that had been passed down from the apostles apart from scripture.[3] There was widespread agreement that no new doctrines could have been revealed since the death of the last apostle, but in some quarters there was a feeling that new revelations had been made since then.[4] Another vexed question was the relationship between the Church and scripture. From primitive times until the Middle Ages the two were seen as intimately connected, in what has been called 'coinherence'.[5] It was this concept that lay behind Augustine's well-known claim that he would not believe the Gospel unless the Church compelled him to do so.[6] But the wealth and corruption of the medieval Church impressed many with a sense of the gulf between it and the Church of the New Testament. Fourteenth-century theologians such as Henry of Ghent began to see the possibility of conflict between the scriptural ideal and the worldly reality of the Church. And this potential became actual in the writings of Wycliffe, who used the New Testament against the Church as an institution.[7] It was at about this time that heretical movements first began to appeal to scripture alone. Gerson observed that this was characteristic of the Hussites.[8] Gerson himself, a prominent reformer, was led to reverse the famous dictum of Augustine by remarking that he would not believe in the Church unless the Gospel compelled him to do so.[9] However, despite the growing concern with the moral corruption of the Church and especially of its hierarchy, all accepted that the Church as a whole could not err in its teaching on faith and morals. Nevertheless, there remained room for conflict over the scope and expression of that infallibility. All agreed that it was vested in general councils, most also agreed that it resided in particular with the local church of Rome, and some that it lay with the bishop of Rome, the pope, by virtue of his office. But it was the role of the papacy that was the most contentious issue in late medieval ecclesiology. The crisis of the Great Schism had been resolved only through a general council, and that crisis had fostered the full development of the corporationist view of the Church, traceable to canonist origins and now known as conciliarism, which for the first time subjected the bishop of Rome to the judgment of other clerics.[10] Even within the ranks of the conciliarists there was a variety of views, although the distinguishing common tenet was the jurisdictional supremacy of a general council over a pope. Against this doctrine stood that of papal monarchy or sovereignty and the derivative doctrine of papal infallibility, which agreed in seeing the pope as the absolute head of the Church by divine right.

In this relatively new, yet already highly contentious, field Luther wrought nothing less than a revolution, overthrowing established authorities with a combination of radical theology and popular violence. This ecclesiological revolution grew out of his conflict with the papacy in the later 1510s. Although Luther at first proclaimed his intention of remaining a loyal subject of the pope,[11] curial theologians read his attack on indulgences as an implicit assault on the papacy. They had been rendered wary by a controversy earlier that decade with the university of Paris, where resurgent conciliarism emerged to support the king of France, Louis XII, in a political dispute with Julius II. The irrelevance of that debate to Luther's ideas is best illustrated by the fact that the Paris theology faculty, whatever its ecclesiological perspective, was to condemn Luther in 1521.[12] But it was easy for the curial, and mostly Dominican, theologians such as Sylvester Prierias, the *Magistri Sacri Palatii* (the pope's personal theological adviser), to see Luther as just another conciliarist. Prierias reduced the discussion to a flat demand for submission to papal authority. Luther's convictions outweighed his avowed loyalty, and he demanded arguments from scripture to show why he should submit. His challenge was picked up by John Eck, who faced Luther in public disputation at Leipzig in June 1519. Each side claimed victory, as was customary in such disputations and indeed inevitable when the combatants were as stiff-necked as Luther and Eck.[13] But Eck certainly succeeded in forcing Luther to recognise the implications of his arguments, which extended to the rejection of both papal and conciliar authority. Luther was also compelled to increase the weight he attached to scripture as opposed to tradition in matters of doctrine. Henceforth Luther's insistence on the word of scripture against all other authorities grew ever more pronounced, leading him to formulate his principle of appeal to scripture alone in 1520.[14] This development was a corollary of his deteriorating view of the capacities of the fallen human race. One of his favourite texts at this time was 'Omnis homo mendax' (Ps 115:11), a maxim he applied rigorously to all human authors and authorities except himself.[15] The only authority which could survive such acidic scepticism was scripture, whose human authors were but instruments of divine dictation. This radical doctrine necessitated a reappraisal of the traditional concept of 'apostolicity'. Since the end of the first century, the 'apostolic' had meant anything derived from the apostles, whether on paper or through oral tradition via the apostolic succession of bishops.[16] Though this concept was of course underpinned by belief in the Holy Spirit's guidance of the Church, it was far too human for Luther. He replaced it with a concept of the apostolic as that which cohered with the evangelical message originally and authentically preached by the apostles, namely the saving passion, death and resurrection of Christ. This transference of apostolicity from the medium to the message had the disconcerting effect of undermining even parts of the New Testament itself. Luther was to argue flatly that the epistle of James was not apostolic because it contained no references to the central mysteries of salvation.[17]

From the start, Fisher appreciated that Luther's views on doctrinal authority occupied a central place in his theology. His sermon of 1521 had identified both the denial of the papacy (to which we shall return later in the chapter) and the assertion of the sole sufficiency of scripture as foundations of Luther's position. In reply he emphasised, 'it shal appeere that more testimony must be admytted for sufficyent authoryte. than only that that is wryten in the byble. whiche one thynge yf we may establysshe. it wyl cast downe a grete nombre of Martyn luthers artycles.'[18] His case against Luther was reproduced in a fuller and better organised way in the *Confutatio* on which he was already at work. The preface to the *Confutatio* presented ten propositions ('decem veritates') which together demonstrated the need for tradition and a definitive authority in disputes over doctrine and the meaning of scripture.[19] The propositions were:

i Many who have relied on their own abilities in interpreting scripture have gone sadly astray

ii Even today those who follow their own notions in interpreting scripture could easily fall into error

iii It is fitting that there should be some judge competent to decide controversies about scripture or about truths relating to the Church

iv Such controversies have not always been resolved by reference to scripture alone

v The Holy Spirit was sent to abide with the Church forever so that when errors arose, she should always be made certain of the truth

vi The Holy Spirit has always used the tongues of the orthodox fathers to eradicate heresy and to instruct the Church in doubtful matters, and shall always do so

vii Those who reject the orthodox fathers scorn the teaching of the Holy Spirit and do not have that Spirit in them

viii If the Spirit has spoken through the mouths of individual fathers, then *a fortiori* he has spoken through general councils

ix Apostolic traditions are to be observed by all true Christians even when they are not set out in scripture

x Christians are to follow not only such traditions but also such customs as are universally accepted by the Church.

The argumentation for these propositions reworked and expanded many of the ideas of the 1521 sermon. For example, the list of heretics used to substantiate the first proposition was identical to that given in the sermon: Arius, Macedonius, Nestorius, Eutyches, Elvidius, Donatus, Jovinian, Pelagius and Wycliffe.[20] It is interesting to note that he cited Origen not in his list of heretics (as Longland was to do later in the 1520s), but in support of his concept of apostolic tradition, using the same lengthy extract in each work.[21] In both the sermon and the *Confutatio*, he outlined a tripartite division of the history of revelation into the ages of the Father, who spoke to the prophets; of the Son, who spoke to the apostles; and of the Holy Spirit, who spoke and still speaks through the fathers and doctors of the Church.[22] It is obvious from the 'decem veritates' that the active intervention of the Holy Spirit for the protection of the faith was of great importance in Fisher's theology. The Spirit, which in his view spoke not only through individual fathers, but also through general councils, was thus for him the connection between the authority and the tradition of the Church. It therefore provides the unifying theme both for his doctrine of authority, and for our analysis of it in this chapter.

Between delivering his sermon at St Paul's and completing the *Confutatio*, Fisher was exposed to the writings of an early father ('priscus auctor') who was to add a new dimension to his theology of scripture and tradition. That author was Tertullian, whose works became available in print for the first time in June 1521 in an edition by Beatus Rhenanus, the friend of Erasmus and former pupil of Lefèvre. The treatise which especially impressed Fisher was the *De Praescriptionibus Haereticorum*, which laid down principles according to which the orthodox ought to regulate their dealings with heretics. The first was that heretics were *ipso facto* disbarred from discussions about scripture because the scriptures simply did not belong to them – they belonged to the Church, which alone was competent to expound them. Tertullian founded this principle on Paul's admonition to have nothing to do with heretics after giving them two warnings (2 Tit 3:10–11 – a text that Fisher himself cited in the opening lines of the *Confutatio*).[23] The second principle was that discussions with heretics over scripture were doomed to failure because the heretics would either reject whole books of the Bible, or mutilate them, or insist on adopting distorted interpretations.[24] Fisher's employment of Tertullian is a mark not only of his enthusiasm for the fathers, but also of his ability to overcome natural prejudice. Tertullian, like Origen, had a dubious reputation in the Middle Ages because of his lapse into heresy and his posthumous condemnation by Pope Gelasius. As a result, Tertullian's works were almost unknown until the sixteenth century. If this were not enough, Rhenanus's first edition was strongly sympathetic to the Reformers. Indeed, Rhenanus pegged an attack on the papacy onto the *De Praescriptionibus*.[25] Yet Fisher was able to ignore these extraneous considerations and take advantage of a useful argument from however unlikely a source.

Rhenanus's Tertullian may have reminded Fisher of another patristic illustration of the relationship between scripture and tradition, one which he had already used in the *Eversio Munitionis*. This was the case of the heretic Elvidius and his denial of the perpetual virginity of Our Lady. Tertullian had been one of the authorities Elvidius cited against this doctrine, and Rhenanus referred in a note to Jerome's refutation of Elvidius, alleging that it was based on 'ecclesiasticum dogma'.[26] In the *Confutatio* Fisher expounded the case more fully than he had done in the *Eversio*, and gave it a twist that suggests strongly that his immediate source was Erasmus's edition of Jerome. For his strategy in refuting Elvidius was different from Jerome's. Jerome had simply analysed the texts cited by his opponent in the light of parallel scriptural phrases and usages in order to demonstrate that they did not entail the conclusion Elvidius drew. But Fisher, having recited the various texts from which Elvidius argued, departed from Jerome by conceding that their apparent meaning did indeed suggest that Mary had not remained a virgin after giving birth to Christ, but had borne several children to Joseph. He added that not a jot of scripture could be found that positively pointed in the other direction. Only the constant teaching of the Church could be adduced to prove that Mary had indeed remained a virgin.[27] Both Fisher and Rhenanus were almost certainly following Erasmus's edition of Jerome, in which a note stated that Jerome's case was based on tradition rather than scripture.[28] To be fair to all three scholars, they were perhaps compensating for the undeniable lacuna in Jerome's case – for though he demolished Elvidius's arguments against the doctrine, he did not put forward any convincing arguments in its favour. Fisher's special contribution was to apply this case to the new dispute over the sole sufficiency of scripture, and his argument was to become a commonplace of Catholic polemic. Curiously enough, the Protestant Reformers seem to have been highly sensitive to this argument, for they often took pains to affirm their commitment to the doctrine of Mary's perpetual virginity, despite both its lack of clear scriptural evidence and its close association with the Catholic cult of Mary that they repudiated so decidedly.[29]

In Fisher's use of the example of Elvidius we seem to find a distinctly dualist approach to the problem of doctrinal authority. Certain truths can be ascertained from scripture. Others, like the perpetual virginity of Our Lady, are known only from the tradition of the Church. Yet this did not prevent Fisher from signing up to an apparently different account of authority, embodied in the traditional dictum that all truths necessary to salvation were contained in scripture. In article 37 of the *Confutatio*, discussing purgatory, he stated 'since scripture is a kind of treasure-chest of all truths that a Christian need know, nobody can doubt that the truth of purgatory is contained in it and can be proved from it'. He even went so far as to say 'it is not credible that purgatory should not be demonstrable from scripture, since it is a matter that all Christians must know of'.[30] Yet this hardly squared with his assertion in the same article that even if the doctrine of purgatory could not be demonstrated from scripture, it ought nevertheless to be accepted by Christians because of the antiquity of the ecclesiastical custom behind it.[31] Fisher is clearly in some discomfort over the doctrine of purgatory which, as he acknowledged, had appeared relatively late in the Church's history. Nevertheless he was able to find more scriptural support for it than he could for the rather older doctrine of the perpetual virginity of Our Lady. His problem, one he shared with most other Catholic polemicists, was in dealing with Luther's claim about the sole sufficiency of scripture, which exploited the traditional view that all truths necessary to salvation were to be found in scripture in order to divorce scripture from the tradition of the Church. It is wrong to suggest, as is often in fact suggested, that the Catholic polemicists' emphasis on tradition was somehow derogatory to scripture.[32] Most of them concurred with Fisher in avowing allegiance to the scriptural basis of all truths necessary to salvation.[33] Fisher himself placed an extremely high value on scripture, as we have seen from his preaching and his support for Erasmus and Reuchlin, and as we shall see below in chapters 8 and 9. His problem was not with Luther's exaltation of scripture but with his denigration of tradition. Fisher and his successors were united in rejecting Luther's simplistic appeal to scripture alone, but were for the moment unable to produce a coherent explanation of the role of tradition with respect to scripture – an inability they shared with the fathers of the Council of Trent. But this was not to deter them from maintaining the importance of both scripture and tradition in authorising the doctrine of the Church.

Further light is shed on Fisher's concept of tradition by his assimilation to it of the concept of the Cabbala, in which, as we have already observed, he took a close interest. In his sermon of 1521 he drew an analogy between the apostolic tradition of the Church and the role of the Cabbala in the time of the Old Testament.[34] A clue to his meaning can be found in a later work, a treatise on the Septuagint in which he made passing allusion to Hilary of Poitier's affirmation of the divine inspiration of that translation. While he gave no full reference, it is certain that he had in mind a passage in the commentary on the psalms where Hilary identified the seventy translators of the Septuagint with the institution of the seventy elders who preserved the oral tradition handed down from Moses. Hilary described this tradition as 'certain secret mysteries from the arcana of the law', by which he apparently envisaged a kind of mystical or spiritual interpretation of scripture rather than a separate vehicle of truth.[35] It is probably this interpretative role that Fisher, here at least, wished to ascribe to the apostolic tradition. And in theological disputes he tended to use tradition to expound scripture rather than to supply information it did not contain. In his arguments over the papacy, purgatory, the real presence in the eucharist, or whatever, he drew on the fathers and councils to explain the meaning of disputed scriptural texts rather than to establish doctrines in their own right. When the scriptural evidence was tenuous, however, tradition could assume a more dominant role. And in his theory, as we have seen, he left open the possibility that a doctrine could rest on tradition and custom rather than on scripture.

The main expression of Fisher's recourse to tradition was appeal to the fathers. Throughout his polemical career he showed an increasing sophistication and discrimination in this. He was never so naive as to believe that the fathers were individually infallible, a view attributed to him on the basis of a passage in which he spoke in general terms of the divine inspiration of the fathers.[36] Although, as he said in the 'ten truths', he believed that the Holy Spirit spoke through the mouths of the orthodox fathers, he did not believe that they uttered nothing but the Spirit's promptings. He made it perfectly clear that their inspiration was of a general nature, and that, as they were only human, they inevitably erred on occasion.[37] He was quite happy to acknowledge that Jerome had erred in his translation of the scriptures, and it was one of his basic principles that anybody, however exalted or learned, could err.[38] But in his earliest polemical composition, the *De Unica Magdalena*, the evidence he assembled from patristic and medieval authors was, as we have seen, uncritically arranged and presented. The most glaring difference between this and his later works was the suspicion with which he viewed the Greek fathers. His first reasons for ruling out the testimony of Origen and Chrysostom looked quite plausible: the former was dismissed because of his tendency to concentrate on the allegorical to the exclusion of the literal sense of scripture, and the latter because he was writing homilies rather than commentaries. But when he went on to dismiss the Greek tradition in general because of the inherent tendency of the Greek church to doctrinal error, prejudice overcame criticism. It may have been the disciplined marshalling of patristic authority in Clichtove's *Defensio* that awoke Fisher to the need to approach the fathers with more discrimination and judgment.[39] Certainly his use of the fathers against Luther was more broad-minded, as we have seen from his appeal to Tertullian, and more logically ordered, as we shall see later in this chapter in his treatment of the papacy. Moreover, he put a distinct premium in the *Confutatio* on earlier testimony where possible. He hardly cited an author later than Bede, and gave full weight to the Greeks. In the *Convulsio Calumniarum*, written shortly afterwards, we see Fisher for the first time paying attention to problems of attribution, questioning the authenticity of the suppositious correspondence between Paul and Seneca, and admitting doubts about the Dionysian corpus and the Donation of Constantine.[40]

Tradition was not restricted in Fisher's mind to the writings of the Church's intellectuals, the fathers and the doctors. The guidance of the Holy Spirit could be expressed though humbler agents, monks, nuns or even laypeople, by the medium of direct revelation. Fisher drew regularly on such revelations in his polemics, and was of course to be implicated in the 1530s in the alleged treasons of the Holy Maid of Kent, whose revelations were a source of intense political embarrassment to Henry VIII. That he was still intrigued by such revelations this late in his career shows that his belief in their potential value did not diminish as he grew older.[41] His lax terminology in dealing with such revelations (the description of them as 'private', as opposed to the 'public' revelation of scripture, was a later development) has led one recent critic to conclude that he regarded them as an extension or continuation of the scriptural revelation, a method by which new truths could be added to the deposit of faith handed down from the apostles.[42] This is a serious mis-apprehension of his position. Fisher explicitly dismissed the concept of a new stage of revelation in his sermon of 1521, wryly suggesting that if such a thing were possible, then one might suspect that Luther had received his doctrine from that source.[43] As for private revelations, he subordinated them firmly to the Church, insisting that they required papal approval if they were to be held as authoritative.[44] Since he followed Scotus in limiting the power of popes and councils to declaring explicitly what was already part of the faith, and in refusing to accept that this power could add new truths to the faith, there is no reason to assume that he gave wider scope to those very revelations that he subordinated to ecclesiastical authority.[45] In practice he seems to have regarded these revelations, much as he regarded tradition, as a means of expounding rather than adding to scripture. In the *Confutatio* he explained that the doctrine of purgatory, which was hardly known in the primitive Church, developed 'partly from revelations, and partly from the scriptures', which implies that the revelations were not so much introducing a new doctrine as helping to extract the doctrine from scripture.[46] Such a view of private revelations is also to be seen in his comment to Cochlaeus around 1525 that Revelations was such an obscure book that it could scarcely be understood without a further revelation to explain its author's intentions.[47]

Tradition was for Fisher, in effect, the record of the Holy Spirit's activity in leading the Church into all truth. Nowhere could this activity be seen more clearly than in the authoritative teachings of the popes and councils. Like most theologians before him, he believed that the Church as a whole was infallible in matters of faith and morals: 'no thinge may be more certayne to vs than it whiche is taught by holy chyrche'.[48] And only of the Church as a whole did he ever explicitly predicate the gift of infallibility, talking of her as 'infallibly guided by the spirit of truth'.[49] His concept of the Church was not restrictively clericalist. He saw the Church as the body of the faithful, not merely as the clergy. Yet the Church as a whole was clearly not in any practical position to decide disputes, because it was not possible for the whole Church to gather in one place to discuss them. So her infallibility was vested in general councils by representation.[50] There was no doubt in Fisher's mind that a pope with a general council 'convoked in the Holy Spirit' represented the universal Church, and that it was therefore forbidden for any Christian to dissent from whatever they decreed to be a matter of faith.[51] The proviso about the Holy Spirit enabled him to deal with such apparently 'general' councils as might have promulgated dubious doctrines or decrees. Should such errors be committed, the Holy Spirit would soon intervene to rectify them.[52] The emphasis on the whole Church and on conciliar representation might seem at first to indicate that Fisher was a conciliarist. However, such notions were by no means the monopoly of conciliarists, and Fisher himself emphatically did not hold the fundamental conciliarist tenet, namely the superiority of the general council over the pope. He nowhere so much as suggested, as Thomas More of course did, that a council could depose a pope.[53] Although he did assert that the Church could admonish and call back to the right path a pope who had deviated from the straight and narrow, such language falls a long way short of the power of judgment.[54] And when he wrote that there was nothing on earth superior to a pope, his use of 'nihil' rather than 'nullus' goes further than the 'maior singulis, minor universis' supremacy that even a conciliarist such as John Major was prepared to concede.[55] This language is more redolent of a papal monarchist than of a conciliarist. Nor would any conciliarist have had any doubts about where fault might lie in a conflict between a pope and a council. Fisher, in contrast, thought any such disagreement a cause for grave concern unless it arose through the blatant fault of the pope.[56] He diverged further from the conciliarists in seeing papal convocation as a prerequisite of an authoritative council.[57] On the whole, though, he avoided uncomfortable questions about the relative powers of popes and councils, opting instead for a more satisfying but less realistic model of consensus. His persistent use of such phrases as 'pontifex cum concilio' indicated a preference for co-operation over conflict, although his occasional short-hand reference to 'pontifex' alone in talking of conciliar acts is possibly a sign of an underlying preference for the papal monarchy. 'Ecclesiae catholicae consensus', however, remained for him, as for many medieval and early modern theologians, the crucial dogmatic concept. This consensus might be explicit or implicit, the former being whatever a council had defined, the latter whatever was held by the faithful without disagreement. As an example of the latter, Fisher proposed the doctrine of the Assumption of the Blessed Virgin Mary.[58] This preference for consensus helps explain why Fisher's ecclesiology failed to address the tensions between popes and councils. Rather as Tudor theorists of king-in-parliament refrained from discussing the possibility of conflict because of their presumption of consensus and unanimity, he was reluctant to admit the possibility of dogmatic conflict within the Church's government. There can be no doubt, though, that Fisher was committed to the divine right papal monarchy of the Middle Ages. His writings contain no hint of the circumspection with which English statesmen (who were often churchmen) were wont to regard papal claims. On the contrary, he was seen as a papal maximalist by so acute an observer as Wolsey, who had cause to consult him over the validity of Henry VIII's marriage to Catherine of Aragon.[59] And while Thomas More's commitment to papal supremacy undoubtedly hardened as the years passed, Fisher's was solid from the start. His opening argument in the *De Unica Magdalena* was that Christians should give pride of place to papal pronouncements in ascertaining the teaching of the Church on any specific matter.[60] He wrote uncompromisingly of the 'supreme authority of the popes within the Church' explaining, as we have already noted, that there was nothing on earth superior to the pope, 'to whom Christians should have recourse in every dispute, and to whose decrees they should give obedience especially in matters concerning the faith of the Gospels'.[61] Thus it was from an already firmly established ecclesiological position that Fisher responded to the challenge that Reformed doctrine posed to the papacy.

Catholic teaching on the papacy was subjected to three lines of attack in the Reformation. Luther led the way by denying the supremacy and also the infallibility of Peter and thus of his successors. The third line of attack was that of Ulrich Velenus, who endeavoured to break the connection between Peter and the papacy by denying that Peter had ever been to Rome. Fisher took issue with only two of these three lines of attack. He defended the supremacy of Peter and the papacy in his *Confutatio*, and argued in the *Convulsio Calumniarum* that Peter had indeed resided and ministered at Rome. He kept a meaningful silence, however, over the attack on papal infallibility. His case against Velenus was especially strong. The essence of Velenus's work was the argument from silence: he claimed that there was no scriptural or contemporary evidence that Peter had been to Rome; he dismissed the testimony of tradition to Peter's residence at Rome on the grounds that the authorities could not agree over the date; and he conjectured instead that Peter had died at Jerusalem at the same time as James the Just.[62] In reply Fisher countered Velenus's argument from silence with an appeal to the traditional view that the 'Babylon' from which Peter's first epistle purported to be addressed was in fact Rome (1 Pet 5:13).[63] He also remarked that the argument from silence weighed far more heavily against Velenus's suggestion that Peter died at Jerusalem because this was mentioned neither in scripture nor in any tradition.[64] As for the discrepancies in dating, he argued that these did not invalidate the underlying unanimity of tradition on Peter's ministry and martyrdom in Rome.[65] He proposed an analogy with the crucifixion, whose fact nobody disagreed with, even though the commentators differed widely over its precise date – although this was not entirely fair as the crucifixion was, unlike Peter's residence in Rome, explicitly described in scripture.[66] In this controversy, tradition was definitely the essence of Fisher's case, and he displayed impressive erudition in marshalling it. Among the Latins he cited Tertullian, Cyprian, Ambrose, Leo and Bede; and among the Greeks, 'Hegesippus', Irenaeus (at second-hand from Eusebius), Eusebius himself, Chrysostom and Theophylact. He implicitly undermined the humanist pretensions of his opponent by drawing on a far wider range of patristic sources. Yet to avoid making his case look dated, he referred to such modern humanist historians as Platina, Sabellicus, Volaterranus and Mantuanus.[67] Modern scriptural scholarship was also brought into play. Erasmus's *Novum Instrumentum* and *Annotationes* gave him useful material, as did Lefèvre's edition of Paul.[68] And he also made use of the Hebrew text of Genesis, presumably from the Complutensian Polyglot that had recently been published.[69] His references, which we have already noticed, to Erasmus's doubts about the authenticity of the letters between Seneca and Paul (to which Velenus appealed) and of the Dionysian treatises, and to the doubts of Valla about the Donation of Constantine, served to emphasise his acquaintance with and commitment to humanist criticism, and implicitly to expose the limitations of Velenus's scholarship. As a demolition of Velenus's case, the *Convulsio* was highly effective. One cannot tell how big a part it played in ensuring that Velenus's theory failed to attract widespread support among the Reformers, but one can agree with a recent judgment that the *Convulsio* 'marked a culminating point' in the controversy.[70]

The main line of attack on the papacy remained that pursued by Luther, namely the denial of the supremacy, and thus of the infallibility, of Peter and his successors. As we have seen, Fisher identified this denial as one of the three pillars of Luther's theology as early as his sermon of 1521. The defence of the papacy he constructed there was largely founded on scripture, giving a prominent place to the two customary 'petrine texts' (Mt 16:18 and Jn 21:15–17), and to a typological interpretation of the high priesthood of the Old Testament as a forerunner of the papacy. The essentials of this argument were reproduced in the fuller discussion of the papacy in the *Confutatio*. The basis of this was a mass of testimony from both scripture and tradition in favour of Peter's primacy among the apostles. Fisher began by describing ten 'prerogatives' of Peter that could be deduced from the Gospels. These 'prerogatives' – even the word, coming from an Englishman, is rich in monarchical resonances – were occasions when, or indications that, Peter exercised leadership among the apostles. They included not only the two petrine texts, but the paying of the Temple tax (Mt 17:23–6), the prayer for Peter's faith (Lk 22:32) and the observation that Peter was always named first in lists of the apostles. The ten prerogatives were confirmed with a further ten instances or proofs of Peter's leadership taken from the Acts and Epistles, such as his decision to recruit a new apostle in place of Judas (Acts 1:16–26), his place as the first to preach the risen Christ (Acts 2:14–40), and his revelation about God's will to extend salvation to the Gentiles (Acts 10). Fisher mixed hypothesis with fact in these ten instances, deducing that Peter had played the leading role in the election of the seven deacons (Acts 6:1–6), and claiming, on Chrysostom's authority, that he had appointed James bishop of Jerusalem.[71] Moving from scripture to tradition, he then brought forward first the Latin fathers and then the Greeks.[72] The whole section was rounded off with an appeal to the Council of Florence, where representatives of the Greek Church had signed a declaration that the pope was the head of the Church by divine right.[73] Fisher's case for the primacy makes an illuminating contrast with that presented by Cardinal Cajetan in his *De Divina Institutione Romani Pontificis*. The difference is between a patristic or historical method on the one hand, and a scholastic or dialectical method on the other. Fisher founded his case on a broad scriptural basis, relying on the cumulative effect of twenty texts supported by a catena of patristic citations. Cajetan concentrated on the two central petrine texts (Mt 16:18 and Jn 21:15–17), exploring their possible meanings in eleven out of fourteen chapters, and concluding that the papal interpretation was the most likely. For him the fathers were of purely illustrative value. He produced a range of patristic citations in his final chapter, but they were nearly all from Latin authors, mostly second-hand, and often spurious.[74] Though Cajetan's dialectical analysis is very powerful, Fisher's contextual approach probably held more for the sixteenth-century reader. Certainly subsequent Catholic polemic on the papacy was to tend more towards the latter course.

Much recent historical work on the doctrine of the papacy, work which has itself often seemed to be polemically charged, has been anxious to establish that papal supremacy does not entail papal infallibility.[75] Clearly this is undeniable as a matter of pure logic. Whether it is true as a fact of history is a more contentious issue. In the case of John Fisher and his opinions on the papacy it is a particularly knotty problem, for there seems to be a deep-seated ambiguity or ambivalence in his comments on the papacy. While he unambiguously affirms papal supremacy on several occasions, he never ascribes infallibility as such to the pope, and even states that popes can make mistakes (an opinion, it should be remembered, shared by most exponents of papal infallibility). It would be easy to conclude from this that papal infallibility was far from his mind. But the idea was undoubtedly in the air at the time. Ambrosius Catharinus upheld the doctrine at some length in his *Apologia pro Veritate Catholicae et Apostolicae Fidei*,[76] and Luther accused Catholics of believing it. Fisher's ambivalence can be detected in his reply to this accusation, for he neither denied the doctrine nor defended it. He simply ignored it.[77] Yet many of his arguments in favour of papal supremacy can be read as implicitly tending towards an assertion of infallibility. This is especially true of his typological interpretation of the relationship between Moses and Aaron as prefiguring that between Christ and Peter. According to Fisher, Moses had established Aaron and his successors as supreme and omnicompetent judges over Israel. It was not therefore credible that Christ should have left his Church worse equipped than Moses had left the Jews, that is, that he should have left the Church without some leader capable of resolving controversies over articles of the faith.[78] In fact, he continued, such supreme judicial power was vested in the papacy, which occupied under the new law the place of the high priesthood under the old. Just as the Jews had been instructed to set their doubts and problems before the High Priest in the see of Moses at Jerusalem (Deut 17:8), so Christians were obliged to go to the see of Peter.[79] The argument so far was a commonplace among papal theorists.[80] The ingenious twist Fisher put on it was to refer this to the famous unintentional prophecy of Caiaphas, 'it is expedient for us, that one man should die for the people', which John glossed with the remark that Caiaphas spoke truth not of his own volition, but because he was high priest for that year (Jn 11:49–51). Fisher further glossed that if the high priest of the Jews, though guilty of avarice and ambition, pronounced the truth despite himself by virtue of his office, then surely the pope, the high priest of the Christians, would enjoy the same privilege.[81] A similar argument can be found in Thomas Aquinas's *Quaestiones Quodlibetales*, where the analogy of Caiaphas's prophecy was used to establish that the pope could not err in the canonisation of saints.[82] Fisher himself argued elsewhere for the inerrancy of canonisation, and took the canonisation of Thomas as his example.[83] It seems then that the analogy of the see of Peter with the see of Moses took him to the verge of affirming papal infallibility. In the *De Unica Magdalena* he wrote that there was nowhere that certainty about any matter of faith could be more readily ascertained than at the apostolic see, because it was there, in the place chosen by the Lord, that the high priest sat (an echo of Deut 17:8).[84] He went even further in the *Confutatio*, explicitly attributing to the papacy divine assistance in passing judgment in disputes about the faith: 'To which judge shall we go, if not to the see of Peter? For that see will never lack divine assistance in handing down to us the certain truth about doubtful matters, especially matters concerning the faith.'[85] He unhesitatingly attributed to the pope the power to interpret not only papal and also conciliar decrees, but even scripture itself.[86] Other things being equal (though as we shall see in a moment, they are not) one would be hard pressed to say how such statements fell short of accepting papal infallibility. Admittedly, Fisher never explicitly predicated infallibility of the papacy as Catharinus did. Yet far from this being, as has recently been suggested, 'no surprise', it is highly surprising in view of the character of Fisher's defence of the papacy.[87] Equally surprising is the fact that he never explicitly predicated infallibility of a general council either. Since, as we have seen, be dismissed as impossible the idea of consulting the Church as a whole on disputed issues, this would lead us to the absurd conclusion that Fisher attributed to the Church an infallibility he thought she had no means of expressing. For all that, however, the fact remains that he shied away from affirming and defending papal infallibility when Luther gave him the chance to do so. And elsewhere he admitted the possibility of licitly resisting decisions taken by the pope with the advice of his cardinals even in matters of faith and morals: 'When he who is the foremost leader of the whole Church, to whom the care ['cura'] of the whole world has been entrusted by Christ's decree, has, together with the other princes of the Church, approved this or that interpretation, then everyone else should follow them unless they have overwhelming arguments to the contrary.'[88] We can add to this Fisher's frequent assertions of human fallibility, often applied directly to the papacy. The fullest statement of this theme is found in his last surviving treatise against Henry VIII's divorce, the 'Brevis Apologia', where he writes:

We certainly do not deny that popes can err. For they are human, and thus can lapse, unless they wholeheartedly rely on divine assistance. When they do rely on this, there is no doubt that they are guided by the Holy Spirit in all judgments on matters that concern the welfare of the souls entrusted to them. But if by chance they occasionally deviate from the straight path, then provided that their error is flagrant and glaring, especially in a matter of the faith, they can be admonished and called back by the Church.[89]

We are thus faced with an apparent inconsistency. The most plausible explanation for it is that Fisher was wary of attributing infallibility as such to any human being or group because he foresaw the erroneous impressions which such a claim could give – the false idea, for example, that Catholics believe their spiritual leader on earth to be omniscient and impeccable. From this perspective, his remark about the distant possibility of resistance to a papal doctrinal decree might be interpreted as allowing for the case, dealt with in canon law, of a pope who fell into heresy and was therefore *ipso facto* deposed. Hence perhaps his insistence that the pope's error be flagrant ('manifestarius'). It is interesting to note, moreover, that the assertion that popes can err unless they are guided by the Holy Spirit is akin to his remark that councils, in order to be authoritative, must be convoked 'in the Holy Spirit'. In each case, the proviso about the Holy Spirit is a sort of escape clause to deal with embarrassing anomalies. In each case also, though, there is an underlying claim that the authority in question, be it pope or council, is under normal circumstances guided by the Holy Spirit and therefore able to give judgment with the infallibility vested in the Church as a whole. In conclusion to this intricate discussion, we can perhaps say that Fisher saw both popes and councils as organs of the Church's infallible teaching authority, although not upon each and every occasion nor under all circumstances. And we can certainly say that his teaching on both papal and conciliar infallibility lacked the fine distinctions introduced by later theologians to resolve the anomalies raised by those councils and popes that had in some way taught error.

This absence of fine distinctions was apparent in other areas of Fisher's ecclesiology, and is itself an argument against categorising him too readily as a scholastic. The absence of scholastic rigour is perhaps best illustrated by his confusion between the 'potestas ordinis' and the 'potestas jurisdictionis' of the clergy. When he wrote 'Do we not see how Christians are born of priests,

priests of bishops, and bishops – as often as is necessary – of the pope himself?', he confuses the sacramental and universal power of baptism (which could of course be validly administered even by lay men and women) with the sacramental and episcopal power of ordination, and also with the jurisdictional power to nominate or appoint bishops (who, like priests, were of course *ordained* by other bishops).[90] A similar confusion is evident in his comments on the power of the keys, where he indiscriminately referred to the sacramental and sacerdotal power of absolution, the peculiarly papal power of granting indulgences, and the jurisdictional clerical power of excommunication as if all three were the same kind of thing.[91] The former confusion is perhaps best accounted for as the expression of a highly clerical mentality, a mentality that was to be typical of the Counter-Reformation; the latter as an expression of a highly scriptural theology, which traced all three powers to the entrusting of the keys to Peter and the apostles by Christ. But in each case confusion of a kind unusual in a scholastic theologian is undeniably present.

Whatever confusion there may have been at the margins of Fisher's ecclesiology, there is no doubt that a belief in the guidance of the Holy Spirit lay at the heart of it. He saw this guidance as operative in different ways through a variety of channels, primarily through the fathers, whether individually or gathered in councils. It is worth remarking that his use of the term 'fathers' was not as restricted as that current in contemporary theology (hence my avoidance of the customary initial capital). In his eyes 'fathers' were not only the primitive authors, but also the bishops of every age, a blurring which demonstrates his conviction that the primitive Church was essentially identical with the Church of his own day. Thus anyone who rejected the teaching of the fathers or councils of any age was guilty of rejecting the Holy Spirit that spoke through them. This was not to suggest that individual fathers were infallible, nor even that every utterance of popes or councils was necessarily so. But the consensus of the fathers could be relied upon, as could the decrees of councils when they were harmonious and convoked by the papacy in the Holy Spirit. This guidance by the Holy Spirit extended beyond the sphere of authoritative teaching into that of the practices and customs of the Church. Finally, since the Holy Spirit could not be trammelled by human institutions, even simple lay Christian men or women could be the providential vehicle of this guidance. This explains Fisher's readiness to accept the validity of special revelations, although he tempered this with the insistence that such revelations were subject to the approval of the ecclesiastical authorities. The theological foundation of this ecclesiology lay in the promises concerning the Holy Spirit that Christ made to the apostles at the Last Supper: namely that he would send the Paraclete to dwell with the Church for ever, to announce the things that were to come, to interpret Christ's words and to guide the Church into all truth.[92] The fulfilment of these promises became in a curious way a double issue of credibility.

It was important to Christ's credibility that they were seen to be fulfilled – we have seen a similar concern in Fisher's treatment of Christ's promise about the perpetual memory of the woman who anointed him, and we shall see it again in his treatment of Malachi's prophecy about the eucharist.[93] If the Church should fall for some time into grave doctrinal error, then the Holy Spirit would not be with her for ever and would not have guided her into all truth, in which case Christ's own credibility would be irreparably damaged. But the credibility of the Church was also at stake. For if she could be convicted of grave error, why should anyone ever trust her again? Given the weakness of the fallen human race, an infallible Church was necessary to convince them of truth, and only the intervention of the Holy Spirit on a regular basis could produce that infallibility and thus guarantee the Church as the vehicle of Christ's saving grace.

This examination of Fisher's concept of authority in the Church has produced few surprises. The martyr for papal supremacy was indeed a lifelong advocate of papal primacy in the Church. Yet his theology of the papacy was not of great originality. He relied on the same scriptural texts as most medieval and early modern papalists, although he did break new ground with his wide appeal to both Greek and Latin fathers. His patristic erudition enabled him to demolish the insecure cavils of Ulrich Velenus against the tradition of Peter's ministry and martyrdom at Rome. And his demonstration of the constant tradition from the New Testament onwards of Peter's primacy among the apostles pointed the way for future defences of papal supremacy. His contribution to the debate over scripture and tradition was of a higher order. His crucial insight was into the importance which the principle of scripture as the sole doctrinal authority occupied in Luther's system. By devoting serious and lengthy attention to this problem, Fisher again showed the way to future polemicists. From the *Confutatio* onwards it was standard practice for large-scale refutations of Reformed theology to begin with an analysis of scripture, tradition and authority in the Church. Even though his account left unclear just how far tradition was independent of scripture, it emphasised that scripture could not be read without reference to that tradition, and it did not betray itself into denigration of scripture. On the contrary, his continuing sympathy with much of the humanist scriptural programme remained clear. Equally, he remained firmly committed to the authority of the Church. The relationships he worked out between scripture and tradition, and authority and scholarship, were to be perfectly illustrated in his handling of other theological issues in the Reformation debates. And it is to one of those debates, over justification, which Fisher identified as the third pillar of Luther's system, that we now turn.

7
Faith, grace and justification

THE DEBATE ON justification sparked off by Luther in the early sixteenth century is by no means over yet. Ecumenical dialogue has largely, though not entirely, replaced polemic as the medium of debate, but passions still run high. The whole domain is a theological minefield which the historian is, or ought to be, nervous of entering. There is no universal agreement on the content and development of Luther's teaching, and still less on how authentically Christian, Pauline or Augustinian it may have been, or on how well his opponents (not to mention his adherents) understood it. Indeed, despite the return *ad fontes* characteristic of the historiography since the 'Luther renaissance' began earlier this century, the study of Luther and his opponents remains bedevilled by misconceptions born either of dogmatic presuppositions or of traditional mis-representations. His opponents have suffered even more from this than has Luther himself. Ecumenical concerns have led to the paying of disproportionate attention to the so-called 'irenicists' among the Catholic theologians, and to the consequent denigration of the polemicists. This has in turn fostered a tendency to dismiss the early polemical opponents of Luther on justification as Pelagians who failed even to appreciate, much less to understand, the issues – a tendency that reflects both an uncritical acceptance of Luther's own evaluation of his opponents and a naive identification of the doctrine he preached with that of Augustine. There have been harbingers of a more balanced approach. For example, an exhaustive analysis of the debate on free will between Erasmus and Luther has finally laid to rest the myth of the Pelagian Erasmus. Yet despite 'l'accord profond' that was detected between the teaching of Fisher and Erasmus,[1] and despite Edward Surtz's argument that Fisher was no Pelagian,[2] it remains possible for a recent critic to remark, 'Fisher's defence of free will scarcely avoids overt Pelagianism.'[3] The primary objective of this chapter is to put this apodictic judgment to the test. It is also meant to redress the historio-graphical balance to some extent by investigating how well one early polemicist understood and grappled with his opponent. Such objectives cannot be at-tempted, though, without a preliminary look at the distant and immediate background against which Fisher wrote. This chapter shall therefore begin with the dispute between Augustine and Pelagius which set the scene for all subsequent discussions of justification. After a brief look at scholastic opinions, and at the 'Augustinian renaissance' of the late Middle Ages, it will present a picture of Luther that differs in some respects from the most common contemporary view. Only then will it proceed to an analysis of Fisher's own teaching that should enable us to ascertain where he stood on the doctrinal spectrum that runs from Pelagius at one end, through the Semipelagians and the scholastics, to Augustine and finally Luther at the other. The consequential revision of the conventional image of the 'Pelagian Fisher' will in turn suggest a new assessment of his part in the Reformation debate on justification.

Between the time of Paul and Augustine, justification was not a major preoccupation of Christian writers. Concerned with the defence of free will against pagan determinists, they placed a premium on personal effort in achieving salvation, although they did not ignore the role of grace. They certainly did not treat of justification systematically.[4] The first to do so was Augustine who, in response to questions put to him in the 390s by Simplicianus (Ambrose's successor as bishop of Milan), affirmed the primacy of grace in justification. Thus the foundations of his soteriology were laid before he came across the ideas of Pelagius that provoked him to expand his doctrine in the course of a voluminous controversy.[5] Pelagius was a moral reformer who feared that concepts such as grace and original sin undermined free will and encouraged people to deny their own responsibility for doing good and avoiding evil. He therefore taught that it was entirely within human power to avoid sin and live a moral life; and that divine grace was either a reward for so doing, by which the moral life became easier, or else nothing other than the law revealed in scripture, by which the essentials of the moral life could be more readily ascertained. Such teaching was, Augustine maintained, a flagrant contradiction of St Paul. In a series of books against Pelagius and his disciples, he elaborated a comprehensive doctrine of sin and grace on a strictly Pauline basis.[6] Each person was flawed by original sin and was therefore precluded from performing authentically good works without first undergoing regeneration by the grace of God, through faith and baptism (the 'sacramentum fidei'). This regeneration was in Augustine's view an intrinsic process, that is, a process by which God not only treated the regenerate as if they were just, but really made them just. Hence the significance of the term 'justificare' which he derived from the phrase 'justum facere'.[7] Baptism cleansed away the guilt of sin, leaving only concupiscence, a proclivity of the flesh to sin that could not become actual sin without the consent of the free will. Without baptism, salvation was unattainable. In the heat of controversy, Augustine spelled out in merciless detail his views on the dominance of sin in the souls of the unregenerate, and adopted an increasingly arbitrary interpretation of predestination and election. But he never even suggested that salvation was possible without the co-operation of the free will. Although free will prior to baptism had power only to sin, grace enabled it to co-operate in acts of faith, hope and charity. Augustine's assault on the Pelagians won general acceptance, but his harsh attitude to the unregenerate will provoked some theologians to seek a middle way. Accepting the indispensability of grace for salvation, these 'Semipelagians' nevertheless affirmed that the beginning of the salvific process, the 'initum fidei', lay in the unaided will, and that morally good acts (though not acts meritorious of eternal reward) could be performed without grace. They also mitigated Augustine's predestinarian doctrines. In the event, Augustine's arguments prevailed against both Pelagians and Semipelagians, and his doctrine was posthumously vindicated at the Second Council of Orange.

Augustine's theology of justification shaped that of the whole Middle Ages. In the twelfth century, both the 'last of the fathers' (Bernard) and the 'first of the scholastics' (Peter Lombard) provided impeccably Augustinian accounts of the subject.[8] However, the picture became far more complicated in the scholastic period. The condemnation of Semipelagian teachings at Orange II was unknown from the tenth to the sixteenth centuries.[9] At the same time, some surviving Pelagian and Semipelagian writings were unwittingly circulated under such names as Jerome and even Augustine, to infiltrate and adulterate the Augustinian legacy.[10] From about 1200, medieval theologians can be divided into two camps on justification. The majority tended to limit the role of grace in the interests of preserving free will, granting more to the unaided will than Augustine would have done, though less than Pelagius would have liked. Concerned with the problem of the good pagan, they allowed that morally good acts could be performed without the help of grace, though they denied that such acts could merit eternal life. From here it was a short step to admit that God could award grace to sinners or pagans in respect of their unaided best efforts. Hence the famous tag, 'facientibus quod in se est deus non denegat gratiam', 'God does not deny grace to those who do what lies in them [namely, their best]'. This gift of grace was not earned by the merit of the act itself ('meritum ex condigno') but by the merit which God freely chose to ascribe to the act despite its inherent worthlessness ('meritum ex congruo'). These teachings were characteristic of the early Thomas Aquinas, of Giles of Rome, Scotus and Ockham, and thus permeated all the main schools. Even Luther upheld them in his early days.[11] However, among a substantial minority, a more authentic Augustinianism flourished.[12] The later writings of Aquinas stood at the head of this somewhat nebulous tradition. Although his early commentary on the *Sentences* had been in the mainstream, his mature writings reflected a fuller knowledge of Augustine's anti-Pelagian works and shied away from Semipelagian tendencies.[13] But the contradictions between his earlier and later writings enabled both views to find followers in the Thomist school. Not until the pioneering work of John Capreolus (himself an Augustinian Thomist) was the superior authority of Thomas's later writings established as an hermeneutical principle, and it was not until Cajetan's definitive edition of the *Summa Theologiae* that this principle won general acceptance.[14] Outside the Dominicans, the Austin friars were the chief upholders of their patron's thought – although not to such an extent that Augustinianism can be regarded as the order's official theology.[15] The most famous Augustinian was Gregory of Rimini, who was heavily influenced by the later Aquinas. He and his contemporary Thomas Bradwardine (a secular priest) went so far as to accuse their opponents of Pelagianism. While Bradwardine's work soon sank into obscurity, Gregory's remained a force to be reckoned with throughout the Middle Ages;[16] and Augustinian themes ran through the writings of such successors in the order as Dionysius of Montina, Hugolino of Orvieto and Diego Perez of Valencia.[17] On the eve of the Reformation, the tension between the two poles was increasing. The cause of free will was energetically and influentially taken up by Gabriel Biel. Thinking that Gregory of Rimini attributed too little to free will, Biel adopted a position so liberal as to have been termed Pelagian by Heiko Oberman.[18] Even in the Thomist camp, Cajetan diluted the Augustinianism of the *Summa* in his epoch-making commentary.[19] But as the scholastic tradition slewed away from Augustine, the growing humanist preference for the fathers over the scholastics combined with the appearance of the first complete edition of Augustine's works to produce an anti-Pelagian reaction, a veritable Augustinian renaissance.[20] This can be seen in the work of several early sixteenth-century theologians, mostly of a reformist cast of mind. Johann Staupitz's *Sermones in Iob* betray marked Augustinian influence, as do John Colet's lectures on Paul.[21]

This Augustinian renaissance of the early sixteenth century provides the immediate context for the emergence of Martin Luther's theology. Though his nominalist mentors at Erfurt were of Biel's school, his lectures on scripture at Wittenberg soon took on a 'strongly anti-Pelagian cast',[22] apparently as a direct result of his reading of Augustine. Nevertheless, the obsession with the 'young Luther' that has characterised twentieth-century Luther studies has led to a misunderstanding of the importance of Augustine in his development, as well as to confusion over the nature and date of his 'Reformation breakthrough'. The consensus of scholarly opinion locates the crucial insight in his early lectures on the Psalms, identifying its substance, as Luther himself did, with the perception of the righteousness of God ('iustitia dei') as the gift of salvation rather than as the exaction or infliction of punishment, which Luther claimed was the teaching of all the theologians.[23] This consensus sees the lectures on Romans, delivered shortly afterwards, as the first full exposition of Reformation teaching on justification. Because of the unquestionable importance of Augustine to this phase of Luther's development, the myths of Augustine as the 'first Protestant', and of Reformed doctrine as essentially Augustinian, have been unwarrantably perpetuated. Unfortunately, as was conclusively demonstrated eighty years ago, the interpretation of the 'iustitia dei' as salvific rather than punitive was a medieval commonplace.[24] This crucial insight can thus hardly be regarded as a turning-point, whatever Luther may have thought. Besides, this early dating of Luther's breakthrough sits uncomfortably with other remarks of Luther's which tend to place it as late as 1518–19.[25] Either Luther's dating or his identification of the insight must give, and the consensus doubts his dating. A minority school of conservative Lutherans prefers instead to doubt his identification, maintaining that his breakthrough lay in exchanging the concept of intrinsic righteousness for that of extrinsic righteousness. That is, he replaced the Augustinian notion of the real appropriation of Christ's justice to the sinner with that of its 'imputation' – the justified sinner was called, rather than made, just. While this has long been a distinguishing feature of Protestant theology, there is no explicit trace of it in the early writings of Luther though it may perhaps have been implicit. Luther talks frequently of the 'imputation' of sin, but not of the imputation of justice. The 'Reformation breakthrough' is clearly a knotty problem, and one which can hardly be resolved here.

What is clear is that the understanding of justification with which Luther emerged from the 1510s constituted a complete break with the Augustinian tradition of Catholicism.[26] This disjunction has been blurred by tendencies in recent scholarship to play down the extremism of Luther's repudiation of free will in salvation and the significance of his new interpretation of sin and concupiscence, tendencies themselves motivated by ecumenical attempts to reconcile Catholic and Lutheran doctrines of justification. The concentration on the young Luther has fostered such tendencies, for there is more scope for reconciliation in the Augustinian Luther of the 1510s than in the 'Post-Augustinian' Luther of the 1520s.[27] Although Luther long kept up his appeal to Augustine (claiming to have re-read *De Spiritu et Littera* after his breakthrough, and to have found there many of his own ideas),[28] his theology went far beyond the polemic of the anti-Pelagian writings, often taking up positions falsely ascribed to Augustine by his opponents and indignantly repudiated by Augustine himself. The break with Augustine can be seen most clearly over sin and baptism. Luther's reflection on his experience in the light of scripture led him to a radically pessimistic view of fallen human nature. Through Adam sin had penetrated so deeply that nobody in this life could be wholly liberated from its dominion. Even baptism did not wipe away sins completely, because the concupiscence of the flesh it left behind was itself sin in the full sense of the word[29] – it was simply not 'imputed' as sin to those who had faith. Augustine, on the other hand, despite his gloomy view of concupiscence and his identification of it with sexual arousal, always stressed that it was not sin as such, and could become so only through the consent of the will to its promptings in a sinful act. He insisted that baptism cleansed away all sin, and denied the Pelagian accusation that he did not believe this.[30] For him, the rite of baptism itself was to be regarded with the utmost awe, whereas for Luther the rite was overshadowed by the faith of which it was the sacramental sign.[31] Luther's denial of free will, and in particular of the co-operative role of free will in salvation, was poles apart from Augustine's position. While they agreed on the impotence of the will to do good before grace, they disagreed on its power after regeneration. The notion that every good work was inevitably flawed by sin, summed up in Luther's thesis 'the just person sins in every good work',[32] represented another break with Augustine, for whom such phrases as this and 'simul iustus et peccator' would have had no meaning.[33] Finally, Luther's assertion of the subjective certainty of being in a state of grace ('in statu salutis'), which he identified with the state of faith or belief, was in flat contradiction of Augustine. Thus, even prescinding from Augustine's ecclesiology and philosophy, as found in his polemics against the Donatists and Manicheans, there is precious little of Augustine left after such a thorough purge. In his later years, Luther was to claim that he had moved on from Augustine to St Paul, and that Augustine had said only two worthwhile things: 'Peccatum dimittitur, non ut non sit, sed ut non damnet et dominetur'; and 'Lex impletur, cum quod non fit, ignoscitur' – texts which recur throughout Luther's writings.[34] The first of these texts, which Luther repeated in many different forms, was a garbled version of a comment Augustine made in the *De Nuptiis et Concupiscentia*, a comment which, by distinguishing concupiscence from sin, utterly undermined Luther's identification of them.[35] The other, garbled from the *Retractationes*, was given a meaning quite different from anything Augustine ever intended.[36]

John Fisher, like Staupitz, Colet and the young Luther, can be placed in the early sixteenth-century Augustinian renaissance. His commitment to Augustine emerged most clearly in the *Confutatio*, not only in explicit appeals to his authority, but in extensive citations from his works and in the theological foundations of the argument. In article 3 he expressed a preference for the teaching of Augustine over that of the scholastics on original sin.[37] The only scholastic he cited on justification was the fiercely Augustinian and anti-Pelagian Gregory of Rimini,[38] whom he followed in rejecting the scholastic consensus on the possibility of morally good acts without the assistance of grace. Moreover, he explicitly repudiated the theory of 'meritum ex congruo' favoured by the Scotists, some Thomists and almost the entire *via moderna*.[39] Luther's Augustinian pretensions, however, did not impress him. In his sermon of 1521, he claimed that many scholars thought that Luther 'lytle regardeth Austyn', and in the *Confutatio* he dismissed Luther's claim to Augustine's mantle as empty boasting.[40] Fisher's own frequent recourse to Augustine was expressly intended to show up the vanity of Luther's claim.[41] Augustine was indeed far and away the most frequently cited authority in the *Confutatio*.[42] Given Augustine's standing, and the sheer volume of his works, this might not seem surprising. But while it would have been easy for Fisher to concentrate on the polemics against Donatists and Manicheans which told so heavily against Luther, the fact is that he relied more on the very anti-Pelagian tracts which might be presumed to have most closely approached Luther's teachings. Most of the major anti-Pelagian polemics appear in the *Confutatio* – *De Peccatorum Meritis et Remissione, De Natura et Gratia, De Spiritu et Littera, De Nuptiis et Concupiscentia, De Gratia et Libero Arbitrio, Contra Duas Epistolas Pelagianorum, De Gratia Christi et de Peccato Originali, De Praedestinatione Sanctorum* and *Contra Julianum*.[43] Should it be thought that Fisher adopted an Augustinian position only in reaction to Luther's violent attack on Pelagian or Semipelagian tendencies in scholastic theology, recourse to his sermons on the penitential psalms readily shows this to be a misconception. A work whose pastoral agenda was the encouragement of sinners to repentance, and which therefore laid great stress on personal effort, might not seem a likely place to find evidence of Augustinian concerns. Yet such is the case. Fisher made use of Augustine's famous prayer from the *Confessions*, 'Da quod iubes: iube quod vis',[44] and stated that 'no creature of himself hath power to do good werkes without the grace and helpe of god'.[45] While this remark could conceivably refer only to meritorious works (and could thus be echoed by any exponent of 'meritum ex congruo'), Fisher made it clear that even the process of preparation for grace was itself stimulated by grace: 'These thre thynges that we have spoken of cometh without doubte of the gracyous pyte of god. Thou arte sory for thy synne, it is a gyfte of almyghty god. Thou makest knowledge of thy synne wepynge and waylynge for it, it is a gyfte of almyghty god. Thou arte besy in good werkes to do satysfaccyon, whiche also is a gyfte of almyghty god.'[46] Despite the limitations of Fisher's Augustinianism – chiefly that he, in common with most other scholars, accepted a host of spurious attributions – there can be no doubt that his approach to the problem of justification was shaped by an authentic interpretation of Augustine.

One of the criticisms most frequently levelled against the early opponents of Luther – by Luther himself, among countless others – is that they failed to appreciate the central issues in the debate and thus failed to understand what they were attacking. Apart from observing that, since their difficulty in interpreting Luther seems to be shared by a great many recent scholars, the criticism is perhaps not especially damaging, we can nevertheless propose Fisher as at least a partial exception to the rule. Even in the sermon of 1521 he drew attention to the role of justification by faith alone in Luther's theology, describing it as one of the three 'great groundes' of his system.[47] As far as I have been able to ascertain, this sermon was the first Catholic critique to identify that doctrine explicitly as fundamental to Luther's teaching. Previous polemical literature had largely ignored it, concentrating instead on papal primacy, penance, or indulgences. Jacob Latomus, for example, overlooked 'sola fides' entirely, and gave the related question of free will a mere two pages in his *Contra Articulos*.[48] Catharinus picked up the phrase 'sola fides' in his *Apologia* of

December 1520, but his brief notice of it came at the end of a vast treatise on papal primacy and infallibility, in the immediate context of a discussion of penance, and gave no sign of seeing its crucial importance. Luther's denial of free will was introduced not as a subject for argument but as clear proof of heretical depravity.[49] The various treatises of Sylvester Prierias, Cardinal Cajetan and John Eck were almost exclusively concerned with ecclesiological matters. Even Henry's *Assertio* did not hint at the doctrine of faith that under-pinned Luther's theology of the sacraments – a strong indication that Fisher was not involved in its production. Most notably of all, justification by faith alone did not figure among the forty-one articles condemned in *Exsurge Domine* by Leo X. Fisher's sermon of 1521 therefore marks an important stage in the emergence of the Catholic response to Luther. It was followed up by the *Confutatio*, which gave 'sola fides' prominent and extensive consideration under article 1 (an article that in fact concerned the sacraments as channels of grace – for which Fisher referred his readers to Henry's *Assertio*).[50] The *Confutatio* took the question further by, again for the first time, dealing at length with Luther's denial of free will.[51] And in article 23 Fisher spelled out how Luther's initial error over faith led on to his other heresies. He explained that the doctrine of justification by faith alone entailed the denial of the efficacy of the sacraments; made indulgences, satisfaction, contrition and even confession practically useless; and culminated in contempt for excommunication.[52] The *Confutatio* thus assumes fresh significance as the first polemic to present Luther's teaching as a coherent body of theology erected upon a firm doctrinal foundation.

The *Confutatio* showed an unusually wide knowledge of Luther's writings, and indeed an unusual concern to understand as well as to refute them. The treatment of justification began by trying to give some account of Luther's view of faith. Though not entirely successful, Fisher took some trouble over this, adducing a number of citations from a range of Luther's works, starting with the *De Libertate Christiana*, and including the *Acta Augustana*, the *De Fide et Operibus*, the *Resolutiones contra Eckium*, the 1519 commentary on Galatians, and the *De Captivitate Babylonica*.[53] The texts he chose were those in which Luther's remarks were framed in the style of definitions. Given such a selection of passages, it is not surprising that he felt able to accuse Luther of deliberate equivocation. At times, he argued, Luther seemed to reduce faith to a bare assent to the truths of revelation, such as no Christian could be thought to lack; yet at other times he equated it with a contrition and charity, such as hardly any Christian could be imagined to have.[54] The problem was, of course, that Fisher made no concessions to the vagaries of expression of a man who has never been held up as a model of consistency, and that he failed to allow for the rapid development of his opponent's beliefs between 1517 and 1520. The works he cited contained passages capable of orthodox interpretation as well as passages characteristic of Luther's mature thought – as, *mutatis mutandis*, Luther himself

117

was to observe in reprinting them in 1546.[55] The contradictions identified by Fisher illustrated the transition from an Augustinian to a Lutheran account of faith. Nevertheless, his presentation of Luther's doctrine was far from a travesty. Fisher himself was satisfied with it, using it again in the *Defensio* of 1525 and alluding to it in his second sermon against Luther in 1526.[56] The attention that he gave to the *De Libertate Christiana* is of particular significance.[57] It shows that he looked in the right place, and helps explain how he came to appreciate the centrality of faith in Luther's system. He read it, rightly enough, as an attack on the notions of sanctification and merit, under which good works performed in a state of grace were seen as making satisfaction for sin, reducing the power of concupiscence and earning an eternal reward. He was particularly scornful of Luther's claim that, apart from a text or two in James, the whole of scripture ascribed justification to faith rather than works. In reply, expanding an argument from his earlier sermon against Luther, he adduced sixteen New Testament texts that made eternal reward contingent in some way upon the performance of good works.[58] However, in common with many other Catholic polemicists, he did not attend to Luther's insistence that good works, although unnecessary to justification, were nevertheless its inevitable fruit. Like Latomus before him, he saw Luther's teaching as frankly antinomian – a conclusion Luther himself always rebutted. To be fair, though, it remains a weakness of Luther's case that while he provided reasons why good works might be expected to be performed, he provided no reasons or motives for performing them. His protestations were therefore hardly an adequate disclaimer of the inherent antinomian potential of his position.

The polemical strategy with which Fisher attacked Luther's teaching has become familiar from centuries of controversy. To Luther's emphasis on Paul's preference for faith over works (Romans 3:20–5:2, and so forth) he opposed the contrary preference of James (James 2:14–26), adding Paul's encomium of charity (1 Cor 13:1–2). Latomus had already adumbrated a similar case in his treatment of good works in the *Contra Articulos*, and Fisher may perhaps have been influenced by him.[59] Yet our familiarity with this case should not blind us to its novelty at the time, when there was an urgent need for a simple and scriptural answer to Luther's arguments – an answer which the *Confutatio* did much to popularise, if not to originate. Fisher elaborated his reply into a theory of 'double justification'.[60] By this he meant that the first stage of justification was accomplished by grace or faith, while the second stage, 'sanctification', was a growth in grace through good works and the sacraments, a process he ascribed to the 'faith which works by love' of Paul (Gal 5:6, 'fides quae per dilectionem operatur'). In discussing Paul's own concept of faith, he emphasised that this comprised not so much mere assent of the mind to truth as 'spes fiduciaque', a reading reminiscent of Colet's lectures on Romans.[61] Like Colet, Fisher saw Paul as a stern moralist who enjoined the avoidance of sin and the performance of good works, and he emphasised the importance of 'charity' in Paul's thought.[62] Turning to the contradiction of Paul by James, Fisher based his reconciliation of them on Augustine, on whose authority he observed that in the early Church certain heretics had derived a doctrine like Luther's (that is, antinomianism) from a misapprehension of Romans, and that Peter, James and Jude had all written to forestall this. Taking Augustine's distinction between works done before and works done after justification, he argued that Paul was referring to the former and James to the latter.[63] Whether or not this is a proper reading of Paul, it is a fair representation of Augustine's own views. By seizing on Paul's 'faith which works through love' he placed himself firmly in the Augustinian tradition of the Western Church.

The second stage of Fisher's 'double justification' was sanctification, that is, progress in justice through good works, and pre-eminently through the sacraments. Luther did not deny that believers continued to make progress in justification throughout their lives, but he did not see good works as contributing directly to their spiritual growth. This was made clear in his *De Libertate Christiana*, where he gave several analogies to show that doing good works could not make people good or better. The most illuminating of these analogies was that of the builder who, according to Luther, did not become any more of a builder by building more houses, because building was the effect of his skill rather than the cause of it.[64] This argument was of course a flat rejection of the whole edifice of Aristotelian ethics against which, as incorporated into Christian theology by Thomas Aquinas and other scholastics, he had been fulminating for several years. In the Thomist–Aristotelian scheme, a virtuous person was one who did virtuous acts and thus became more virtuous through doing so – just as builders and other artisans became more skilled through practical experience in their trade.[65] Fisher seized upon Luther's analogy as supporting the traditional view rather than Luther's (few people, after all, would deny that practice hones skills). In doing so he enounced the highly Aristotelian principle, 'the just man becomes more just by doing just works'.[66] But here we should observe how Fisher avoids the intrinsically Pelagian cast of Aristotle's own claim, 'we become just by doing just actions', by making it comparative and thus clearly posterior to and dependent on the primary justification by grace. His 'baptism' of Aristotle, though, is poles apart from Luther's absolute and explicit repudiation of the Aristotelian ethical heritage, which extended even to the fundamental Aristotelian principle that all human actions are ordained towards some good. Their different attitudes to this principle can be best seen in the opening paragraphs of their respective commentaries on the Psalms. Fisher began with the remark, 'There is nobody who does not desire happiness, although not everybody seeks the same happiness. For it is perfectly clear that many seek it in things in which it is scarcely to be found. Some hope to find it in the pleasures of the flesh, others in riches, and others still in wickedness.'[67]

This was a clear echo of Aristotle's own comments on happiness in the *Ethics*: 'with regard to what happiness is they differ, and the many do not give the same account as the wise. For the former think it is some plain and obvious thing, like pleasure, wealth, or honour.'[68] Luther, in contrast, ruthlessly undercut this Aristotelian theme with an attack on the vanity of the philosophers who 'located happiness in virtue or in acts of virtue, thus making themselves the unhappiest people of all, depriving themselves of the goods of both this life and the next'.[69]

In Fisher's view, Luther's refrain of 'sola fides' represented a demand for perfect faith that could only drive sinners to despair or else license them to presumption.[70] Luther insisted that true faith was an absolute certainty of acceptability to God,[71] while Fisher could not see how such certainty could be attained without an immediate divine revelation.[72] The problem of certainty of grace, however, was an important one for Fisher, and in his solution he drifted closer to Luther than Catholic orthodoxy was subsequently to allow. In doing so, he showed that he took seriously the genuine concerns of the Reformers, and that he was not purely intent on proving them wrong at every turn. For although he denied that certainty about grace was possible *per se* (barring a direct divine revelation), he believed that the sacraments were instituted to compensate for this human uncertainty. This belief became stronger in his later polemical works. In article 10 of the *Confutatio* he denied the possibility of total certainty in the sacrament of penance, since even if one could go through contrition and confession with sufficient certainty, one could never be sure beyond all doubt that the priest was validly ordained, or that he was performing the sacrament with a proper intention.[73] This position was subtly modified, however, by the argument that Christ had instituted the sacraments so that 'since nobody could be certain through faith alone of their own justification, whatever was lacking to the sufficiency of faith should be supplied by the sacraments'. This left unclear, though, whether it was a defect of faith or of certainty that was to be supplied – it was more probably the former than the latter.[74] By the time he wrote *De Veritate* he seems to have come down firmly in favour of certainty through the sacraments. He maintained there that the sacraments had been established so that through their use Christians might be sure beyond all doubt that they had acquired grace.[75] And without the sacraments, there was no prospect of such certainty.[76] He even made the use of the sacraments an alternative to special revelation as a means of obtaining certain knowledge of being in a state of grace.[77] It must be emphasised at this point that Fisher in no way suggests that the sacraments can give certainty of ultimate salvation, in other words of final perseverance. His concern is purely with the present state of the believer.[78] Although he was probably more concerned with the sacraments as infallible channels of grace in themselves than with the subjective certainty of the recipient, Fisher's rhetoric was strong, and directed towards encouraging his readers to have confidence, at least, in grace.[79] This shift was accompanied by an increasing emphasis on 'fiducia' in his writings. We have already noticed his concern with 'fiducia' in the *Confutatio*, but in the psalm commentary and the *De Veritate* the word appears much more often. The commentary on Psalm 26 interprets it as a call to the exercise and development of trust in Christ, and that on Psalm 21 urges on its readers 'certainty' that they belong to the flock of Christ.[80] 'Fiducia' was of course presented as a gift of God, but it was something that could become stronger 'through our assent and co-operation'.[81] It is tempting to see this new direction in Fisher's theology as a response to Luther's offer of certainty of grace, which was presumably one of the most intellectually appealing features of Lutheran doctrine. But at the Council of Trent, the judgment of the Church went against the possibility of certainty about either grace or salvation (unless by means of a special revelation), although Fisher was adduced among the authorities for the contrary view.[82]

Underlying the Reformation debate about justification by faith alone was a deeper disagreement over what justification actually meant and perhaps over what it was. The Catholic view rested on the Augustinian concept of justification as a real and intrinsic process in which the sinner was cleansed of sin and made righteous through the reception by grace of Christ's 'iustitia'. As we have already hinted, there is disagreement over precisely what Luther's view of justice and justification was. Whether the doctrine of 'imputed justification' which became characteristic of Lutheranism was originated by him or Melanchthon is a matter of some dispute. But it is unnecessary to enter upon that dispute here as Luther had clearly not arrived at such a view within the period (up to 1525) that concerns us. At this stage, Luther's view of 'iustitia' seems to have remained 'real' or 'intrinsic', and he himself regarded the perception that the 'iustitia dei' was salvific rather than merely punitive as the crucial insight. Indeed, on this question of what 'iustitia' actually was there was a striking resemblance between Luther's position and Fisher's. For Fisher maintained with equal insistence that what made people just was not their own justice, but a justice conferred by God.[83] In his sermons on the penitential psalms he stated that the same justice which damned the unrepentant saved the repentant sinner.[84] And, like Luther, he made the preaching of this 'iustitia' the heart of the evangelical message. It was closely tied in his thought to Christ's mediation with the Father, and thus to the eucharist, which made that mediation present to the faithful. This connection was spelled out in his commentary on Psalm 21, which said of the eucharist: 'This is the new generation, which is gracious in the eyes of God insofar as it will be justified by the justice of the Gospel which the apostles will preach throughout the world. Christ will be the mediator and advocate between them and the Father. Whatever good they do he will announce to the Father, and he will see in turn that the justice of the Father is unceasingly proclaimed to them through the apostles and their successors.'[85] He even came close to Luther's concept of the 'fröhlich Wechsel', the joyous exchange of human sin for Christ's justice: 'For as without doubt he [Christ] has conferred upon us his justice, so that it really becomes ours, so in turn he has taken our sins upon himself, and they really become his own, not as if he had committed them himself, but so that the pain of conscience owed on their account is handed over to be suffered by him.'[86] If there is a difference between this and Luther's position, it is to be found in the clause 'so that it really becomes ours', which drives home the real appropriation of Christ's justice, rather than its mere imputation, to the convert or repentant sinner. But whether or not Luther had yet arrived at the concept of imputed justice, what was undoubtedly new in his doctrine was his view of the relationship of 'iustitia' to 'peccatum' in the justified sinner. For he did not accept that justification cleansed the person from sin, merely that it precluded that person's sin from being 'imputed' or accounted as such. Thus it was possible for him to assert, 'every person is at once just and a sinner'. The substantial co-existence of sin and justice in the person in a state of grace was a radical innovation, and one that made little sense within the Augustinian perspective, in which sin and grace are mutually exclusive. If it did not amount to a full doctrine of 'imputed justification', it was definitely pointing in that direction. And it was this that underpinned Luther's doctrine that in every good work the justified person was still committing sin. Fisher perceived how important it was to Luther to establish the compatibility of sin and grace, but at the same time he was frankly incredulous.[87] Yet despite 'scarcely understanding' what Luther was driving at, he managed to formulate what was to become the standard Catholic reply: since God was truth, then if he did not account something as sin, it could not be sin.[88] He thus later felt able to dismiss as mere contradiction his opponent's claims that on the one hand one could never be certain that one was not committing mortal sin, and that on the other, when receiving sacramental absolution, one must with utter certainty believe oneself to be genuinely absolved and therefore acceptable to God. Indeed, his refutation at this point (art. 35) was devastating. Luther had proposed that nobody could ever be certain that they were not in a state of sin because of the insidious danger of pride, often unperceived by its victims. Fisher, however, taking up what was perhaps the only passage of James that Luther approved, reminded him that 'God resists the proud, but gives grace to the humble' (James 4:6). As pride and grace were thus demonstrably incompatible, it was impossible to be both certain of being in a state of grace and uncertain about whether or not one was guilty of pride.[89]

Luther's doctrine of the compatibility of sin and justice entailed not only a new understanding of justification, but a new understanding of sin. Fisher dealt with this chiefly in article 2, where Luther argued that 'To deny that sin remains in the just even after baptism is to ride roughshod over the teaching of Christ and St Paul.' This argument was based on St Paul's remark about 'the sin that is in me' (Rom 7:17), which Luther took literally as an assertion of the survival of sin and guilt in the saint justified by grace. He identified this sin with the concupiscence of the flesh. Fisher accepted that Paul was referring to concupiscence, but took issue with Luther's unequivocal acceptance of Paul's usage of 'sin' to describe it. He therefore began by observing that Paul used the word 'sin' in several different senses. It could mean firstly the 'fomes carnis', or concupiscence, that is, the flaw left in the flesh as a result of original sin; secondly the 'motus impurus carnis', that is, the temptation experienced as the promptings of the 'fomes carnis'; and thirdly the 'consensus mentis motibus carnis impuris', that is, the free consent of the will to such temptation, which alone constituted sin in the full sense of the word. When Paul talked of 'the sin that is in me', Fisher maintained, he meant not a sinful act of the will, but the sinful tendencies and promptings of the flesh that incurred guilt only when given the consent of the will.[90] He sought to clarify this analysis with the aid of Augustine, drawing on the genuine and thoroughly anti-Pelagian *De Nuptiis et Concupiscentia*, in which Augustine first adumbrated the distinction between the 'actus' and the 'reatus' of sin that was to become central to scholastic tradition. According to this distinction, every actual sin comprised two components, the deed itself ('actus'), which was inevitably transient; and the guilt of that crime ('reatus'), which , unless remitted, endured forever. Original sin, however, was different from 'actual sin' in that its 'actus' was not transient but endured as the 'fomes carnis' until the flesh itself was dissolved in death. Its 'reatus', though, along with that of any actual sins, was fully remitted in baptism. Since it was 'reatus' that in Augustine's eyes was alone to be properly regarded as sin,[91] baptism washed all sin away. With this equipment it was easy for Fisher to dismiss Luther's case for the permanence of sin after baptism. Luther of course rejected the validity of the distinction between 'actus' and 'reatus' on the grounds that it was not to be found in scripture. Fisher's reply that the word 'reatus' did in fact occur in scripture (Ex 32:35 and Deut 21:8) was hardly adequate.[92] Luther was right to say that the distinction was not explicitly drawn in scripture: the real question was whether or not the distinction was an authentic interpretation of scripture. The crux was whether concupiscence was sin *qua* guilt, in which case Luther's thesis would stand; or whether it was sin only *qua* effect, in which case baptism really did remit all sin. Luther made a disingenuous attempt to recruit Augustine's support, seizing on Augustine's admission that baptism did not remove the 'actus' of original sin and suggesting that he therefore did not believe that baptism remitted all sin. Fisher was able to refute this with a crushing chain of anti-Pelagian citations explicitly confining sin in its strict sense to 'reatus' and allowing it to apply only in a loose sense to 'actus' or concupiscence.[93] He pointed to Augustine's frequent observation that Paul called concupiscence 'sin' in the same way that people referred to hand-writing as a 'hand' and to language as a 'tongue' – that is, by extension from cause to effect, rather than by nature.[94] The culmination of this was the citation of Augustine's indignant rebuttal of Pelagius's allegation that Catholics did not accept the eradication of sin by baptism.[95] From Paul himself, Fisher cited the remark 'nihil ergo damnationis est his qui sunt Christo Iesu' (Romans 8:1). But since he interpreted this to mean that no sin remained in those in a state of grace, while Luther argued that this same text showed that, even though sin remained, it was not imputed as guilt to those in a state of grace, this was hardly conclusive.[96] Nevertheless, Fisher was able to call upon an impressive patristic consensus for the remission of all sin in baptism, citing not only Augustine, but Jerome, Ambrose, Origen, Cyprian and Chrysostom.[97] While the debate over what Paul meant must go on, there can be no doubt that Fisher had the better of Luther in interpreting Augustine and the tradition of the Church.

The reason why concupiscence of the flesh could not be identified with sin as such by Fisher or Augustine was their shared belief that there could be no sin without the consent of the will, which in turn could be accorded only if the will was genuinely free.[98] It is therefore consistent of Luther to have abandoned not only the traditional teaching on sin and concupiscence but also that on free will. Article 36 of his *Assertio Omnium Articulorum* took the denial of free will further than any other of his writings – 'omnia de absoluta necessitate eveniunt', 'all things happen by absolute necessity' – and it was against this article that Erasmus was to direct the attack of *De Libero Arbitrio*. Fisher's defence of free will was, like Erasmus's, solidly scriptural and patristic. It was founded on a threefold distinction of human freedom as dealt with in scripture: the liberty of nature, available to all, 'which in Paul is called the power of doing this or that', which included the freedom to commit sin as well as to pursue material goods; the liberty of grace, available to those in a state of grace, to perform meritorious acts; and the liberty of glory, available to the souls of the just in heaven, the freedom to love God absolutely (Rom 8:21).[99] Although it has been described as scholastic,[100] this tripartite division is not to be found in the pages of Aquinas, Scotus or even Peter Lombard. In fact it derives from Bernard of Clairvaux's treatise *De Gratia et Libero Arbitrio*, a highly Augustinian and far from scholastic work.[101] The point of this distinction, for Fisher, was to explain how freedom of the will could exist without grace, even though without grace the free will was unable to attain or pursue certain ends. To his argument from scripture Fisher added the usual catena of patristic testimony.[102] Directing his attack against a position which was not merely anti-Pelagian but frankly determinist, he was concerned as much with human freedom to commit sin as freedom to do good. His fear was that Luther's attribution of all events to absolute necessity meant making God rather than people morally responsible for sin – an error he thought worse than that of the Manicheans, who had at least explained evil by postulating an anti-God.[103] Once free will was denied, moreover, he could not see how sinners could ever be persuaded to attend the sermons which might inspire them to repentance.[104] The pastoral agenda underlying this position emerged in his exposition of Psalm 35, which he interpreted as an affirmation of free will against determinism. Here he emphasised to his readers that their sins were their own free acts and not the workings of an irresistible destiny.[105] There remained of course a problem in reconciling divine prescience with human liberty, and it cannot be said that Fisher made any original contribution to resolving it. His was after all a practical rather than a speculative intellect. He contented himself with the patristic consensus that the two were indeed reconcilable.[106]

Fisher's dependence on Augustine, already quite clear, becomes still more apparent if we consider his teaching on justification in its own right rather than as a response to Luther. His starting-point, as Surtz correctly concluded, was the absolute and prior necessity of grace for salvation. But he insisted on the cooperation of free will with grace. He affirmed the indispensability of grace unequivocally, speaking of grace as 'the only salvation of the soul'.[107] If he spoke happily of the role of free will in preparing sinners for grace, he made it perfectly plain that this preparation itself required God's special help.[108] He referred to this variously as 'primary', 'auxiliary' and 'prevenient' grace[109] – and taught that it could not be merited, but was freely offered by God to sinners. When he talked of the sinner 'doing what lay in him', he was careful to qualify this with the words 'through the assistance of grace'.[110] He firmly rejected the theory of 'meritum ex congruo' favoured by the Scotists and the *via moderna*, denying that those in a state of mortal sin could, without the aid of grace, perform morally good acts or prepare themselves for justifying grace.[111] Instead he associated himself with Gregory of Rimini's theory, which was itself based on Augustine's,[112] and expressed a preference for the patristic over the scholastic account of justification. Although other theologians sometimes left it unclear whether, in affirming the necessity of God's help in doing good, they were referring to the help of grace or merely to the 'general influence' by which God sustained the whole of creation, Fisher put his own position beyond all possible doubt: 'The fathers taught that nobody could wish anything good without the special help of God, and that the general influence of God was not enough. On the other hand, several scholastics argued that this influence was enough to enable people to behave morally and do good works without that special help.' He then rejected the scholastic view on the grounds that it would mean that even Pharaoh, after God had hardened his heart, would have been able to do good – which he found incredible.[113] Ths shows that he did not espouse the doctrine of the universal availability of auxiliary grace, adopting instead the argument of Augustine and the fathers that in certain cases (such as Pharaoh's) God withdrew even this grace from those who had consistently and utterly spurned it.[114] This was not a view that won universal acceptance among subsequent Catholic theologians.[115] In its main outlines, however, his doctrine of grace was that of post-Tridentine orthodoxy. Justification depended not only on experiencing the initial auxiliary grace, but on responding correctly to it. It was open to the will to accept or reject it.[116] The required response was either faith and repentance (in the case of the pagan) or repentance (in the case of the Christian who had relapsed into sin), followed by either baptism or penance, which would compensate for the inadequacy and uncertainty of merely human faith and contrition, and convey to the recipient the fullness of saving or justifying grace. Fisher conceded that the sacraments were not indispensable – as was demonstrated by the example of the penitent thief to whom Christ promised a place in paradise.[117] But he saw this as the exception rather than the rule, and reckoned that Luther's insistence on 'faith alone' made the sacraments redundant. Since Luther argued that Christ's words 'Anyone who believes and is baptised will be saved' (Mk 16:16) amounted to a statement of justification by faith alone, Fisher could not see why he thought that Christ had mentioned baptism at all.[118] In short, he reminded Luther of the difference between a necessary and a sufficient cause. Saving grace was necessary and sufficient; faith was necessary, but not usually sufficient; baptism was sufficient but not invariably necessary.[119] Similarly he could not see what room Luther's emphasis on personal faith in the sacrament of penance left for the role of sacerdotal absolution.[120] Luther was of course eventually to abandon the doctrine of sacramental penance. But although his doctrine of faith, if taken to its extreme, would indeed have reduced even baptism and the eucharist to mere symbols, his commitment to the literal sense of scripture – which inculcated the necessity of these two sacraments – kept him from going that far. Other Protestants did of course reduce the role of these two sacraments from the real and effectual to the declaratory or symbolic.

At the end of article 36 Fisher concluded his treatment of free will with a brief but coherent summary of his theology of justification, based upon the story of the centurion Cornelius (Acts 10:1–48) and on the parable of the publican and the pharisee (Lk 18:10–14), which respectively concerned the justification of an unbeliever and of a fallen believer. In the case of the publican and the pharisee, Fisher argued that their decisions to go to the Temple had both been made freely at the prompting of divine grace. But only the publican had responded properly to that grace by acknowledging his sin and begging forgiveness, and therefore he alone was granted forgiveness and grace and went down from the Temple justified. From this parable Fisher concluded that by acknowledging sin, praying and doing anything else that lay in his power, the sinner could, with the help of auxiliary grace, not only avoid mortal sin but also perform morally good acts and thus merit forgiveness.[121] The position of the centurion Cornelius before the angel was sent to him was like that of the catechumen – he was endowed with grace enough to do works and live well, but not enough to reach the kingdom of heaven. Only afterwards was he fully incorporated into the Church through the sacraments. Fisher drew this exegesis directly from Augustine, borrowing the simile that initial grace was to the grace of baptismal rebirth as conception was to natural birth.[122] He therefore concluded that it would be impudence to dismiss as mortal sins the works which Cornelius performed before he received sanctifying grace, even though he insisted that those works were the fruit of a prior grace.[123] Yet at this point, within sight as it were of the final fence, Fisher seems to fall, because he tries to tie up his argument with long citations from the *De Ecclesiasticis Dogmatibus*, a work widely attributed to Augustine but in fact composed by Gennadius of Marseilles, a late fifth-century Semipelagian with a low opinion of Augustine.[124] Worse still, the chosen passages are, to the reader aware of their authorship, shot through with Semipelagian observations. They entirely avoid the word 'grace' and make divine assistance secondary to and contingent upon the correct exercise of free will. Nevertheless, Fisher's profound Augustinianism redeemed even such infelicitous texts, glossing them according to the mind of Augustine rather than that of their true author. The first text hinted at the Pelagian teaching that God invited sinners to salvation not through grace, but through revealing his law: 'Free will (that is, a rational will) manages to pursue salvation, given the prior admonition and invitation of God.' Fisher, though, sanitised this with the gloss 'which comes about through primary grace'.[125] In the second text, Gennadius expanded on his theme by placing the 'beginning of salvation' ('initium salutis') firmly within human power. He admitted that salvation was God's gift, but it was clearly there for the taking, and perseverance was a matter of personal responsibility with merely the assistance of God:

We have the beginning of our salvation by the mercy of God. Assent to his saving inspiration is within our power. That we receive what we desire by assenting to his warning, is a gift of God. That we do not fall away from this state of salvation is at once a matter for our concern and for God's assistance. If we do fall away, that is the result of our own choice and idleness.[126]

Again, Fisher's paraphrase introduced the priority and necessity of grace:

First comes the beginning of our salvation, by which we understand the primary grace which incites us to do good. Then comes the assent of our will, by which we follow that stimulus. He says that this lies within our power. Third is saving grace, by which we are made pleasing to God. This is a gift of God alone. Fourth is perseverance in grace, which is a matter not only for our concern, but also for the divine assistance. Fifth is the fall from grace, which is purely a matter of our will, done by ourselves alone.[127]

A scholar who could 'Augustinise' such an unsuitable passage was never going to be an acute textual critic. But he was clearly neither a Pelagian nor a Semipelagian. The only point on which Fisher really agreed with Gennadius was that on which Augustine really agreed with Pelagius, namely the individual's full responsibility for sin. Fisher's final words on justification are therefore authentically Augustinian. He presents a process in four stages: first the 'prima gratia', knocking on the door of the sinner's heart; then the free acceptance of that grace by the will, in repentance of past sins; next the reception of justifying grace conferred through the sacraments of baptism or penance; and finally the perseverance in grace through the co-operation of free will with grace.

The analysis of Fisher's handling of justification has been especially rewarding. The discussion has raised many issues, and has cast light on a number of vexed questions concerning the early Reformation. The main conclusion with respect to Fisher's theology has been to demolish the notion that he was a Pelagian. It has been possible to go beyond this and demonstrate his dissociation not only from Pelagius, but also from the Semipelagians and even from the scholastics with whom he has too often and too casually been classified.[128] On the contrary, his teaching was unequivocally Augustinian in its commitment both to the freedom of the will and to the indispensability of grace, in its interpretation of 'iustitia', and in its account of sin, baptism and concupiscence. This in turn confirms one of the emerging themes of this study, namely the fundamentally patristic orientation of Fisher's theology. In passing, the Augustinian quality of Fisher's critique of Luther has raised doubts about the mature Luther's affiliation to Augustine. However, even in such an Augustinian mode, Fisher definitely showed many signs of his scholastic background, notably an essentially Aristotelian approach to moral acts. The most unexpected finding, though, is a certain convergence with Luther's thought, apparent most of all in his emphasis on fiduciary faith and in his growing tendency to affirm the possibility of certainty about grace – a development which perhaps reflected the response of a pastoral theologian to one of Luther's more attractive doctrines. The focus of this development was in the sacraments, and in particular in the sacrament of the eucharist. It will be the task of the next chapter to explore his theology of this central sacrament, and to assess the importance that it occupied in his theological system.

8

The eucharist

JOHN FISHER'S THEOLOGY of justification, unlike that of Luther and the Reformers, left room for the sacraments to play an active part in the Christian life. For him, as for the Christian tradition since the earliest times, the eucharist was pre-eminent among the sacraments. A considerable body of theological speculation, as well as of devotional practice, had grown up around this sacrament, especially in the Middle Ages. It is therefore no surprise that the eucharist should have rapidly become one of the most bitterly contested issues of the Reformation. Nowhere was this more true than in England, where the eucharist probably provoked more debate between Catholics and Protestants than any other single question. Three of Fisher's polemical works deal largely with aspects of the eucharistic controversy. The *Defensio Regiae Assertionis* and the *Sacri Sacerdotii Defensio* defend the sacrifice of the mass and the concomitant doctrine of the sacrificing priesthood against Luther, and the *De Veritate* is a defence of the real presence in the eucharist against the Swiss Reformer Oecolampadius. These three books provide the framework of this chapter, which thus looks first at the mass, then at the priesthood and finally at the sacrament in itself. Since this analysis also amounts to a chronological approach, it affords us an opportunity to examine the development of Fisher's response to Reformed eucharistic doctrine. For the new challenges posed at successive stages of the debate elicited from him new responses in a process of development which again undermines the notion that he was an entirely conventional theologian. This notion is further undermined by the assessment of the relative role of the scholastics and the fathers in his eucharistic theology, and from the identification of the authorities to whom he owed a particular debt. Finally, the chance survival of a devotional treatise on the eucharist helps us to put some flesh on the dry bones of his theology and to see how doctrine and devotion were related in his thinking on the sacrament.

The concept of eucharistic sacrifice had been the subject of remarkable unanimity since the very dawn of the Church. The language of sacrifice and oblation had been applied to the sacrament by Paul himself (1 Cor 10:16–21), as well as in such post-apostolic writings as the *Didache* and the Ignatian epistles. The doctrine underwent especially extensive development in the West, where sacrifice became the dominant motif of the Latin eucharistic rite. This led, in the later Middle Ages, to an emphasis in Catholic liturgical practice on the mass as a work of satisfaction for sin, and ultimately to the almost mechanical multiplication of masses, a custom or abuse which may have tended to compromise the doctrine of the sufficiency of Christ's sacrifice on the cross. Luther's repudiation of eucharistic sacrifice was thus a complete break with traditional theology and liturgy. But it was a logical consequence of his fundamental principles. The doctrine of justification by faith alone rendered satisfaction for sin not merely redundant but a presumptuous blasphemy. Reliance on scripture alone led Luther to question a doctrine for which he, at least, could find no scriptural warrant. The core of his case against the sacrifice of the mass lay in his new theory of the sacraments, according to which the essence of a sacrament was a 'word of promise' ('verbum promissionis') by which Christ assured forgiveness of sins to those who had faith in him and thus in his words and promises. From this perspective, what mattered about the last supper were Christ's words 'this is the new testament in my blood, which will be shed for the forgiveness of sins'. On this Luther based his claim that the mass was not a sacrifice but a testament, an analogy which he expounded by casting Christ as a testator, bequeathing forgiveness to his heirs. Luther maintained that this 'new testament' was Christ's blood as such, because Luke had written 'hoc poculum novum testamentum in meo sanguine'.[1] Since the fruit of this new testament was the forgiveness of sins, Luther saw communion as a sacrament in which sins were forgiven.[2] All that was necessary was to believe Christ's promise and accept his bequest. Faith alone attained the good offered by the eucharist. Later on Luther and other Protestants added to this theory a reading of Hebrews 7:27 (which described Christ's sacrifice on the cross as done 'once and for all'), by which they laid such emphasis on the sole sufficiency of the cross that any further sacrifice was rendered superfluous. On the principle that the function of the priest was to offer sacrifice (Heb 5:1), it was a short step to argue that Christ was the only priest and that all Christians, to the extent that they participated in Christ, participated in his unique priesthood and sacrifice. Hence came the doctrine of the priesthood of all believers, and the denial of the sacrificing priesthood of the Catholic ministry.

Fisher first grappled with Luther's eucharistic theology in the *Confutatio*, where he outlined arguments in favour of sacrifice and priesthood that he was to explore further in the *Defensio* and the *Sacri Sacerdotii*. Discussion of sacrifice arose in the course of article 15 where Luther argued that faith alone, rather than examination of conscience and confession, was the prerequisite of receiving communion. The problem, in Fisher's eyes, originated with Luther's identification of the new testament with Christ's blood and the forgiveness of sins.[3] To him this represented a complete misapprehension of the nature of the covenant, and of its relationship with sacrifice. In reply, he gave his own definition of the new testament in an overtly scholastic form which is for that very reason noteworthy. The new testament, he declared, was 'a new law, laid down by Christ and sealed in his blood, whose followers are made heirs to the kingdom of heaven'.[4] On this basis he then drew out the parallels between the old and the new testaments. The old concerned the law of Moses, inscribed on stone; the new concerned the law of Christ, the law of grace, the Gospel, inscribed on human hearts. Each covenant was sealed in blood – the old in that of a goat, the new in that of Christ himself. And each was commemorated in a memorial sacrifice – the old in the Passover, the new in the mass. Fisher noted in particular the parallel between the words of Moses, 'This is the blood of the testament which God has imposed on you' (Exod 24:8), and those of Christ, 'This cup is the new testament in my blood' (Lk 22:20). The former blood, he maintained, although powerless in itself, was the 'figure' of Christ's blood, in which there was redemption and the forgiveness of sins.[5]

Fisher's treatment of the sacrifice of the mass brings out once more the strongly patristic orientation of his theology. He was primarily anxious to establish that the Church had always believed the eucharist to be in a real sense a sacrifice offered to the Father in propitiation for sins. To this effect he produced a dozen patristic citations describing the Christian liturgy as a sacrifice or offering. In the systematic way that characterised his mature writings, he gave first the Greek fathers and then the Latins, adding the spurious Acts of Andrew and Life of Matthew, as well as some early (that is, pseudo-Isidorean) papal decretals.[6] The Reformers of course did not deny that the language of sacrifice had long been applied to the eucharist. Rather, they held that the sacrifice consisted not in propitiation but in praise and thanksgiving. Fisher's reply was their own contention that since Christ's sacrifice was 'once and for all', no other sacrifice was possible. If the mass was any sort of a sacrifice, he argued, it could be none other than the sacrifice of the cross itself. Otherwise it must inevitably compromise the sufficiency of that sacrifice.[7] The identity of the sacrifice of the mass with that of the cross was an ancient theme in Catholic theology, though it had perhaps become obscured in the later Middle Ages. But Fisher, taking it up from patristic sources, put it at the heart of his polemic. Seeking to corroborate his theory from scripture, he pursued further the correspondence between the sacrifices of the old testament and that of Christ. Drawing on Paul, he explored the concept of Christ as the fulfilment of paschal sacrifice by pointing out that under the old law the paschal lamb had to be eaten as well as sacrificially killed by the faithful. While Christ's death on the cross fulfilled the first aspect of the sacrifice, it was the eucharistic meal, in which Christ gave himself to be eaten by his followers, that fulfilled the second aspect. He found confirmation of this in Paul's argument that if eating pagan sacrifices was to participate with demons, then eating the eucharist was to participate in Christ (1 Cor 10:16–21). The force of this analogy for Fisher was to prove that the eucharist was as much a sacrifice as were the animal offerings of the pagans.[8] Evidence of a different kind was derived from the fulfilment of prophecy. Taking up the prophecies that Christ was to be a priest according to the order of Melchisedek (Ps 109:4), and that a sacrifice would be offered everywhere in his name (Mal 1:11), he emphasised the traditional association of the eucharist with Melchisedek's sacrifice of bread and wine. If the mass was not that universal sacrifice, he contended, then Malachi's prophecy had not been fulfilled.[9] His only entirely original argument was the erroneous derivation of the word 'missa' for the eucharist from a Hebrew root implying sacrifice. This was based on an etymology in Reuchlin's *De Rudimentis Hebraicis*, and proved surprisingly popular among Fisher's polemical heirs.[10]

The reputation for die-hard conservatism that has clung to Fisher has given rise to the misrepresentation of his views on the eucharist as on other matters. In a recent study of early sixteenth-century English teaching on eucharistic sacrifice, his writings have been adduced as evidence that a number of theologically dubious positions were then prevalent, namely:

i that the priest's sacrifice on the altar was separate from Christ's sacrifice on the cross;
ii that the priest was a mediator between Christ and the congregation;
iii that the sacrifice of the mass was located not in the consecration but in a separate act of offering by the priest.[11]

They all revolve around whether or not the mass is essentially identical with the sacrifice of the cross. If it is not, then the priest is clearly a mediator other than Christ and there is no necessary connection between the words of consecration, which make the body and blood of Christ present, and whatever other action might be taken to constitute the offering. These propositions thus provide an excellent route by which to approach Fisher's actual teaching. As we shall see, they rest on a narrow and casual reading of Fisher's works. The claim that he separated the sacrifice of the mass from that of the cross is particularly hard to justify as he explicitly stated on several occasions that the two sacrifices were essentially one and the same.[12] In explanation he cited Chrysostom to the effect that the last supper (and thus the mass) was the same sacrifice as that of the cross, because the latter completed what the former had begun.[13] The assertion that Fisher located the sacrifice of the mass elsewhere than in the consecration is disproved by his own definition of the mass as 'a ceremony or action of a priest [such that] while the eucharist is consecrated upon the altar, at the same time the sacrifice of the crucified Christ is proclaimed'.[14] He made this even clearer with such comments as 'the consecration of the eucharist really is a sacrifice' and 'as often as we consecrate the bread and wine, we make them holy, and we sacrifice, and we in every way perform a sacrifice'.[15] Indeed, one of his favourite arguments for the reality of the sacrifice of the mass was that since Christ used the present tense in saying that his blood 'is shed for you' and that his body 'is given for you', he was identifying the essence of the last supper with the essence of the crucifixion.[16] The firmness with which Fisher located both consecration and oblation in the words of institution helps us in addition to appreciate his view of Christ as the operative priest in the mass. He undoubtedly saw the celebrant as a mediator. But he insisted that *qua* mediator the priest's action was not distinct from that of Christ.[17] Nor for that matter did he exclude the congregation from the act of offering (although they could not join in the offering without a priest to celebrate). In his exposition of Psalm 19:4 he affirmed that those hearing mass should join with all their hearts in offering the sacrifice to God.[18]

Underpinning this traditional yet unconventional account of eucharistic sacrifice was a thorough acquaintance with the writings of John Chrysostom. Fisher's argument in the *De Veritate* that the mass and the cross were one sacrifice was wholly dependent on him. Citing a long passage which propounded the essential unity of the sacrifice of the altar with that of the cross, he noted that Chrysostom 'labours to explain how it can be that this sacrificial victim which was offered for us upon the cross is altogether the same as that which we offer daily'.[19] The passage in question read:

Do we not offer [sacrifice] every day? Indeed we do, as a memorial of his death. It is one victim not many. How can it be one and not many? Because that which was once offered, was offered in the holy of holies. This sacrifice is an instantiation ['exemplar'] of that one. We always offer the selfsame thing, not one lamb today and another tomorrow, but always the same.[20]

As a graduate of the Aristotelian tradition, Fisher did not altogether grasp or accept the Platonic metaphysics of ideal and exemplar on which Chrysostom's analysis was founded. Instead he explained that Chrysostom was postulating a difference of manner or relation rather than of matter ('non rei quidem, sed rationis') between the sacrifices. But although he was unable to cast off the scholastic apparatus with which he came to Chrysostom, he was able to break away from the tendencies in late medieval theology to separate the mass from the cross. The same authority was employed to establish the identification of the priestly words of consecration with the words of Christ at the last supper. Chrysostom had argued that since the words Christ spoke were the same as those that the priests recited the sacrifice was also the same. This enabled Fisher to link the sacrifice directly to the words of consecration, and thus to present the priest as a mere channel or vehicle for the priestly action of Christ. This final link in the chain was itself forged with the aid of a further citation from Chrysostom: 'It is not men who sanctify this, but Christ, who sacrificed before. As the words that Christ spoke are the same as those that priests now utter, so too the offering is the same.' And a little later: 'This is the body of Christ, and so is that. Anyone who thinks that the one is at all inferior to the other does not know that it is Christ himself who is present and who acts.'

Fisher's typical gloss on this ('now you can see, reader, that it is Christ who is present and offers the sacrifice') shows that he fully appreciated the implication that Christ was priest and victim in the mass: precisely because it was Christ rather than the priest who really performed the sacrifice, no more was offered by a good and holy minister than by a sinful one.[21]

The argument so far has indicated that the doctrine of eucharistic sacrifice is inextricably bound up with that of the special priesthood. It was therefore inevitable that in abandoning the former, Luther should have abandoned the latter, although this consequence was not made entirely clear until the publication of the *De Abroganda Missa Privata* in 1522. There was thus a good deal of sense in Fisher's decision to publish his defence of the priesthood together with his defence of the mass. The *Sacri Sacerdotii Defensio* was an economical refutation of Luther divided into three sections or 'congressus' ('attacks'), which corresponded with the familiar scholastic triad of authority, scripture and reason. In the first he adduced an impressive array of Latin and Greek fathers in evidence of the constant teaching of the Church.[22] The second section proceeded to the scriptures, developing an argument in ten axioms which progressed from the necessity of a special ministry of some sort to the conclusion that Christ had ordained the apostles as priests to offer the sacrifice he instituted at the last supper. Proving first that there was indeed a scriptural ministry established in the New Testament (axiom 1) by Christ (axiom 2), he argued that this ministry needed to be, and had in fact been, endowed with special grace adequate to its performance (axioms 3 and 4). This ministry, he continued, must have been meant to endure (axiom 5). It was clear from the New Testament that Christian ministers had to be called by the Church and the Holy Spirit, and had to receive ordination and mission (axioms 6 and 7). The crucial stages of the argument were those in which he proposed that ordination was a sacrament conferred in the rite of laying on of hands (axioms 8 and 9). In conclusion (axiom 10), he identified this ministry with the priesthood on the grounds that this was necessary to fulfil the prophecy of Malachi. Identifying the messianic sacrifice with that of Melchisedek, offered by Christ in bread and wine at the last supper, he took Christ's injunction to the apostles, 'Hoc facite in meam commemorationem', as tantamount to ordination.[23]

The most important feature of Fisher's defence of the sacrament of ordination is his concentration on the laying on of hands. This is yet another instance of his preference for the fathers over the scholastics. The theologians of the schools had mostly come to believe that ordination, like the other sacraments, must have 'matter' and 'form'. Assuming (out of ignorance of history) that the medieval ordination rite was that of the early Church, they found 'matter' in the 'tradition of the implements', the relatively late practice by which the ordinand was ceremonially handed some object related to the order he was about to receive (a copy of the gospels for a deacon, or a chalice and paten for a priest). This view was enshrined in the decree of the Council of Florence that secured reunion with the Armenians, by which the latter were obliged to add the tradition of the implements to their ordination rite (which of course already included the laying on of hands).[24] As representative a sixteenth-century theologian as Ruard Tapper was of the opinion that this decree was definitive, although he was in fact aware that the practice had been unknown in the early Church. He even claimed that the laying on of hands was not essential to the sacrament.[25] Fisher, in departing from that consensus, was taking a stand upon the scriptures and the primitive Church. The use of the laying on of hands for the appointment of ministers occurs throughout Acts and the Pauline epistles, and was frequently mentioned by the early fathers. The evidence Fisher cited was in fact drawn mostly from scripture, although he also referred to Jerome, and can hardly have been ignorant of the patristic view.[26]

The third congressus, corresponding to reason in the scholastic triad, was a refutation of selected arguments proposed by Luther. Fisher's main objection was that Luther proved too much. In Luther's rhetorical question 'what need is there of a priest, when there is no need of a mediator or teacher?' he saw an argument for dispensing with any kind of ministry, not merely with a sacrificing priesthood.[27] And in reply he had no difficulty in demonstrating from scripture the need at least for preachers and teachers even under the new law.[28] In cooler moments, of course, Luther upheld the need for some ministry, but there is no doubt that on this occasion, as so often, his rhetoric ran away with him. Luther's more telling argument based on the priesthood of all believers was defused by Fisher's acceptance of it. Admitting that Peter had described Christians as 'a royal priesthood, an holy nation' (1 Pet 2:9), he observed that Peter was merely repeating terms that had been applied to the people of Israel (Exod 19:6). Since this common priesthood had not kept the Jews from having in addition a special priesthood, charged with specifically sacerdotal duties, Fisher could not see why it should prevent the Christian Church from having a similar special priesthood. Making some capital out of the equally implausible deduction that the common kingship of all believers would dispense with the need for government in a Christian society, he emphasised that the common priesthood, like the common kingship, was something which individuals exercised over themselves alone, and which involved no authority over others.[29] He showed similar critical ability in dealing with some of the other scriptural texts and arguments which Luther produced in support of his position. The fact that the New Testament did not use the word 'priests' of Christian ministers did not disturb him, as he had little time for the argument from silence.[30] It was clear to him that the 'presbyteroi' and 'episkopoi' of the New Testament corresponded roughly to priests and bishops, and he was not deterred by the apparently undifferentiated use of the two terms in the Acts and the Epistles. That the term 'presbyter' implied seniority by rank rather than by age (as the literal sense of 'old man' would suggest) was proved for him by Paul's reference to ordaining 'elders' (Titus 1:4), and by the fact that Timothy, who was a young man (1 Tim 4:12), was clearly himself an elder or bishop.[31] The confusion between 'presbyteroi' and 'episkopoi' was no more serious for him than that in the Gospels between disciples and apostles. The fact that John nowhere used the term 'apostle' did not imply that there was no difference between them and the other disciples.[32] As for the avoidance of the term 'hiereus' (priest) for Christian ministers, he argued that this reflected a deliberate decision by the early Christians to avoid giving offence to the priests who were still officiating under the old law in the Temple, and to preclude confusion between the two bodies.[33] He did not accept, however, Luther's claim that the New Testament in no way suggested that Christian ministers offered sacrifice. Interpreting Acts 13:2 with the aid of Erasmus, he noted that the Greek term 'leitourgiantes' used here could be rendered as 'making sacrifice'.[34] This was perhaps a little disingenuous, as the sacrifice Erasmus had in mind at this point was the sacrifice of a holy life. But Fisher was justified in his reading since in the Greek scriptures 'leitourgia' usually refers to specifically priestly, sacrificial functions.[35] This shows an interesting ability to use Erasmus rather than merely to follow him slavishly. And it would be wrong to think that Fisher's view of sacrifice failed to link holiness of life with the offering of the mass. Commenting on Ps 19:4 he stated that any virtuous action done with a pure heart in a state of grace was an acceptable sacrifice to God, and he immediately linked this to the eucharist by proceeding to talk about the sacrifice of the altar.[36] This turning of Erasmus to advantage was seized upon by many of Fisher's polemical heirs, including Alfonso Salmeron, who introduced it into the Tridentine debates, and was frank enough to admit that Fisher's interpretation had not been in Erasmus's mind. Predictably, he concluded that Fisher was nevertheless correct.[37]

The distinctive contribution of the South German Reformers to the Reformation debates on the eucharist was the denial of the real presence therein of Christ's body and blood. Led by Zwingli, they worked out a symbolic interpretation of the crucial words 'hoc est corpus meum' that famously kept Luther from abandoning a doctrine which on *a priori* grounds he had been inclined to suspect as a popish imposture, and for which his doctrine of justification left little room.[38] But the symbolic interpretation was highly problematic, being contrary to the interpretation of the majority of Christian writers since the second century. If the new doctrine was to retain credibility, some reinterpretation of that tradition was clearly necessary, and this was what in 1525 Oecolampadius set out to provide with his *De Genuina Interpretatione*. This lengthy and learned essay proposed that the 'realist' language of the fathers should be read in the light of the 'symbolic' language that they also used of the sacrament. This convenient exegetical contrivance enabled him to evade the realist implications of all but the most uncompromising authorities. There

were three important refutations of his work. The Lutheran Bilibald Pirckheimer (who subsequently returned to Catholicism) produced a pamphlet in
1526, and the Catholic Josse Clichtove issued a rather longer reply the following year.[39] But by far the most substantial and successful attack was Fisher's
De Veritate Corporis et Sanguinis Christi in Eucharistia, his longest single work.
Because of its great length (about 220,000 words), Fisher divided it, along with
his opponent's original essay, into five sections or books, to each of which
he attached a separate preface. These prefaces, which together amounted to
nearly a sixth of the work, were self-contained treatises on various aspects of
eucharistic theology. Unconstrained by the exigencies of detailed refutation,
they were more readable than the books they introduced. This is probably why
most of the references to the work by subsequent writers are in fact to the
prefaces, and why Cochlaeus confined his attention to them when he published
a German translation in 1528.[40] It is also why we shall concentrate on the
prefaces, which provide a more coherent account of Fisher's own eucharistic
theology, in our examination of the *De Veritate*.

The first preface was a general introduction in which Fisher made two main
points. First he emphasised the differences over the eucharist that had arisen
primarily between Luther and Oecolampadius, but also between other Reformers such as Zwingli, Carlstadt, Melanchthon, Capito, Lambert and
Hubmaier. In their internecine dissensions he claimed to see the vengeance
and judgment of God on those who had broken the unity of the Church.[41]
Secondly, and with more direct relevance to what was to come, he warned the
reader against the fraudulent disputative techniques of Oecolampadius himself
who, he alleged, systematically mutilated his patristic citations, ripped them
from their true context and misrepresented their implications.[42] Such accusa-
tions were of course common in Reformation polemic, and were facilitated by
the lack of established texts over which to argue, but on this occasion they were
not entirely unjustified. Fisher was a careful reader, and any such charges he
made were not made lightly, and should not be taken so. Although some of the
misquotations of which he convicted Oecolampadius are doubtless mere errors
of transcription, and often have little bearing on the argument, others are too
convenient to allow such a generous explanation, and strongly suggest
dishonesty. Several instances can be shown where an omission facilitated
Oecolampadius's case: the omission of 'why one and not many?' from the
passage of Chrysostom which argued the identity of the liturgical sacrifice with
that of the cross; of the crucial clause 'iuxta anagogen' from a text of Jerome
which interpreted Christ's injunction to 'eat my flesh' *anagogically* as a reference
to reading the scriptures; of 'that is, Christ' from Cyprian's exposition of 'daily
bread' in the Lord's Prayer; and of 'the flesh of the Lord' from Ignatius of
Antioch's description of the eucharist.[43] On the other hand, the omission of a
line from Hilary's *De Trinitate* was most probably a slip of the eye.[44] Fisher's

charge of citation out of context was borne out most notably in Oecolampadius's selection of a passage from Ambrose's sermons on the Psalms without so much as a hint that it followed immediately upon one of the most realist of all patristic comments on the sacrament.[45] Wilful misrepresentation can be observed by anyone who cares to check Oecolampadius's claim that Augustine equated unworthy reception of the sacrament with not paying due attention to scripture readings. His source shows that the issue was careless or negligent reception – dropping or spilling the sacred species – rather than communion made in sin.[46]

The second preface was one of Fisher's most original conceptions, an exploration of the nature of the sacrament through the multifarious names applied to it by various fathers. Inspired by 'Dionysius's' excursus on the many names of God, and perhaps also by Cabbalistic exegesis,[47] it proposed that just as the nature of God could not be exhaustively described by any or all of the myriad names and titles used of him, so likewise the mystery of the eucharist was too profound to be plumbed by any or all of its names and titles. The titles that he listed manifested a wide acquaintance with the fathers: 'corpus domini' (Paul); 'sacramentum corporis et sanguinis Christi' (Augustine); 'mysteria' (Chrysostom); 'synaxis' or 'communio' ('Dionysius'); 'eucharistia', which for him had a twofold signification as 'bona gratia' and 'gratiarum actio'; 'sacrificium'; 'panis supersubstantialis' (Augustine again); 'cibus dominicus' (Hilary); 'viaticum'; 'supplementum vivificum' (Augustine yet again); 'benedictio mystica' (Cyril); 'convivium' (Jerome); and 'exemplar' (Basil the Great).[48] While his interpretation of those titles adumbrated many of the themes of his eucharistic spirituality, his main point was to emphasise the ineffability of the sacrament, and thus to associate it by analogy with the divine. The diversity of its titles served to emphasise the sacrament's transcendence, an argument he had already introduced against Oecolampadius's reduction of it to mere symbol.[49] The preface moreover illustrates perfectly the distance between the mind of Fisher and that of the scholastic whose theology he most closely approached, Thomas Aquinas. Thomas had regarded the multiplicity of names as a problem to be explained rather than a point to be exploited. Where he divided a narrower selection of titles into three specific categories of significance, related to the sacrament as Christ's presence, as sacrifice and as symbol of unity, Fisher in contrast found an indication of its unfathomable riches.[50]

This is not to suggest that Fisher was endeavouring to break away from the scholastic heritage. In other ways his eucharistic theology stands particularly close to that of Thomas. Whereas most scholastics from Scotus onwards regarded transubstantiation as an antecedently improbable explanation of the real presence, accepting it only on the authority of the Lateran Council,[51] Thomas had thought it the only coherent explanation, a view with which Fisher concurred. Even in the second preface, where his approach to the names of the eucharist diverged from that of Thomas, Fisher made use of the Thomistic analysis of the threefold signification of the sacrament, in which the separation of the species signified Christ's sacrifice on the cross, and communion signified both the unity of Christians in Christ and the messianic banquet in heaven.[52] He adopted these distinctions in order to combat one of Oecolampadius's most plausible arguments against the real presence, namely that a thing could not be both a sign and the reality it signified. Fisher was able to evade the dilemma of having something acting as the sign of itself by making the species of bread and wine a sign of the reality of the body and blood they contained. He was also able to explain why the fathers had used the symbolic language that Oecolampadius turned to advantage against the real presence. Where Oecolampadius insisted on reinterpreting the realist language according to the symbolic, Fisher reconciled the two as describing the sacrament under different aspects. The *locus classicus* for their difference in approach was the interpretation of Tertullian's remark that Christ 'having taken bread and given it to his disciples, made it his body by saying "this is my body", that is, "a figure of my body"'.[53] Oecolampadius argued that 'figure' so qualified the remark 'made it his body' as to deprive the latter of its apparent literal meaning. Fisher, on the other hand, maintained that Tertullian was speaking about the sacrament under its two aspects as both reality and sign. Neither explanation is entirely satisfactory. Tertullian was obviously trying to deal with the problem of why Christ should have called something his body when to all appearances it was not. But his solution is obscure and remains a matter for debate.[54] However, from our perspective it is interesting to note that the interpretations of Fisher and Oecolampadius both betrayed their authors' training in an Aristotelian tradition that firmly distinguished sign from signified. Oecolampadius cut the knot by reducing the sacrament to a sign, on the grounds that relations such as signification could exist only between separate substances. Observing that this would raise serious difficulties with the doctrine of the Trinity, Fisher fell back on the scholastic supposition of a difference 'rationis, non rei'.[55] He could not see what room Oecolampadius's symbolic account left for the act of communion itself. For if the eucharist was a mere memorial sign, whose true meaning lay solely in the words 'Do this in memory of me', then simply witnessing the eucharist would be as good a reminder of Christ as partaking of it.[56] Eating bread and wine did not seem to him an effective stimulant for memory. Indeed, it was a less natural and effective sign than the paschal lamb of the Jews that it was supposed to supplant.[57] And the crucifix was a still more effective reminder of Christ's sacrifice.[58] This is not to imply that Fisher minimised the role of the eucharist as memorial. On the contrary, he believed that the doctrine of the real presence made people more, not less, mindful of Christ's sacrifice.[59] He deftly inverted a common Protestant argument which compared Christ's gift of the eucharist to his Church with the practice by which lovers give their beloved a token, or kings give their favourites a portrait.

According to Fisher, Christ, as the most loving of all men and the most power-ful of all kings, would not leave his bride the Church with such a poor memento as bread and wine, but would leave the best memento possible, namely his own flesh and blood – concealed beneath the appearances of bread and wine so as not to offend decency.[60]

The third preface is in its own way as much a *tour de force* as the second, although since it chiefly summarises arguments which are found in more detail elsewhere in the *De Veritate*, it does not call for close analysis here. It put forward fourteen arguments, termed 'corroborations', for the real presence. The first two were drawn from scripture, one from a literal exegesis of Christ's words at the last supper and at the feeding of the five thousand (an argument expanded in preface V); and the other (outlined above) moving from the evidence of God's perfect love for his people to the conclusion that he would leave them with a perfect memorial.[61] This was followed by an appeal to the unanimous testimony of the fathers (presented more fully in preface IV).[62] After outlining his familiar argument for the infallibility of the Church (corroboration 4), he cited the decrees of various councils (corroboration 5), and then turned to the evidence of miracles and revelations (corroborations 6 and 7).[63] The eighth corroboration was drawn from Church history, which showed, according to him, that whenever heresies had arisen in the Church they had been met with instant opposition. His conclusion from this was that the doctrine of the real presence could not be a heresy as it had never been condemned, and had scarcely been opposed other then by stray individuals.[64] Still in historical vein he explained lastly (corroboration 9) that the various rises and falls in the level of the spiritual life in the history of the Church could be correlated closely with the rise and fall of devotion to the sacrament, which thus became a sort of spiritual barometer.[65]

In the fourth preface we are presented with Fisher's patristic scholarship at its best. Setting out to demonstrate that the real presence was the constant teaching of the Church, he divided Church history into five periods of three-hundred years, and adduced a cloud of witnesses to the doctrine from each one. As the doctrine was undeniably the current consensus of the Church, he worked backwards from the fifth and latest period, and felt that there was no need to do more than list names until he reached the second period. Only here did he start to substantiate his claims with citations, producing texts from Gregory the Great, Cassiodorus, Fulgentius, Leo, Eucherius of Lyons, Sedulius, Iuvencus, Cyril of Alexandria, Augustine, Cassian, Chrysostom, Jerome, Ambrose and (anachronistically) Theophylact and John Damascene.[66] Entering on the first period, Fisher introduced some conscious anachronism, admitting that several of his selected authors did not truly belong there but were entitled to rank with the earliest writers because of their learning and sanctity. Thus he cited Gregory Nazianzen, Gregory of Nyssa, Basil the Great and Hilary of Poitiers as well as Cyprian, Clement of Alexandria, Origen, Tertullian, Irenaeus, Ignatius, Clement of Rome and 'Dionysius'.[67] He also quoted the epicleses from what he believed to be the early Christian liturgies of Clement and James (at second-hand, from Bessarion's sermon on the eucharist).[68] This preface was especially relevant to the book it preceded, because in this section Oecolampadius took great trouble to reinterpret the patristic tradition. His chief technique was to pick out from patristic texts words or phrases implying figurative or symbolic expression, and to make them qualify whatever realist terminology an author might otherwise employ. He ruled out of court any works that he could not revise in this way. Thus, for example, he rejected as spurious, with neither evidence nor argument, the undeniably realist *De Sacramentis* and *De Mysteriis* attributed to Ambrose. Fisher objected to this cavalier behaviour, noting that Augustine had referred to a book by Ambrose on the sacraments,[69] and showing with citations from his other writings that Ambrose did indeed uphold the real presence in the eucharist.[70] It would be tedious to bring forward all the passages over which Fisher and Oecolampadius disagreed, especially as many of them are still the subject of dispute. Nevertheless, it would be hard to disagree with Fisher's realist reading of Ambrose, Chrysostom, Cyril of Alexandria, Hilary and Jerome; while Oecolampadius was on firmer ground with Irenaeus, Tertullian, Cyprian, Origen and perhaps Augustine – in short with the more ambiguous authorities. On the whole, Fisher's reading of the fathers is less strained than his opponent's, although he did have difficulties with Tertullian.

The fifth and final preface dealt with the scriptural arguments in favour of the real presence, and in particular with the interpretation of the sixth chapter of John's Gospel. Christ's warning 'unless you eat the flesh of the Son of Man and drink his blood, you shall not have life in you' (Jn 6:54) created special problems for the Zwinglian school. The dominant Catholic tradition on these words was that they were a barely veiled reference to eucharistic reception, although there was a minority school, including such influential figures as Augustine, Aquinas and Cajetan, that gave them (at least some of the time) a spiritual interpretation on the grounds of Christ's words 'the spirit gives life, the flesh avails nothing' (Jn 6:64).[71] The Zwinglians of course seized on this Augustinian view to escape the realist implications for the eucharist. Fisher, however, maintained that it was Christ's words about the flesh availing nothing, rather than his words about eating his flesh, that should be taken metaphorically. Otherwise, he observed a little later, those words would undermine the doctrine of the Incarnation – if the flesh literally achieved nothing, why should the Word have become flesh?[72] He derived what he saw as convincing proof of the sacramental interpretation from an earlier remark of Christ's, 'the bread which I shall give you is my flesh, which I shall give for the life of the world' ('panem quem ego dabo, caro mea est, quam dabo pro mundi vita', Jn 6:52). In fact the repetition of the phrase 'which I shall give' is not found in the Vulgate, but does appear in both the Greek and the Latin texts of the *Novum Instrumentum*.[73] Putting rather too much weight on what was perhaps merely a scribal duplication, Fisher suggested that 'dabo' referred in the first instance to the eucharistic gift of Christ's flesh under the form of bread, and in the second instance to the sacrificial gift of his flesh upon the cross.[74] Whatever the merits of this argument (which like so many of his was widely adopted by subsequent polemicists), he was able to confirm his sacramental reading of John 6 with a mass of patristic, especially Greek, support.[75] And, as we shall now see, this sacramental interpretation held a special place in his eucharistic theology.

Oecolampadius's attack on Catholic teaching consisted in large part of arguments against the spiritual necessity or value of the real presence. He claimed that since eternal life was offered for believing in Christ, and faith alone thus sufficed for salvation, there could be no role for the eucharist beyond reviving the memory of Christ and confirming the believer's faith. If Fisher was to defend the real presence against this line, it was essential for him to develop a convincing account of its role in the spiritual life. At the heart of the spirituality that he opposed to Oecolampadius lay the necessity for the believer to eat Christ's flesh, a necessity he deduced from John 6:54 and its patristic expositions,[76] and perhaps especially from such authors as Paschasius Radbert and the pre-scholastic opponents of Berengar of Tours.[77] This led him to affirm the necessity, or at least desirability, of frequent communion, a position which was remarkable in an age in which most Christians received communion only once a year, at Easter. The emphasis on frequent communion which appears in the *De Veritate* had not been a feature of his earlier writings. Indeed his concern with the dangers of unworthy reception tended to militate in quite the opposite direction. Even as late as his commentary on Psalm 22, where he extolled communion highly, he acknowledged that, as lay people, many readers might feel they could hardly aspire to daily communion. To them he offered the assurance that it was equally meritorious merely to assist at the mass with pious intentions and to make an act of spiritual communion, a position he justified with the Augustinian tag, 'believe and you have eaten'.[78] Yet the *De Veritate*, with its polemical concern to distinguish spiritual from sacramental communion and to uphold the special value of the latter, argued that there were real spiritual benefits to be gained from sacramental communion. Positing the case of two people starting on an equal footing in terms of piety and grace, one of whom was a frequent communicant while the other was not, Fisher stated that there was no doubt that the former would scale greater spiritual heights.[79] Without the regular nourishment of Christ's body and blood, he wrote, one's faith might well simply evaporate.[80] The authority of Cyril of Alexandria was adduced in support of this.[81] That there was a real change in Fisher's approach is apparent from the new attitude to Augustine's dictum that he revealed in the

De Veritate. 'Crede et manducasti' was now said not to be any kind of discouragement to sacramental communion, and another text was produced to show that Augustine too was in favour of frequent reception.[82] It is in this context of an increasing awareness of the value of sacramental communion that we should place Fisher's devotional treatise on the eucharist, a work described in the materials assembled by his first biographer as 'ten considerations of faith, hope and charity encouraging people's hearts to receive the eucharist with greater devotion'.[83] This work has previously been thought entirely lost, but in fact some surviving fragments in Fisher's hand can be identified. Calendared vaguely as fragments of a theological treatise, they in fact deal with Paul's exposition of the eucharist (1 Cor 11), but are clearly part of a devotional tract rather than a scriptural commentary.[84] The final words of the treatise, 'may the whole soul be more clearly illuminated by faith, more firmly corroborated by hope, and finally more and more enkindled and inflamed with charity, so that at last it may fail in itself, dissolve in the love of Christ, and be altogether absorbed and transformed into him', are strongly reminiscent of the lost work's title, and demonstrate its devotional nature. The numbering of some of the surviving sections fits the brief description given by the first biographer. And the theme of mystical absorption into Christ that emerges in those final words is a central theme in the eucharistic spirituality of the *De Veritate*.[85] Equally interesting is the way that this treatise sets up communion as the most perfect form of justification available in this life. We saw in the previous chapter how Fisher, like Luther and Augustine, emphasised that Christians were justified by Christ's justice, and not their own. Here he presents the reception of communion as an actual eating of Christ's justice.[86]

Even in his controversy with Luther, Fisher had stressed that the eucharist was primarily the sacrament of union with Christ, effecting the unity which it signified.[87] In the *De Veritate* he took this further. The sacrament was the consummation of the union in Christ inaugurated by the Incarnation. By taking flesh, Christ had participated in human nature, and had thus brought about union with the human race in a general sense. But this general union was common to both sinners and the justified alike.[88] The nature he took was the nature of the sinners he had come to save. The eucharist supplemented this with a particular union offered only to the justified. Having taken a share in human nature, Christ went further and offered the faithful a share in his perfect nature by giving them his flesh to eat.[89] By this double bond, Christ was in the faithful and they were in him, just as he had promised.[90] This argument put especial weight on the fleshiness of both the Incarnation and the eucharistic presence. Yet this heavily 'carnal' interpretation was no medieval corruption, as the Reformers alleged. Its origins lay in the writings of Hilary of Poitiers and Cyril of Alexandria, and it appeared in a muted form in some of Augustine's works. For the Western tradition Hilary was the main source, and he had arrived at his position in the course of his controversies with the Arians. Drawing a parallel between the unity of Christ with the Father, and the unity of the faithful in Christ, he maintained that in each case the unity in question was no mere coincidence of will or purpose, but a true union of nature.[91] This view, to which Fisher was impelled by polemical exigencies, was mediated to him through the writings of the eleventh-century opponents of Berengar of Tours, who had themselves derived it in part through Paschasius Radbert. It is easy to see why a tradition which laid so much emphasis on the physical participation in Christ's nature which the eucharist made possible should have brow-beaten Berengar with remarks about 'munching' the flesh of Christ.

Fisher's wider acquaintance with the fathers, and in particular with the Greeks, enabled him to pursue this theme much further than the pre-scholastics had done. He was able to bring the real presence into even closer relationship with the Incarnation through a passage of Cyril which compared the effects of communion on the recipient with the miracles that Christ had worked by the power of touch (for example, the healing of the blind man at the pool, Jn 9:1–7). Fisher concluded that when Christ's flesh was joined to that of the believer in communion, the eternal Word hypostatically united to that flesh was likewise joined to the believer, who was thus caught up into the very life of God.[92] His understanding of how this unity was effected was conditioned by his reading of Augustine, from whom he took the notion that the eucharistic meal differed from ordinary food in that, rather than being absorbed into the substance of its recipient, it converted its recipient into its own substance.[93] A similar idea underlay the theme he took from Irenaeus, that the eucharist was a seed which, after the body died, germinated into eternal life.[94] Fisher himself added a new twist to these ideas with the analogy of the medicinal use of gold or ground pearls by contemporary physicians. The theory was that these medicines, when swallowed, changed the condition of the patient without themselves undergoing change.[95] In modern terms, their action was catalytic. Oecolampadius, however, even granting the real presence, did not accept that the sacrament could be spiritual food, on the grounds that flesh could not feed souls. Instead, he argued, the soul was fed on the Word of God, as were the angels in heaven. While the angels fed by direct contemplation, Christians fed by faith, that is, by hearing and believing God's Word in scripture.[96] Fisher in fact agreed with him that scripture was spiritual food. In his psalm commentary he wrote, 'First is the food of the soul, namely the sacred scriptures, on which the soul is nourished just as the body is fed on material bread.'[97] But he objected to his opponent's facile move from the scriptural to the eternal Word. For him, the eucharist itself was the Word *par excellence*, since it contained Christ's body, blood, soul and divinity.[98] It was therefore the pre-eminent spiritual food. Reception of the sacrament achieved an intimacy of physical union for which the best analogy he could find was that of marriage. This in turn enabled him to put a eucharistic interpretation on Paul's description of marriage as a 'magnum mysterium', and to apply to Christ's relationship with his Church what Paul said about the relationship of man and wife, namely that a husband would care as much for his wife as for his own body.[99]

Oecolampadius's symbolic interpretation of the eucharist tended to reduce communion to an essentially intellectual act. For Fisher, on the other hand, it was also a physical and emotional experience. The tears he used to shed at mass are proof enough of this, but the *De Veritate* itself shows signs of an emotional and almost mystical devotion which reaches its climax towards the end of book III. There Fisher told how in communion 'the whole person is taken up [rapitur] and transformed into Christ; the minds of the faithful are filled by the presence of this flesh with a sort of cream or oil of devotion, and are fattened with a sweetness beyond words'.[100] The 'dulcedo' of the sacrament was a recurrent theme in his argument, reminiscent of the medieval tradition of St Bernard.[101] The use of the concept of eucharistic rapture reminds the reader of the 'ecstatic' spirituality recently identified in a study of Erasmus's *Encomium Moriae*. There are striking resemblances between Erasmus's attitude to the eucharist, and that of the *De Veritate*: 'Erasmus places the emphasis on the eucharist as synaxis. Spiritual communicants become one with God and with each other.'[102] Erasmus's observation that the Christian in communion is 'taken up [rapitur] to things eternal, invisible, spiritual' is clearly close to Fisher's view.[103] And it may not be without significance that the work to which Erasmus's concern with Christian rapture and ecstasy has been traced is the very fragment of Basil on Isaiah that Erasmus had originally translated for Fisher.[104] However, the suggestion that these two men were close in their eucharistic theology may seem somewhat ambitious in view of the widespread idea that Erasmus was not entirely happy with Catholic eucharistic doctrine. Some scholars have even claimed that Erasmus's views were, at least for a while, more akin to those of Oecolampadius, with whom he was closely associated in work on editions of the fathers for Froben at Basel when the *De Genuina Interpretatione* appeared.[105] Though something has been made of Erasmus's favourable remarks about the *De Genuina Interpretatione* on its publication,[106] it should be noted that he was impressed by its scholarship rather than won over by its case – he went so far as to dismiss Oecolampadius's thesis as 'error' as early as October 1525.[107] Anxious as he was to prevent the Paris faculty of theology from gathering further ammunition against him, he acted promptly to disabuse some forward sacramentarians of the idea that he agreed with them. The *Detectio Praestigiarum* (Basel: Froben, 1526) committed him firmly to the orthodox line. In 1530 he struck another blow with his edition of the twelfth-century tract on the sacrament by Alger of Liège, thus resorting like Fisher to the pre-scholastic opponents of Berengar.[108] But while there are undoubtedly similarities between the eucharistic theologies of Fisher and

Erasmus, it would be hasty to conclude that Erasmus was significantly influenced by Fisher.[109] Although of the three replies to Oecolampadius, Fisher's is the one that Erasmus is most likely to have read, it is clear that he was already dissociating himself from Oecolampadius before the *De Veritate* appeared. And as with the question of justification, it was possible for him to hold very similar views to Fisher without deriving them from him. What we can say is that in this matter, as in many others, there was a fundamental accord between the two scholars that goes some way towards explaining their mutual respect and friendship.

Fisher's eucharistic theology has been a rich and fruitful source for this study, providing confirmation of its themes and offering new insights into its subject. Once more the image of dull conventionality has been found wanting. The Fisher of this chapter remains an essentially patristic rather than scholastic theologian, owing special debts to a few particular fathers. His account of eucharistic sacrifice was shaped by the homilies of John Chrysostom, although the latter's essentially Platonic approach was not fully appropriated by a mind schooled in Aristotelian categories. Nevertheless, Fisher did assimilate Chrysostom's insistence on the real and numerical identity of Christ's sacrifice on the cross with the sacrifice of the mass, and on the purely ministerial or instrumental role of the ordained priest. These emphases marked a departure from the sophisticated 'mass machinery' of the later scholastics and offered a chance of escape from the dilemmas posed by the Reformers. On the sacrament of holy orders, Fisher's exclusive concentration on the imposition of hands placed him with the consensus of the fathers against the consensus of the scholastics with their 'tradition of the implements'. The debate about eucharistic presence saw Fisher make special appeal to a number of fathers. From Hilary he borrowed the theme of 'natural union'; from Augustine, that of Christ's body as food assimilating those who ate it; and from Cyril the importance of frequent communion. These and many other patristic themes were woven together in a coherent whole which was one of his most original and impressive achievements. Although Fisher was clearly closer to Thomas Aquinas than to any other scholastic, he had equally clearly moved beyond the confines of scholastic theology in his approach to the eucharist. The almost Baroque luxuriance of Fisher's preface to book II of the *De Veritate* is a striking contrast to the Gothic simplicity of Aquinas's attempt to reduce the many names of the sacrament to a rigid order. And his emphasis on the eucharist as communion reveals yet another point at which his theology was remarkably close to that of Erasmus – probably because of their shared admiration for the fathers rather than because of any direct dependence of one on the other. This emphasis on sacramental communion was the most 'modern' feature of Fisher's eucharistic theology, placing him at the start of the movement towards frequent communion that was to become so strong after the Council of Trent. Although undoubtedly an essentially conservative figure, Fisher was, as we shall see again in the next chapter, far from isolated from contemporary developments of genuine spiritual value.

9
The inspiration and translation of scripture

IN THE COURSE of the 1520s, Fisher's interest in what we now call Christian humanism was overshadowed by his zeal in defending orthodoxy against the Protestant Reformers. His humanism has therefore been hidden from the eyes of historians, and it would be tempting to presume that it was no longer there at all. The committed defence of traditional Catholic doctrine inevitably engaged him more closely with the teachings of the scholastics, although it is in fact remarkable how in his polemical writings he strove to go beyond them to the pre-scholastics and the fathers. Later in the 1520s, however, the Christian humanist in Fisher re-emerged in a controversy which has not merely been neglected by previous historians, but has remained completely unknown to them. The protagonist in this affair was a friend of his, the talented humanist and diplomat Richard Pace, dean of St Paul's. The issue at stake was the status of the Septuagint version of the Old Testament which, according to Pace, was a purely human artefact. However, to Fisher, it was itself, like the original Hebrew Old Testament, the product of immediate divine inspiration. Each party could call on a tradition of respectable antiquity in support of their view – the same issue had been debated between Jerome and Augustine. Moreover, Pace's view enjoyed considerable contemporary vogue, upheld not only by his and Fisher's tutor in Hebrew, Robert Wakefield, but also by Fisher's friends Erasmus and Reuchlin. It is at first sight surprising that Fisher should have taken exception to an opinion with such a pedigree. Nevertheless, as in the Magdalene controversy, he detected here a subtle yet powerful threat to the very trustworthiness of the scriptures and the Church. He knew from his wide reading among the early fathers that they had held the inspiration of the Septuagint if not unanimously then certainly *nemine contradicente*, and that they had without exception relied on it in their preaching and their writing. As if this were not enough, the authors of the New Testament had given citations from the Old Testament almost entirely in Septuagint wording. Thus the authority of the Septuagint was confirmed both by the practice of the Church and by the inspiration of the Holy Spirit in the Apostles and Evangelists. Even so, it might seem a relatively trivial dispute until it is recalled that there were a large number of discrepancies, of varying degrees of importance, between the Hebrew and the Greek versions of the scriptures. To reject the inspiration of the Septuagint was thus to admit the possibility that its discrepancies from the Hebrew were errors. This in turn was to suggest, in Fisher's view, that the Apostles and early fathers, in relying upon the Septuagint, had built upon sand – exactly the sort of threat that he could not overlook. The resulting controversy is of considerable interest to the historian of scholarship in early Tudor England. It casts new light on English theology on the eve of the Reformation. For example, we learn from it what we should otherwise hardly suspect, that Fisher was an advocate, in principle at least, of the vernacular translation of scripture. In order to attain a deeper understanding of the significance of this controversy, this chapter will sketch its background in the changing Christian attitudes to the Septuagint from the emergence of the Church through to the Renaissance. Only then will it be possible to assess with confidence the quality and implications of the arguments adduced by Fisher and Pace. But before proceeding to the prehistory and history of this debate, it is necessary to review the evidence which enables us to identify its participants and to date its occurrence.

Our first hint about the controversy between Fisher and Pace comes from a letter written to Erasmus by one John Crucius early in 1528. His record of the affair was brief and unilluminating:

There was a heated argument between the bishop of Rochester and Pace over the Septuagint translation. But this will be old news to you, because it happened last August while I was still living practically as one of the family with Pace, who was then at Syon Priory recovering from illness.[1]

Led by P.S. Allen, previous historians have seen this as a passing reference to some aspect of the early debate over the validity of Henry VIII's marriage to Catherine of Aragon. This explanation was rendered plausible by the fact that it was at this time that the two men were drawn into that debate. With a piece of typically inspired conjecture Allen was even able to suggest that perhaps the dispute revolved around the discrepancies between the Hebrew and the Greek.[2] Nevertheless, it is now clear that the controversy was purely theological, arising out of the authors' academic and doctrinal concerns rather than out of immediate political circumstances. This conclusion has been made possible by the identification, as their respective contributions to the controversy, of an extremely rare printed book of Pace's and of a manuscript of Fisher's.

The first of these contributions is Pace's *Praefatio in Ecclesiasten Recognitum ad Hebraicam Veritatem* (London: Pynson, n.d.), a book which has failed to attract the attention it deserves. Tentatively ascribed by the editors of the *Short-Title Catalogue* to 1526, it was actually written and published the following year. For it can be identified with a book that Pace was reported in July 1527 as being on the verge of publishing. On 30 July Gasparo Spinelli sent his brother Lodovico the following account of a recent visit he had paid to Syon Priory:

I have been at Syon visiting the reverend Pace, who is leading the life of the blessed in that lovely spot. Arrayed in his clerical garb, he is surrounded by a mass of books such as I have never before seen assembled in one place. He has become expert in Hebrew and Chaldaic, and now, armed with this knowledge, he is embarking on a corrected edition of the Old Testament, in which he has found so many errors, especially in the Psalter, that it is quite amazing. He has already corrected the whole of Ecclesiasticus, and this will be published within a few days. He will then go on to the prophets, and so the work will be of the highest value, and will make him immortal. When the first part has appeared, I will take care that you receive a copy.[3]

Granted that 'Ecclesiasticus' is manifestly a misreading at some point for 'Ecclesiastes', the identification of the *Praefatio* with the book Spinelli describes is irresistible.[4] Equally convincing is the association of this book with the quarrel which Crucius recalled had broken out in August 1527. For the *Praefatio* consists of a manifesto and apologia for the correction of the Vulgate text of Ecclesiastes (and indeed of the whole Old Testament) by collation against the 'hebraica veritas'.[5] Pace realised that his enterprise would expose him to attack and foresaw that the strongest argument against him would be that the Septuagint, on which the Vulgate Ecclesiastes was based, was directly inspired by God.[6] This argument had recently been revived by the Carthusian theologian Peter Sutor (formerly of the Sorbonne) as part of the Parisian theology faculty's campaign against the scriptural enterprises of Erasmus and Lefèvre. In the *Praefatio*, which was almost certainly written with Sutor in mind, Pace therefore secured himself against such an attack with a pre-emptive strike against the inspiration doctrine. The resultant playing off of the Hebrew against the Greek makes the work perfectly compatible with Crucius's exiguous account of the controversy.

Fisher's reply to the *Praefatio* survives as an incomplete manuscript, 'Pro Assertione Septuaginta Interpretum Translationis', found in the Public Record Office among the theological tracts which were once in Thomas Cromwell's possession.[7] Its survival is almost certainly owed to the fact that in its first few pages it makes frequent use of the words 'rex' and 'pontifex', which led an early but casual reader to label it 'Arguments from the Old and New Testament for the proof of the pope's authority.'[8] The treatise consists of thirty-eight leaves, divided into twenty-four axioms numbered one to twenty-six (with numbers eighteen and twenty-four missing). Although most of the text is in a scribe's hands, the survival of two axioms in Fisher's hand and the presence of amendments in his hand on the scribal drafts show that the work is indeed his.[9] Its thesis is that the translation of the Old Testament carried out by seventy-two Hebrew elders at the request of King Ptolemy of Egypt and with the permission of the High Priest Eleazar was inspired both in conception and execution by the Holy Spirit, and is therefore equal in authority to the Hebrew original even though it often diverges from it. The identification of this treatise with Fisher's reply to Pace is almost certain. The external evidence is very strong. Crucius recorded that Fisher wrote against Pace on the Septuagint, and it is hardly likely that he should have written on it twice without publishing on either occasion. The internal evidence, however, is somewhat problematic. Nowhere does Fisher name his opponent or opponents. On the other hand, his jibe at those who 'after one or two weeks' study of Hebrew reckon they know more than Jerome' looks remarkably like an allusion to Pace's boast of having learned Hebrew in less than a month, and fulfils his prediction that his relative lack of experience with the language would be cast in his teeth by his adversaries.[10] Besides, it is clear that 'Pro Assertione' cannot have been written before 1527, as it cites passages from Irenaeus, an author whom Fisher had lamented lacking from his library in the *De Veritate*.[11] Equally, it is unlikely to have been written later than mid-1529 because it does not cite Sanctus Pagninus's literal translation of the Hebrew Old Testament (published at Lyons in 1528), which was certainly in Fisher's possession by June that year.[12] It is another citation, from the commentary on the Psalms of Euthymius Zigabenus, that raises the only problem with the otherwise straightforward dating – Fisher cites him in the version by Filippo Sauli published in 1530. But since Sauli had probably died in 1528, it is in fact probable that he had completed his translation well before then, and that Fisher had managed to get hold of it in manuscript form.[13] Given that from late 1527 Fisher was almost wholly preoccupied with the controversy over Henry VIII's divorce, it seems most likely that 'Pro Assertione' is the reply to Pace's *Praefatio* that he wrote in August 1527.

The quarrel between Fisher and Pace had a long prehistory. The doctrine of the inspiration of the Septuagint was of pre-Christian origin, emerging, like the Septuagint itself, from the Jewish community at Alexandria under the Ptolemies. The earliest legends about the Septuagint are found in the so-called *Aristeas Letter*, a rhetorical exercise from early second-century BC Alexandria which purported to give an eye-witness account of the production of the translation.[14] The letter told how Ptolemy Philadelphus sought from the High Priest at Jerusalem a translation of the books of the Law for his library at Alexandria. By freeing Jewish slaves and sending gifts for the Temple, Ptolemy secured the co-operation of Eleazar, who deputed seventy-two elders to attend on Ptolemy and carry out his wishes. Although the letter makes no mention of inspiration, it testifies to the high regard in which the Septuagint was held by the Hellenised Jews of the diaspora.[15] The doctrine of inspiration was in circulation by the first century AD, when it appears in the writings of Philo of Alexandria, and it is therefore not surprising that it was adopted by the early Christian Church, then spreading among the Jews and the Gentiles of the Hellenic world.[16] In the context of the deteriorating relations between Church and Synagogue, the discrepancies between the Hebrew version (by now being canonised in the Massoretic text) and the Greek (which often preferred more radically messianic readings) assumed polemical significance, and allegiance to the Septuagint became a party badge of Christianity. The early Christian fathers were unanimous in their reliance upon the Septuagint and effusive in their praise for it. Not until Jerome did an orthodox Christian question its inspiration, and he was sharply controverted on the point by Rufinus and Augustine.[17] Since Jerome's views circulated in his prefaces to the books of the Bible, and Augustine's in his *De Civitate Dei*, both opinions were available in the Middle Ages.[18] Early on, the inspiration doctrine remained prevalent, passed on for example in the work of Isidore of Seville. But by the twelfth century Jerome's opinion was in the ascendant, and even such writers as Hugh of St Victor and Peter Comestor, who gave both sides of the question, tended to evince a preference for Jerome.

The authoritative status of the Septuagint was central to the early sixteenth-century debate over the humanist approach to the sacred text, a debate sparked off by Erasmus's *Novum Instrumentum*. Erasmus himself appealed to Jerome's debunking of the Septuagint to justify his own critical work on the New Testament,[19] and such prominent humanists as Reuchlin and Vives shared his view, as did Fisher's protégé Robert Wakefield.[20] Nevertheless, the revival of Greek and patristic studies in the Renaissance stimulated a revival of belief in the inspiration of the Septuagint. An important stage in this was the rendering into Latin in the mid-fifteenth century of the *Aristeas Letter*, which was subsequently included in several editions of the Bible.[21] Further impetus was added to the revival by Pico, who was led to take a high view of the Septuagint by his interest in the Cabbala.[22] Petrus Galatinus, another leading Cabbalist, also subscribed to the doctrine, and it may be that the Cabbalistic connotations of the doctrine increased its attraction to Fisher.[23] But the most influential restatement of the inspiration doctrine was Peter Sutor's *De Tralatione Bibliae*, a discourse on scriptural translation provoked by Erasmus's criticism of the Vulgate New Testament.[24] Since Sutor's principal objective was to establish the Vulgate as the authoritative translation of scripture, his insistence on the inspiration of the Septuagint might seem at first sight somewhat inconsistent. The explanation for it lies in Sutor's desire to deprive Erasmus of the example of Jerome to which he appealed, by proving that Jerome himself in fact upheld the inspiration doctrine. Sutor's opening lay in Jerome's own contradictory statements about the Septuagint, which gave him scope to 'interpret' Jerome in the light of Augustine. But Jerome and Augustine were almost the only authorities he cited,[25] and his ignorance of Greek and Hebrew prevented him from assessing either the discrepancies between the Massoretic and the Septuagint, or the extent to which the New Testament followed the one rather than the other. In explaining the discrepancies between the two recensions he was therefore wholly reliant on what little he could glean from Jerome and Augustine.[26] Ruling out error on the part of the translators and malicious distortion of the Hebrew by the Jews, he was left with scribal error and divine inspiration as possible explanations. His rule for distinguishing between the two was the *a priori* principle that in cases of contradiction, scribal error must be presumed; whereas in cases of mere difference, inspiration might be invoked.[27] Hopelessly ignorant of critical techniques for telling probable errors in transmission from genuine alternative traditions, he was thus utterly incompetent to address the issue at all, and his work is vastly inferior to Fisher's.

Unimpressive though it was, Sutor's pamphlet was widely read and set the scene for Pace's *Praefatio*. With the weight of the Paris theology faculty behind him, even Sutor was formidable, as one can see from the sheer length of Erasmus's reply.[28] Pace's desire to protect himself and his critical endeavour is understandable. Anticipating the charges of temerity that his attempt to emend the scriptural text would evoke, especially from those who regarded the Septuagint as inspired, he set out to expose that doctrine as a myth. Aware of the patristic consensus behind the doctrine, he disposed of it at a stroke by ruling out of court any author who was not an expert in all three relevant languages.[29] This in effect eliminated all testimony but that of Origen and Jerome, neither of whom, he maintained, accepted the doctrine of inspiration.[30] Turning to specific instances, he argued that the doctrine was inconsistent with the Septuagint's erroneous renderings of certain passages directly prophetic of Christ. Among them he included, with astonishing audacity, Isaiah 7:13 – 'Behold, a virgin shall conceive and bear a son, and he shall be called Emmanuel.' Pace dwelt on the trivial discrepancy between 'he shall be called' (Massoretic and Vulgate) and 'he shall call' (Septuagint), totally ignoring that between 'virgin' (Septuagint and Vulgate) and 'young girl' (Massoretic) which is the most important single discrepancy in the entire canon, but which of course told heavily against him.[31] However, his assault on the Septuagint concluded with the more plausible argument that the Church had never entirely accepted the Septuagint, preferring, for example, Theodotion's rendering of Daniel; and that Jerome had often preferred the readings of Theodotion, Aquila and Symacchus to those of the Septuagint. In a further swipe at Sutor he observed that the Vulgate as read in the contemporary Church was not in fact wholly or purely the work of Jerome.[32]

It is ironic that Pace's pre-emptive strike, which was designed to forestall attacks on his textual criticism, probably brought down upon him the wrath of a personal friend who would otherwise in all likelihood have had no quarrel with what he was attempting. Fisher, after all, had looked with favour on the similar textual endeavours of Erasmus and Reuchlin, and was deeply committed to the cultivation of the original languages of scripture. Unlike Sutor and the Paris theology faculty, he saw no intrinsic threat to the Vulgate in the study of the Hebrew and Greek scriptures. But he did attach considerable doctrinal importance to the Septuagint, for much the same reasons that the early fathers had done. His defence of the Septuagint in the 'Pro Assertione' is a cogent piece of reasoning, implicitly embodying an ambitious and successful strategy which aimed to steer between Sutor's ignorant contempt for humanism and Pace's blithe disregard for ancient tradition. The argument was founded upon a wide range of classical and patristic texts and upon the collation of Greek and Hebrew renderings of various passages of scripture. Although the 'Pro Assertione' was not without similarities to Sutor's *De Tralatione*, it was more substantial and more sophisticated. From the start Fisher went more deeply into the issues than Sutor had done, resorting for historical information not to medieval compilations such as those of Peter Comestor and Platina, but to original sources. And he put his historical account into a strongly patristic theological perspective. He made use of all the four themes used by the fathers in their defence of the Septuagint: the probity and scholarship of the seventy-two translators; the providential dispensation by which the translation had been accomplished before the advent of Christ; the parallel between the work of the seventy-two and that of the prophet Esdras, who was supposed to have restored the Hebrew scriptures to their pristine condition from the corruption into which they had fallen during the Babylonian captivity; and the reception of the Septuagint by the Church.[33] But it was the theme of divine providence which gave unity to the argument as a whole. The very first axiom emphasised that the human origin of the translation in Ptolemy Philadelphus's love of books (a characteristic which Fisher substantiated from a variety of classical and patristic authors) was itself a proof of the wonderful providence of God.[34] This love of books, he continued, led Ptolemy to desire translations of the books of the Law in order to complete his collection. Here he observed that the pharaoh's desire extended not merely to the Pentateuch but to the whole of scripture. Conceding that Josephus had written only of the Law in recounting the labours of the translators, he argued with some plausibility that in Josephus's time this term often embraced the books of wisdom and prophecy as well.[35] Evidence of the divine impetus behind Ptolemy's desire was found in the gifts and favours which, according to Josephus, he has heaped upon the Jewish people. The liberation of thousands of slaves and the donation of masses of gold and silver to the Temple were an excessive price for a few volumes, and could be explained, Fisher believed, only in terms of the instigation of the Holy Spirit. He adduced the scriptural examples of the divinely inspired favours of Cyrus, Darius and Artaxerxes as analogies.[36] Ptolemy's request for a number of expert translators was thus providentially inspired, as was Eleazar's favourable response.[37] Divine providence could also be detected in Eleazar's selection of so many and learned scholars for the task. Their erudition was sufficiently attested by their performance in disputation with Ptolemy's Egyptian philosophers, whose leader, Menedemus, himself thought that the visitors' extempore responses were divine.[38] Having thus established the credentials of the translators, Fisher proceeded to examine Pace's claim that they had been deceived in their work by the similarities between various characters of the Hebrew alphabet. He concluded that the number and ability of the translators made such error unlikely, and that the possibility was ruled out by the Jewish practice of reading the scriptures in public every Sabbath. If the translators had deviated from the text as known through public reading, then their error would have been pointed out. In addition, Fisher observed that by no means all the discrepancies could be explained as errors about characters.[39] Turning next to the notion, raised and dismissed by Sutor, that the translators might have deliberately or even maliciously produced an inaccurate translation, he answered that fear of God would have deterred them, or at least fear of detection and punishment in a country where there were still thousands of Jews, many in close attendance on the pharaoh.[40] With folly and malice eliminated, this left only religious discretion or divine inspiration as possible explanations. Jerome had suggested that the seventy suppressed Christological and Trinitarian texts in the Old Testament in order to avoid giving scandal to readers who might wrongly assume that these compromised monotheism. Yet Fisher could not conceive that they would have risked incurring the Deuteronomical curses pronounced against those who tampered with the word of God's law.[41] This left only divine inspiration, a theory that received strong support from that element of the Septuagint story that had the seventy-two translators each doing their work in a separate cell, and finding at the end of each day, on comparing their efforts, that they had miraculously translated their passages into the selfsame words. Fisher was aware that Jerome had dismissed this part of the story as mere fiction, but was inclined to accept it on the testimony of Justin Martyr, who claimed to have been shown near Alexandria the traces of buildings held by local tradition – the 'vera lex historiae' – to be the seventy-two cells.[42] He was not disturbed by the absence of the cells from the Aristean account, as Aristeas did at least record that Ptolemy had allocated a special building to the translators for their work.[43]

At this point history gave way entirely to theology in Fisher's account as he moved on from the providential origin to the providential purpose of the translation. Given that it was the divine plan to spread the true religion to all the peoples of the world, it was necessary that the scriptures should be made available in a language more widely known than Hebrew. Otherwise the gentiles could never be certain that Christ fulfilled the law, figures and prophecies of the Old Testament. It was further necessary that this translation be accomplished before the advent of Christ, lest the gentiles have cause to suspect the integrity of a translation made after the event by the apostles themselves.[44] The translation had to be seen to be divine, because its testimony to Christ could not be any less authoritative than that of the Hebrew original if it was to convince its audience. That the Septuagint was indeed regarded as divine Fisher deduced from the use made of it in the writings of the New Testament by the apostles, and especially by Paul (an observation which he borrowed from Origen.) If it had not been accepted as authoritative, he argued, then Paul would never have drawn upon it in his epistles, for fear that the Jews might find reason therefrom to impugn his witness.[45] Furthermore, the translation had to be carried out before the coming of Christ in case the Jews might subsequently corrupt the original Hebrew out of hatred for Christ in order to frustrate the preaching of the Gospel (an argument hardly consistent with his earlier certainty that the seventy would be deterred by Deuteronomy from altering the text!).[46] Indeed, the corruptions that the Jews had subsequently introduced into the text – an allegation put about by, among others, Irenaeus, Lyra and Giustiniani – were an indication of what they might have done had no authoritative translation already been performed.[47] The production of the Greek version obviated another potential obstacle to the propagation of the Gospel, namely the ambiguity of the Hebrew language. Since the Jews were able to exploit ambiguities in order to evade the force of those passages which Christians took as prophetic of Jesus Christ, it was essential that a divinely authenticated and unambiguous rendering of the scriptures be made before Christ's birth.[48] Finally, some accessible version of the Bible had to be available if Christians, like Jews, were to be able to make progress in the knowledge of the scriptures.[49]

In the third phase of his argument, Fisher attempted to prove directly the authority of the Septuagint. The foundation of his case was the frequent preference in the New Testament for the Greek over the Hebrew where the two recensions diverged, a preference he demonstrated with a dozen examples.[50] Scarcely less important to him was the reliance of the early fathers on the Septuagint. Until the time of Aquila in the second century there was no alternative version at all. Even after the production of rival versions by Jews and Judaising Christians, the Greek fathers continued to depend on it entirely. In the West, the *Vetus Editio* (the Latin translation of the Septuagint) held undisputed sway until the appearance of Jerome's version, which even then was far from universally received by the bishops.[51] Thus the authority of the Septuagint was confirmed by the universal practice and general consensus of the early Church.[52] However, Fisher was careful to emphasise, the inspiration of the Septuagint was in no sense a derogation from the authority of the Hebrew original. That, too, was inspired. The discrepancies between the Hebrew and the Greek were therefore comparable to those between the Gospels: the accounts might differ in detail but, emanating from the same Spirit, were of equal validity. In each case, though, the doctrine of inspiration depended on the teaching of the Church. Without the Church's infallible guidance there would be even less reason to presume the inspiration of the Hebrew text than there would be that of the Greek, because the Hebrew version could be traced back to the labours of a single individual, Esdras, who had restored the scriptures in a new alphabet after the Babylonian captivity. It was manifestly more reasonable to doubt the authority of a single redactor than that of seventy scholarly translators (another dig at Pace, perhaps), yet if God had inspired that redactor, he was just as likely to have inspired the seventy.[53] Thus, with characteristic emphasis on the consensus of the infallible teaching Church, Fisher brought his defence of the Septuagint to a close.[54]

The 'Pro Assertione' was one of Fisher's most deliberate and most successful attempts to align himself with the fashionable currents of Renaissance humanist scholarship. His undoubted sympathy with the cause of *bonae literae*, however, is not enough to explain the systematically humanist approach of this treatise. A more pressing motive was the need to distance himself from the obscurantism of Peter Sutor, to whose *De Tralatione* his 'Pro Assertione' might otherwise seem uncomfortably close. For Erasmus had committed him against Sutor by citing him as a supporter in the *Adversus Petri Sutoris . . . Debacchationem*, a work which had rejected the inspiration of the Septuagint. Fisher and his tutor Melton had been adduced there as examples of impressively learned and impeccably orthodox theologians who nevertheless whole-heartedly approved of the Erasmian scriptural programme – that is, as the opposite of Sutor himself.[55] Fisher's treatise therefore makes a parade of humanist learning in a bid to establish authentic humanist credentials and live up to Erasmus's encomium. Although he referred to classical authors but rarely in his other writings, here he drew in the very first axiom on Plutarch, Aulus Gellius and Eutropius for information about Ptolemy Philadelphus. He showed a far wider acquaintance with patristic literature than Sutor had done, calling on Greeks (Justin, Irenaeus, Origen, Chrysostom and Euthymius) as well as Latins (Tertullian, Hilary, Jerome and Augustine). Moreover, he employed modern editions and translations of the fathers – Vives's Augustine, Erasmus's Jerome and Irenaeus, Trapezuntius's Eusebius, and Palmeri's Aristeas. The catena of versions of the title of the ninth psalm that he produced in axiom 19 – by Jerome, Lyra, an anonymous translator,[56] Reuchlin, Felix de Prato and Agostino Giustinani – showed that he was cognisant of the latest Hebrew scholarship.[57] Detailed arguments about divergences between the Massoretic and the Septuagint demonstrated his competence in both Greek and Hebrew. He was able to show, with the aid of Jonah's prophecy of the fall of Nineveh, which gave the city forty days to repent in the Hebrew but only three in the Greek, that not all such discrepancies could be explained as errors induced by the similarities of Hebrew words and letters – there was no resemblance between the Hebrew words for forty and for three.[58] His best argument, though, was built on the apostles' preference for the Greek over the Hebrew text where the two diverged. In this implicit attack on the opinion of Jerome, Fisher followed instead the lead of Origen, and substantiated his case with a chain of examples from the New Testament. Citing both Hebrew and Greek – and following Erasmus's *Novum Instrumentum* for the New Testament

Greek – he made a brief but effective statement of a thesis that has on the whole been vindicated by subsequent biblical criticism.[59]

The argument of the 'Pro Assertione', however, forces us to modify one of the elements of Edward Surtz's account of Fisher's humanism. Relying on a passage in the *De Causa Matrimonii*, he reasonably enough concluded that Fisher attributed only to the Hebrew version of the Old Testament the authority of immediate divine inspiration, while ascribing to the Septuagint and Vulgate a merely doctrinal infallibility because of their approval by the infallible Church.[60] Unfortunately, Surtz was misled by a classic typographical error. The text of *De Causa* affirmed that the Latin translation of scripture was of less authority than the Hebrew or the Greek. However, *De Causa* was in fact summarising the argument of an earlier treatise on Henry VIII's divorce, the brief 'Ne qua fiat' presented to the legatine tribunal of Wolsey and Campeggio in 1529.[61] At this particular point, *De Causa* was drawing on it almost verbatim. But both manuscripts of that earlier treatise affirmed that the Latin translation was of *no* less authority than the Hebrew or the Greek.[62] Miguel de Eguia, or his typesetter, simply omitted 'non'. Once this emendation is made, Fisher's argument becomes far more coherent. His point was that even though only the Hebrew and the Greek versions were inspired, it was inconceivable that the Latin version should disagree with them on a matter of faith or morals because it had been approved by the authority of the infallible Church. In both treatises on the divorce, this argument was confirmed by a lengthy demonstration that the Hebrew, Greek and Latin versions were indeed in agreement on the matter of marriage to a brother's wife. But this ecclesiastical guarantee of the Vulgate did not extend to its transmission. Fisher was happy to acknowledge that errors had crept in since Jerome's time, and was happy to see them corrected.[63] It is interesting to note, however, that his argument for the inspiration of the Septuagint found its way into two of his treatises on the divorce, where he deployed it as part of his broader contention that the various renderings of the crucial scriptural texts did not differ in essentials.

The most surprising feature of Fisher's treatise is without doubt the strong argument he elaborates in favour of making scripture available to clergy and laity alike in a language they can understand. To some extent this can be seen as part of his strategy for dissociating himself from Sutor, who had dismissed the vernacular translation of scripture as neither necessary nor useful. Such repudiation of vernacular scripture was a common theme of polemics against Erasmus, who had recommended Bible reading for the laity in his *Paraclesis*.[64] But Fisher can hardly have adopted such a position out of mere reaction against Sutor. Rather we should see his stance as further confirmation of his essential commitment to the Erasmian scriptural programme. His argument for vernacular scripture is not made in passing, but is given an entire axiom to itself (axiom 20), and comes as the culmination of an argument developed since axiom 14 for the providential necessity of an authentic translation of scripture in the primitive Church. Fisher began, like so many sixteenth-century proponents of vernacular scripture, with Christ's injunction to scrutinise the scriptures for evidence about him (Jn 5:39), asking 'who can scrutinise the scriptures if they do not have them written in some language they understand?'[65] He continued with Peter's instruction to priests to feed their flocks (1 Pet 5:2), commenting that the flock would be ill fed if it was not able to taste the food it was given.[66] In the early Church, he observed, few among the clergy or laity would have known Hebrew.[67] It was therefore necessary that the scriptures be translated into some language they did know so that they could attain certain knowledge of the Christian revelation. The lack of such a translation, he maintained, would have made nonsense of Paul's admonition to the faithful to keep the Word of God ever upon their lips, 'singing hymns, psalms, and spiritual canticles' (Col 3:16).[68] He concluded by claiming that laity and clergy alike were obliged to make daily progress in the knowledge of the scriptures: if the Jews had listened to the scriptures every Sabbath, how much more attentively ought Christians to hear or read them.[69] Although Fisher's argument was specifically concerned with establishing the need for a translation in the primitive Church, his texts and reasoning amounted to a justification in principle of vernacular scripture. Confirmation of this can be seen in the obvious approval with which the opening axioms of the treatise speak of Ptolemy's pious desire to translate the scriptures, a desire Fisher significantly attributes to the prompting of the Holy Spirit. Indeed, those opening axioms could in another context have been taken as a manifesto for the Authorised Version. He cannot have been blind to the implications of his argument at a time when the English episcopate was taking firm action to suppress the translation of scripture recently produced by Tyndale. This is not to suggest that he was seeking to subvert the policy of his fellow bishops. His friend Tunstall had presided the previous year over the incineration of a bundle of Tyndale New Testaments, and there is no reason to suppose that Fisher disapproved. Nor is it to suggest that there was no opposition to vernacular scripture in principle. The prior of the Cambridge Dominicans, Robert Buckenham, who preached against Latimer in 1529, argued that the laity would tend to adopt absurdly literalistic readings of scripture which might endanger not only their prospects of eternal life, but even their chances of earthly happiness.[70] Rather it is to argue, against the consensus of Reformation historians, that the bishops and their supporters were sincere in protesting that their opposition to Lollard and Protestant translations of scripture was based not on opposition to translation in principle, but on the theological distortions they claimed to see in those particular versions and on the inopportuneness of publishing vernacular scripture at a time when heretics were seeking to turn it against the Church. Nowhere in his surviving writings does Fisher voice any criticism of the private reading of scripture. On the contrary, he encourages it – even in his vernacular sermons on the penitential psalms.[71] What he did oppose was the private, or in other words idiosyncratic, interpretation of scripture.[72] It is quite clear that for Fisher scripture was certainly to be read, even perhaps in the vernacular, but it was to be read according to the mind of the Church.

When the prejudices derived from Protestant polemic are put aside, the evidence that the bishops really did accept vernacular scripture in principle looks remarkably strong. Erasmus's support for vernacular scripture was undisguised, and he counted the most influential English bishops among his friends (Warham, Wolsey, Fox, Fisher, Tunstall and Longland). Similar views were put into the mouth of Reginald Pole by Thomas Starkey, and there is no particular reason to believe that he misrepresented his patron's views.[73] Henry VIII himself, in his most orthodox phase, was careful to emphasise that the reading of scripture was good in any language – but that it was dangerous to read translations carried out by heretics.[74] Thomas More's avowal of support in principle for scriptural translation, and his claim that bishops of his acquaintance were happy to sanction accurate translations, have impressed few historians, but look more plausible in the light of Fisher's treatise.[75] The distinctions More drew between the utility, necessity and expediency of a vernacular translation were echoed by William Barlow in 1531,[76] and also appear in Henry VIII's proclamation of 1530 against heretical books. The proclamation, which offered the prospect of a vernacular Bible provided that the people abandoned heresy, was the result of work done by a committee of theologians from Oxford and Cambridge which included delegates of a conservative as well as a Reformist tendency – among them were Fisher's friends John Watson and Ralph Baynes.[77] Fisher's own chaplain, Dr Addison, who became after his patron's execution a loyal though strongly conservative Henrician Catholic, owned English copies of both the New Testament and the whole Bible at his death in 1540.[78]

The controversy over the Septuagint, then, has cast new and occasionally unexpected light upon the intellectual and theological stance of John Fisher, and upon the environment in which he worked. The mere occurrence of such a dispute is of interest, in that it shows us the flickering of a kind of critical scholarship which was hardly to be seen again in England for fifty years, as first the divorce and then kaleidoscopic religious change brought more pressing concerns before the academic community. That the dispute took place between two figures as close as Fisher and Pace shows that we should take seriously the point that English humanism on the eve of the Reformation was by no means ideologically homogeneous.[79] With regard to Fisher himself, his affirmation of the inspiration of the Septuagint strikes a blow at the essentially medieval image often drawn of him. He was able to stand aside from the medieval or 'Hieronymian' consensus against the doctrine, aligning himself instead with an older patristic tradition. Yet he simultaneously avoided the bias against the Hebrew which often accompanied that older tradition, and the anti-Erasmian use to which that tradition was being put in his own day. The way in which Fisher argued his case demonstrates better than any other of his works the nature and extent of his commitment to Renaissance humanism. As Erasmus had already observed, his interests in this direction were shaped entirely by his pursuit of a better understanding of the scriptures.[80] Secular literature as such held no appeal for him, although he was prepared to draw on it in order to further his theological purposes. In this treatise, Hebrew, Greek, the classics and the fathers were deftly arranged in an elegant and coherent argument, during which Fisher played one of his most surprising cards, a concern for the vernacular translation of scripture. There could be no stronger testimony to the fact that years of controversy against the Protestant Reformers had not closed his mind. In the event, however, the treatise was not published, though it was undoubtedly written with publication in mind. It is tempting to speculate that Pace and Fisher may have made their peace and agreed not to publish – this might explain why there are only two copies of *Praefatio* (one of them belonged to Pace's friend Sir Thomas Elyot, who might have received his, as it were, hot from the press) and why the revised text of Ecclesiastes does not survive at all.[81] Alternatively, both men may have been distracted from the issue by their entanglement in a dispute of far greater immediate importance, the debate over the validity of Henry VIII's marriage to Catherine of Aragon. As we shall see in the following chapter, Fisher had already been consulted on this when Pace's *Praefatio* first came to his attention, and it was Pace's presentation of a dedication copy to Henry VIII himself that brought him and Robert Wakefield into the discussion. It is this case, and in particular Fisher's role in it, that now demands our attention.

10

The controversy over Henry VIII's first marriage

TOWARDS THE END of his life, Fisher was to remark that of all the controversies in which he had become embroiled, none had cost him more effort than that over Henry VIII's marriage to Catherine of Aragon. In total, he reckoned he had written seven or eight books on it – which may well have been an underestimate.[1] This certainly represented in quantity and probably also in quality a more significant contribution to the debate than that of any other single individual. Although several of these books are lost, four are known to survive, and we can deduce a fair amount about the contents of another and the outline of a further two.[2] The examination of the arguments he developed in this series of treatises provides the basis of this chapter. But besides an immense contribution to the literature of the divorce, Fisher also played a central, though not a controlling, part in the opposition to the divorce in English academic and ecclesiastical circles. There is a certain similarity here to his part in the English campaign against Luther: leadership by example rather than by the overt exercise of authority. It is remarkable how many of the English opponents of the divorce, like the English opponents of Luther, were friends or clients of the bishop of Rochester. The attitude of his friends in Cambridge did not escape the attention of the king's commissioners when with some difficulty they extracted from the university in 1530 a judgment in favour of the king.[3] The interrogatories put to Fisher during his confinement in the Tower of London are ample testimony to the suspicion with which Henry's Council regarded his activities, even though his answers undoubtedly disappointed their expectations. This chapter will seek to assess the importance of Fisher in the story of Henry's divorce from Catherine of Aragon. As we are led to expect from the fact that he was without doubt England's best known theologian, his importance was considerable. His writings were praised by supporters of the Queen as diverse as Chapuys himself, Cochlaeus and Agrippa. Henry's advisers, though expressing little but contempt for his contributions, paid him the backhanded compliment of writing more refutations of his works than of anybody else's. Indeed, until the appearance of *Gravissimae Censurae* in 1531, Fisher's works determined the direction of the controversy. Even as late as 1534 he was regarded as the man to beat, with two refutations of his arguments being published. There can be no doubt that he had the best of the controversy on theological grounds, whether in the exegesis of the Hebrew, in the evaluation and collation of scriptural texts, in the interpretation of patristic and scholastic writers, or in the application of theological and philosophical concepts of law to the discussion. By 1531, as *Censurae* made abundantly clear, his adversaries had been reduced to the basest techniques of misrepresentation and special pleading. But the cause was not to be resolved by dispassionate argument and impartial process. Policy and force were to be the decisive agents, and interest the decisive motive. Nevertheless, it is with the academic aspects of the king's great matter that this chapter is primarily concerned, and before we proceed to the analysis of the controversy, it is worth reminding ourselves of its historical and theological background.

Shortly after his accession in 1509, Henry VIII decided to solemnise the marriage to Catherine of Aragon to which he had been contracted for several years. During the first decade of their marriage Catherine was frequently pregnant, but of all her children only one, Princess Mary, lived more than a few months.[4] By 1519 Henry was beginning to despair of a male heir, and by 1524 his relationship with Catherine had broken down irretrievably. He had already had a few mistresses, and had acknowledged one illegitimate son, when he fell in love with Anne Boleyn. Her sister Mary had been one of Henry's earlier mistresses, but Anne herself played hard to get, and it was around this time that the idea of securing an annulment of his marriage to Catherine first entered Henry's mind.[5] He began to attribute his misfortunes as a father to a divine judgment on him for marrying his sister-in-law – Catherine had of course been previously married to his elder brother Arthur, who had died in 1502 a few months after their wedding. Since such marriages had been forbidden under ecclesiastical law since the days of the early Church, a dispensation had been necessary, and had been easily obtained, from the pope, Julius II. Yet such marriages were also apparently prohibited by the book of Leviticus in the following terms: 'Thou shalt not take thy brother's wife. Thou shalt not uncover the nakedness of thy brother's wife: it is thy brother's nakedness' (Lev 18:16); and 'If a man shall take his brother's wife, it is an unclean thing: he hath uncovered his brother's nakedness: and they shall be childless' (Lev 20:21). An initially attractive case against the marriage could be made on the grounds of the scholastic commonplace that the pope could not grant dispensations from provisions of divine law.[6] Exploiting the inherent ambiguities of the term 'divine law', which in this context meant the natural, moral or immutable law, but which could also mean any law promulgated by God, Leviticus 18:16 could be seen as divine law, and could therefore be deemed outside the jurisdiction of the pope. Unfortunately for Henry, there was an equally well-known text (Deut 25:5) which stipulated that where a man died leaving a widow but no children, his widow should marry his brother so that they could bring up a child in the name of the deceased. It was upon the contradiction between these two texts that the whole controversy turned.

There was a long tradition of exegesis upon these texts, the starting-point of which is found in Augustine's *Quaestiones in Heptateuchum,* where he proposed that in the light of the Deuteronomical provision, the Levitical prohibition must be understood as prohibiting marriage in one of three ways: either simply between a man and the wife of his living brother; or also between a man and the divorced wife of his living brother; or in addition between a man and the widow of his dead brother unless that brother had died childless.[7] Little was added to the work of Augustine until the high Middle Ages, when the Levitical marriage legislation attracted closer interest with the development of the Church's own increasingly complex legislation on matrimony. Most scholars opted either for Augustine's first alternative or for his third. There was also much discussion of the legal status of the Levitical prohibition. Was it part of the natural law (that is, the immutable law by which God created and sustained the universe, some-times also called the 'divine' or 'moral' law) or not? Five schools of thought on the matter can be identified. To those various theologians who restricted the prohibition to the wives of living brothers, it was undoubtedly a matter of divine law as it was a special case of the prohibition of adultery.[8] Among those who applied the prohibition to widows as well as to wives, there was general agree-ment that it was not a matter of natural law. The Victorine school held that only marriages between parents and their children were contrary to natural law.[9] The Thomists deemed the prohibition on levirate marriage binding except in the case covered by the Deuteronomical provision.[10] The Scotists, however, held that impediments to matrimony on the grounds of affinity (that is, relation-ship by law) rather than by consanguinity (that is, by blood) rested entirely on ecclesiastical authority, and were therefore dispensable.[11] A minority school, which originated with Peter of Paluda, believed the Levitical prohibition on levirate marriage to be a matter of divine (that is, immutable) law, and thus indispensable.[12] But this drastic position, the only one which could be honestly brought forward by Henry VIII's advisers, was flawed in two ways. First of all, Innocent III had dispensed a number of Livonian converts to Christianity to retain wives married under a levirate custom of their people (although not to contract such marriages in the future), and dispensations within a parallel degree of affinity had been given in recent years (notably in 1500 to King Manuel I of Portugal, enabling him to marry his deceased wife's sister).[13] Secondly, and more tellingly, Peter of Paluda himself retracted his opinion in a subsequent commentary on Leviticus.[14] Thus the underlying theological consensus was undoubtedly in favour of the validity of the marriage between Catherine and Henry. But the variety of positions available and of arguments adduced, together with the ambiguity of many of the terms of the debate (such as 'divine law'), left Henry's supporters with plenty of ammunition.

By early 1527 Henry had already set his heart on divorcing Catherine in order to marry Anne Boleyn. The first practical steps were taken in May, when Wolsey convoked an informal gathering of canon lawyers to examine the question. However, attempts to get Henry out of his marriage by technicalities of canon law were abandoned either because they were deemed unlikely to succeed, or because Henry himself was anxious to achieve victory on the theological rather than the canonical level.[15] For whichever reason, the debate over the divorce rapidly resolved itself into a debate over the question of divine law, and a wider sampling of opinion was soon under way. As England's most accomplished theologian, Fisher was among the first to be consulted. Towards the end of May, Wolsey asked him for an opinion on whether or not the Levitical prohibition on marriage to a brother's wife was a matter of natural law. Fisher's brief reply, which is no longer extant, merely observed that the authorities were divided. A few days later Wolsey broached the matter with him in person, calling at Rochester on his way to France. Fisher's fuller reply is recapitulated in a second letter, which argued that the reasons for seeing the prohibition as a matter of divine law were far from cogent. He was content to rest his case on the authority of the pope to pass judgment in disputes over the interpretation of scripture. Since popes had issued several dispensations from this prohibition, he concluded, they had *de facto* decided that it was not a matter of natural law.[16] It is probably to some point soon after this that we should date a personal interview he had with Henry in the Long Gallery at Westminster on the subject of the marriage. Despite the intimidating presence of the dukes of Norfolk and Suffolk and a number of other spiritual and temporal lords, Fisher's nerve did not break, and he advised the king to brush aside the conscientious scruple that was bothering him. Henry can hardly have liked what he heard, but nevertheless asked him to produce a full assessment of the case.[17] It is worth observing that at this stage Fisher seems to have taken Henry's talk of conscience at face value. In a letter written about a year later he repudiated the notion that Henry had any other desire in this affair than to resolve a conscientious scruple, and voiced his confidence that Henry, like the pious and orthodox king he was, would properly submit to the judgment of the pope.[18] Yet his turn of phrase barely conceals fears about the king's intentions, and seems to express hopes about Henry rather than expectations. The comment that kings are apt to imagine, because of the extent of their power, that they can do whatever they like, and the description of the decrees of the Church as bonds which prevent them from doing so, remind the reader of occasional private remarks by others of Henry's servants.[19]

In Wolsey's absence, Henry continued the collection of scholarly opinions on his marriage. It was as a result of a discussion with Richard Pace, probably when he presented his *Praefatio in Ecclesiasten* to the king in August 1527, that Henry recruited the scholar who was to produce some of the best arguments for the divorce in the early years of the controversy – Robert Wakefield. When Pace was granted an audience, he was apparently faced with questions about the marriage, and about the relative authority of Leviticus and Deuteronomy, to which he replied in a letter the next day. But this letter was more important for its strong recommendation of the services of Wakefield, who, it reported, was unwilling to interfere in the matter directly without the express permission of the king.[20] Some time afterwards Wakefield was visited at Syon Priory, where he was staying with Pace, by Edward Foxe and John Bell (an agent of Wolsey). They presented him with three propositions that the king wanted him to establish, namely that the Levitical prohibitions forbade not so much illicit intercourse as irregular marriage; that they were moral precepts; and that they applied as much to the wives of dead relatives as to the wives of the living.[21] Although his reply does not survive, we can tell from his later writings and from the course of events that his interpretation of the texts made the question of the consummation of the first marriage crucial. A little later he was summoned to the royal presence to be informed that Catherine's previous marriage to Prince Arthur had indeed been consummated, and it is to this meeting that we can date his recruitment to Henry's 'spiritual learned counsel' and the beginning of his defection from the clientage of Bishop Fisher. Wakefield himself admitted that until he learned that the first marriage had been consummated, he had supported Queen Catherine, and that he had in the meantime assisted Pace in a work in defence of the marriage. But the outcome of his meeting with the king was a commission to refute a treatise by Fisher which had now come into the king's hands.[22] This marked the commencement of a lengthy polemical battle that was the most significant of all the early debates on the divorce.

Fisher's first treatise has regrettably not come down to us, but we are fortunate in being able to reconstruct from later sources the general lines of its argument. The book, vaguely described by its author and its opponent as 'Liber', was cast in the form of a scholastic 'quaestio'. The question was 'Whether a marriage in which the pope has granted a dispensation for a man to marry his brother's wife is firm and indissoluble?'[23] Yet despite the scholastic format, there was a decidedly humanist strain in the 'Liber' as Fisher's first move was to grapple with the Hebrew and Greek renderings of the relevant scriptural texts. He observed correctly enough that one of the crucial sentences in the Vulgate rendering of Leviticus 18:16, 'Nobody may marry his brother's wife', was not to be found in the original Hebrew or Greek, and he conjectured that it was an annotation that had crept into the text through scribal error.[24] The scholastic character soon came to the fore, however, as Fisher distinguished four possible meanings of the term 'divine law': canon law, divine by virtue of the authority with which God had endowed its framers, the apostles and their successors the bishops; the law of the Gospel, the rules for belief and conduct promulgated by Christ; 'positive' divine law, that part of the law of

Moses which endured only until the promulgation of the Gospel; and finally, 'natural' law which, unlike the other three, was perpetually binding. Having elaborated this distinction, he observed that the marriage in question had manifestly not been forbidden in the Gospel, and set out to demonstrate that it was not forbidden under natural law either.[25] It is to this section of the work that we should ascribe his argument, briefly recapitulated in the later 'Licitum fuisse', about the discernibility of natural law. His principle was that any statement of natural law was capable of being instantly recognised as true by anyone of sound mind and good will through the natural light of reason.[26] Having thus defined natural law, he proposed a number of 'obstacles' which precluded the Levitical prohibition on marriage to a brother's wife from being accepted as part of it. The first was the principle that even where a particular act is enjoined by natural law, its contrary is not thereby necessarily rendered absolutely illicit.[27] The second was more cogent. It was simply the Deutero- nomical provision that a man should marry his childless brother's widow in order to raise a child in the dead brother's name.[28] Fisher's conclusion that God would not have commanded such a marriage were it indeed forbidden under natural law (and thus absolutely and intrinsically immoral) remains a compelling and irrefutable objection to the case that Henry and his advisers were attempting to establish.[29] The 'Liber' apparently went on to dismiss the trivial objections that the Deuteronomical provision was a dispensation rather than a commandment, and that it was ordained solely towards the procreation of a single heir to the deceased brother.[30] The final obstacle that Fisher brought forward was based on the exact parallel in degrees of affinity between, on the one hand, a man and his brother's wife and, on the other, a woman and her sister's husband. This parallel was made relevant by Leviticus 18:18 which, while it forbade marriage between a man and his wife's sister, made this contingent on the first wife's remaining alive. Since the limiting clause 'while the former is alive' ('illa vivente') implied that such a marriage was permissible after the death of the first wife, Fisher deduced that the degree of affinity established by the first marriage was not such as to render marriage within that degree intrinsically immoral. The same could therefore be said of the case of a man and his brother's wife, in which case the Levitical prohibition was neither absolute nor indispensable.[31] Once it had been established that the Levitical prohibition was not part of the natural or the evangelical law, and was therefore not immutable, it could remain binding on Christians only in so far as it was sanctioned by the canon law of the Church.[32] It was then undeniable that the pope could dispense with canon law, and that he had done so validly in the case of Henry and Catherine. Fisher developed this argument in a series of 'assertions'. He first dismissed the Henrician claim that the Levitical penalty of childlessness had in fact been exacted of couples who contracted marriage under the Deuteronomical provision, observing that scripture itself contained examples to the contrary.[33] Then he pointed out that popes had dispensed for such marriages in the past, notably Innocent III for the natives of Livonia and Alexander VI for King Manuel of Portugal. Fisher's third precedent, that Martin V had dispensed a man to retain a wife whom he had discovered after the marriage to be his sister, was a *canard* derived from the writings of the canonist Antoninus of Florence.[34] He buttressed this with the thesis of an unspecified 'Antonius' (perhaps de Rosellis) that while dispensations should not be granted to marry a woman where a sexual relationship had already existed with her mother or sister, if such a marriage were to take place, it should be presumed valid and allowed to stand.[35] In conclusion, he reiterated his confidence that neither God nor Moses could have commanded an action condemned as immoral in Leviticus, and that therefore marriage contracted under the Deuteronomical provision could in no sense be contrary to natural law.[36]

It is doubly regrettable that Wakefield's original reply to Fisher's 'Liber' is also lost. But large portions of it do survive in summary or slightly redrafted form, and these enable us to reconstruct not only Fisher's 'Liber' but also Wakefield's reply, the 'Codex'. In addition we have the covering letter under which Wakefield sent Fisher his reply late in 1527 – although until now this letter has been thought to date from 1534. It reads as a *pièce justificative* excusing its author's defection to Henry VIII.[37] Wakefield was already finding that there were disadvantages to his decision. His letter is dated from London rather than from Syon Priory, and his past-tense reference to his stay at Syon confirms that he was no longer resident there. Since Syon was a centre of support for Catherine, and Wakefield laments the loss of Catherine's favour, it is possible that changing sides had led to his eviction. His detailed account of how Edward Foxe and Henry himself recruited him, his concern at the loss of his anonymity as an opponent of Catherine's (which he had certainly lost by late 1528), and his distress about popular disapproval of his position, all read like an exercise in damage control. But after the first quarter of 1528 he ceased to receive the stipend of the Hebrew lecturer on Fisher's private foundation at St John's.[38] His replacement, Ralph Baynes, was an outspoken supporter of Catherine. It is hard to resist the conclusion that Fisher withdrew patronage from Wakefield as soon as he heard of his *volte face*. The respectful and almost conciliatory tone of the covering letter is in marked contrast to the arrogant and contemptuous tone Wakefield later adopted. An explanation of this might be found in his loss of the Hebrew lectureship.

Wakefield's 'Codex' survives in three incomplete sections or versions. The earliest is found in the manuscript 'Eruditi cuiusdam responsio' (henceforth 'Responsio'), which appears to be a summary of the 'Codex'.[39] Much of this 'Responsio' reappears in Wakefield's *Syntagma de Incorruptione Hebraeorum Codicum*, published some time in 1534. The third source for the 'Codex' is

Wakefield's *Kotser Codicis*, also published in 1534, a work whose title – 'a fragment of a Codex' – betrays its relationship to the original treatise, and whose text also exhibits parallels with the 'Responsio'.[40] The 'Responsio' was a reply not to Fisher's original 'Liber', though, but to a summary of it that Fisher had himself provided.[41] Moreover, it was originally drafted in the king's name, and only later amended into anonymity.[42] Its tone is from the start markedly offensive, which suggests that the relationship between Fisher and Wakefield had deteriorated since the original composition of the 'Codex'. It begins by making cheap capital out of Fisher's choice of the 'quaestio' genre, disdainfully remarking that there is in the work 'much that is to my mind superfluous, excessively scholastic, and insufficiently solid and robust'.[43] The final dismissal of Fisher's effort as 'parergis tuis' ('your triflings') is a long way from the polite deference of the covering letter of the 'Codex'.[44] And it stands in stark contrast to the extravagant praise which Wakefield, taking advantage of the cloak of anonymous or pseudonymous authorship, chose to shower upon himself: 'he is uncommonly learned in scripture, an ornament not only to this kingdom but also to the whole of Christendom, a match for any number of Jews in his knowledge of the Hebrew tongue'.[45] The chief importance of the 'Responsio', though, as almost certainly of the 'Codex' too, was in its original solution to the problem of the contradictory texts and in its reply to Fisher's claim that Leviticus 18:16 did not forbid *marriage* to a brother's wife. Wakefield's argument, preserved in both the 'Responsio' and the *Syntagma*, was that the term 'revelare turpitudinem' used throughout Leviticus 18 was a synonym for marriage.[46] Since its primary implication was plainly sexual intercourse, Wakefield had to conclude that it meant specifically a consummated marriage, and not merely marital consent. His solution to the Deuteronomical exception was simple – it applied only where the first marriage had not been consummated.[47] It is to this exegesis that we can trace the importance attached by the king's side throughout the controversy to the alleged consummation of Catherine's marriage to Arthur. Only if that marriage had been consummated could the full force of Leviticus 18:16 be brought to bear on the case.

The controversy between Fisher and Wakefield extended into 1528, by which time diplomatic moves were afoot to secure from the pope a commission under which the question of the marriage could be resolved by a court in England. The advantage that such a commission would have given to Henry hardly needs spelling out. Louis XII of France, anxious to extricate himself from marriage to the ugly Jeanne de Valois (daughter of Louis XI) in order to marry the heiress Anne de Bretagne, had obtained just such a commission in 1498 from the pliable Alexander VI. Although Louis had a slightly stronger case than Henry VIII, the affairs were in many ways very similar. Jeanne never stood a chance, and was widely perceived as the victim of injustice. Henry's papal commission was procured after tortuous negotiations, and was brought to

England by Cardinal Campeggio in September 1528. At first, Campeggio tried to arrange a compromise settlement by which Catherine would retire to a nunnery. But this solution, itself of dubious canonical legitimacy, was firmly repudiated by Catherine, at which point Campeggio resorted to delaying tactics, presumably at Clement VII's instigation.[48] The tribunal over which he was to preside with Wolsey did not meet until June 1529. In the meantime, Catherine had recruited counsel to represent her. Fisher was of course the leader of this group, which included two other bishops who had already written in her favour – Nicholas West (bishop of Ely) and Cuthbert Tunstall (bishop of London, soon translated to Durham). Besides these three, she also obtained the services of John Clerk (bishop of Bath and Wells), John Veysey (bishop of Exeter), Henry Standish (bishop of St Asaphs), George de Athequa (bishop of Llandaff and Catherine's confessor), William Warham (archbishop of Canterbury), Thomas Abel (Catherine's chaplain), Robert Ridley (Tunstall's cousin and secretary), Edward Powell (canon of Salisbury), Richard Featherstone (Princess Mary's chaplain) and Robert Cliff (West's chancellor).[49] The overlap of this group with the opponents first of Luther in the 1520s and then of Henry's religious policies in the 1530s is striking. While it is manifestly not the case that religious conservatives invariably supported Catherine, it is clear that her supporters were almost invariably from the more papalist wing of the English Church. The fate of her dozen counsellors is illuminating. Four lost their lives and one (de Athequa) went into exile for refusing the royal supremacy; a further three (West, Clerk and Ridley) spent some time in prison for opposing the king's religious policy, one (Warham) died on the brink of resistance, and one (Tunstall) conformed under intimidation. Only Standish and the aged Veysey conformed without demur.

When the legatine tribunal at last convened on 31 May, its proceedings were immediately and irretrievably marred by Catherine's total refusal to co-operate. She appeared in person at only the second and third sittings (18 and 21 June) to protest against the impossibility of receiving a fair hearing in England and to lodge her appeal to Rome.[50] Although proceedings continued in her absence, they were of dubious legality. Her case was argued, unofficially in view of her appeal, by her counsel. It was Fisher who breathed the first life into the dull routine of the court with an impassioned oration delivered at the fifth session on 28 June. Taking his cue from the Church calendar (it was the eve of the nativity of John the Baptist), he offered to give his life in defence of the marriage bond just as the Baptist had.[51] This irritated the king for two reasons. First it cast him in the unsympathetic role of Herod (for which, as time was to tell, he was admirably suited). Secondly, it glossed over one of the planks of the royal case, namely that the sin for which Herod had been upbraided by the Baptist was that of marrying the wife (Herodias) of his brother (Philip). Together with this thunderbolt, Fisher threw down his written challenge in the form of his treatise

'Licitum fuisse', a work of about 16,000 words divided into six axioms of unequal length. The first and longest dealt with the central question of whether or not marriage to a brother's widow was forbidden by divine law. The second covered the theory and practice of papal dispensations, and the remaining four briefly spelled out that if the marriage was dispensable and had in this case been dispensed, then Henry's marriage to Catherine had been properly arranged, contracted and sacramentally sealed, and was thus indissoluble by any earthly authority.[52] Only the first of these axioms, an extended consideration of the basic scriptural texts, need detain us long. It began, again in highly scholastic fashion, with two syllogisms. The premisses of the first were that the impediment between the persons in this case was a matter of human rather than divine law (major premiss); and that the pope could dispense any impediment under human law (minor premiss). Postponing consideration of the minor until later, Fisher set about demonstrating the major premiss with a further syllogism: nowhere in scripture other than in Leviticus was marriage between a brother and his deceased brother's wife forbidden (major premiss); but the case in hand did not fall under the Levitical prohibition (minor premiss). [53] The crux of the argument was thus the minor premiss of the second syllogism, and this was the subject of the first axiom. Fisher commenced by laying down three principles in turn: that the same act could not be both moral and immoral; nor both compulsory and forbidden; nor finally deserving of both praise and blame, of both reward and punishment.[54] To illustrate the first principle, Fisher undertook to prove that although Leviticus forbade marriage to a brother's wife, marriage to a childless brother's widow was considered righteous 'before, under, and even until the consummation of, the Law'.[55] His main evidence was the case of Thamar and the sons of Judah (Gen 38). When Thamar's first husband, Er, died before they had had children, his father Judah gave her his second son, Onan, in marriage. When he too died without children, Judah contracted his third son, Shelah, to marry her when he should come of age, although he was reluctant to fulfil his pledge lest Shelah should share the fate of his brothers. When he failed to deliver Shelah, Thamar enticed Judah himself into intercourse by masquerading as a prostitute. She become pregnant, and when her condition became known, Judah hoped to eliminate the danger to Shelah by having her executed for adultery, although he changed his mind and admitted his guilt when she told him he was the father. The importance of this episode for Fisher was its testimony to the practice of levirate marriage among the Jews before Moses. Judah's betrothal of Shelah to Thamar despite his fears, and his subsequent admission of guilt for not fulfilling his agreement, showed that the custom was deemed an obligation. And his attempt to have Thamar condemned for adultery – rather than for fornication – showed that her marriage to Shelah was recognised.[56] The case of Thamar was undoubtedly the strongest that could be alleged for the exegesis of the Deuteronomical provision, the very wording of which was echoed in Judah's instruction to Onan to marry Thamar (Gen 38:8).[57] Throughout the controversy it remained an embarrassment to Henry's advisers, who tried all sorts of shifts to escape its significance. Fisher's illustration for the practice of the levirate under the Law was provided by the case of the marriage of Ruth to her cousin Boaz, and its practice even at the consummation of the Law (that is, at the time of Christ's birth) by a conjectural argument about the parentage of Joseph, the husband of the Virgin Mary. The genealogies of Christ presented by Matthew and Luke disagreed about the identity of Joseph's father, but Fisher argued that this discrepancy could be resolved if it were assumed that his mother had married two brothers under the law of the levirate, and that therefore one evangelist named his natural, and the other his legal, father.[58]

The remaining principles under which Fisher examined the contradiction between Leviticus and Deuteronomy tended to become repetitive. His chief arguments were as follows. The royal claim that Deuteronomy 25:5 constituted a dispensation rather than a commandment was rebutted with an impressive list of authorities as well as the observation that dispensations did not commonly impose penalties for non-compliance.[59] Nobody denied that Leviticus was a prohibition. But if Deuteronomy was a commandment, it followed that the two texts could not be talking of the same thing.[60] Since Leviticus 18:16 threatened those who contravened it with childlessness and infamy, while Deuteronomy 25:5 promised a perpetual posterity and praise to those who obeyed it, Fisher concluded that the two provisions could not be contemplating one and the same act.[61] The advantage of this line of attack was that he could prescind from the knotty problem of whether or not Leviticus 18:16 was binding under natural law. He did not concede that it was, but irrespective of that question, he was able to conclude that the Levitical prohibition was merely a general statement to which Deuteronomy made an exception.[62] To lend plausibility to this, he drew analogies with the fourth and sixth commandments. The general prohibition of work on the Sabbath had not prevented the performance of circumcision and other liturgical acts on that day under the old law, and the general prohibition of homicide did not render capital punishment immoral.[63] The remainder of the axiom dealt with various objections that could be levelled against this position. He decisively dismissed the contention that Deuteronomy was inherently of less authority than Leviticus.[64] Although he conceded that the Deuteronomical imposition of the levirate had lost its force since the pro-clamation of the Gospel, he insisted that the laws of Leviticus (except where they expressed natural law) had likewise lost their force.[65] A number of trivial objections regarding the case of the Livonians were easily brushed aside, but more attention was given to the claim that the Levitical prohibition had been promulgated afresh in the New Testament by John the Baptist. Henry's counsel recurred throughout the controversy to the Baptist's condemnation of Herod for marrying his brother's wife. Their argument turned on the assumption that Philip the Tetrarch was dead when Herod married Herodias, but Chrysostom alone among the fathers was of this opinion.[66] The consensus, as Fisher rightly observed, was that Philip was still alive. Moreover, he continued, even if Philip was dead he had left a surviving child (a daughter), and the law of the levirate was therefore inapplicable. This in turn meant that the Baptist's condemnation of Herod was in no way prejudicial to levirate marriage.[67] The last objection was a desperate attempt to argue that the marriage forbidden by Leviticus must have been intrinsically immoral because it was described by Moses as an 'abomination'.[68] Fisher replied that many things thus described in Leviticus were widely practised among Christians, specifying transvestitism (permitted in plays) and the eating of eels (prized as a delicacy).[69] He wound up his case with a recapitulation of the various arguments and authorities he had adduced in the course of the axiom.[70]

Several months before the commencement of the tribunal, rumours had reached Fisher that Wakefield had found something new in the Hebrew to support Henry's case. We learn of this from a letter, to one 'Paul', who appears to have been shaken by a report that Wakefield's discovery had caused all the bishops who previously opposed Henry's wishes to swing into line behind him.[71] Fisher assured him that he could not see anything in the Hebrew capable of assisting the King's case.[72] Wakefield's discovery was in fact to be sprung upon an unsuspecting world in the early days of the legatine tribunal. If it had been true, it would have completely undermined the reliance of the Queen's counsel on the exception to the Levitical prohibition provided by Deuteronomy. For Wakefield quite simply denied that the Hebrew text of Deuteronomy pre-scribed marriage between a widow and the *brother* of her first husband. Instead, he maintained, the true signification of the Hebrew word was any near, male relative ('cousin' in the sixteeth-century sense), and the Septuagint and Vulgate versions of this were wrong in rendering it brother. Although his own presenta-tion of this argument is no longer extant, it is easy to see how it would have continued: the Levitical prohibition on marriage to a brother's wife would become a qualification on the text of Deuteronomy, rather than the latter an exception to the former. Fisher rose to the challenge, rapidly extemporising a reply with which he floored Wakefield in what amounted to a verbal scholastic disputation before the court. This reply was later written up and expanded for presentation to the court, and it is to this version that we owe all we know of Wakefield's original case.[73] Fisher took issue with Wakefield on several grounds. Above all, he could not countenance the tactless introduction of such a sensitive issue in front of a gathering that included laymen, because even to hint that the Vulgate contained errors might undermine their faith in it, and thus in the Church that had endorsed it.[74] Nor was he pleased by the attack on the inspiration of the Septuagint.[75] Unfortunately, his written reply was hampered by an undue respect for the talents of his opponent, a man who had taught him all the Hebrew he knew and was not averse to reminding him of that fact. It was probably this that kept Fisher from coming to grips with him on the weakest point of the case, the precise signification of the Hebrew word rendered as 'brother'. For Wakefield's claim was in fact completely without foundation, and Cajetan was later to provide the devastating refutation that the word for 'brother' in Deuteronomy 25:5 was the same as that used in Leviticus 18:16![76] Fisher's line was less dramatic, though equally effective. Accepting Wakefield's philology, he nevertheless insisted that the interpretation and application of Deuteronomy 25:5 remained unchanged, and were to be properly understood in the light of scriptural instances of the levirate, and of patristic comment. The scriptural instances were those of Thamar and the sons of Judah, and of Ruth and Boaz. He gave especially close attention to the latter case. Admitting that Boaz was indeed not the brother but only a close relative of Ruth's first husband, Mahlon, he emphasised that Boaz had initially been prevented from marrying Ruth by the existence of a closer male relative, who therefore had a prior claim. Only when this rival had renounced his claim could Boaz marry Ruth.[77] Pausing only to remind the legates of the chaos that would erupt within the Church should the reliability of the Vulgate be questioned, Fisher embarked on a sophisticated refutation of Wakefield's thesis, divided into five 'collections'. The first was a succinct summary of the argument he had developed against Pace in defence of the inspiration of the Septuagint. He also vindicated the authority of the Vulgate, appealing to its long acceptance by the Latin Church, and especially by the See of Peter. Since both Greek and Latin versions were in different ways infallible, there could be no doubt that they were both correct in rendering the Hebrew as 'brother'.[78] Fisher's second 'collection' rested on the unanimity of the fathers in referring Deuteronomy 25:5 to a brother.[79] The third recycled the familiar argument about the pope's power to pass definitive judgment in disputes over the interpretation of scripture.[80] The fourth corroborated the strict interpretation of 'brother' from the citation by Matthew, Mark and Luke of Deuteronomy 25:5 as applying to brothers.[81] The final collection grappled more closely with the three recensions of the text, comparing literal Latin renderings of the original Hebrew and Greek with the Vulgate. The three versions are placed in parallel columns, and their essential identity is easily demonstrated.[82] In conclusion, Fisher recapitulated the arguments of 'Licitum fuisse' against the absurdities consequent upon assuming that Deuteronomy and Leviticus contradicted each other.[83] Then, widening the scope of the discussion, he argued that the custom codified in Deuteronomy 25:5 had, like many other Jewish laws, been prevalent before the time of Moses, and he equated this ancient law with the Cabbala.[84] The real reason for the complex marital legislation, he continued, was to ensure that the ancestry of Christ remained clear of doubt and stain. If it were not for that legislation, and in particular for the levirate provision, then the conflicting genealogies of Christ given by Matthew and Luke could not be reconciled.[85]

The failure of the legatine tribunal to produce the required judgment brought about Wolsey's downfall later in 1529. With the papal revocation of the divorce case to Rome in the wake of Catherine's appeal, it also brought Henry's policy to an impasse. The next step, suggested by Thomas Cranmer, was to set about consulting a wide range of European universities and theologians in search of support for the royal case. The two English universities were the first to be approached, and it is worth examining the events at Cambridge in some detail because of Fisher's connections there. On 16 February 1530 Henry wrote to Cambridge, and his letter was delivered the following Saturday by Gardiner and Foxe, who at once began to canvass support. However, the opposition began mobilising their party even more effectively. When the king's letter was read to a university congregation on Sunday afternoon, and those present were asked for their opinions, the proceedings soon dissolved in uproar. The vice-chancellor, William Buckmaster, proposed instead that the matter be referred to a committee of 'indifferent men', to be decided by a two-thirds majority. This was agreed, although there was inevitably dispute about who was 'indifferent'. The supporters of the Queen disapproved in particular of the selection of John Salcot, abbot of St Benet's Hulme (Norfolk) and William Repps (or Rugge), subprior of Norwich, rare visitors who had come up specially for the debate – the king's party had clearly tried to pack the congregation with a number of backwoodsmen. But Gardiner overcame the obstacle by pointing out that there was hardly anyone who had not already come to some judgment on the case, and that the university had no choice but to trust the good faith of the committee. We are fortunate in knowing the membership and allegiance of the committee. Besides the vice-chancellor and the two proctors, it comprised ten doctors of divinity and sixteen other theologians, making twenty-nine in total. Sixteen were committed to Henry's cause, and of the remaining thirteen, four were thought to be wavering. Henry's supporters included seven future Henrician bishops (Salcot, Repps, Shaxton, Latimer, Skip, Goodrich and Heath), the other thirteen only one (George Day), besides a Marian bishop (Ralph Baynes). Repps, Heath, Simon Matthew and Buckmaster himself were the only thoroughgoing conservatives among Henry's supporters, although John Skip later retreated from his evangelical associations of the 1530s and was perhaps always a conservative at heart. Half of Henry's supporters were later to adopt strongly reformed positions: Salcot, John Edmunds, Crome, Simon Heynes, Shaxton, Latimer and Goodrich. Catherine's party included a bevy of strong religious conservatives (Watson, Thomson, Venetus, Downes, Longforth, Thixtill, Day and Baynes), and nobody of known Protestant inclinations. It was also strong in associations with the colleges of St John's, Christ's, Michaelhouse, Queens' and Pembroke – which all had close links with

Fisher. There is no obvious pattern to the collegiate associations of Henry's supporters.[86] The limitations of the evidence prevent us from seeing far beneath the surface of this affair. But a stray reference in a letter from Foxe to Buckmaster written in January 1530 casts further light on it. At Christmas 1529 the university had been shocked by a tendentious sermon from Hugh Latimer, and this had evoked pulpit replies from Robert Buckenham (prior of Blackfriars), and Ralph Baynes, John Brickenden and Thomas Greenwood (all fellows of St John's). Foxe, commenting on this, alleged that the Johnians had been egged on by Dr Watson and other friends of the bishop of Rochester because of Latimer's known sympathy for Henry's divorce.[87] Dr Watson and Ralph Baynes (the college lecturer in Hebrew at St John's) wrote in favour of Catherine, as did Dr Robert Shirwood, a prominent hebraist perhaps connected with St John's.[88] The records of an interrogation of Fisher in 1534 reveal the authorities' suspicion that he had egged on Baynes and Day to oppose the royal position. Day had in the event abstained, and had written an apologetic epistle to the bishop justifying his action. Baynes had written to Fisher complaining that the affair in Cambridge had been 'handled by authority and conveyance'. However, our reading of Fisher's involvement must be tempered with reference to his own statement under interrogation that he had not advised anybody to support Catherine's cause.[89] Although the nature of patronage relationships is such that little evidence of active influence has come down to us, we do have some illuminating *aperçus* on the way in which these relationships could work. Dr Buckmaster wrote to John Edmunds shortly after these stirring events to say that his support for the king had cost him a benefice that he had expected from one Mr Throckmorton.[90] If, as is likely, this was none other than Sir George Throckmorton, all becomes clear. George Throckmorton had close connections with Fisher, More and the priory of Syon, and was one of the most active Parliamentary members of what has been termed the 'Aragonese connection'.[91]

In the aftermath of the legatine tribunal, the writings of Fisher made the theological running. His treatise 'Licitum fuisse' opened a new phase in hostilities. It was undoubtedly one of the most cogent presentations of the queen's defence, and it made a great impact when it was so dramatically thrust upon the court in 1529. The threat which it posed to the king's cause seemed so grave that it attracted a thorough refutation from Henry's advisers.[92] It was probably in the light of this that Fisher produced a revised version which, while it expands and rearranges the arguments of 'Licitum', is essentially the same work. This in turn attracted a further three refutations from Henry's advisers. All three take issue with the theological arguments of its first axiom, and so were presumably made by theologians, but there seems to be little hope of identifying the authors.[93] The year following the prorogation of the legatine tribunal saw Fisher compose at least two more tracts on Catherine's behalf.

Only one, the *De Causa Matrimonii*, survives, but it contains evidence about another, which for convenience we shall call 'Decem rationes'. *De Causa* explicitly summarises from an earlier work ten reasons for believing that the Levitical prohibition on marriage to a brother's wife was meant to apply only during the lifetime of that brother.[94] These reasons appear neither in 'Licitum' nor in 'Ne qua fiat', nor (so far as we can tell from the limited evidence) in his original 'Liber'. Indeed, there is hardly place for such arguments in any of them, as they all assume that the Levitical prohibition in general applies as much after the death of the brother as before. We may therefore conclude that the ten reasons represent a new stage in Fisher's appreciation of the issues raised by Henry's divorce, and that they formed the central theme of a distinct treatise produced after the tribunal but before the *De Causa* (printed by August 1530, and presumably finished several months previously). The ten reasons are easily summarised. They begin with an argument from authority which listed the principal exponents of this interpretation. But the strongest argument is the parallel drawn with the prohibition on marriage to a deceased wife's sister (Lev 18:18), which made the explicit proviso 'vivente sorore'. Fisher proposed that the proviso 'vivente fratre' ought to be presumed in reading Leviticus 18:16. A further analogy with the prohibition against marriage to a neighbour's wife provided powerful corroboration. Although it was not specified that the neighbour must still be alive, nobody imagined that remarriage was absolutely forbidden for widows. The nature of the marriage bond itself was the fourth reason. Since the unity of flesh between man and wife was broken irretrievably by the death of either partner, after a man's death there could be no real relation between his widow and his brother, and thus there was no real reason why they should not marry. The remaining six reasons all ring familiar changes on the theme of the difficulties consequent upon allowing an actual contradiction between Leviticus and Deuteronomy. In each case, the novel step is the resolution of the contradiction. Since Deuteronomy 25:5 prescribed marriage to a childless brother's widow, such marriages could not be immoral. Such marriages could not therefore be forbidden by Leviticus 18:16, which must consequently be taken as forbidding simply marriage to a brother's *wife*, leaving open the question of marriage to his *widow*. The whole argument is highly plausible, and offers the most elegant solution to the whole problem. It is interesting to note the suspicion of Fisher's interrogators in 1534 that he had first been alerted to the value of this approach by John Clerk, the bishop of Bath and Wells. Pressing him about a letter from Clerk on this subject that they had found among his papers, they asked 'Whether he has followed in his books this interpretation of the bishop of Bath?' Fisher's reply evaded the question, doubtless in order to keep Clerk out of trouble, merely observing that many scholars had adopted that interpretation, and that he himself had not based his case entirely upon it.[95]

The *De Causa Matrimonii* of 1530 was Fisher's most comprehensive treatment of the problem to date. Divided into five sections, it went over most of the ground covered in his previous writings, but also explored new areas. The first two sections, proving that Deuteronomy 25:5 was indeed a commandment and that it should be understood primarily of brothers, do little more than recast the arguments of 'Licitum fuisse' and 'Ne qua fiat.'[96] But Fisher examined the question of Christ's genealogy in detail for the first time, discovering in it, on the authority of the early father Julius Africanus, two instances of the levirate. The first concerned Joseph, the husband of the Virgin Mary. Where Matthew had written 'Jacob begat Joseph' (Mt 1:16), Luke wrote 'Joseph was the son of Heli' (Lk 3:23). Julius had reconciled these with the deduction that Matthew was referring to natural, and Luke to legal paternity. This would be possible if Jacob and Heli were brothers, and Heli had died before his wife had borne him any children. For thus Jacob would have been obliged to marry his widow and raise children in Heli's name. Unfortunately, this solution entailed a fresh problem, how Heli and Jacob could be brothers. For Matthew had written 'Matthan begat Jacob', while Luke had written 'Heli was the son of Mathat'. But Julius had a ready answer. Jacob and Heli were sons of the same woman by successive husbands. She had married first Matthan, of the line of Solomon, and then Mathat (or Melchi, according to Julius), of the line of Nathan. Despite its complexity, this theory is not impossible, and Julius claimed for it the additional authority of having been handed down by Christ's collateral descendants. Fisher simply took over Julius's argument wholesale, citing him at considerable length.[97] The second instance of the levirate in Christ's ancestry was that of Salatiel, described by Luke as the son of Neri (Lk 3:27), but said by Matthew to have been begotten by Jechonias. It was solved in much the same way.[98] The third section of *De Causa* takes its departure from Augustine's three alternative interpretations of Leviticus 18:16 as prohibiting marriage to a living brother's wife, to a living brother's divorced wife, or to a dead brother's widow. Fisher drew especial attention to Augustine's remark that it was difficult to decide which was the correct interpretation. Insuring himself against refutation, he claimed that irrespective of which sense was preferred, the Deuteronomical provision could still not be thought to contradict it. He began with the case of a living brother's wife. If this were correct, he argued on the authority of the Scotist tradition, then the relationship between a man and his brother's widow was merely one of affinity, and was therefore a matter of canon law subject to papal dispensation.[99] If the alternative interpretation were correct and the prohibition also applied to brothers' widows then, he argued, resorting to the Thomist tradition, it was merely judicial and not a matter of natural law; and the Deuteronomical provision was therefore a perfectly licit exception from it.[100] In the fourth stage of his work, Fisher returned to the interpretation of Leviticus as referring only to a living brother's wife, inclining towards it on the familiar grounds that God could not have commanded an immoral act.[101] Since God had commanded marriage to a childless brother's widow, marriage to a brother's widow could not be intrinsically evil. In support of this, he introduced the almost universal medieval opinion that no marriage was absolutely contrary to natural law except for one contracted between parent and child.[102] The crucial scriptural test-case for this was the marriage of Abraham to his half-sister Sarah. Although the royal advisers were able to make something of the undoubted fact that he used to call her his sister as a ruse, Abraham's statement to Abimelech that Sarah was the daughter of his father but not of his mother was unequivocal.[103] The final part of the work returned to the argument that the pope had the power to dispense in such cases as the king's. At this point Fisher invoked the concept of 'ratio legis', the reason underlying any particular law, in order to make the papal power to dispense from Leviticus 18:16 more acceptable.[104] The reason for this law, Fisher maintained (following Chrysostom), was to spread the social bonds established by matrimony as widely as possible, and thus to diffuse love and peace throughout society.[105] He drew his case to a close with a series of canonical and theological opinions in favour of the papal dispensing power, and concluded with a summary of the whole work.[106]

The dominance achieved in controversy by Fisher's 'Licitum' and its derivatives was short-lived. In 1531 'Licitum' was to be displaced as the definitive statement of the case by a book produced on Henry's side, the *Gravissimae Censurae*.[107] The opinions of foreign universities to which the title *Censurae* alluded in fact occupied only a small part of this book. The bulk consisted of seven chapters of detailed argument from scripture, tradition and canon law against the validity of marriage to a brother's wife or widow. Several refutations were produced over the next couple of years by Catherine's friends and supporters. The most accessible of these was the *Invicta Veritas* of her chaplain Thomas Abel. Despite its Latin title, the treatise was actually written in English, and it was a powerful presentation of the case for the defence. It is noteworthy that Fisher's interrogators in 1534 thought that Abel's work was derived almost wholly from his.[108] Another reply, published anonymously, was the *Non esse neque divino, neque naturae iure prohibitum*. This was thought by Henry VIII's advisers to have been compiled either by the Dutch humanist and savant, Heinrich Cornelius Agrippa, or less probably by Juan Luis Vives.[109] But a close perusal reveals that it too was the work of an Englishman – quite possibly Sir Thomas Elyot.[110] Abroad, Dr Ortiz, an agent of Charles V who acted for Catherine in Rome, composed a reply to *Censurae* at the request of the pope. Fisher hoped that the Spanish theologian Moscoso would do likewise; and Chapuys unsuccessfully urged the same task on Agrippa.

It must be emphasised that despite Fisher's importance in the English opposition to the divorce, his was not the organising role. That belonged to

Eustace Chapuys, Charles V's ambassador to Henry VIII.[111] Nevertheless, Fisher was especially closely associated with Chapuys until his arrest in 1534, and the records of his interrogations show that the government entertained grave suspicions, which they were never able to substantiate, about the nature of this connection.[112] It began shortly after Chapuys's arrival in October 1529. Chapuys was soon busy smuggling treatises in favour of Catherine out of the country. Early in 1530 he reported to Charles that he had already despatched one by Fisher, who had recently completed another, which Catherine had ordered Chapuys to pass on. Significantly enough, he also reported that Fisher was afraid to be known as it author.[113] These works can probably be identified with 'Licitum' and De Causa Matrimonii. By November 1530 Chapuys was hoping to publish two further books by Fisher – if Fisher had no objections – and in December he sent them forward.[114] 1531 saw him export Fisher's 'Brevis Apologia' (his reply to Gravissimae Censurae) in three parts between June and November. Fisher's writings were not the only ones Chapuys handled. He sent out a treatise by Tunstall early on, and the English authorities suspected Fisher of assisting in smuggling out works by John Clerk and Nicholas Wilson.[115] In 1531 he devoted a great deal of energy to persuading Agrippa to write against the divorce, but though Agrippa was not unwilling, his personal troubles prevented him from doing so.[116] In 1532 Chapuys went a stage further. As the divorce controversy reached its climax he arranged for the clandestine publication abroad of works in Catherine's favour. Three of these are known, all by English authors, and all published under the fictitious imprint of Sebastian Golsen of Luneburg. There was in fact no press at Luneburg in the sixteenth century, nor was there anywhere a printer with the name of Golsen, and the books were probably printed in Antwerp by Martin Keyser.[117] One of them, the Non esse, was dedicated to Chapuys. The second, Thomas Abel's Invicta Veritas, has no apparent connection with the ambassador. Yet it was the first work to reveal the existence of Peter of Paluda's commentary on Leviticus, which contradicted his earlier commentary on the Sentences which had pronounced levirate marriage to be contrary to divine law. And Chapuys was reported in January 1531 as having written to Mai, his counterpart in Rome, about just such a work of Paluda's, said to be in the library of the Paris Blackfriars.[118] But the most interesting of the three works was the reply to A Glasse of the Trouthe, the work entitled Parasceve, which appeared beneath the pseudonym 'Philalethes Hyperboreus' – 'lover of truth from the north'.[119] According to the information which reached Cromwell, the book was the work of Fisher, who had given it to two Spanish friars to smuggle out of the country. They had prepared it for the press, and two English Observant Franciscans, William Peto and Henry Elstow, had carried copies back to England.[120] In fact this information was wildly inaccurate. The book in question was undoubtedly Parasceve, but Fisher could not have been the author, who claimed to have spent some time studying in Paris.[121] And as Fisher had been under house arrest at Lambeth since 6 April it is unlikely that he had anything to do with its production.[122] It is far more likely that Chapuys was behind it.

One is at a loss to explain why Fisher's reply to *Gravissimae Censurae*, his 'Brevis Apologia', was never published.[123] It was successfully smuggled out of the country, and was easily Fisher's most important treatise on the divorce. Despite its length (some 60,000 words), there is little new in it, apart from a tantalising reference to yet another lost work on the divorce, which apparently marshalled the various authorities under six separate headings.[124] 'Brevis Apologia' is divided into seven chapters which answer precisely to the seven chapters of *Censurae*. Thus the first deals with the evidence from the Old Testament about the scope of the Levitical and Deuteronomical legislation, and the second with the evidence from the New Testament, chiefly the case of Herod and Herodias. The third and fourth chapters refute arguments built respectively on patristic and medieval authorities. The fifth considers whether, and if so in what sense, the Levitical prohibition is to be regarded as a matter of natural, divine and moral law according to the definitions of those laws elaborated in *Censurae*. Chapter six deals with further argumentation designed to prove from the customs and writings of the pagans that marriage to a brother's wife is against natural law, and the final chapter meets the case that the pope is unable to dispense for a marriage contrary to the Levitical prohibition. The most significant theme in the book is that the Levitical prohibition should be read as implicitly qualified by the proviso that it forbids marriage to a living brother's wife, and not to a dead brother's widow. As we have seen, Fisher had been inclined towards this exegesis since late 1529 or early 1530. Even so, he continued to hedge his bets, arguing that if this qualification were not to be approved by the Church, then one of the other two qualifications proposed by Augustine must be accepted instead. But his less guarded comments show that he was personally convinced on the matter. This can be seen in the proliferation of reasons he adduced in support of it. From ten in 1530 they had now become sixteen and, he remarked later, 'the prohibitions of Leviticus 20 show clearly that they should all be understood of living spouses'.[125] The most important advance on his previous treatises is the emphasis given to the idea that the Levitical prohibitions are directed against not so much unlawful marriage as illicit sexual intercourse. This underlies the extra six arguments for his preferred reading. Otherwise, the interest of the 'Brevis Apologia' lies in the light it casts on Fisher's changing attitudes to Henry and his advisers. There is a studious failure to remark on Henry's motives which contrasts strongly with his earlier confidence in the king's good faith. Where his previous writings had been not merely polite but even friendly towards his opponents, and were clearly written on the assumption that both parties were engaged in a dispassionate quest for truth, the 'Apologia' makes no such concessions. The persistent use of the term 'these learned fellows' – 'hii doctissimi' – to describe the authors of *Censurae* smacks of sarcasm. As Fisher exposes one blatant misrepresentation after another, he is astonished at their manifest dishonesty. 'Blessed Jesus, what sort of conscience do these learned fellows have, who so grievously mutilate and distort the sayings of so weighty an author in a matter of such importance, in order to establish their error – to use no stronger term for it – any way they can', he laments when his opponents, through the judicious omission of a passage from the middle of a citation, disguise from their readers the fact that Hesychius interpreted the Levitical prohibitions as condemning illicit sex rather than improper marriage.[126] By this time, Fisher had come to appreciate that the divorce meant more to Henry and his supporters than loyalty to the papacy. Since he had been present at the events surrounding the first submission of the clergy in January 1531, and had been told then by Thomas Boleyn that Christ had left no vicar on earth, this is perhaps no startling insight.[127] But even at that late date a break with Rome probably seemed barely imaginable to most of Henry's supporters. When Fisher commented, 'These learned fellows do not seem to care how narrowly they restrict papal authority as long as they can secure the divorce', and accused his opponents of setting themselves in judgment over the pope, it is unlikely that he saw where things would end.[128] But he certainly caught the drift of the argument towards the conclusion that Henry should have the matter settled in his kingdom without any reference to the pope.[129] And he detected the implication that the papal dispensing power extended no further than that of an ordinary priest, namely to the forgiveness of sins.[130] Already his defence of the marriage was merging into the stand for papal primacy that was to bring him to the scaffold.

The end of the divorce controversy, when it came, was swift. Anne Boleyn conceived by the king around Christmas 1532 and Henry, claiming to have a dispensation from Rome, tricked one of his chaplains (Roland Lee) into solemnising their marriage secretly on 25 January.[131] The legal steps necessary to confirm the marriage were soon under way. The act in restraint of appeals was pushed through Parliament, and Convocation was presented with two theses for approval, in order to pave the way for Cranmer to act. The first was that marriage to the widow of a childless deceased brother was, if the first marriage had been consummated, contrary to divine law and therefore outside the pope's dispensing power. The second was that the marriage between Catherine and Prince Arthur had been consummated. These were passed by large majorities on 5 April.[132] John Fisher led the few dissidents, and the following day spoke in support of Catherine. He was promptly put under house arrest.[133] A month later, Cranmer convened his court at Dunstable, and after due process annulled Henry's marriage to Catherine on 23 May. After Anne's coronation on 31 May, Fisher was allowed to return to Rochester, where he stayed until recalled to London in April next year to begin the life sentence for misprision of treason imposed on him by the act of attainder against the Holy Maid of Kent. The true reason for his inclusion in this act is not hard to find. He had concealed nothing, for Henry VIII himself had already heard from the Maid in person the import of her predictions and admonitions. The decision to proceed by attainder rather than judicial process is a sufficient comment on the government's confidence in its case under the law. The truth was that no Englishman had done more to oppose and obstruct the divorce. The zeal with which Henry's advisers controverted his writings shows just how dangerous they were seen to be. It is likely that they occupied just as prominent a place upon the European stage. Although many scholars wrote at varying lengths on either side, few could be easily cleared from the charge of writing as their superiors desired or dictated. The scholars of Spain and the Netherlands, for example, judged to the last man in Catherine's favour. The opinions from Germany largely upheld Catherine because of Imperial influence among the Catholics, and because the Lutherans were reluctant to make the Levitical law binding on Christians in a state of evangelical liberty (although Zwinglians did make Leviticus 18 the foundation of their marriage law). The scholars of France, though by no means unanimous, were urged by François I to support Henry. The bribery was such on both sides in France and Italy that the hard-bought opinions of the universities carried little moral weight. Amid a debate in which the search for truth was so blatantly subordinated to the pursuit of interest, Fisher's stand against his own king, closely argued and maintained despite the losses and dangers it risked, was of a rare cast. Just as in England he carried with him many of his friends, so too in Europe it is likely that he took with him many of his admirers. Nevertheless he found himself on the losing side, as power and self-interest trampled on truth and decency. His early hagiographers were to present him in the guise of a latter-day John the Baptist, as a martyr to the indissolubility of the marriage bond. Since his condemnation was a direct result of denying the royal supremacy, this was not strictly true. Yet his opposition to the divorce had helped make necessary the anti-papal legislation under which he was to die, and it certainly evoked in Henry the bitterness which was to pursue a dying man to the Tower and to the scaffold.

11

Conclusion

THE CONCLUSION to a study of this nature is inevitably an attempt to draw together the threads, to spell out ideas which may have become obscured by the weight of the argument. We can best begin by recalling that this study has been intended as a contribution to three discussions. It is primarily an effort to understand the mind of John Fisher himself, and I shall return to this a little later. But the study of Fisher's writings has more general implications, firstly for historians of the English Reformation, and secondly for historians of the Counter-Reformation, the Catholic response to the challenge of Protestantism. For England, its importance lies in the evidence that Fisher's writings provide about the intellectual vitality of the Church of England on the eve of the Reformation. In this regard, it can be seen as part of that wider reassessment of the English Reformation which is often assimilated to the movement of 'revisionism'. Over the last twenty years, a succession of studies has revised our ideas about the late medieval Church. Its bishops have emerged as an altogether more impressive group than that so unsympathetically portrayed by John Foxe. Its popular appeal has been demonstrated beyond all possible doubt. Doubt has been cast instead on the significance of Lollardy and 'anti-clericalism' as symptoms of popular dissatisfaction with the established religion – doubt which remains undispersed even by recent trenchant restatements of the Foxean tradition.[1] Moreover, the resilience of the native Catholic tradition in the face of determined governmental and later clerical repression has been powerfully argued in number of works. This study would claim only a modest place in that debate, proposing that we can add intellectual muscle to the growing list of the strengths of late medieval English Catholicism. As I have argued elsewhere, there was a vigorous English response to the emergence of Reforming theology in the 1520s.[2] Fisher was by far the most talented and productive of the English opponents of the Reformers, but it is important to remember that he was by no means alone. The theologians of England – that is, of Oxford and Cambridge – came out strongly against the new doctrines at first. And unlike their Parisian counterparts, these theologians, with Fisher pre-eminent among them, were far from hostile to

184

the new currents of humanism stirring their intellectual waters. This must make us question the conventional but casual identification of humanism with Protestantism which has been facilitated by the posthumous recruitment of Erasmus as an honorary Anglican, and by the enduring misreading of the term 'new learning' as a synonym for humanist scholarship (its original connotation being doctrinal deviation). Large numbers of those who welcomed the new studies of Greek, Hebrew and the fathers were to remain loyal to the 'old learning' of Catholicism, even if they found themselves able to stomach schism. John Fisher's willingness both to call upon the resources of humanist scholarship and to criticise the scholastic tradition in the light of scripture and the fathers is hardly redolent of the 'fifteenth-century patterns of thought' attributed to him and his kind in the most influential account of the English Reformation. The fathers of the Council of Trent and the many others who in turn drew on Fisher's works in their theological endeavours would indeed have been surprised to be told, as the same authority suggests, that they had discarded Fisher's patterns of thought.[3] Fisher's willingness to contemplate, in principle at least, vernacular translations of the Bible stands in marked contrast to the total repudiation of the concept that is usually ascribed to the English hierarchy. His commitment to frequent communion puts him near the head of a Catholic devotional movement that was to gain in strength continuously over the next two centuries. His was certainly not a closed mind. One can argue about how representative of the late medieval Church he may have been. But one can hardly adduce him as evidence of its stagnation and incapacity for reform. The reception accorded his vernacular writings gives us reason to believe that the Catholicism he represented, a theocentric and personal Catholicism with a strongly scriptural content, was welcome in early sixteenth-century England. His commitment to humane learning suggests that it was open to change. And his polemical writings tell us that it was able and willing to defend itself.

John Fisher's life ended in the worldly defeat of martyrdom, which in his case, as in so many others, proved in the longer term a worldly as well as a spiritual triumph. The impact even on contemporaries of the unjust and vindictive execution of England's two best-known scholars was considerable. Abroad, Protestants joined with Catholics, and scholastics with humanists, in deploring the killings. Even the tainted but talented pen of Richard Morison could do little to redeem the situation. In England itself, of course, the systematic elimination of Fisher's memory conspired with the ultimate Protestant victory to depress his reputation. Even those English Catholic polemicists who drew on his theological writings did so for the most part without acknowledgment. For Englishmen, he was to live on chiefly through unflattering references in Foxe's *Acts and Monuments*. His fame as a preacher was overshadowed by Latimer.

The man who had been the best-selling native devotional author of the early sixteenth century was forgotten except among a limited circle of learned recusants – a circle from which the first biography emerged. Yet it was his association with a defeated cause, rather than any intrinsic weakness in the variety of religion for which he stood, that accounts for the oblivion into which he fell. The curious Anglican afterlife of his private prayers, the *Psalmi seu Precationes*, regularly reprinted without attribution as *The King's Psalms*, illustrates the genuinely contemporary appeal and Christian core of his theology and piety.[4] There can hardly have been much late medieval decadence in a devotional work that could be used happily by seventeenth-century English Protestants.

This study of Fisher also has implications for historians of the Counter-Reformation. On the European stage, Fisher was but one of many early Catholic opponents of Luther and the Protestant Reformers. These men have for long been dismissed, in accordance with Luther's own judgment of them, as obscurantist and reactionary. In a more mellow and ecumenical age, they have sometimes been held up to ridicule for allegedly failing to appreciate the true nature of Luther's ideas and for responding to them in a purely negative spirit. Indeed, in the rush to exculpate Luther from causing the tragic division of Western Christendom, his opponents have done useful service as alternative scapegoats. Recent studies, especially in Germany, have done much to rehabilitate them. Fisher's reputation has, of course, always stood high in Catholic circles. Edward Surtz's account unfortunately failed to make the impact it deserved outside (and sometimes even within) those circles. This study is therefore intended to find its place in the general re-evaluation of Luther's opponents, and in particular in succession to Surtz's pioneering efforts on Fisher. The figure who has emerged certainly does not fit into the simplistic categories of obscurantism and mere reaction. Fisher's understanding of Luther was neither perfect nor sympathetic, but he strove for objectivity and identified at any rate the central themes of Luther's message. The importance of Luther's attack on the papacy had been recognised, perhaps even overemphasised, from the start. But Fisher's sermon of 1521 was the first polemical effort to attach due weight to the roles of 'sola scriptura' and 'sola fides' in Luther's teaching. And his *Assertionis Lutheranae Confutatio* took this analysis further and made it a commonplace among the Catholic controversialists. His refutation of Oecolampadius's eucharistic teaching was no essay in obscurantism. Fisher met Oecolampadius on his chosen ground of scripture and the fathers, and dealt him some telling blows. In this controversy, as in his controversy with Luther, Fisher concentrated on the essential issues, in effect pushing to one side such arcane late medieval debates as that about the value and application of the merits of the sacrifice of the mass. Taking up patristic and early medieval parallels between the real presence and the Incarnation (parallels themselves based on a reading of John 6), he knit the doctrines of transubstantiation and communion into an incarnational ecclesiology that made the real presence an indispensable part of the economy of salvation.

As we have already seen, on the Continent Fisher's fame was not eclipsed but enhanced by his martyrdom. Although More (thanks to Erasmus's letters) may have been better known, Fisher was certainly more widely read. Indeed, he may well have been more widely read abroad than any other English author of that century. The English humanists, though gifted, were little known beyond these shores. The leading native Anglicans, such as Jewel, Whitgift, Cartwright, Hooker and Perkins, were hardly known in Europe. Only the Catholic exile Stapleton and the Puritan Whitaker were truly international figures as authors. But Fisher's influence on Catholic polemicists and on the debates and decrees of Trent was enormous. His refutations of Luther and Oecolampadius served as handbooks for the relevant issues. Lainez and Salmeron, the two Jesuits who played such an important part at the council, were both addicted to his writings. And most of those participating seem to have had some acquaintance with Fisher's works. There can no longer be room for doubt about Fisher's stature. He may not have been in the same league as Aquinas or Scotus, Bellarmine or Suarez, but he came the nearest to them among the Englishmen of his time.

The primary concern of this study, however, is with Fisher himself. It has shown us, if it needed to be shown, that Fisher was no 'intellectual'. He was above all a bishop and a doctor of divinity. Apart from the category of sinner, with which this study is not concerned, these were the only two labels under which he ever discussed himself. In these capacities, he regarded himself as obliged to preach the Word of God and to combat heresy. This study has investigated the way he fulfilled these obligations. Scripture of course held pride of place in Fisher's theology, and his attitude to scripture was in many respects old-fashioned. He was content, for example, to employ allegorical interpretation of scripture, although he did this more in his devotional and pastoral works than in his polemical endeavours. It is a pity, though, that we have so little from his hand in the way of scriptural commentary as such. His commentary on the Psalms is admittedly dominated by non-literal readings (moral, Christological and ecclesiological) – but even Protestant commentators interpreted the Psalms along these lines. It would be more revealing if we had some portion of Fisher's harmony of the gospels, which if anything would have shown the extent to which the researches of Lefèvre and Erasmus on the New Testament made an impact on him. Fisher's traditionalism was also apparent in his defence of the authority of the Vulgate because of its reception by the Church, and especially in his attack on Robert Wakefield for calling the Vulgate into question before a lay audience. Yet we can qualify this by reference to his interest in the scriptural endeavours of Erasmus and Reuchlin on the original Greek and Hebrew texts of the Bible, and by his promotion of the study of those languages in Cambridge, especially in his own college of St John's. Moreover, he was himself prepared to admit in a scholarly context that Jerome could have made mistakes in his translation, and that errors had crept into the manuscript tradition of the Vulgate. He made regular use of Erasmus's version of the Greek New Testament, even citing it on one occasion during a vernacular sermon (delivered in 1526 at the recantation of Robert Barnes). He was certainly not afraid of introducing lay audiences to the text of scripture. His sermons on the penitential psalms are testimony enough to this, but his affirmation of the value of vernacular translations of scripture puts it beyond doubt.

As we saw earlier, Fisher gave weight in principle as well as in practice to the tradition of the Church's fathers and doctors in theology. He was particularly widely read in the early fathers, not only the Latins, but also the Greeks (albeit in Latin translations), citing them frequently in the course of his writings. He usually cited them, moreover, from Renaissance translations or editions, and clearly sought *editiones principes* as they came off the press. He was of some assistance to Erasmus himself in his preparation of the 1530 edition of Chrysostom, receiving a mention in the dedication to that work as he had also received a mention in the dedication to Erasmus's Augustine. Amid the wide range of fathers Fisher cited, several stand out as of particular importance in his theology. Augustine was his favourite theologian. There was nothing distinctive about this in itself, as Augustine was the dominant theologian of the Latin Church. But Fisher was perhaps less typical among Catholics in modelling his theology of justification on Augustine's anti-Pelagian treatises. Chrysostom was probably the next most important influence on him, especially in his theology of the mass and the priesthood. And Fisher's account of the real presence was shaped most of all by John 6, and by Hilary of Poitiers and his later followers, Paschasius Radbert and the opponents of Berengar. Besides these, he made telling use of Tertullian, Origen, Cyprian, Eusebius, Jerome and Gregory among many others. His defence of the Septuagint against the assault of Richard Pace was motivated not by any such fear of humanist endeavour as fired the Frenchman Peter Sutor, but by a firm commitment to the consensus of the early fathers, and a disinclination to allow that they could have based their teachings on a defective Bible.

Fisher emphatically did not share the contempt of some of his humanist and even more of his Protestant contemporaries for the work of the scholastics. He was acquainted with the writings of all the major scholastics, and treated them with respect. It is obvious from his references and citations that he was not enamoured of the later scholastics. He never cited William of Ockham, and referred to Gabriel Biel only very rarely. Fifteenth-century scholastics appeared for the most part only in his writings on Henry VIII's divorce, and their role was almost entirely illustrative. On the whole he preferred the earlier scholastics, most notably Thomas Aquinas (the 'flower of theology') and Duns Scotus. These were the dominant figures in the theology course he had himself pursued at Cambridge, with Scotus probably the more popular of the two. His statutes for St John's College manifested a similar slight preference for Scotus, and Fisher's allegiance was marked enough for Robert Barnes to dismiss him as a 'Dunce' man. Yet he stood too far from Scotus on such matters as justification and penance for the cap to fit. It was in ecclesiological matters that Fisher stood closest to him, following his line on the Church's power to declare rather than to create doctrine, and on the concept that the Levitical marriage prohibitions were not matters of divine law, but owed their contemporary authority to the Church's legislation. His eucharistic theology was closer to Aquinas than to Scotus, and his essentially Augustinian theology of justification was closer to the later Aquinas and Gregory of Rimini than to the other scholastics. Besides, Fisher was acquainted with contemporary currents in Thomism, which represented the most important development in scholasticism in the sixteenth century. He referred to Cardinal Cajetan's edition and commentary on the *Summa*, and himself drew more often on the *Summa* than on Aquinas's earlier commentary on the *Sentences*. But it would be a mistake to deduce from this that Fisher was a Thomist. The relatively small place of the scholastics in his writings prevents us from reaching any such conclusion. While Fisher always recognised that the dialectical finesse of the scholastics gave them some advantages in certain matters (such as those raised by Henry VIII's divorce), he always claimed to prefer the fathers, and the evidence of his writings bears him out.

It was for their logical rather than their literary skills that Fisher admired the scholastics, and he felt the force of the humanist critique of their barbarous style. His intellectual programme made plenty of room for humanism, as can be seen not only from his own private studies, but also from his patronage of such men as Erasmus, Croke, and Wakefield, and from his statutes for St John's College. His own literary style was praised by critics as acute as Juan Luis Vives and Erasmus, but it must be said that his interest in rhetoric was entirely practical. He evinced no taste for classical literature for its own sake and, except for a few commonplace tags, the classics are conspicuously absent from his writings in an age when it was *de rigueur* to parade one's erudition. He was committed to languages and letters only in so far as they would promote the study and application of theology. He wanted his theologians to have a thorough knowledge of the Bible, if possible in its original languages, and to be able to put their learning to good use in writing or preaching through an understanding of the best rhetorical practice. Even the exotic Cabbala was for him nothing more than another angle on the scriptures. But he had no intention of allowing his theologians to discard the scholastics or the study of logic. His later statutes for St John's expressed concern that the fashion for rhetoric had distracted students from logic – a failing to which he was perhaps made doubly sensitive by the flagrant fallacies he detected in the works of Luther and Oecolampadius. Without rescinding any of the humanist provisions of the earlier statutes, he laid fresh emphasis on the necessity of logical and dialectical studies. His even-handed approach is best illustrated in his provision that the College lectureship in Hebrew should be turned into a course on Scotus's theology, if on the one hand no Hebrew lecturer should be available, and on the other somebody could put Scotus into better Latin.

Fisher's involvement in various humanist controversies compels us to put another qualification on his commitment to humanism, namely his overriding commitment to the consensus of the Church. This was no mere obscurantist, anti-intellectual fideism. Nor was it an option for expediency at the expense of truth. His belief in the infallible teaching authority of the Church was a reasoned position, founded on his prior acceptance of the indefectibility of Christ's promises to the Church. Since Christ had promised to send the Holy Spirit upon the Church to guide her into all truth, he argued, the Church could not teach falsehood and must be empowered to distinguish true from false teaching without risk of error. The consensus of the Church, be it implicit or explicit, was in his eyes trustworthy for this reason. Where teachings came into dispute, of course, implicit consensus was of little intrinsic evidential value. What ultimately mattered was explicit consensus, which could be voiced through conciliar or papal definitions. The extent to which he regarded either of these as infallible is open to question, as he did not commit himself in print. But he undoubtedly believed that the Church's infallibility had some means of expression. In practice, he allowed that conciliar and papal decrees could be ignored for overwhelming or pressing reasons. But he gave no clear idea of what might constitute reasons of adequate weight. His underlying problem was that of papal and conciliar statements which had in fact erred. He seems to have lacked the technical conceptual equipment with which later theorists of papal and conciliar infallibility were to address this problem. When, however, Fisher took a stand upon the consensus of the Church against the conclusions of a humanist, he did so without impugning the critical approach of humanism in the manner of Erasmus's enemies at Paris, Louvain and Cologne. He tried to join battle as far as possible on the humanists' own ground of Greek, Hebrew and the fathers. And where the conclusions of the humanists were not in-compatible with the consensus, he was happy to accept them. In the controversy over Mary Magdalene, for example, he was at the same time unshakeable in his allegiance to what he saw as the genuine teaching of the Church about her, and receptive to Lefèvre's arguments against a popular tradition about St Anne that he saw as unfounded in scripture, tradition and the liturgy.

More than anything, however, it was Fisher's vocation as a bishop that dominated his theological as well as his ecclesiastical career. The main implication of this was that his interest even in theology was practical rather than speculative. His statutes and objectives for St John's College again illustrate this, for he was concerned that his students should not waste time in abstract theological disputations, but should learn to argue and preach on matters of practical benefit to Christians. His own writings were designed either to defend the doctrines of Catholicism or else to encourage Christians in their devotions. Controversy and the sermon are therefore his preferred genres. Even his commentary on the Psalms was primarily a devotional work, albeit a highly sophisticated one with a distinct polemical undercurrent. Although his harmony on the Gospels has not survived, we can be confident that it would have been more a devotional than an academic exercise. This preference for the practical over the theoretical was clearly perceived by Fisher himself as an integral part of his episcopal role. As we have seen, he associated himself with the bishops among the fathers – Hilary, Ambrose and Augustine – rather than with the scholar Jerome who was unburdened by a cure of souls. It is a similar difference in vocation that explains the genuine differences in approach and emphasis between Fisher and Erasmus, despite their friendship and agreement over essentials. It is significant that whereas Fisher chose the bishops as his models, and declared that he would rather side with Augustine than with any other theologian, Erasmus chose instead to model himself upon Jerome, so many of whose temperamental characteristics he shared. Even in a matter as specific as the inspiration of the Septuagint, Fisher followed Augustine, but Erasmus followed Jerome. Fisher, in short, took seriously his responsibilities as a bishop towards his particular and the universal Church. He believed he would have to give account for his stewardship, and dreaded that any spiritual damage to his charges should be put down to his negligence. It is worth remembering that Fisher's polemical writings belong exclusively to his time as a bishop – a matter in which he might be taken as having followed the patristic examples of Irenaeus, Athanasius, Hilary and Chrysostom. He certainly saw his polemical works as a fulfilment of his episcopal role. There is no sign that he, unlike say Thomas More, took any pleasure in the genre for its own sake. In the event, Fisher's discharge of his episcopal duties evoked the admiration of his contemporaries and of his successors. His diligence as a bishop led him to be ranked later in the century with the likes of Giberti of Verona as a model of Catholic episcopacy. At the same time he commanded, as a controversial theologian, an esteem equal or superior to that of an Eck or a Cochlaeus. What was unusual about Fisher was not simply that, following patristic example, he combined the roles of pastor and polemicist, but that he did so to such good effect as to become a model in both areas of endeavour for the leaders of the Counter-Reformation.

Appendix

John Fisher's library

The following list names all the separate works John Fisher owned, cited, mentioned or (in a very few cases) clearly alluded to, in the course of his surviving writings. Where possible, suggestions are made as to the precise editions, translations or recensions he used. The fact that Fisher refers to a work is not in itself conclusive proof that he had read, or indeed that he owned, the work in question. We know of cases where he borrowed books from friends, and it is often clear that his citations are drawn indirectly from compilations, such as the *Sentences* of Peter Lombard, Gratian's *Decretum* or Thomas Aquinas's *Catena Aurea*, rather than directly from the originals. Nevertheless, Fisher exhibits a strong sense of the importance of verifying citations and of providing verifiable references. This is implicit in his own common practice of citing by author, title, book and chapter which, moreover, suggests that he worked from originals rather than compilations. The spread of this practice, of course, owed much to printing, which made identical or at least very similar copies of books widely available for the first time. The importance he attached to verification is confirmed by explicit remarks addressed to polemical opponents. In the *Eversio Munitionis* he criticised Clichtove for taking a text of Theophilus from the *Catena Aurea* inaccurately and without naming his source.[1] He regularly convicted Oecolampadius of selective and defective quotation. And at one point he lamented that he was unable to verify a passage from Irenaeus because he did not have a copy himself – a lacuna in his collection that he was soon to remedy. As Fisher's library was almost legendary in its scope – when it was conveyed away by royal commissioners in 1535 it was carried in 'XXXII great pypes' – it seems reasonable to assume that a good proportion of the books he cited in the course of his writings were actually in his possession.[2] This list will inevitably represent only a portion of his collection. But while one can hazard a guess at many books he may have possessed in addition, such as Thomas More's *Utopia*, to do so would detract from the value of this exercise, which is to give a conspectus of the scholarship on which Fisher drew.

Author	Title[3]	Source
PATRISTICS		
Ambrose	Sermones[4]	*DUM* 1407
	De Officiis	*EM* G.4.v
	In Psalmos	*ALC* 288
	*In Epistolas Pauli[5]	*ALC* 460
	De Iacob et Vita Beata	*ALC* 609
	In Lucam	*ALC* 627
	*De Vocatione Omnium Gentium	*ALC* 693
	De Sacramentis	*DRA* 194
	*De Dignitate Sacerdotali	*SSD* 1234
	De Benedictionibus Patriarcharum	*DVC* 1004
	De Mysteriis	*DVC* 1005
	Epistolae[6]	
Arnobius	In Psalmos[7]	*SSD* 1235
Athanasius	Epistolae	*ALC* 663
Augustine[8]	De Consensu Evangelistarum	*DUM* 1399
	De Sermone Domini in Monte	*DUM* 1407
	Retractationes	*DUM* 1446
	Contra Epistolam Manichaei . . . Fundamenti	*EM* a.3.r
	*Quaestiones in Veteri et Novum Testamentum[9]	*ALC* 282
	De Baptismo Parvulorum	*ALC* 295
	De Nuptiis et Concupiscentia	*ALC* 344
	Confessiones	*ALC* 351
	Contra Iulianum	*ALC* 353
	De Peccatorum Meritis et Remissione	*ALC* 356
	Contra Duas Epistolas Pelagianorum	*ALC* 357
	De Gratia Christi et de Peccato Originali[10]	*ALC* 367
	Sermones de Tempore	*ALC* 368
	Ad Bonifacium de Correctione Donatistarum	*ALC* 371
	Tractatus super Iohannem	*ALC* 403
	*De Vera et Falsa Poenitentia	*ALC* 413
	*De Visitatione Infirmorum	*ALC* 423
	Sermo de Coena Domini	*ALC* 464
	Enchiridion Christianae Fidei	*ALC* 488

	Contra Epistolam Donati	*ALC* 554
	Contra Fortunatum	*ALC* 608
	De Natura et Gratia	*ALC* 626
	Homiliae super Iohannem	*ALC* 661
	De Vera Religione	*ALC* 661
	*Hyponosticon	*ALC* 668
	De Spiritu et Littera	*ALC* 668
	De Praedestinatione et Gratia	*ALC* 693
	De Civitate Dei	*ALC* 696
	De Gratia et Libero Arbitrio	*ALC* 705
	Sermones de Sanctis	*ALC* 705
	Contra Felicem	*ALC* 706
	Ad Simplicianum	*ALC* 713
	De Cura pro Mortuis Agenda	*ALC* 724
	De Doctrina Christiana	*CC* 1303
	Ad Dardanum de Praesentia Dei	*SSD* 1211
	*De Vera Innocentia	*DVC* 764
	De Trinitate	*DVC* 769
	Super Apocalypsim	*DVC* 770
	Contra Literas Petiliani	*DVC* 778
	Contra Cresconium Grammaticum	*DVC* 778
	Ad Ianuarium	*DVC* 815
	*De Utilitate Agendae Poenitentiae	*DVC* 857
	Ad Marcellinum	*DVC* 900
	*De Haeresibus	*DVC* 924
	Ad Iulianum Comitem	*DVC* 992
	Sermones de Verbo Domini	*DVC* 1126
	Contra Faustum	*DVC* 1139
	Quaestiones in Heptateuchum	*DCM* 17.r
	*Speculum Augustini[11]	*DCM* 34.r
Basil the Great	De Institutione Monachorum	*ALC* 419
	Adversus Eunomium	*ALC* 543
	Exhortatio ad Baptismum	*ALC* 708
Bede	In Lucam	*DUM* 1413
	In Actis	*ALC* 549
	Historia Ecclesiastica	*ALC* 729
	De Temporibus	*CC* 1303
	In Petrum	*CC* 1351
Cassian	Collationes	*DUM* 1417
	De Institutione Coenobiorum	*ALC* 400
Cassiodorus	In Psalmos	*DVC* 991

Chrysostom[12]	Sermo de Proditione Iudae	*DUM* 1440
	Homiliae in Matthaeum	*EM* V.1.r
	Sermones contra Iudaeos[13]	
	Homiliae in Iohannem	*ALC* 359
	Sermo de Poenitentia	*ALC* 391
	Sermo de Compunctione Cordis	*ALC* 403
	De Dignitate Sacerdotum	*ALC* 529
	Sermones de Laudibus Pauli	*ALC* 702
	Homiliae in Epistolas Pauli[14]	*DRA* 193
	Sermo de . . . mysteriorum	*DVC* 1206
	Homiliae in Genesim[15]	
Clement	Epistolae[16]	*DRA* 193
Cyprian	Epistolae	*DRA* 153
	De Ablutione Pedum	*ALC* 294
	De Lapsis	*ALC* 392
	De Unctione Chrismatis	*ALC* 450
	De Unitate Ecclesiae[17]	*ALC* 540
	De Cardinalibus Operibus Christi	*DVC* 1185
Cyril of Alexandria[18]	In Iohannem	*DUM* 1404
	In Leviticum	*ALC* 419
Damascene	De Fide Orthodoxa	*DVC* 1185
'Dionysius'	Ecclesiastica Hierarchia	*DRA* 180
	Ad Demophilum	*ALC* 419
	De Divinis Nominibus	*DVC* 991
Eucherius of Lyons	De Quaestionibus[19]	*DVC* 992
Eusebius of Caesarea	Canones Evangeliorum	*DUM* 1450
	Historia Ecclesiastica	*EM* B.4.v
	Adversus Hieroclem	*DVC* 800
	De Praeparatione Evangelica[20]	
Eutropius	Historia Romae	*CC* 1343
Fulgentius	Ad Quaestionem Momini	*DVC* 991
Gennadius	De Ecclesiasticis Dogmatibus[21]	*ALC* 715
Gregory I	Registrum	*ALC* 540
	Homiliae	*ALC* 540
	Moralia In Iob	*ALC* 623
	Dialogi	*ALC* 717
Gregory Nazianzen	De Miraculis Evangeliorum	*DUM* 1455
	Apologeticus	*ALC* 449
	Carmina	*DVC* 994

Gregory of Nyssa	De Mystica Vita Moysi	*DVC* 994
'Hegesippus'		*CC* 1313
Hesychius	In Leviticum	*DCM* 5.v
Hilary of Poitiers[22]	De Trinitate	*CC* 1328
	Adversus Constantinum Caesarem	*DVC* 1234
	[In Psalmos][23]	
	In Matthaeum	*DCM* 5.v
Ignatius of Antioch	Epistolae[24]	*DRA* 192
Irenaeus	Adversus Haereses[25]	
Iuvencus	Carmina	*DVC* 992
Jerome[26]	In Marcum	*DUM* 1417
	Adversus Helvidium	*DUM* 1439
	Epistolae[27]	*DUM* 1454
	In Galatas	*EM* D.4.v
	In Matthaeum	*EM* K.2.v
	Adversus Vigilantium	*EM* N.3.r
	Adversus Montanum	*EM* Y.4.v
	Apologia contra Ruffinum	*EM* a.4.r
	Quaestiones ad Algasiam	*ALC* 306
	In Malachiam	*ALC* 392
	In Esaiam	*ALC* 403
	In Ecclesiasten	*ALC* 420
	In Corinthios	*ALC* 464
	In Danielem	*ALC* 511
	Adversus Pelagianos	*ALC* 610
	Adversus Critobolum	*ALC* 615
	In Hieremiam	*ALC* 694
	In Ezechielem	*ALC* 694
	In Philomonem	*CC* 1317
	Catalogus Virorum Illustrium	*CC* 1339
	Catalogus ad Desiderium	*DRA* 248
	In Titum	*DVC* 993
	In Ephesios	*DVC* 1197
Lactantius Firmianus	De Divinis Officiis	*CC* 1302
Leo I	Sermones[28]	*DUM* 1454
	Epistolae	*ALC* 283
Origen[29]	In Iohannem	*DUM* 1440
	In Matthaeum	*DUM* 1447
	In Ezechielem	*EM* D.3.r
	In Iosue	*ALC* 359

	In Leviticum	*ALC* 391
	Super Psalmos	*ALC* 408
	Super Numeros	*ALC* 514
	In Exodum	*ALC* 555
	In Lucam	*ALC* 627
	De Principiis	*ALC* 664
	In Romanos	*ALC* 694
	In Iob	*DRA* 192
	Contra Celsum[30]	*DVC* 841
Orosius	Historia	*CC* 1343
Paulinus of Nola	Vita Ambrosii	*DVC* 1011
Polycarp of Smyrna	Epistola ad Philippenses	*DVC* 1239
Sedulius	Carmina	*DVC* 992
	In Epistolas Pauli	*DCM* 21.r
Tertullian[31]	De Praescriptionibus Haereticorum	*ALC* 278
	Adversus Iudaeos	*CC* 1302
	De Corona Militis	*DRA* 192
	De Cultu Foeminarum	*DRA* 193
	Adversus Marcionem	*DVC* 662
	De Monogamia	*DVC* 663
	De Resurrectione Carnis	*DVC* 996
Theophylact	In Epistolas Pauli[32]	*ALC* 294
	In Lucam	*ALC* 543
	In Marcum	*DVC* 993
	In Matthaeum[33]	*DCM* 6.r

CLASSICS

Aemilius Probus	De Vitis Imperatorum[34]	
Aristeas	Epistola[35]	
Aristotle	Rhetoric	*ALC* 742
	Ethics[36]	
	Opera Graeca[37]	
Aulus Gellius	Atticae Noctes[38]	
Cicero	De Oratore	*EW* 285
	De Rhetorica[39]	
Eutropius	Historia Romae	*CC* 1343
Josephus	Antiquitates Iudaeorum	*CC* 1335
Laertius	De Vita et Moribus Philosophorum	*DVC* 833
Plutarch	Vita Caesaris	*ALC* 562

Pomponius Mela	De Situ Orbis	*DVC* 754

MEDIEVAL AND SCHOLASTIC

Adelmann Brixiensis[40]		*DVC* 991
Aegidius Romanus		*DVC* 990
Albert the Great	In Lucam	*DUM* 1443
	In Marcum	*DCM* 22.r
	In Matthaeum[41]	
Alexander of Hales	Summa	*DCM* 19.r
Almarius Minatensis	De Divinis Officiis	*EM* &.3.r
Alueredus abbas[42]		*DVC* 990
Andrew of St Victor	In Genesim[43]	
Angelomus	In Libros Regum[44]	*DVC* 991
Angelus de Clavasio	Summa Angelica de casibus conscientiae	*DCM* 39.r
Anselm of Bec	De Passione Christi	*DUM* 1445
Antonine of Florence	Summa	*EM* M.4.v
Antonius de Rosellis[45]		*DCM* 24.v
Bartramus Strabus[46]		*DVC* 991
Bernard of Clairvaux[47]	[De Gratia et Libero Arbitrio][48]	*ALC* 664
	Ad Eugenium (De Consideratione)	*EM* Z.2.r
Bonaventure	In Libros Sententiarum	*DCM* 19.v
Bridget of Sweden	Revelationes[49]	*DUM* 1456
Clement of Lanthony	[Unum ex Quatuor][50]	*DUM* 1447
Druthmar[51]	In Matthaeum	*DUM* 1445
Duns Scotus	In Libros Sententiarum	*ALC* 338
Durandus		*DVC* 990
Eadmer	Vita Dunstani[52]	
Ekbert		*DVC* 990
Elizabeth of Schöngau	Revelationes[53]	*ALC* 577
Euthymius Zigabenus	Praefatio in Psalmos[54]	
Francis Maro	In Libros Sententiarum	*DCM* 21.v
	In Genesim	*DCM* 29.r
Gabriel Biel	In Libros Sententiarum[55]	*OO* 1707
Gerson	De Perfectione Cordis	*OO* 1707
	De Probatione Spirituum[56]	

Gilbert de la Porrée		*DVC* 990
Gilbert of Citeaux		*DVC* 990
Gislebertus		*EM* M.1.v
Gregory of Rimini	In Libros Sententiarum	*ALC* 672
Guido Lenfredi		*DVC* 991
Guimund of Aversa	De Veritate Corporis Christi[57]	*DVC* 760
Haymo of Halberstadt	In Marcum[58]	
Henry of Ghent	Quodlibeta[59]	
Henry of Huntingdon	Historia[60]	
Heriger		*DVC* 990
Hildebert of Tours		*DVC* 990
Hildegard of Bingen	Sciviae	*DVC* 922
Honorius of Autun		*DVC* 990
Hugh of St Cher	In Matthaeum	*DCM* 19.r
	In Genesim[61]	
	In Leviticum[62]	
Hugh of St Victor	De Sacramentis	*DVC* 1221
Iacobus Bergamensis	Historia	*EM* M.4.v
Iacobus de Lausanna	In Leviticum	*DCM* 26.r
Iacobus de Voragine	Legenda Aurea	*EM* M.4.v
Iohannes Andreas[63]		
Iohannes Bacho[64]		*DVC* 990
Iohannes de Mola[65]		
Iohannes de Tabia[66]		
Isidore of Seville	Etymologia	*DVC* 832
Ivo of Chartres	Collectiones[67]	*SSD* 1297
John of Salisbury		*DVC* 990
Lanfranc of Bec	De Eucharistia[68]	*DVC* 991
Lotario de Segni (Innocent III)		*DVC* 990
Ludolphus of Saxony	(Vita Christi)	*EM* &.3.r
Mechtild	Revelationes	*EM* S.3.r
Moses Maimonides	De Dubiis et Perplexis	*DCM* 7.r
Nicholas of Cusa	Dialogus de Remissione Peccatorum	*DUM* 1451
Nicholas of Gorran	In Epistolas Pauli[69]	
Nicholas of Lyra[70]		*EM* K.1.r

Panormitanus	In Decretis	*ALC* 599
Paschasius Radbertus	De Corpore et Sanguine Domini	*DVC* 922
Paulus Burgensis	In Scripturam Sacram	*DCM* 29.v
Peter of Blois	Epistolae	*DCM* 18.v
Peter Cantor		*DVC* 990
Peter Comestor	Historia Scholastica	*DCM* 25.r
Peter Damian		*DVC* 990
Peter Lombard	Sententiarum Libri	*DVC* 1188
Peter of Paluda	In Libros Sententiarum In Leviticum[71]	*DCM* 39.v
Peter of Riga		*DVC* 990
Peter of Tarentasia (Innocent IV)		*DCM* 21.r
Rabanus Maurus	In Matthaeum	*DUM* 1445
Ralph of Flaix	In Leviticum[72]	*DCM* 18.r
Ratherius Veronensis		*DVC* 991
Remigius Antisiodorensis		*DVC* 991
Richard of Middleton	In Libros Sententiarum	*DCM* 39.r
Richard of St Victor		*DVC* 990
Robert Grosseteste	In Leviticum	*DCM* 26.r
Robert Kilwardby		*DCM* 21.r
Roger Bacon	Ad Clementem Papam	*CC* 1333
Rupert of Deutz[73]	In Genesim In Apocalypsim De Glorificatione Trinitatis	*DVC* 1134
Sigibertus	Chronicon[74]	*EM* M.2.v
Simon de Cassia	De Gestis Christi[75]	*DUM* 1444
Smaragdus		*DVC* 991
Strabo	Geographia[76]	
Theodore of Canterbury		*DVC* 991
Thomas Aquinas	In Iohannem Catena Aurea In Libros Sententiarum In Epistolas Pauli Summa Theologiae	*DUM* 1444 *EM* I.3.r *OO* 1707 *OO* 1707 *DCM* 23.v
Thomas Netter of Walden[77]		
Ubertino de Casale	Arbor Christi Crucifixi	*DUM* 1444

Vincent of Beauvais	Speculum Historiae	*DUM* 1457
William of Ockham		*DVC* 990
William of Paris	De Vitiis et Virtutibus[78]	
William of St Thierry		*DVC* 990
William Varro		*DVC* 990
William of Wodeford[79]		
Zachary of Besançon	[De Concordia Evangelistarum][80]	*DUM* 1447

RENAISSANCE AND REFORMATION

R. Agricola	De Inventione Dialectica[81]	
J. Almain[82]		
J. Annius of Viterbo	Antiquitates[83]	
Antonius	Summa	*DCM* 39.v
T. de Argentina	In Libros Sententiarum	*DCM* 27.v
J. Bessarion	De Eucharistiae Sacramento	*DVC* 928
F. Biondo		*EM* S.4.v
J. Boemus	Omnium Gentium Mores Leges et Ritus[84]	
M. Bucer	De Caena Dominica	*DRA* 257
J. Bugenhagen	Librum Psalmorum Interpretatio (n.p., 1524)[85]	
T. de Vio Cajetan	Commentarii in Summa	*DCM* 27.v
J. Clichtove	Disceptationis de Magdalena Defensio	*EM* A.1.1
J. Cochlaeus	Adversus Latrocinantes[86] Fasciculus Calumniarum[87]	
D. Erasmus	Adagia[88] Apologia contra Fabrum[89] Diatriba de Libero Arbitrio[90]	*DVC* 1108
D. Erasmus (ed.)	Lucubrationes Senecae (Basel: Froben, 1515)	*CC* 1330
	Theodore of Gaza's Grammatica Graeca[91]	
	Novum Instrumentum (Basel: Froben, 1516)[92]	
	Noveum Testamentum (Basel: Froben, 1519)	*SSD* 1281
	Opera Omnia Hieronymi	
	Lucubrationes Hilarii	

	Irenaeus, Adversus Haereses (Basel: Froben, 1526)	
	Opera Omnia Augustini	
	Opera Omnia Chrysostomi[93]	
Felix de Prato	Psalmi ab Hebreo[94]	
P. Galatinus	De Arcanis Catholicae Fidei[95]	*SSD* 1266
A. Giustiniani	Octaplus super Psalterium[96]	
M. de Grandval	Apologia seu Defensorium	*EM* a.2.r
Henry VIII	Assertio Septem Sacramentorum[97]	*ALC* 274
	Gravissimae Censurae (London: Berthelet, 1530)[98]	
J. Lefèvre d'Etaples	De Maria Magdalena (Paris: Estienne, 1517)	*DUM* 1395
	De Maria Magdalena (Paris: Estienne, 1518)	*DUM* 1395
	Secunda Disceptatio (Paris: Estienne, 1519)	*CSD* a.1.r
	In Epistolas Pauli (Paris: Estienne, 1513 or 1515)	*EM* F.4.r
	Liber Trium Spiritualium Virginum (Paris, 1513)	*EM* S.3.r
M. Luther	Operationes in Psalmos	*DRA* 107
	Sermo de Eucharistia	*ALC* 407
	Acta Augustana	*ALC* 443
	Resolutiones . . . de indulgentiarum	*ALC* 503
	Resolutiones contra Eckium	*ALC* 328
	Resolutiones . . . Lipsie Disputatis	*ALC* 291
	Resolutio . . . de Potestate Papae	*ALC* 565
	Contra Sylvestrum	*ALC* 495
	Sermo de Virtute Excommunicationis[99]	*ALC* 527
	Assertio Omnium Articulorum	*ALC* 274
	In Epistolam Pauli ad Galatas	*ALC* 305
	De Libertate Christiana	*ALC* 314
	De Captivitate Babylonica	*ALC* 466
	De Abroganda Missa Privata	*SSD* 1232
	Contra Henricum Regem Angliae	*DRA* 112
	Enarrationes in Epistolas Petri	*DRA* 104
	'De Fide et Operibus'[100]	*DRA* 119
	Epistolarum Farrago (Hagenau, 1525)[101]	*DVC* 1229

M. Makerel (ed.)	Sermones Odonis (Paris: Bade, 1520)[102]	
P. Melanchthon	Rhetorica et Dialectica[103]	
	Proverbiae Salomonis (Hagenau, 1525)	*DVC* 791
S. Munster	Dictionarium Chaldaicum (Basel: Froben, 1527)[104]	
J. Oecolampadius	Sermo de Eucharistia	*DVC* 749
	De Genuina Verborum . . . Expositione	*DVC* 749
R. Pace	Praefatio in Ecclesiasten (London: Pynson, 1527)[105]	
S. Pagninus	Lexicon Hebraicum[106]	
	Sacra Biblia (Lyons: du Ry, 1528)[107]	
F. Petrarch	Carmina	*DUM* 1453
A.S. Piccolomini (Pius II)	Europa	*EM* B.4.v
G. Pico della Mirandola	Oratio (or Apologia)	*DVC* 758
G.F. Pico	Vita Ioannis Pici Comitis Mirandulae	*ALC* 544
B. Platina	Vitae Pontificum	*ALC* 492
J. Reuchlin	De Verbo Mirifico[108]	
	De Rudimentis Hebraicis (Pforzheim: Anshelm, 1506)[109]	
	Oculum Speculare[110]	
	De Arte Cabalistica[111]	
M.A. Sabellicus	Enneades	*EM* M.3.v
	Liber Exemplorum	*EM* M.4.r
G. Savonarola	Opuscula	*ALC* 637
W. Steinbach	Supplementum Gabrielis	*DCM* 22.r
Theodore of Gaza	See under D. Erasmus (ed.)	
J. Turrecremata	Super Decretis	*DCM* 24.r
	Summa de Ecclesia	*DCM* 40.r
U. Velenus	Libellus	*CC* 1299
M. Vigerio	Decachordum Christianum	*DUM* 1451
P. Vergil	De Oratione Dominica[112]	
R. Volaterranus		*CC* 1344
J. Wessel	Sermo de Eucharistia	*DVC* 1206
Ximenez	Complutensian Polyglot[113]	

Notes

Introduction

1 For a full discussion of the date and authorship of the first biography, see *Vie*, x, pp. 186–201, esp. pp. 200–1 for the suggestion of Young. In his popular edition of the life, P. Hughes resolves a problem Van Ortroy raised about Watson's involvement. See *Saint John Fisher: the earliest English life*, ed. P. Hughes (London, 1935), pp. 10–13.

2 T. Bailey, *The Life and Death of that Renowned John Fisher Bishop of Rochester* (London, 1655).

3 J. Lewis, *The Life of Dr. John Fisher*, ed. T.H. Turner, 2 vols. (London, 1855).

4 *The Funeral Sermon of Margaret Countess of Richmond and Derby*, ed. J. Hymers (Cambridge, 1840); *The English Works of John Fisher*, Part I, ed. J.E.B. Mayor, EETS extra ser. 27 (London, 1876).

5 T.E. Bridgett, *Life of Blessed John Fisher* (London, 1888).

6 *Vie du Bienheureux Martyr Jean Fisher*, ed. F. Van Ortroy, *Analecta Bollandiana*, x (1891), pp. 121–365, and xii (1893), pp. 97–287. Also reprinted separately (Brussels, 1893).

7 *The Defence of the Priesthood*, tr. P.E. Hallett (London, 1935). This is a version of *SSD* which had been critically edited by H.K. Schmeink, Corpus Catholicorum 9 (Münster, 1925). *Saint John Fisher: the earliest English life*.

8 E.E. Reynolds, *St John Fisher* (London, 1955; revised edn. London, 1972). M. Macklem's *God Have Mercy: the life of John Fisher of Rochester* (Oberon Press, 1967), though based on a re-examination of the original sources, does not represent any advance on Reynolds's work.

9 J. Rouschausse, *La Vie et l'Oeuvre de John Fisher Evêque de Rochester* (Nieuwkoop, 1973).

10 J. Rouschausse (ed.), *Saint John Fisher: discours, traité de la prière, écrits de prison* (Namur, 1964); and *Erasmus and Fisher: their correspondence 1511–1524* (Paris, 1968).

11 B. Bradshaw and E. Duffy (eds.), *Humanism, Reform and the Reformation: the career of Bishop John Fisher* (Cambridge, 1989).

12 J.W. Blench, *Preaching in England in the late Fifteenth and Sixteenth Centuries: a study of English sermons 1450–c. 1600* (Oxford, 1964).

13 B. Gogan, *The Common Corps of Christendom: ecclesiological themes in the writings of Sir Thomas More*, SHCT 26 (Leiden, 1982).

14 J.J. Scarisbrick, *Henry VIII* (London, 1968), chs. 7–8; H.A. Kelly, *The Matrimonial Trials of Henry VIII* (Stanford, 1976); and V. Murphy's unpublished Cambridge Ph. D. dissertation, 'The debate over Henry VIII's first divorce: an analysis of the contemporary treatises' (1984).

15 Criticisms along these lines were raised in the reviews of Surtz's book by P.

Collinson in *English Historical Review* 84 (1968), pp. 841–2, and T.M. Parker in *History* 54 (1969), pp. 94–5.

16 Although he was later elected a fellow there, he need not necessarily have been a member of that college beforehand.

17 Vatican Archives, Index Brevium, 4 Julius II, fol. 112.r, records an indult (6 Jan 1506) releasing him from the obligation of residence on solemn feast days so that he could see to the spiritual needs of Lady Margaret.

18 See especially S. Thompson, 'The bishop in his diocese', in *HRR*, pp. 67–80.

19 C.N.L. Brooke, R. Rex, S. Thompson and M. Underwood, 'Fisher's career and itinerary, c. 1469–1535', *HRR*, pp. 235–49.

20 S. Ehses, *Römische Dokumente zur Geschichte der Ehescheidung Heinrichs VIII. von England, 1527–1534* (Paderborn, 1893), no. 132, pp. 202–3. In view of the fact that it was more pleasing to God that Fisher should spend his time in reading the scriptures and writing against the heretics of the time, Clement VII conceded 'ut quoad vixerit et in studiis aut compositionibus huiusmodi occupata fuerit, loco horarum pro tempore dici ab eadem [namely, 'Fraternitas Tua', Fisher] solitarum aliquas quantumvis breves et paucas orationes per eam eligendas, quod totum arbitrio tuo remittimus, recitare libere et licite possit nec ad horas canonicas aliter recitandas teneatur'.

21 *OO*, c. 1703.

22 For the harmony, which is sadly not extant, see below, ch. 3, pp. 55–6. For the psalm commentary, which survives in substantial but badly damaged fragments, see below, ch. 5, pp. 81–2.

23 *LP* 8. 666, Chapuys to Charles V, 5 May 1535. Cromwell and other councillors had visited More in the Tower on 30 April (*LP* 8. 659, More to Meg Roper, early May 1535), so they probably put the oath to Fisher that day. The oath was presumably the oath to the succession in the special version imposed on the clergy, which amounted to an oath to the supremacy. See G.R. Elton, *Reform and Reformation: England, 1509–1558* (London, 1977), p. 186.

24 This is the essence of Fisher's indictment, as printed by J. Bruce in 'Observations on the circumstances which occasioned the death of John Fisher, bishop of Rochester', *Archaeologia* 25 (1834), pp. 61–99, at pp. 94–5, from a later copy. See also *Third Report of the Deputy Keeper of the Public Records* (London, 1842), p. 239, for a digest of the original indictment as found in PRO Baga de Secretis, pouch VII, bundle 2. *LP* 8. 856, p. 326, records that Cromwell and other councillors examined Fisher on 'Friday after Ascension' (7 May). Thomas More was interrogated that same day by Cromwell, Bedyll, Tregonwell and others. See *Third Report*, p. 240, indictment of Thomas More.

25 In the fragments of Rastell's biography of More, printed in N. Harpsfield, *The Life and Death of Sir Thomas Moore, Knight*, ed. E.V. Hitchcock and R.W. Chambers, EETS orig. ser. 186 (1932), pp. 232–5. Rastell's chronology is also dubious as he transfers to 4 May Fisher's interrogation of 3 June in which he took up More's analogy of the 'two-edged sword' for the act of supremacy. However, Rastell does date his denial of the supremacy correctly to 7 May.

26 G.R. Elton, *Policy and Police: the enforcement of the Reformation in the age of Thomas Cromwell* (Cambridge, 1972), p. 408, rightly rejects Rastell's lengthy speeches as 'artifice rather than report'.

27 On which I differ from Elton, *Policy and Police*, p. 408, and Van Ortroy, *Vie*, xii, pp. 176–9, n. 1. If the story is pure invention, it is remarkably imaginative. The fact that the whole episode does not appear in Fisher's indictment is hardly surprising,

as all that mattered was the unequivocal denial of the supremacy he had undoubtedly uttered. We have no detailed record of Fisher's trial other than that of
Rastell (Harpsfield, *More*, pp. 237–40), from which that of the *Vie* (xii, pp. 170–83)
is derived. But Rastell was after all not only a contemporary of the events described
but also a judge, which must lend some credibility to his account of the judicial
proceedings.

28 See *Third Report*, p. 241, More's indictment; and *LP* 8. 856 and 858–9 for
interrogations relating to the correspondence.

29 *LP* 8. 742, notes that the decree announcing the creation of the cardinals was
issued on 20 May. *LP* 8. 787 notes that the titles were bestowed on 31 May.

30 *LP* 8. 856, interrogations of servants in the Tower, June 1535. George Gold, on 8
June, said that he had heard of Fisher's promotion ten days earlier (p. 329). And on
10 June a servant of Antonio Bonvisi recalled that he had heard Florens Volusenus
discussing the news in Bonvisi's house twelve days earlier (p. 330). Both reports
point to 30 May.

31 *LP* 8. 948, Chapuys to Charles V, 30 June 1535, reports Cromwell as blaming Paul
III. Bruce, 'Observations', p. 85, was of the opinion that the news of Fisher's
elevation could not have reached London before the legal process began, and that
the claim was pure fiction. But as we have seen, the news had indeed arrived.
Chapuys's letter to Charles of 16 June reported Henry's rage and his decision to
prosecute Fisher immediately (*LP* 8. 876).

32 *Third Report*, pp. 239–40, gives the dates for the various stages of the legal process.

33 *LP* 8. 876, Chapuys to Charles V, 16 June 1535.

34 *LP* 8. 921. Henry VIII, circular letter, 25 June 1535.

35 P.L. Hughes and J.F. Larkin (eds.) *Tudor Royal Proclamations* (3 vols. New Haven
and London, 1964–9), i, no. 161, pp. 235–7, 1 Jan 1536.

36 *LP* 9. 1041, John Barlow to Cromwell, 11 Nov 1536, reports the arrest of a priest
named William Norton for, among other things, owning a book by Fisher in
defence of the papacy.

37 *LP* 8. 1125, Bedyll to Cromwell, 28 July 1535.

38 *LP* 9. 157, Cromwell to Sir John Wallop, 23 Aug 1535; and 213, instructions to
Edward Fox, ambassador to Germany.

39 *LP* 9. 46, H. Schukborough to Sir T. Inglefield, 7 Aug 1535, reported Richard
Crowley, the vicar of Broughton (Oxfordshire), as calling Fisher and More martyrs.
LP 9. 100, T. Clerk to Cromwell, 15 Aug 1535, similarly reported Oliver Bromley,
curate of Exton.

40 *LP* 8. 932, 27 June 1535, records the story. *LP* 9. 681, Ortiz to the Empress, 24 Oct
1535, shows that it had reached Rome and reports Cromwell's attempt at
suppression.

41 R. Morison, *Apomaxis Calumniarum* (London: Berthelet, 1537; *STC* 18109), fol.
93.v.

42 R.F. Scott, *Records of St John's College, Cambridge*, 4th ser. (Cambridge, privately
printed, 1934), p. 281.

43 J.E.B. Mayor (ed.), *Early Statutes of St John's College Cambridge* (Cambridge, 1858),
pp. 238–45 and 254–8 put the 1530 and 1545 statutes side by side for comparison.

1 Humanism and scholasticism in late fifteenth-century Cambridge

1 *Grace Book A*, ed. S.M. Leathes (Cambridge, 1897), pp. 211 and 215; and *Grace
Book B, Part I*, ed. M. Bateson (Cambridge, 1903), pp. 25–6. For his ordination
on 17 Dec 1491, see Reynolds, *St John Fisher*, p. 6.

2 *Grace Book B, Part I*, p. 68.
3 *Grace Book B, Part I*, pp. 104–5. No precise date can be given for his appointment as confessor.
4 *Grace Book B, Part I*, p. 162. SJC D 5.14, foundation deed of Lady Margaret readership.
5 Henry VII to Lady Margaret, in C.H. Cooper, *Memoir of Margaret, Countess of Richmond and Derby* (Cambridge, 1874), pp. 95–6, for the king's decision to nominate Fisher to Rochester. For the chancellorship, see *Grace Book B, Part I*, p. 203, and C.N.L. Brooke, 'The University Chancellor', *HRR*, pp. 47–66, at p. 63, n. 32.
6 Fisher's letter to R. Croke, n.d. (but *c.* 1525–6) reminds Croke how Fisher had resigned the post and then accepted it again at the request of the university. See SJC, Thin Red Book, fol. 50.r-v, printed in Hymers, *Funeral Sermon*, pp. 215–16. For the correspondence between Fisher and the university, see CUL, University Archives, Lett. 1, 'Epistolae Academicae I', pp. 25–6 (to Fisher, 24 May 1514), pp. 29–30 (from Fisher, 26 May), and pp. 32–3 (to Fisher, n.d.), printed in Lewis, *Dr Fisher*, ii, pp. 282–5. Notice of Fisher's re-election during the proctorship of Norris and Martin (17 Oct 1514–17 Oct 1515) is at *Grace Book B, Part II*, ed. M. Bateson (Cambridge, 1905), p. 36.
7 F. Seebohm, *The Oxford Reformers* (3rd edn., London, 1887), *passim*.
8 R Weiss, *Humanism in Fifteenth-Century England* (3rd edn., Oxford, 1965), esp. pp. 160–7 on Cambridge.
9 D.R. Leader, 'Professorships and Academic Reform at Cambridge: 1488–1520', *Sixteenth Century Journal* 14 (1983), pp. 215–27. See also his 'Teaching in Tudor Cambridge', *History of Education*, 13 (1984), pp. 105–19, and his *A History of the University of Cambridge* (Cambridge, 1988), pp. 235–42, and, more generally, chs. 11–12 (pp. 233–319).
10 Luther to Spalatin, 10 Dec 1520, *WA Briefwechsel* 2, p. 234, describes the bonfire. See also Melanchthon's 'Intimatio' of this event (*WA* 7, p. 183).
11 For the scholastics in private collections, see E.S. Leedham-Green, *Books in Cambridge Inventories* (2 vols., Cambridge, 1986), *passim*.
12 Weiss, *Humanism*, pp. 13–18 (Poggio), 122–7 (Gunthorpe) and 153–9 (Selling).
13 C.H. Cooper, *Annals of Cambridge* (5 vols., Cambridge, 1842–1908), i, p. 240.
14 *Grace Book A*, pp. 185, 202 and 219; *Grace Book B, Part I*, p. 196 (paid for lecturing, 1503–4).
15 *BRUC*, pp. 566–7. Surigone graduated D.Cn.L. in Cambridge, 1476. See also Weiss, *Humanism*, pp. 153–4.
16 J. Ruysschaert, 'Lorenzo Guglielmo Traversagni di Savona (1425–1503): un humaniste franciscain oublié', *Archivum Franciscanum Historicum* 46 (1953), pp. 195–210, surveys his career. P.O. Kristeller, *Iter Italicum* (London, 1963 –), i, pp. 148–9, describes some of his surviving MSS still at Savona. G. Farris, *Umanesimo e Religione in Lorenzo Guglielmo Traversagni di Savona* (Milan, 1972), is a brief study of his work which prints some of Traversagni's orations and prefaces.
17 Farris, *Traversagni*, p. 6.
18 Farris, *Traversagni*, pp. 9–14, and Ruysschaert, 'Traversagni', *passim*.
19 Printed by Farris, *Traversagni*, pp. 71–81.
20 Farris, *Traversagni*, p. 80.
21 *Margarita Eloquentie Castigate*, (London: Caxton, 1478, *STC* 24188.5; and St Alban's: 'Schoolmaster's press', 1480, *STC* 24190). *Epitonia sive Isagogicum Margarite Castigate Eloquencie* (London: Caxton, 1480), *STC* 24190.3.

22 *Margarita* (St Alban's, 1480), preface, sigg. a.1.v–a.7.v.

23 *Margarita*, sig. a.7.v, 'vir eruditissimus divinarum humanarumque litterarum'.

24 Weiss, *Humanism*, pp. 162–3.

25 Farris, *Traversagni*, pp. 23–42.

26 Ruysschaert, 'Traversagni', pp. 208–9.

27 Leader, *Cambridge*, pp. 93–4 and 'Professorships', p. 218. See his *Cambridge*, chs. 3–6, pp. 89–169 for a more detailed study of the arts curriculum.

28 Leader, *Cambridge*, p. 95, and 'Professorships', p. 224.

29 *EE* II, ep. 456, to Henry Bullock, 22 Aug 1516, p. 328, 'Ante annos ferme triginta nihil tradebatur in schola Cantabrigiensi praeter Alexandrum, Parva Logicalia, ut vocant, et vetera illa Aristotelis dictata Scoticasque questiones. Progessu temporis accesserunt bonae literae: accessit matheseos cognitio: accessit novus aut certe novatus Aristoteles: accessit Graecarum literarum peritia: accesserunt autores tam multi, quorum olim ne nomina tenebantur.'

30 Lewis, *Dr Fisher*, ii, pp. 263–72, esp. p. 264.

31 *EE* II, ep. 336, from Fisher, *c.* May 1515, p. 90, 'Utinam iuvenis praeceptorem illum fuissem nactus!'

32 *EE* IV, ep. 1111, to Vives, *c.* June 1520, p. 281; and VIII, ep. 2157, to Alfonso Fonseca, *c.* May 1529, p. 160.

33 Leader, *Cambridge*, pp. 249–50, and 'Professorships', pp. 218–19.

34 *Grace Book A*, pp. 219–20; *Grace Book B, Part I*, pp. 51, 138, 159, 175 and 196.

35 *Grace Book B, Part I*, p. 171. See also P.L. Rose, 'Erasmians and Mathematicians at Cambridge in the early sixteenth century', *Sixteenth Century Journal* 8 (1977), pp. 47–59.

36 *BRUC*, p. 149. Roger was probably a brother, cousin or nephew of Ralph Collingwood (*BRUC*, p. 149), on whose connection with Fisher see below, p. 26.

37 See *Letters of Richard Fox 1486–1527*, ed. P.S. and H.M. Allen (Oxford, 1920), pp. 40–1, where the dedication is printed.

38 *DVC* V, preface, fol. CXXXIIII.r (p. 1128).

39 M.R. James, *A Descriptive Catalogue of the Manuscripts other than Oriental in the Library of King's College Cambridge* (Cambridge, 1895), p. 74.

40 R. Croke, *Orationes Ricardi Croci Duae* (Paris: Colinaeus, 1520), sig. c.1.r, 'Ioannem Canonicum probo.' A copy of John Canonicus was bought for Fisher's nephew, Matthew White, a student at St John's College, Cambridge, as late as the end of 1532. See SJC, Master's Accounts, D 106.6, fol. 62.r.

41 Farris, *Traversagni*, p. 73.

42 See G.F. Warner and J.P. Gilson, *A Catalogue of the Manuscripts in the Royal Library* (4 vols., London, 1921), i, p. 294. For Reynoldson, see *BRUC*, p. 479.

43 Leedham-Green, *Cambridge Inventories*, i, p. 596.

44 *Grace Book B, Part I*, pp. xi and 140. John Camberton bequeathed a Latin Plato to Pembroke around 1506 (*BRUC*, p. 118).

45 The records of an Oxford bookseller reveal that Lefèvre's editions of Aristotle were common in Oxford by 1520. See 'The Day Book of John Dorne', ed. F. Madan Oxford Historical Society, *Collectanea* I (Oxford, 1885), p. 158 (twenty-four copies identified). See also p. 148, identifying seven copies of Argyropoulos's version of the *Ethics*.

46 Leader, *Cambridge*, ch. 7, pp. 170–91.

47 CUL, MS Kk. 1. 18. Mentioned by J. Bale in *Index Britanniae Scriptorum*, ed. R.L. Poole and M. Bateson, Anecdota Oxoniensia, Medieval and Modern Series 9 (Oxford, 1902), pp. 149 and 515.

48 *EE* I, ep. 227, to Colet, 13 Sept 1511, p. 467; see also ep. 237, 29 Oct 1511, p. 477.

49 For Songar, see *BRUC*, p. 542. For Gower and Walkden, see *Grace Book Γ*, ed. W.G. Searle (Cambridge, 1908), pp. 181 and 185. For the Franciscans, see Leader, *Cambridge*, p. 182.

50 S. Baron, *Sermones declamati coram alma universitate Cantibrigiensi* (London: de Worde, n.d.) *STC* 1497, *passim*, e.g., sigg. A.5.v (Richard), B.3.v–4.v (Bonaventure, Scotus and Thomas).

51 These figures are based on data collected from *BRUC*, Leedham-Green's *Cambridge Inventories*, the *Grace Books* (books were often deposited as cautions against the fulfilment of academic obligations), and various published fifteenth-century inventories of the Cambridge university and college libraries.

52 For Lyra see *New Catholic Encyclopedia* 10, pp. 453–4.

53 The material cited so far in this paragraph is mostly drawn from the relevant entries in *BRUC*. For Mennall's books see Leedham-Green, *Cambridge Inventories*, i, p. 594.

54 *Catalogue of the Library of Syon Monastery*, ed. M. Bateson (Cambridge, 1898), p. xxvi.

55 *Vie*, x, pp. 216–17. See S. Thompson, 'The bishop in his diocese', in *HRR*, pp. 67–80.

56 *Grace Book A*, pp. 189 and 193; *Grace Book B, Part I*, pp. 2 and 5. This was first pointed out by W.R. Godfrey, 'John Colet of Cambridge', *Archiv für Reformations-geschichte* 65 (1975). pp. 6–17, esp. p. 17, and has been recently confirmed in the authoritative biography by J.B. Gleason, *John Colet* (Berkeley, 1989) pp. 39–42.

57 *Grace Book A*, p. 193. See also Erasmus's record of Colet's bitter attack on Aquinas in a conversation, *EE* IV, ep. 1211, to J. Jonas, 13 June 1521, p. 520.

58 Gleason, *Colet*, pp. 202–3.

59 For which see B. Bradshaw, 'The Christian Humanism of Erasmus', *Journal of Theological Studies* 33 (1982), pp. 411–47, esp. pp. 413–15.

60 J.H. Lupton, *A Life of John Colet, DD.* (London, 1887), p. 279.

61 See Lupton, *Colet*, p. 215, on Colet's plan to retire to the Charterhouse of Sheen; and p. 275 on his position as rector of the Guild of Jesus at St Paul's. On his study of Greek, see *EE* II, ep. 471, to Reuchlin, 29 Sept 1516, p. 351.

62 A.G. Dickens, *The English Reformation* (2nd edn. London, 1989), p. 112.

63 *DVC* I, preface, sig. BB.4.r (p. 749); and V, preface, fol. CXXXIIII.r (p. 1128).

64 *Vie*, x, p. 205. *Grace Book B, Part I*, pp. 80 (probably 11 March 1496) and 81 (6 June 1496).

65 J.J. Scarisbrick, 'The Conservative Episcopate in England 1529–1535' (unpublished Ph. D. dissertation, Cambridge, 1955), pp. 348–9.

66 W. Melton, *Sermo Exhortatorius* (London: de Worde, n.d.), *STC* 17806.

67 *Sermo*, sigg. a.3.r and a.4.r.

68 *Sermo*, sig. a.7.v, 'Precipuum autem contra inertem torporem prestat remedium lectio assidua et revolucio librorum legis dei et scripturarum: quos ante nos sancti patres et doctores ediderunt. In quorum opusculis iam per impressionem habundantibus possunt vel mediocriter eruditi/varium et iocundum colligere solatium.'

69 *Sermo*, final page.

70 *Testamenta Eboracensia V*, Surtees Soc. 79 (1884), p. 254.

71 D. Knowles, *The Religious Orders in England* (3 vols., Cambridge, 1948–59), iii, p. 239, referring to Lincoln Cathedral Library MS A. 6. 8. Like Knowles, I am

grateful to Dom Philip Jebb OSB, MA, headmaster and archivist of Downside College, for allowing me to consult his transcripts of these prefaces. The treatises, by John Norton, prior of Mount Grace (died *c.* 1520), were edited by one Robert Fletcher, who persuaded Melton to contribute the prefaces. Melton left money for masses to be said at the altar of the Name of Jesus in York Minster (*Testamenta Eboracensia V*, p. 251).

72 *The Historians of the Church of York and its Archbishops*, ed. J. Raines, Rolls Series (3 vols., London, 1886–94), ii, pp. xxv and 422–55. A.G. Dickens, *Lollards and Protestants in the Diocese of York 1509–1558* (Oxford, 1959), pp. 16–17.

73 *DVC* I, preface, sig. BB.4.r (p. 749).

74 P. Heath, *The English Parish Clergy on the Eve of the Reformation* (London, 1969), p. 71.

75 *Testamenta Eboracensia V*, pp. 258–9, summarised, not always accurately, at *BRUC*, p. 401. See p. 259 for 'Ruffenc contra Lutherium', 'Liber, sacri Sacerdotii defencio' and 'Liber de Veritate Corporis Christi', easily recognisable as *ALC*, *SSD* and *DVC*.

76 SJC D 56.45, Watson to Metcalfe, 29 March 1519, where Watson also planned to send copies of *DUM* to the priors of the Gilbertines at Watton and the Carthusians at Hull: 'Vellem ex opusculis patroni nostri [de M]agdalene assertione quinque aut sex ut ea [sint quam]primum perlata in nostratem regionem ad patres [conventorum] de Watton et hulle priores ac Meltonum.'

77 SJC D 56.18.

78 Melton endowed masses for his and Rotherham's souls, *Testamenta Eboracensia V*, pp. 251–2. For a letter from Traversagni to Rotherham (as bishop of Lincoln) see Kristeller, *Iter Italicum*, i, p. 149.

79 Erasmus, *Adversus Petri Sutoris ... debacchationem Apologia* (Basel: Froben, 1525), sig. K.2.r-v, 'At ego multos novi candidos Theologos ... qui ... hortabuntur ... tyrones Theologiae, ut linguas ac bonas literas amplecterentur ... Ex his unum nominabo, quem in Anglia plurimi norunt, et arbitror adhuc superesse. Nomen erat Melton, cancellarius ecclesiae Eboracensis. Aedidit libellum de examinandis his, qui sacris cupiunt initiari. Erat vir impeditiore lingua, sed impense doctus ... R.P. Ioannem episcopum Roffensem, nec ipse Sutor, opinor, audebit contemnere ... Et tamen is iam vergens ad annum quadragesimum, magno studio didicit Graecas et Hebraicas literas, et idem faciant instigat alios, ac sumptibus iuvat: non ut intelligant Homerum aut Lucianum, nihil minus illi cordi est, sed ut plenius intelligant divinas scripturas.'

80 Fisher cited Spagnuoli (as 'Mantuanus') in *DUM* III, fols. L.II.v–L.III.r (cc. 1461–2); Colet included 'Baptista Mantuanus' among the authors suitable for use at St Paul's (Lupton, *Colet*, p. 279 and Gleason, *Colet*, pp. 227–8); and Melton's inventory includes 'Opera Mantuani' (*Testamenta Eboracensia V*, p. 259).

81 Agnes Constable and Dam Elizabeth Melton were both described as nieces of Sir Thomas Cumberworth in his will of 15 Feb 1450. See *Lincoln Diocese Documents 1450–1544*, ed. A. Clark, EETS orig. ser. 149 (1914), pp. 45–57, at pp. 49–50. Another connection between Meltons and Constables is suggested by the naming of John Melton esq. as an executor of Sir John Constable's will (20 Dec 1472). See *Testamenta Eboracensia III*, Surtees Soc. 45 (1864), p. 278.

82 *Grace Book B, Part I*, p. 170 (Lent 1502).

83 SJC D 56.9, Sir M. Constable to Fisher, n.d., about Ralph's conduct. *Testamenta Eboracensia V*, will of Sir M. Constable (1 May 1518, proved 27 April 1520),

p. 93, provided 'for foundyng of certeyn scolers in Cambridge'. SJC D 58.4 for foundation deed, 4 July 1524.

84 He was granted a dispensation on 9 July 1478, at the age of seventeen, to hold a benefice despite being under the canonical age. See *Calendar of Papal Registers: Papal Letters* 13, part 2, p. 616.

85 *BRUC*, p. 155. *Grace Book B, Part I*, p. 81. Other Constables who studied at Cambridge included his uncle William, a canon lawyer (*BRUC*, p. 155); and his nephew Marmaduke, son of his brother Robert and Beatrix, Lady Greystoke. See *Testamenta Eboracensia IV*, Surtees Soc. 53 (1869), pp. 195 and 236–9 for their wills, each providing for their son's education at Cambridge.

86 C.H. and T. Cooper, *Athenae Cantabrigienses* (2 vols., Cambridge, 1858–61), i, p. 35.

87 M. Bowker, *Secular Clergy in the Diocese of Lincoln* (Cambridge, 1968), pp. 162–4, and *The Henrician Reformation: the diocese of Lincoln under John Longland 1521–1547* (Cambridge, 1981), pp. 31–2. Despite the evidence for Constable's importance in the campaign for residence, Bowker herself attributes the responsibility for it to Longland and his treasurer Parker, who of course remained in office after Constable's death, when residence was declining again.

88 Emden missed this (*BRUC*, p. 155). George Fitzhugh had vacated the mastership in March 1489 (*BRUC*, p. 219), and was succeeded by Constable who, as master, nominated W. Leyceter to the rectory of St Denis, York, on 2 Oct 1489 (*Rotherham's Register* I, p. 120).

89 J.J. Scarisbrick, *The Reformation and the English People* (Oxford, 1984), p. 53.

90 J.A.H. Moran, *The Growth of English Schooling: learning, literacy, and laicization in pre-Reformation York diocese* (Princeton, 1985), p. 106.

91 SJC D 56.10, Constable to Fisher, 27 Jan 1512 or 1515 – plans for Fisher to attend the Council were twice frustrated. *EE* I, ep. 252, to Anthony of Bergen, 6 Feb 1512, p. 498, 'Episcopus Rophensis . . . me . . . huius itineris comitem volebat.'

92 SJC D 56.18, Constable to Fisher, 12 Nov, no year given. Constable also apologised because other business had prevented him from working upon his own book.

93 *BRUC*, p. 149. BL Lansdowne MS 978 (Kennett's Collections, vol. 44), fol. 218. William Whitlocke's 'Continuatio Historiae Lichfeldensis', in *Anglia Sacra*, ed. H. Wharton (2 vols., London, 1691), i, pp. 448–59, at p. 456.

94 Lupton, *Colet*, p. 114. See also Colet's *Letters on the Mosaic Account of Creation*, ed. J.H. Lupton (London, 1876), pp. xviii–xix. The Register of Doctors Commons (London, Lambeth Palace Library MS DC1) has entries for 'Radulphus Colyngwod s.p.p.' (without signature) on fol. 7.v and 'Johannes Colett s.p.p.' (with signature) on fol. 8.r. On Doctors Commons see McConica, *English Humanists*, pp. 52–3.

95 BL Royal MS 3. D. i, fol. 234.v, 'Hunc librum dedit conventui fratris minorum Lichefeldie magister Radulphus Collingwood quondam huius venerabilis clausi decanus qui erat famosus predicator et sacre theologie doctor.' The note must be contemporary as the volume had found its way into Henry VIII's collection by 1542 (*Manuscripts in the Royal Library*, i, p. 76). *Anglia Sacra*, i, p. 456.

96 *BRUC*, pp. 51–2, 221, 238, 313–14 and 525–6. See M. Underwood, 'The Lady Margaret and her Cambridge Connections', *Sixteenth Century Journal* 13 (1982), pp. 67–81.

97 R.W. Pfaff, *New Liturgical Feasts in Later Medieval England* (Oxford, 1970), p. 82

(and, for the feast in general, ch. 4, pp. 62–83). Hornby owned copies of Lyra, Hugh of Vienne, Cassiodorus and *De Civitate Dei*.

98 SJC D 105.89 and 91–4, letters from Hornby to Fisher, printed by Scott in 'Notes from the College Records', *The Eagle* 16 (1891), pp. 341–57, at pp. 343–51.

99 *Records of the Reformation: the divorce 1527–1533*, ed. N. Pocock (2 vols., Oxford, 1870), ii, p. 457, notes his vote at Southern Convocation on 5 April 1533 against the proposition that the marriage was contrary to natural law and indispensable by the pope.

100 W.G. Searle, *The History of the Queens' College of St Margaret and St Bernard, Part I, 1446–1560* (Cambridge Antiquarian Society Publications 9, 1867), pp. 137–40 prints a series of letters on this matter from the College to Fisher, Lady Margaret and Bekynsall, from June and July 1508.

101 SJC D 105.102, printed in Scott, 'Notes from the College Records', *The Eagle* 16, pp. 355–6, about a dispute over tenure of a fellowship at Michaelhouse.

102 *Grace Book Γ*, p. 59. For his career, see *BRUC*, p. 403.

103 *The Scholemaster*, in R. Ascham, *English Works*, ed. W.A. Wright (Cambridge, 1904), pp. 278–9.

104 *DUM*, letter from Didymus Lycoucarus to Metcalfe, title page verso (c. 1393). SJC D 105.41, Sharpe to Metcalfe, 20 Oct, no year given. Printed in Scott, 'Notes from the College Records', *The Eagle* 17 (1893), pp. 470–1; and G.J. Gray, 'Letters of Bishop Fisher, 1521–3', *The Library*, 3rd. ser., 4 (1913), pp. 133–45, at pp. 134–5.

105 J. Foxe, *Acts and Monuments*, ed. G. Townsend (8 vols., London, 1843–9), vii, p. 451. *Records of the Reformation*, ii, p. 458, for his vote in favour of Catherine's marriage in 1533. See P. Friedmann, *Anne Boleyn* (2 vols., London, 1884), i, p. 142, for Metcalfe's and Shorton's signatures to a protestation of May 1531 against conceding the title of supreme head to the king.

106 R.F. Scott, 'Notes from the College Records', *The Eagle* 31 (1910), pp. 323–58, at p. 332.

107 W. Stubbs, *Registrum Sacrum Anglicanum* (2nd edn., Oxford, 1897), pp. 97–8. The other three were Vesey of Exeter (6 Nov 1519), Longland of Lincoln (5 May 1521) and Rawlins of St Davids (26 April 1523).

108 *DRA*, dedication to West, 6th leaf verso (p. 101). Mayor, *Early Statutes*, p. 394. The office is still exercised by the bishop of Ely.

109 *LP* 6. 625, inventory of West, 11 June 1533, gives totals of 199 books bound in boards and 50 bound otherwise.

110 Both bishops received dedications from Siberch: West of Baldwin of Canterbury's *De Sacramento Altaris* and Fisher of Erasmus, *De Conscribendis Epistolis* (both Cambridge: Siberch, 1521; *STC* 1242 and 10496). Croke's *Orationes Duae* was dedicated to West. Croke recalled 'quibus verbis … me, ad latinam eloquentiam fueris adhortatus' when he had been a scholar at King's (sigg. a.3.r–4.v). See also sig. c.4.r, 'Eliensi, qui quantum bonis literis faveat.'

111 See below, ch. 5, p. 86, n. 66 and ch. 10, p. 170.

112 M. Thomas, 'Tunstall – Trimmer or Martyr?', *Journal of Ecclesiastical History* 24 (1983), pp. 337–55, at p. 340.

113 *STC* 277–87.

114 *LP* 2. i, pp. 1445, 1450, 1454, 1460, 1466, 1470 and 1474, for 1510–17 (except 1514).

115 J. Fabri, *De Intercessione Sanctorum*, in *Opuscula* (Leipzig: Wolrab, 1538), sig. d.6.r.

2 The preaching bishop

1 J.W. Blench, *Preaching in England in the late Fifteenth and Sixteenth Centuries* (Oxford, 1964), is the best introduction to the subject of preaching in general.

2 *Vie*, x, pp. 217, 219 and 221. J. Fabri, *De Intercessione Sanctorum*, in *Opuscula*, sig. d.6.r. *EE* XI, ep. 3036, to Christopher von Stadion, 6 Aug 1535, p. 191.

3 As Surtz also observes (*Works and Days*, p. 56). Fisher's commitment to preaching finds a mention in most of the biographies, as do most of the things mentioned in this paragraph.

4 Mayor, *Early Statutes*, p. 377, recalling that Lady Margaret had founded the college to produce 'ex hoc coetu theologi qui suorum studiorum fructum populo communicent'. This clause of the 1516 statutes is repeated verbatim but for the omission of 'populo' in the statutes of 1524 (p. 313), 1530 (p. 96) and 1545 (p. 97).

5 Sundays, feast days and certain other days excepted. The exposition could be in Latin or English, but had to be literal. The preachers were to do this on a rota of eight weeks each. Mayor, *Early Statutes*, pp. 315–16 (1524), 100 (1530) and 103 (1545).

6 *EE* XI, ep. 3036, to C. von Stadion, 6 Aug 1533, p. 191. The misconception that Fisher had founded *three* colleges first appeared in Erasmus's dedication to Alfonso Fonseca of Augustine's *Opera Omnia* (10 vols., Basel: Froben, 1528–9), *EE* VIII, ep. 2157, *c.* May 1529, p. 160. This letter also praises Fisher as a preacher (p. 161).

7 *EE* V, ep. 1332, to Christopher von Utenheim, *c.* Jan 1523, p. 162, reports Fisher's importunacy; and ep. 1489, to Fisher, 4 Sept 1425, p. 538, promises him the dedication. See also *EE* XI, ep. 3036, which is in fact the dedication of *Ecclesiastes Libri IV sive de Ratione Concionandi* (Basel: Froben, 1535), recalling Fisher's enthusiasm for the work (p. 191).

8 Leader, *History*, pp. 278–81, with further evidence of patronage of preaching in late fifteenth-century Cambridge. There is no direct evidence that Fisher suggested this enterprise to Lady Margaret, but as he was her confessor and chief adviser at the time it is a reasonable conclusion.

9 The text of the bull is not currently known, although it may turn up in the Vatican archives. Its date is recited in the licences issued to the preachers, e.g., CUL, Univ. Archives LIC. A. 1. (1), no. 1. Lewis prints one in *Doctor Fisher*, ii, pp. 261–3.

10 *Grace Book B, Part II*, pp. 16, 77 and 105. See Leader, *History*, pp. 279–81, for the disappearance of the licences (except for a few in 1527) between 1523 and 1532. From 1523 to 1527 I suspect that licences were given but not recorded. There are discrepancies between the licences in CUL, Univ. Archives LIC. A. 1. (1) and the lists in the *Grace Books*. From 1527 to 1532 the gap may reflect a response to the Bilney affair.

11 A. Fuller's introduction to *Calendar of Papal Registers: Papal Letters* 16 (1986), pp. xxxv–xxxviii, suggests that most requests were processed within a matter of months rather than years. Allowing for travel to Rome, the university's petition was almost certainly made in 1502.

12 *EW*, p. 199.

13 *ALC* 36, fol. 209.r (c. 692), 'Et frustra quoque tot conciones quotidie fiunt, ob convertendos peccatores ... Nam si necessitate peccator quisquam est, non voluntate, frustra conabitur, quisquis ipsum convertere studebit. Nec desunt exempla plurima, quae proferamus, eorum qui per conciones ab erroribus, ad viam rectam, a turpi luxu, ad vitae sanctitatem, et a maximis demum sceleribus ad virtutem capescendam sunt conversi.'

14 *A sermon had at Paulis* (London: Berthelet, n.d.), sig. D.2.v. The bulk of the sermon is an exposition of the parable of the sower as applying to the preaching of the faith.

15 The first edition of these sermons was dated 16 June 1508. The third sermon was delivered on the Nativity of the Blessed Virgin (8 Sept), which means that 1507 is the latest year for their delivery. This is the year proposed by W. Stafford in his 'Repentance on the Eve of the Reformation: John Fisher's sermons of 1508 and 1509', *Historical Magazine of the Protestant Episcopal Church* 54 (1985), pp. 297–338, at p. 316. Surtz argued for 1504 because only then in that decade did the Nativity fall on a Sunday (*Works and Days*, p. 402). Rouschausse was not convinced that it had to be a Sunday (*La Vie et l'Oeuvre*, p. 69). I concur with Surtz. Since one sermon refers to the next as to be delivered on 'sondaye nexte comynge' (*EW*, p. 137), the sermons probably were given on Sundays. Moreover, in some later writings, Fisher refers to episcopal duties and makes it clear that he feels them keenly. In these sermons he refers to these duties with no suggestion that he had himself assumed that dignity (pp. 76–7). But he does feel the burden of 'the offyce of a doctour or techer of goddes lawes', referring to the danger of intellectual pride in such a way as to suggest an academic perspective (p. 124). Since he took his DD in June 1504, but was not consecrated bishop until Nov 1504, this could mean that the sermons date from mid-1504.

16 The date generally agreed is 1520. This is based on the allusions to the Field of Cloth of Gold, 'the goodly syghtes whiche were shewed of late beyonde the see' (*Two Fruytfull Sermons*, sig. A.3.r). But 'of late' need not imply that very year. The reference to the treason and punishment of 'great Erles & Dukes' (sig. F.4.r.) could be an allusion to the fate of Buckingham, executed in May 1521. On the other hand, there are no hints about Lutheranism, which one might expect after 1521. 1520 remains the most likely year, but it is not certain.

17 *Two Fruytfull Sermons*, ed. M.D. Sullivan (Ann Arbor, 1965), sig. C.3.r. This edition is my source for these very rare sermons, but references are given to the foliation of the original edition. A Latin translation of these sermons was included in the *OO* of 1597.

18 Brooke *et al.*, 'Fisher's itinerary', *HRR*, p. 244 (Rochester); *LP* 5. 1109, Chapuys to Charles V, 21 June 1532.

19 *Vie*, xii, p. 270, citing fragments of Rastell's life of Thomas More, preserved in BL Arundel MS 152.

20 J.J. Scarisbrick, 'Fisher, Henry VIII and the Reformation crisis', *HRR*, pp. 155–68, at p. 164.

21 For explicit pauses see *EW*, pp. 51 (for the 'Salve Regina'?), 209 ('De Profundis' for the souls in Purgatory), 281 and 303 ('Pater Nosters' for Henry VII and Lady Margaret) and 396 (prayer for light of grace); *A sermon had at Paulis*, sig. C.3.r; *Two Fruytfull Sermons*, sig. A.2.v ('Pater Noster'). In some of the sermons on the psalms, Fisher regards his exposition as itself a prayer (*EW*, pp. 94 and 237).

22 G.R. Owst, *Preaching in Medieval England: an introduction to sermon manuscripts of the period c. 1350–1450* (Cambridge, 1926), pp. 312–30, for a description of this 'new' style, and an explanation of the technical terms. Blench deals in more detail with Fisher's style (*Preaching*, pp. 76–7 and 81–3).

23 Blench identifies these sermons as 'old' style, despite observing their tripartite structure (*Preaching*, p. 76).

24 Blench, *Preaching*, p. 86. He finds further evidence for classical influences in Fisher's attempts to imitate Ciceronian periods (pp. 129–31) and his use of classical allusion (pp. 213–15).

25 *STC* 10902–8 records seven editions between 1508 and 1529, with a further edition in 1555.
26 *EW*, pp. 90–3.
27 *EW*, p. 93.
28 I owe my knowledge of Lewis's criticisms to Eamon Duffy's excellent essay on Fisher's spirituality, to which this chapter is heavily indebted in other respects. Dr Duffy also takes issue with Lewis's reading of Fisher. (See his 'The spirituality of John Fisher', in *HRR*, pp. 205–32, esp. pp. 205–7).
29 *EW*, pp. 93–4.
30 W. Stafford, 'Repentance on the Eve of the Reformation', p. 319.
31 J. Bossy, *Christianity in the West* (Oxford, 1985), p. 38.
32 Duffy, 'Spirituality', p. 208.
33 *EW*, p. 283.
34 *EW*, p. 97.
35 Duffy, 'Spirituality', p. 208.
36 *EW*, pp. 95–7.
37 *EW*, p. 247.
38 *EW*, p. 259.
39 *EW*, p. 259. The Latin tag is 'Da quod iubes: et iube quod vis', but Fisher or his printer garbled this slightly as 'Iubes domine: & iube quod vis.'
40 *EW*, p. 176.
41 *EW*, p. 88, 'yf the helpe of his grace be not redy at all seasons we must nedes sagge & bowe'.
42 *EW*, p. 160, 'almyghty god is not to be accused yf he at ony tyme do his good wyl to lyfte vs vp in to the hygh state of grace, & we in the meane season by the weyght of our frowarde and peruerse wyll fall downe from his handes'.
43 *EW*, pp. 222, 233 and elsewhere.
44 *EW*, pp. 216 and 217.
45 *EW*, p. 219.
46 *EW*, p. 127.
47 *EW*, p. 238.
48 *EW*, p. 282.
49 *EW*, p. 238, 'Lorde here me gracyously lyke as thou arte true and ryghtwyse of thy promyse.'
50 *EW*, p. 221.
51 *EW*, pp. 103–6, esp. p. 106.
52 *EW*, p. 138.
53 Ezech 18:30. *EW*, p. 221.
54 *EW*, p. 222.
55 *EW*, pp. 277 and 307. Fisher based this opinion traditionally enough on Eccles 9:1.
56 Duffy's loose paraphrase, that Fisher wanted them to 'perform good works' (Spirituality', p. 209), might in the context of sixteenth-century polemic appear as a mere call to ceremonial duties. In fact Fisher appealed to the text 'if thou wilt enter into life, keep the commandments' (Mt 19:17).
57 *EW*, p. 98.
58 *EW*, p. 211, 'truly confessyon without contrycyon had before profyteth very lytell or no thynge'.
59 *EW*, p. 32, 'Onely contrycyon with a full purpose of confessyon taketh awaye the gylte of synne.'

60 *EW*, pp. 30 and 223.

61 *ALC* 6, fol. 67.r (c. 404), where Fisher accuses Luther of wilfully ignoring the distinction made by the scholastics between attrition and contrition. He expands on this at fol. 68.r (c. 407). On each occasion, he is careful to explain that he is presenting the views of the scholastics, and he gives no reason to conclude that he subscribes to those views.

62 *ALC* 6, fol. 68.r (c. 407), 'Existimant [namely, the scholastics] enim peccatorum, ex naturalibus, cum generali influxu, et auxilio Dei posse considerare peccatum ab se commissum . . . detestari. Et in hoc detestationis motu pergere, donec ex congruo tandem infundatur gratia.' Fisher did not subscribe to the theory of merit 'ex congruo'.

63 *EW*, p. 26.

64 *EW*, pp. 210–11. For the role of 'profounde consyderacyon' see also p. 37.

65 *EW*, p. 25. See also p. 101, 'Truly almyghty god wyll not knowe our synne and trespasse, yf we our selfe wyll knowe them', and further dilation on this theme.

66 *ALC* 5, fol. 60.v (c. 391), citing 'Poenitentem nunquam oportet oblivioni peccatum tradere, sed deum quidem rogare, ne eius meminerit, ipsum vero nunquam ipsius oblivisci. Si nos eius non recordemur, deus ipsius non obliviscetur. Si nos eius meminerimus, deus obliviscetur', as from 'homilia XLI de poenitentia'. I have been unable to trace this in *PG*, but it can be found in *Tomus Quartus Divi Ioannis Chrysostomi* (Basel: Cratander, 1525), in sermon 41, 'De Poenitentia', of 'Homiliae LXXX ad populum Antiochenum', at fol. 88.v, in a translation by Bernard Brixianus. This is clearly the version, though not the edition, Fisher was using.

67 *EW*, pp. 33 and 85–6.

68 *EW*, p. 24.

69 *EW*, p. 211. Prayer is said to include the virtues of fasting and almsgiving, as it tires the body like fasting and is, when done on behalf of others, the best sort of alms, 'spyrytuall almesse vnto theyr soules'. Besides, prayer is a sacrifice of the most noble thing people have, namely of the soul, and is open to all Christians, not simply to the rich (alms) or the healthy (fasting) (*EW*, pp. 211–12).

70 *EW*, p. 37.

71 *EW*, pp. 25–6.

72 Surtz, *Works and Days*, ch. 13, pp. 235–73. See also Blench, *Preaching*, pp. 131–4.

73 *EW*, p. 176.

74 *EW*, p. 158.

75 *EW*, p. 102.

76 *EW*, pp. 273 and 295.

77 *EW*, p. 120.

78 *EW*, p. 153.

79 *EW*, p. 37.

80 *EW*, p. 324.

81 *EW*, pp. 324–6.

82 *EW*, p. 8.

83 *EW*, pp. 45–51, esp. p. 49.

84 They are summarised by Surtz in *Works and Days*, pp. 266–73.

85 *EW*, p. 269. Blench (*Preaching*, p. 86) and Surtz (*Works and Days*, p. 267) draw attention to this.

86 As Blench (*Preaching*, p. 86) and Surtz (*Works and Days*, p. 267) observe.

87 *EW*, p. 289. Mayor wrongly identifies the gospel with Lk 10:38–9, the other occasion on which Christ is recorded as conversing with Martha. Surtz notes the

use of the gospel in the sermon (*Works and Days*, p. 270), but fails to appreciate the full force of the analogy Fisher draws between Martha and Margaret.

88 *EW*, p. 297, 'For the poore creatures, albeit she dyd not receyue in to her house our sauyour in his owne persone as the blessyd Martha dyde, she neuertheles receyued theim that dothe represent his persone.'

89 *EW*, p. 309.

90 *EW*, p. 273; Lewis, *Dr Fisher*, ii, p. 264.

91 *EW*, p. 271.

92 Though officially her 'confessor', his role seems to have been that of the spiritual director. She made confession to other priests as well as to Fisher, but undertook to follow his advice in matters concerning her spiritual life, as she had previously followed that of Fitzjames (*EW*, pp. 295–6).

93 *EW*, p. 297.

94 *EW*, p. 302.

95 *EW*, pp. 273–4 and 308–9.

96 *EW*, pp. 277 and 300.

97 *EW*, pp. 279 and 300.

98 *EW*, pp. 277 and 307.

99 They are summarised by Surtz, not wholly satisfactorily, in *Works and Days*, pp. 295–301.

100 *Two Fruytfull Sermons*, sig. E.1.r.

101 *Two Fruytfull Sermons*, sig. H.1.r–v.

102 *Two Fruytfull Sermons*, sig. G.1.r–v. Compare, though, the talk of pride, wrath, envy, lechery and avarice (sig. H.1.v) which might look more like the seven deadly sins were, it not for the talk of the commandments on the same page.

103 *Two Fruytfull Sermons*, sig. H.2.r.

104 *Two Fruytfull Sermons*, sig. B.3.v.

105 *Two Fruytfull Sermons*, sigg. B.4.v–C.4.r.

106 *Two Fruytfull Sermons*, sigg. C.4.v–D.1.v.

107 *Two Fruytfull Sermons*, sigg. D.2.v–3.v.

108 *Two Fruytfull Sermons*, sig. D.4.r.

109 *Two Fruytfull Sermons*, sig. D.4.r.

110 *Two Fruytfull Sermons*, sigg. E.3.v–F.3.v.

111 *Two Fruytfull Sermons*, sigg. F.4.v–G.1.r.

112 *Two Fruytfull Sermons*, sigg. G.1.v–4.v.

113 *A Sermon verie fruitfull, godly, and learned, upon thys sentence of the Prophet Ezechiell, Lamentationes, Carmen, et vae, very aptely applyed unto the passion of Christ, EW,* pp. 388–428. See p. 389. Summarised by Blench(*Preaching*, pp. 81–3) and Surtz (*Works and Days*, pp. 380–3). Neither author appreciates the full significance of the parallel Fisher develops at such length in this sermon. The sermon was delivered on a Good Friday, but we do not know the year.

114 Duffy, 'Spirituality', p. 213, finds Fisher's idea in a comment of Richard Rolle's.

115 *EW*, p. 388.

116 *EW*, pp. 390 and 391.

117 *Enchiridion Militis Christiani*, tr. C. Fantazzi, CWE 66 (Toronto, 1988), rule 17, p. 110.

118 *Enchiridion*, rule 5, p. 73.

119 *Enchiridion*, p. 271, n. 13, citing the opinion of Humphrey Monmouth, the London merchant, endeavouring to clear himself of suspicions of heresy in the 1520s.

120 *EW*, p. 390; and *Vie*, xii, p. 193.

121 *EW*, p. 389.

122 *EW*, pp. 393–6.

123 *EW*, pp. 397–407.

124 *EW*, pp. 408–11, reciting at the end a famous passage (attributed to Bernard) which described Christ's head as bowed to kiss, his arms as stretched to embrace, and so forth.

125 *EW*, pp. 413–15 (in the last case applying the image to sin as 'handwriting' in the conscience).

126 *EW*, pp. 415–20, esp. p. 417.

127 *EW*, pp. 421 and 427. Fisher detailed eleven pains, pp. 421–6.

128 *EW*, pp. 427–8.

129 *Works and Days*, p. 238.

130 *STC* 3259–67 (Bonaventure); 23954.7–60 (*Imitation*); and 24873–80.5 (*Legend*). John Mirk's *Liber Festivalis* ran to twenty-four edns. by 1532 (*STC* 17957–75), but it was a handbook for preachers rather than a work of private devotion.

131 See Blench's bibliography for English sermons of this time (*Preaching*, pp. 351–4).

132 See below, ch. 9, pp. 158–60 and compare for example Dickens, *The English Reformation*, pp. 58–9 and 65.

133 *EW*, p. 7.

3 Fisher and the Christian humanists, 1500–1520

1 R. Wakefield, *Oratio de laudibus et utilitate trium linguarum* (London: de Worde, n.d., *c.* 1528), sigg. Q.3.v–4.r, prints a letter from Tübingen university to Fisher praising the latter's devotion to the study of scripture and of its original languages. Wakefield's *Syntagma de hebraeorum codicum incorruptione* (London: Berthelet, n.d., *c.* 1534), is less flattering at sig. D.4.r.

2 Surtz, *Works and Days*, p. 495, n. 28.

3 Erasmus, *De Conscribendis Epistolis*, sig. A.2.v (printer's dedication to John Fisher). For some correspondence between Erasmus and Robert, see *EE* I, eps. 62 (*c.* Aug 1497), p. 188; 71 (*c.* March 1498), pp. 198–9; and 118 (5 Dec 1499), pp. 273–4.

4 *Contemporaries of Erasmus*, ed. P.G. Bietenholz with T.B. Deutscher (3 vols., Toronto, 1985–7), ii, pp. 39–40.

5 *EE* I, app. VI, p. 591. It was presumably during this visit that Erasmus was granted a grace to proceed DD on condition of lecturing on Paul. See *Grace Book Γ*, p. 46.

6 Allen qualifies Fisher's role in Erasmus's decision to come to Cambridge in 1511 with 'perhaps' (*EE* I, p. 465). The theory gains some support from analogy with Richard Croke, see below, n. 49.

7 C.H. Cooper, *Memoir of Margaret*, app. II. 5, accts. of Lady Margaret's executors, p. 200.

8 It is conveniently edited in J. Rouschausse, *Erasmus and Fisher: Their Correspondence 1511–1524*, De Pétrarque à Descartes 16 (Paris, 1968).

9 *EE* I, ep. 278, 31 Oct 1513, p. 537. Surtz, *Works and Days*, p. 134.

10 This is the only volume so far known to survive from Fisher's library. The letter which accompanied it, excusing the changed dedication, is *EE* II, ep. 413, 5 June 1516, pp. 244–6.

11 *EE* II, ep. 432, *c.* June 1516, p. 268.

12 R. Sharpe to N. Metcalfe, SJC D 105.43, printed in Gray, 'Letters of Bishop Fisher', p. 136.

13 *Paraphrases on Romans and Galatians*, ed. R.D. Sider, CWE 42 (Toronto, 1984), pp. xvi–xvii.

14 *EE* V, ep. 1323, to Ferdinand, 29 Nov 1522, p. 143.

15 PRO SP2/R, fols. 28−274.

16 *EE* VI, ep. 1535, to Longland, 5 Jan 1525, p. 2. In fact, he did write paraphrases of some psalms.

17 SP2/R, fol. 157.v, 'Quoniam filius est sermo patris non aliter quam dicendo primogenitus est.' The translation of 'logos' as 'sermo' first appeared in the second edn. of *Annotationes* (Basel: Froben, 1519), p. 162. See R.H. Bainton, *Erasmus of Christendom* (New York, 1969), p. 140, on this.

18 There is no full study of this controversy in English. Even its chronology is obscure, though good outlines are found in *EE* IV, pp. 109−10, and in *Contemporaries of Erasmus*, ii, pp. 311−14 (article by M. O'R. Boyle). But both these accounts prefer Erasmus's version of events to Lee's.

19 Surtz discusses this matter briefly in *Works and Days*, pp. 135−6. E. Lee, *Apologia Edoardi Lei contra quorundam calumnias* (Paris: Gourmont, n.d.), sig. AA.2.r−v. See also More to Lee, *c.* May 1519, in *Epistolae Aliquot Eruditorum Virorum* (Basel: Froben, 1520), pp. 56−75, summarising an earlier letter of Lee's, which (at p. 57) dated the conversation with Erasmus to the time Charles V left the Netherlands for Spain (Sept 1517).

20 Lee, *Apologia*, sigg. AA.2.v−4.r. See *EE* III, ep. 765, to Lee, *c.* Jan 1518, p. 203, for an unconvincing excuse for not using Lee's notes.

21 Lee, *Apologia*, sig. BB.1.r. *EE* III, ep. 886, to Tunstall, 22 Oct 1518, voices Erasmus's suspicion that Lee 'meditatur aduersum nos nescio quid'.

22 Lee, *Apologia*, sig. BB.1.r.

23 *EE* IV, eps. 1061, from Lee, 1 Feb 1520, p. 178; and 1074, to Capito, *c.* Feb. 1520, p. 199.

24 Lee, *Apologia*, sig. BB.3.r.

25 Lee, *Apologia*, sig. CC.1.v. More's letter was the one in *Epistolae Aliquot Eruditorum Virorum*. See *The Correspondence of Sir Thomas More*, ed. E.F. Rogers (Princeton, 1947), pp. 137−54.

26 Lee, *Apologia*, sig. BB.4.r.

27 Lee, *Apologia*, sig. CC.1.r−v.

28 For the embargo and exception of More, see More to Lee in *Epistolae Aliquot Eruditorum Virorum*, p. 57 (*Correspondence*, p. 139). For Erasmus's prior agreement with Fisher that the latter should try to obtain him a copy, see *Apologia ... qua respondet duabus invectivis Eduardi Lei* (Antwerp: Hillenius, 1520), sig. D.1.r, where Erasmus remarked of Lee's embargo, 'Verum id ilico suspicans Lei simplicitas obstitit, ne id illi [Fisher] liceret', and of Fisher's dilemma, 'Cupiebat mihi gratificari vir amicissimus, at noluit Leo fallere fidem vir integerrimus.'

29 *EM*, sigg. D.4.v−G.3.v.

30 Fisher's initiative is summarised by Erasmus in *Apologia qua respondet*, sig. C.1.r−v.

31 *EE* IV, ep. 1053, 13 Dec 1519, pp. 139−52. He later claimed that had Fisher's peace initiative reached him in time, he would not have published (*Apologia qua respondet*, sig. C.1.r−v). But the letter to Lupset opens with a reference to 'a certain great friend' of himself and Lee: 'Ex literis magni cuiusdam amici, sed qui idem Leo non sit inimicus, cognovi isthic late sparsum esse rumorem, et ita sparsum ut plaerisque fidem quoque fecerit, hic mea meorumque opera fieri' (p. 139). Allen conjectures that he meant More, but the description fits Fisher equally well, and the words about a rumour are strikingly similar to a comment Erasmus cited from Fisher's letter: 'Nam rumorem esse tam late sparsum, ipsa etiam re, ut fit, atrociorem, ut expediret magis evulgari quam premi quae scripserat Leus' (*Apologia*

qua respondet, sig. C.1.v). The identification of the friend with Fisher is supported by *The Correspondence of Erasmus 1519–1520*, tr. R.B. Mynors and annotated by P.G. Bietenholz, CWE 7 (Toronto, 1987), pp. 149 and 338.

32 *EE* IV, ep. 1100, *c.* May 1520, p. 259, Erasmus's preface to *Annotationes Lei* (Basel: Froben, 1520).

33 *EE* III, ep. 936, 2 April 1519, p. 524.

34 *Responsio ad Annotationes Eduardi Lei* (Antwerp: Hillenius, 1520), sig. K.1.r, 'Narravi illi [Lee] in familiari colloquio, me cum essem in Anglia tum primum ac recens aedito novo testamento, repperisse Theologum illum [Fisher], quem ille summatem vocat, et merito vocat, occupatum in explicanda genealogia Christi atque hac gratia consuluisse Capnionem per litteras.' This was of course the very occasion on which Erasmus invited Lee's comments on the *Novum Instrumentum*.

35 SJC D 56.18, Constable to Fisher, 12 Nov, no year. Constable may conceivably have meant bk. II of *DUM*.

36 *Secundi Tomi Operum Veneb. Bedae*, ed. J. Bade, ded. to Fisher, 1 June 1521, sig. a.2.v, 'quia te audivimus iampridem habere ad praelum emunctos in Matthaeum commentarios'.

37 *ALC* 31, fol. 166.r (c. 607), 'Caeterum quia super hac re prolixius, in commentariis sermonis eius (quem in monte Christus habuit) disseruimus ista sufficiant.'

38 *DUM* II, fols. XXVIII.r–XXX.v (cc. 1425–43).

39 *CSD*, fol. VI.r–v.

40 *EE* II, ep. 324, to Reuchlin (citing Fisher), 1 March 1515, p. 50. Reuchlin, *De Rudimentis Hebraicis* (Pforzheim: Anshelm, 1506), pp. 19–31.

41 SJC D 105.103, Renatus to Fisher, 6 June 1515. See R.F. Scott, 'Notes from the College Records', *The Eagle* 16, p. 356; and Surtz, *Works and Days*, p. 469, n. 1.

42 *EE* III, ep. 784, to Fisher, 5 March 1518, pp. 237–8.

43 Lambeth Palace Library, MS 2342, fol. 31.r. See below, ch. 10, pp. 174–5.

44 *DCM*, fols. 4.v–5.r and 9.r–12.v.

45 *EE* II, ep. 452, to Ammonius, 17 Aug 1516, pp. 317–18; and ep. 592, from Fisher, June 1517, p. 598.

46 See above, n. 6.

47 Mayor, *Early Statutes*, p. 375.

48 *BRUO* IV, pp. 151–2.

49 R. Croke, *Orationes Duae*, sig. a.5.r, 'non a quolibet huc missus sum, sed a Roffensi episcopo'; 'Iubet heros iste … strenuam operam Graecis navari literis.' Croke explicitly called himself Erasmus's successor as professor of Greek.

50 CUL, Ely Diocesan Archives, G/1/7 (West's Register), records Croke's ordination to the priesthood on 18 June 1519: 'Magister Richardus Crooke in artibus mr. London. dioc. sufficienter dimissus ad ti. domus sive prioratus de Strowde Roffen. dioc. in presbiterum est admissus.'

51 SJC M 3.5 (early accounts).

52 St John's was not the only recipient of Fisher's patronage of Greek. Christ's College also benefited, with the donation of Greek editions of the complete works of Aristotle and of Theophrastus's *De Plantis*. Cambridge, Christ's College Library, MS 22 (Catalogue of donations, compiled 1623, unpaginated).

53 He appears frequently in the *Grace Books* between 1518 and 1525.

54 *LP* 4. i. 1142 and 1144, Croke to Henry Gold, refer to Smith's actions. They belong with letters 1141 and 1143, which concern his plans to proceed DD in 1524, (*Grace Book B, Part II*, p. 15, and *Grace Book Γ*, p. 214).

55 Fisher to Croke, n.d., SJC Thin Red Book, fols. 49.r–50.v, printed in Hymers,

Funeral Sermon, pp. 210–16. T. Baker dated this letter to 1528, connecting it with the university's grant of exequies to Fisher (Hymers, p. 210). He has been followed by other writers, most recently by M. Underwood, 'John Fisher and the promotion of learning', *HRR*, pp. 25–46, esp. p. 38. I have discussed the dating with Mr Underwood who is inclined to accept the following argument. The letter refers to Hugh Ashton as dead (Hymers, p. 213), so must postdate Jan 1523 (*BRUC*, pp. 18–19). The reference to Fox, bishop of Winchester, suggests that he is still alive, which gives Oct 1528 as a *terminus ad quem*. Croke never appears in the *Grace Books* after 1525 (*Grace Book B, Part II*, pp. 124–5 are the latest appearances), and became tutor (a resident post) to the young Henry, duke of Richmond, at Sheriff Hutton in Yorkshire some time in 1526. The abbot of Lanthony gave him a pension at Henry VIII's request, in June, probably the time of his appointment (*LP* 4. ii. 2291). *LP* 4. ii. 1917–8, and 1954, Croke to Wolsey, 6 Feb and 26 May, no year, complaining about his treatment as tutor, cannot date from 1526 as proposed by the editors of *LP* because they refer to Croke's having spent sixty-six weeks in the post, and to Henry's age as eight. These should be dated 26 May 1527 and 6 Feb 1528, as proposed in 'Inventories of the Wardrobes, Plate, Chapel Stuff, etc. of Henry Fitzroy', ed. J.G. Nichols, *Camden Miscellany III* (Camden Soc., 1855), p. xlv. Nichols shows on pp. xxiii and xxx that Palsgrave was Henry's tutor until at least Christmas 1525. Finally, Fisher's references to Lutheran heresy at Cambridge (Hymers, p. 216) were probably inspired by the Barnes affair of Christmas 1525.

56 *EE* II, eps. 468, from More, 22 Sept 1516, p. 347; 520, from Latimer, 30 Jan 1517, pp. 438–42; and 540, to Latimer, *c.* Feb 1517, pp. 485–7.

57 *EE* III, eps. 653 and 667, to Fisher, 8 and 16 Sept 1517, pp. 75 and 91; and 784, to Fisher, 5 March 1518, p. 237.

58 *DUM* I, fols. VI.v–VII.r (c. 1399–1400); and XXXIII.v (c. 1434).

59 G. Lloyd Jones, in *The Discovery of Hebrew in Tudor England: a third language* (Manchester, 1983), does not always correctly disentangle the obscure and convoluted evidence about the study of Hebrew under Henry VIII. J. Friedman's *The Most Ancient Testimony* (Ohio, 1983) is mostly interested in continental hebraism.

60 See above, n. 40.

61 Fisher to Reuchlin, n.d., in *Illustrium Virorum Epistolae* (n.p., 1519), sig. s.3.r. If it had been written prior to 1515 it would presumably have appeared in *Clarorum Virorum Epistolae* (Tubingen: Anshelm, 1514). Its wording shows that it is Fisher's first letter to Reuchlin. In *EE* II, ep. 432, to Erasmus, *c.* June 1516, p. 269, Fisher says that he has received a long letter from Reuchlin and has written back. Thus his first letter probably dates from 1515.

62 *Illustrium Virorum Epistolae*, sig. v.2.r.

63 J. Reuchlin, *De Arte Cabbalistica* (Hagenau: Anshelm, 1517), sig. A.4.r–v. *EE* II, ep. 592, from Fisher, *c.* June 1517, p. 598, 'Liber ille Cabalisticus quo me scribis a Reuchlino donatum, nondum ad me pervenit.'

64 *EE* II, ep. 457, to Reuchlin, 27 Aug 1516, pp. 330–1.

65 *EE* IV, ep. 1129, 2 Aug 1520, pp. 321–2; and VI, ep. 1311, 1 Sept 1522, p. 124.

66 *DRA* VI, fol. LXVI.r (c. 204), 'amicus noster Ioannes Capnion vir in omni literatura celebratissimus'. PRO SP6/5, fol. 62.r, 'vir ipsius linguae suo tempore peritissimus'.

67 Wakefield, *Syntagma*, sig. A.3.v.

68 Wakefield, *Oratio*, sig. C.3.r.

69 R. Pace refers to Stokesley as 'non utriusque modo linguae peritissimo, sed nec hebraicae ignaro' in his *De fructu qui ex doctrina percipitur liber* (Basel: Froben, 1517), p. 101. Croke refers to 'Stopleii triplex lingua' (*Orationes Duae*, sig. c.4.r.).

70 On 14 July. See W.J. Harrison, *Notes on the Masters, Fellows, Scholars and Exhibitioners of Clare College, Cambridge* (Cambridge, 1953), p. 24.

71 *Early Statutes*, p. 375.

72 *Matricule de l'Université de Louvain*, ed. E. Reusens, J. Wils and A. Schillings (10 vols., 1903–67), iii, p. 597. An excerpt from Fisher's register printed in Lewis, *Dr Fisher*, ii, p. 257, shows that Wakefield was at Rochester on 14 July 1519.

73 *Grace Book Γ*, p. 170. H. de Vocht, *History of the Collegium Trilingue Lovaniense*, pt. 1, Université de Louvain Recueil de Travaux d'Histoire et de Philologie, 3rd ser., 42 (Louvain, 1951), pp. 380–1.

74 Baker, *History of St John's*, i, pp. 281–2. *Early Statutes*, pp. 344–5. Underwood, 'Fisher and the promotion of learning', pp. 36–7, has disentangled the following story. The statutes for Fisher's foundation were first incorporated with the College statutes in 1524. But Fisher had made an agreement with the College in 1521 which clearly provided for the financing of lectureships on his chantry foundation within the College, and a revised version of this agreement made in 1525 refers to these lectureships in detail. So the lectureships were probably established *c.* 1521, although further details were hammered out over the next few years.

75 SJC Thin Red Book, fol. 219.r, printed in Baker *History of St John's*, i, p. 358. Wakefield's undated receipt for his commons (£5 4s) and wages (4 marks) for two years in advance, repayable if he returned 'from beyond the sees' is at SJC D 56.180. A receipt for 5 angels (his stipend from Fisher for the Long Vacation term, 'pro termino nativitatis beatae marie'), dated 15 Henry VIII (1523) is SJC D 56.140. This was probably after his return from Tübingen.

76 *EE* V, ep. 1311, 1 Sept 1522, pp. 123–4. Wakefield matriculated at Tübingen on 16 Aug 1522. See *Die Matrikeln der Universität Tübingen*, ed. H. Hermelink (Tübingen, 1906), p. 241.

77 These letters are printed in Wakefield's *Oratio*, sigg. Q.3.r–4.r. The letter from Tübingen omits Fisher's name and diocese, but he was indubitably its recipient. Wakefield later confirms this in his *Kotser Codicis*, sig. P.3.r.

78 Good introductions to the thought of the Christian Cabbalists can be found in Lloyd Jones, *Discovery of Hebrew*, ch. 1, pp. 18–38, Friedman, *Ancient Testimony*, ch. 4, pp. 71–98, and Swietlicki, *Spanish Christian Cabbala*, (Columbia, Missouri, 1986), chs. 1–2, pp. 1–42.

79 *EE* II, ep. 324, to Reuchlin, 1 March 1515, p. 49, citing from a letter of Fisher's the comment 'mihi valde placet hominis [Reuchlin] eruditio, ut, qui vicinius ad Joannem Picum accesserit, alium extare neminem credam'.

80 *DVC* I. 2. fol. II.v (c. 758) cites Pico on the scholastics from the *De Dignitate*. See G. Pico della Mirandola, *De Dignitate Hominis*, ed. E. Garin (Respublica Literaria 1, Berlin, 1968), p. 60, for the passage cited. The gist of the *De Dignitate* (including this text) was included in Pico's *Apologia*.

81 PRO SP2/R, fol. 166.r, on Ps. 8, 'nomen ipsius tetrag[ramaton antequam consonans] adiungeretur, erat inproferribile, adiuncta vero consonanti iam facile profertur ab omnibus' and 'Nomen itaque Ihsuh preter literas nominis tetragramaton interpositam habet consonantem Y quae nostrum S sonat.' This follows Reuchlin's argument that 'Jesus' was the 'Jahweh' rendered pronounceable by the insertion of a consonant, 's'. See Friedman's critique of this etymology in *Ancient Testimony*, pp. 77–8 and 80–1.

82 *SSD* II, fols. XXXII.v–XXXIII.r (cc. 1266–7). Compare P. Galatinus, *De Arcanis Catholicae Fidei* (Ortona: Suncinus, 1518), lib. X, ca. 4–6. I owe this to F. Secret, *Les Kabbalistes Chrétiens de la Renaissance* (Paris, 1964), pp. 228–9.

83 See his sermon against Luther of 1521 (*EW*, p. 332), and his memorandum 'Ne qua fiat', London, Lambeth Palace Library MS 2342, fol. 31.r. Pico had explored the analogy between Cabbala and apostolic tradition in his *Apologia*, q. 5, 'de Magia Naturali: et Cabala Hebraeorum'. See *Opuscula*, sigg. I.5.v–6.r.

84 *Oratio*, sig. E.1.v.

85 Secret, *Kabbalistes*, p. 127. For Zorzi (Giorgi) see Swietlicki, *Spanish Christian Cabala*, pp. 20–2.

86 *BRUC*, pp. 226–7; and CUL, K*.1.21, for Cranmer's copy.

87 Lambeth Palace MS 2342, fol. 29.v, 'Non quod ego profiteor me peritum in his literis esse, quum animarum cura sic semper occupatus fuerim, ut non licuerit multum temporis his impertire. In qua re secutus sum priorum patrum iudicium, nimirum, Augustini, Hillarii, Ambrosii, ceterorumque qui quum curas haberent noluerunt varietate linguarum perdiscendarum, a suis officiis apud plebem, impediri. Quid enim populo profuerit de linguis istis audire quicquam. Quinimo potius apud eos confusionem pariet hauddubie. Hieronimo quod Episcopus non fuisset nec animarum habuisset curam bene licuit illis studiis operam et tempus impendere.'

88 See appendix for the range of books Fisher cited or referred to.

89 *BRUO* II, pp. 717–19. J.K. McConica, *English Humanists and Reformation Politics* (Oxford, 1965), p. 83.

90 *BRUO* II, pp. 828–30.

91 *Testamenta Eboracensia V*, pp. 258–9. See above, ch. 1, p. 24.

92 Bateson, *Catalogue of Syon*, pp. xxiii–xxvii. The contributions of these men (except Reynolds) are summarised under their entries in *BRUC*.

93 See under the relevant headings in appendix, below.

94 *EE* I, ep. 229, to Fisher, Sept 1511, pp. 469–70. The work was spurious.

95 *DVC* III, preface, fol. LXIIII.r (p. 928). See also *EE* I, ep. 227, to Colet, 13 Sept 1511, p. 467, sending the Chrysostom and mentioning the Basil intended for Fisher.

96 R. Sharpe to Metcalfe, 20 Oct (no year), SJC D 105.41. Printed in R.F. Scott, 'Notes from the College Records', *The Eagle* 17 (1893), pp. 470–1; and Gray, 'Letters of Bishop Fisher, 1521–3', pp. 134–5.

97 *EE* IX, eps, 2359, ded. to Christopher von Stadion, 5 Aug 1530, p. 6; and 2413, from E. Schets, 18 Dec 1530, p. 95. Fisher cited Aretino at *DVC* II. 1, fol. XXXII.v (c. 1173). Erasmus had been tipped off about the manuscript by Tunstall, *EE* VIII, ep. 2226, from Tunstall, 24 Oct 1529, p. 292.

98 PRO SP1/64, fol. 244.r–v.

99 Gleason, *Colet*, pp. 143–4 on Erasmus's regard for Aquinas.

100 For Ockham, see *DVC* IV, preface, fol. LXXXIIII.r (p. 990); for Biel, see Gouda, Gemeentlijke Archiefdienst MS 959, unfoliated, Fisher's letter to Lethmaet, side 6 (c. 1707).

101 For Lombard, see *DVC* I. 2. fol. II.v (cc. 757–8); for Gregory, *ALC* 36. fol, 199.r (c. 672).

102 *DCM*, fol. 27.v.

103 *DUM* III, fol. XL.r–v (cc. 1443–4).

104 *ALC* 27, fol. 154.v (c. 583), 'cuius acumen mihi summopere probatur'.

105 *ALC* 10, fol. 82.v (c. 436).

106 *ALC* 27, fol. 154.v (cc. 583–4), on the doctrine of transubstantiation.

107 *ALC* 36, fol. 215.r (c. 704).

108 *Early Statutes*, pp. 110 (1530), 313 (1524) and 376 (1516).

109 *DUM* III, fol. XL.r (c. 1443); *DRA* II, fol. XVIII.v (c. 130); *DVC* I, 2. fol. II.v (c. 758); *DCM*, fol. 27.v.

110 *New Catholic Encyclopedia* 4, pp. 935–8, 'Doctor (Scholastic Title)'.

111 *DVC* I. 1, fol. II.v (c. 758). See above, n. 81. Fisher prefaces the extract with the remark 'Iohannes Picus Myrandulanus, eundem Thomam florem theologiae censet merito vocandum.' I have been unable so far to trace this title in Pico's works, though he does use the cognate phrase 'divo Thoma splendore nostrae theologiae' in his *Heptaplus*.

112 *DVC* IV, preface, fol. LXXXIIII.r (p. 990) says of the scholastics, 'Quibus tametsi defuit eloquentia, doctrina certe non defuit. Sed nec illam a philosophis, hoc est sapientiae studiosis, expectat Cicero', which compares with Pico's 'non defuisse sapientiam, si defuit eloquentia' and 'Non desiderat Tullius eloquentiam in philosopho', *Epistola ad Hermolaum*, in *Prosatori Latini del Quattrocento*, ed. E. Garin (Milan and Naples, 1952), pp. 808 and 814.

113 *Early Statutes*, p. 252.

114 Melton owned Pico's *Disputationes contra Astrologos* and *Heptaplus*, *Testamenta Eboracensia V*, p. 258; Colet's *Letters on the Creation* are modelled on Pico's *Heptaplus*, and his commentaries on the pseudo-Dionysius cite the *Apologia* (see Secret, *Kabbalistes*, p. 228); and More translated into English Gian Francesco's life of his uncle. Other owners of Pico's works included the Cambridge men Thomas Patenson and Brian Rowe (*BRUC*, pp. 444 and 492). For a general survey of Pico's thought and of his following in England see P.O. Kristeller, 'Giovanni Pico della Mirandola and his Sources' and R. Weiss, 'Pico e l'Inghilterra', in *L'Opera e il Pensiero di Giovanni Pico della Mirandola nella Storia dell'Umanesimo* (2 vols., Florence, 1965), i, pp. 35–84 and 143–52.

4 The Magdalene controversy

1 This differentiation of the three women is accepted by modern exegetes.

2 A. Hufstader, 'Lefèvre d'Etaples and the Magdalen', *Studies in the Renaissance* 16 (1969), pp. 31–60, is a good general account of the controversy and underpins this paragraph. Surtz, *Works and Days*, ch. 14, pp. 274–89, summarises Fisher's contributions to the controversy.

3 *De Maria Magdalena, et triduo Christi disceptatio* (Paris: Estienne, 1517). On the French calendar the impress date would permit a date up to Easter 1518. However, the common conjecture of April 1518 (as at Hufstader, 'Magdalen', p. 34) is belied by the references to Lefèvre's book in Erasmus's letters from the middle of January 1518: *EE* III, eps. 765, 766, 18 Jan and 778, 22 Feb, at pp. 203–5 and 226.

4 Lefèvre d'Etaples, *De Maria Magdalena, Triduo Christi, et ex tribus vna Maria, disceptatio* (Paris: Estienne, 1518).

5 P. Renouard, *Bibliographie des Imprimeurs et des Oeuvres de Josse Badius Ascensius* (3 vols., Paris, 1908), ii, pp. 443–4, gives details of the two printings, which share the same date.

6 *EE* III, ep. 936, to Fisher, 2 April 1519, p. 522, said of the book, 'eorum qui legerunt, nemo non fatetur te tota causa superiorem'. This should not be taken as Erasmus's own view. In the same letter he mildly criticised Fisher's bitter tone

and, perhaps under some pressure to come off the fence, pleaded that he had no time to read the book thoroughly. In fact, in letters of January 1518 (see n. 4, above) he had expressed satisfaction with Lefèvre's thesis about the Magdalene.

7 This probably appeared in May, as Grandval later claimed to have received a copy on 16 May. See Grandval's *Tutamentum et Anchora* (Paris: Bade, 1519), sig. a.3.v.

8 The book carries no date, but Fisher refers to it as already in print in his final word on the subject, the *Confutatio Secundae Disceptationis*.

9 *Tutamentum*, sig. a.5.v, 'Quippe de unica Magdalena ille scripsit: et id tam emuncte: tam solide: tam profunde: ut hac etiam Anchora defensorium nostrum minime egeret in tuam defensionem.' See also sig. c.5.v.

10 For which reason *CSD* will not receive specific treatment in this chapter, but will be used only to provide illustrative material. For a brief account of it, refer to Surtz, *Works and Days*, pp. 286–8.

11 The title gives a fair indication of Beda's academic agenda. The dispute flared up again at Paris in early 1521 (J.K. Farge, *Orthodoxy and Reform in Early Reformation France*, SMRT 32, Leiden, 1985, p. 171), by which time Clichtove had repudiated Lefèvre's position. Beda of course was the leader of the Paris theology faculty's prolonged campaign against both Erasmus and Lefèvre.

12 P.E. Hughes, *Lefèvre: Pioneer of Ecclesiastical Reform in France* (Grand Rapids, 1984), p. 123.

13 *CSD*, fol. II.r, 'venit in mentem, sublimitatem dudum tuam rogasse me, quid opinarer ipse de Magdalena ... meque repondisse, duas mihi videri'. While this cannot be dated beyond doubt, we know that Campeggio, having landed in England on Friday 23 July 1518 (*LP* 2. ii. 4333), dined with Fisher at Rochester the following Tuesday (Wolsey to Giglis, 29 July 1518, *LP* 2. ii. 4348). Campeggio had probably become acquainted with the furore over the Magdalene during his three-month journey through France (for which see W.E. Wilkie, *The Cardinal Protectors of England* [Cambridge, 1974] pp. 105–9), and presumably this furnished him with a suitable topic for conversation with his scholarly host. Surtz notices this in passing (*Works and Days*, p. 286), but fails to attach any particular importance to it.

14 *DUM* I, fol. III.r (c. 1395), 'tanta tamen apud me Fabricii nominis existimatio fuerat, ut credere non potuerim illum temere quicquam voluisse adeo asseverare quod sibi non esset compertissimum'.

15 *CSD*, fol. V.r, 'Mihi profecto charissimus uterque fuit, tam Iodocus quam Faber, tametsi nunquam eos viderim, tum ob doctrinam, tum ob vitae probitatem, qua praeditos illos audiverim saepe.' See also fols. II.r, 'Iacobus faber, non minus ob eruditionem quam ob singularem eius probitatem habitus' and II.v, 'Iodocus Clichtoveus, vir alioqui doctus et probus.' Also *EM*, title page verso, 'ab his viris qui sanctimoniam, cum non vulgari doctrina coniunxerint'.

16 SJC Thin Red Book, fol. 18.r (original at D 57.156), printed in Hymers, *Funeral Sermon*, p. 208. *EM*, sig. F.4.r, cites Lefèvre's commentary on the dispute between Peter and Paul in Galatians. See his *In Epistolas Pauli* (2nd edn., Paris: Estienne, 1515), fols. 143.v–4.v. *EM*, sig. S.3.r refers to the revelations of Mechtild 'in eodem volumine una cum Elizabeth visionibus', almost certainly the *Liber Trium Virorum et Trium Spiritualium Virginum*, ed. Lefèvre (Paris: Estienne, 1513). See Surtz, *Works and Days*, p. 429, n. 17.

17 Fisher's citation from Cyril at *DUM* I, fol. X.v (c. 1404) follows the fifteenth-century translation by Trapezuntius. There were several Italian editions, but Clichtove's *Opus Insigne Beati Patris Cyrilli Patriarchae Alexandrini in Evangelium*

Ioannis (Paris: Hopilius, 1508) is more likely to have reached England. See fol. 212.r for the text cited by Fisher.

18 *EM*, sig. A.2.r-v, cites Poncher's letters. The extracts do not tell us why Poncher chose Fisher.

19 *EM*, title page verso, 'qui divam istam veneramini, bono nihilominus animo sitis . . . patronam hanc vestram colite'.

20 *DUM* III, fol. XXVI.v (c. 1425), 'ut miseri peccatores non desperent, sed illius exemplo commoniti resipiscant.' *EW*, pp. 31, 34, 39, 114, 135 and 248.

21 *CSD*, fol. XXXII.v, citing Lefèvre, 'Absit ergo cogitemus hanc consuetudinariam Christi hospitam, aliquando fuisse sordidam infamemque peccatricem' from *De Maria Magdalena*, fol. 17.r. Lefèvre was probably following Origen, who had made a similar remark. See *PG* 13, 1722.

22 *CSD*, fol. XXXIV.r, suggests that Lefèvre's thesis smacks of 'iustitia Pharasaica'.

23 Latimer conflated the Lucan and Marcan accounts, having Mary Magdalene anoint Christ's head and feet in the house of Simon the Pharisee. See his *Sermons*, ed. G.E. Corrie, Parker Soc. (Cambridge, 1844), pp. 15–16. For Zwingli, see G.R. Potter, *Zwingli* (Cambridge, 1972), p. 339.

24 *DUM* II, fols. XXVI.v (c. 1425), 'Quod sane tanto libentius aggredior, quod diuae Magdalenae, cuius tutelae me iam annos multos deuoui, id acceptum fore confido.'

25 SJC D 57.158, schedule to indenture between Fisher and St John's College, 27 Nov 1525, printed by R.F. Scott in 'Notes from the College Records', *The Eagle* 35 (1914), pp. 2–35, at p. 26. The image is described as 'stock', and is one of several. Apart from the references above (n. 20), Fisher mentions the Magdalene only occasionally, e.g., at *ALC* 10, fol. 82.r (cc. 435–6); and 14, fol. 91.r-v (cc. 455–6).

26 *De Maria Magdalena*, part III, fols. 62.v–90.v.

27 N. Beda, *Apologia pro filiabus et nepotibus beatae Annae* (Paris: Bade, 1520). P. Sutor, *De triplici connubio diuae Annae Disceptatio* (Paris: Petit, 1523). K. Wimpina, *De Divae Annae Trinubio*, in his *Farrago Miscellaneorum* (Cologne: Soter, 1531), fols. 137–62.

28 H.C. Agrippa, *De beatissimae Annae monogamia ac unico puerperio propositiones abbreviatae et articulatae iuxta disceptationem Iacobi Fabri Stapulensis in libro de tribus et una*, in *Operum Pars Posterior* (Lyons: Beringi, 1600), pp. 588–93; and *Defensio Propositionum praenarratorum contra quendam Dominicastrum* (pp. 594–663).

29 Could the treatise have been Jean de Fribourg's 'Defensorium Beatae Annae', of which the only extant manuscript is of English provenance? BL Royal MS 6. E. III, fols. 248–50, is a late fifteenth-century copy from the library of Merton College, Oxford. See G. Albert, J.M. Parent and A. Guillemette, 'La légende des trois mariages de Sainte-Anne', *Etudes d'histoire littéraire et doctrinale du XIIIe siècle* (Publications de l'institut d'études médiévales d'Ottawa I, 1932), pp. 165–84. Aquinas is said to have rejected the legend of Anne's three husbands – see Hughes, *Lefèvre*, p. 121.

30 *EM*, sigg. &.2.v–3.r presents Fisher's argument. His point about the liturgy had been made by Lefèvre himself who observed (*De Maria Magdalena*, 2nd edn., fols. 89.v–90.r) that although the official liturgy for St Anne made no mention of three husbands, an unofficial hymn which did mention them (and which he cites in full) had come into use at many places.

31 *EM*, sig. &.3.r.

32 For the extent and significance of the cult of Anne, see J. Bossy, *Christianity*, pp. 9–10.

33 R.H. Bainton, *Here I Stand* (London, 1951), p. 21. For his subsequent doubts see *WA* 1, 415.

34 *The Middle English Stanzaic Versions of the Life of Saint Anne*, ed. R.E. Parker, EETS orig. ser. 174 (1928), at pp. ix–x, xxxii–xxxiv, 79–80, 109 and 110–12. Parker also refers to occasional verses by John Audelay, John Lydgate and Osbern Bokenham (p. xi).

35 J. Stow, *Annales, or a Generall Chronicle of England* (London, 1631), p. 565.

36 Bossy, *Christianity*, pp. 10–11 and 95.

37 *EM*, sig. a.2.r–v (near end of book).

38 *DUM* I, fol. IV.v (c. 1397), 'si mendacium unum quod communi omnium illorum assensu asseveratur compertum fuerit, non video cur in caeteris fides illis a populo adhibeatur'.

39 Fisher summarises these at the start of book II of *DUM*, fols. XXVIII.r–XXX.v (cc. 1427–30).

40 Fisher compares the opinions of Origen, Ambrose, Jerome and Chrysostom in *EM*, secunda veritas, sigg. H.4.v–I.4.r. See Chrysostom, *Homiliae in Matthaeum*, hom. 80, *PG* 57. 723.

41 Origen, *Commentariorum Series in Matthaeum*, *PG* 13, 1722.

42 *PG* 13, 1721, 'Multi quidam existimant de una eademque muliere quatuor evangelistas exposuisse.'

43 *New Catholic Encyclopedia* 9, 'Mary Magdalene', p. 388. Most exegetes now reject the conflation of the Magdelene with Martha's sister and the sinner. Yet the tradition still survives in the Roman liturgy. The office for 22 July (Mary Magdalene) includes references to all three figures.

44 *De Maria Magdalena*, fol. 22.v states that both women were called 'Magdalene', and fols. 23.r–4.v divide the texts between 'Maria Magdalena sorore Marthae' and 'Maria Magdalena, quae erat ex Galilaea.' See Fisher's summary at *DUM* II, fols. XXXVIII.r–XXX.v (cc. 1427–30).

45 *CSD*, fol. XII.r, 'civiliter interpretanda sunt, quae tradiderunt evangelistae, quum illi non solum historias narrent, sed magis ita enarrare studeant, ut pluribus gravidas mysteriis exprimant. Quo fit, ut eandem rem alius alio referat modo et plerunque (nisi generosius interpretentur) videantur asserere sibi repugnantia' See also his treatise on the LXX, PRO SP6/5, fol. 74.r, 'Sicut in tradendis evangeliis quanquam Evangelistae singuli qui non dubitantur afflati spiritu sancto fuisse varient plurimum et gesta parabolasque disceptationes quas cum phariseis et aliis habuit Christus aliter atque aliter enarrent . . . diverso modo rem ipsam quae dicta aut gesta fuerat retulisse videatur.'

46 *DUM* I, fols. VII.r–XII.r (cc. 1400–6).

47 *DUM* II, fol. XXXVII.r (c. 1439), 'Quid ergo prohibet in hoc tam prolixo temporis intervallo Magdalenam, quae prius iuxta crucem fuerat, . . . a cruce longius fuisse repulsam?'

48 *DUM* II, fol. XXXII.v (c. 1433), 'Dilucidum igitur est, Ioannem in exprimendis personis accuratissimum fuisse.'

49 *DUM* II, fol. XXXVIII.r (cc. 1440–1), 'nusquam in evangeliis apud quenquam evangelistarum: istud cognomen Magdalenae, huic mulieri tribuitur, quando vel Bethaniae, vel Marthae sororis eius mentio habita est'.

50 *DUM* I, fol. IIII.r (c. 1396), citing Lefèvre, 'eius rei veritatem a sacris eloquiis potius quam ab auctoribus aut iis qui nunc aut scribunt aut ad populum verba faciunt, esse requirendam' (see *De Maria*, fol. 11.r). Yet in fact Lefèvre goes on to cite Gregory, Ambrose, Origen, Chrysostom and Jerome, 'ne solus sententiae huius

assertor videar esse' (*DUM* I, fol. XII.r, c. 1406; see *De Maria*, fol. 16.r), arguing, 'Perspicuum igitur est, ex sacrorum doctorum sententia, Mariam Magdalenam Marthae sororem, et peccatricem illam, non unam eandemque, sed alteram et alteram' (*DUM* I, fol. XVIII.r, c. 1414; see *De Maria*, fol. 18.r).

51 *DUM* I, fol. IIII.r (c. 1396), 'Verum ego hic illum percontarer, num eloquia sacra sunt cuivis ingenio ubique adeo clara et aperta ut non sit opus interim enarratore aliquo et interprete.'

52 *DUM* I, fol. IIII.v (c. 1397), 'Ego nimirum id genus arbitror summos imprimis pontifices: deinde patres et auctores orthodoxos postremo concionatores ad populum.'

53 *DUM* I, fol. XIIII.r (c. 1409), 'Neque enim cuiquam ambiguum esse potest eos aberrasse, quum in aliis multis, tum de purgatoriis ignibus.'

54 *DUM* I, fol. XIIII.v (c. 1410), 'de Magdalenis suis verba facientes, neque Fabro qui eos introducit, neque secum, neque sibiinvicem conveniunt'.

55 *DUM* III, fols. XL.r–L.r (cc. 1443–57); except for Mantuanus, at fols. LII.v–LIIII.r (cc. 1461–2). See Surtz, *Works and Days*, pp. 277–9 for a fuller summary of this part of *DUM*.

56 Clichtove, *Disceptationis de Magdalena Defensio*, fols. 95.v–6.r. Hufstader, 'Magdalen', pp. 50–1. Surtz, *Works and Days*, p. 282.

57 *EM*, sig. B.1.r, 'Nam apud omnes, qui rem eiusmodi tractant, pro confesso habetur. id ad fidem pertinere, quicquid vel primis verbis in sacris evangeliis continetur, vel ex eisdem primis verbis, quibuscunque veris adiectis, deduci potest.'

58 *EM*, sig. B.3.r. Fisher's summary of Jerome was not entirely correct. Jerome drew chiefly on parallel phrases and usages from elsewhere in the scriptures to argue that Elvidius's case was in fact based on misinterpretation. He succeeded in showing that Elvidius's case was not conclusive, but he fell a long way short of demonstrating his own case. See *Adversus Helvidium*, *PL* 23, pp. 183–206. The controversy is thus strikingly similar to that between Fisher and Lefèvre – though not precisely in the way Fisher imagined.

59 See above, p. 54.

60 *EM*, sigg. D.4.v–F.3.r, esp. E.1.r, 'Constat igitur in controversia fuisse apud istos, num haec reprehensio vera esset, an simulatoria magis, et Hieronymo simulatoriam videri, Augustino contra, veram.' Fisher provides ample citations from Jerome and Augustine.

61 *EM*, sigg. F.4.r–G.1.v, concluding, 'Et quamquam id modis omnibus conetur Faber, ut neutrius videatur partes fuisse secutus...Verumtamen in eo quod est totius quaestionis caput, Augustini partes tam aperte sequitur, ut refragari nemo possit. Affirmat enim quod erraverit Petrus ac noxie simulaverit.' For Lefèvre's comments, see his *In Epistolas Pauli*, fols. 143.v–4.v.

62 *EM*, sig. G.2.r.

63 *EM*, sig. E.1.r, 'Nemo hic expectet nostrum super hanc contentionem iudicium.'

64 *EM*, sigg. G.3.v–end. Surtz, *Works and Days*, pp. 284–5.

65 Hufstader, 'Magdalen', p. 36.

66 *EM*, sig. N.2.r, 'Hoc enim creditu difficillimum erat' and 'hoc Faber admisit, de quo maxime potuit dubitari, nempe quod Maria Marthae soror in has tam remotas a Iudaea partes se recepisset'.

67 PRO SP2/R, fol. 95.v, 'Nam India tam [blank] per Thomam et Bartholomeum Evangelii iugum subierunt. Parthiam per Symonem et Iudam...per Marcum Egiptus, per Dionysium Gallia.'

68 See *CC*, sig. L.4.r (c. 1357) for Fisher's awareness of the attribution problem.

69 *In Epistolas Pauli*, fols. 218.r–21.v.
70 *CC*, sig. G.1.r (c. 1330), 'epistolae dictae, vel eruditissimorum censura, negantur a Paulo Senecaque conscriptae. Testatur hoc inprimis Erasmus, cuius unius in hac parte iudicium, adversus alios mille, mihi sufficeret.' See Seneca, *Lucubrationes Omnes*, ed. Erasmus (Basel: Froben, 1515), pp. 2 and 4. There was a copy of this edition in Rochester Cathedral Priory Library, now at Salisbury Cathedral Library. See *Medieval Libraries of Great Britain: a list of surviving books; supplement to the second edition*, ed. A.G. Watson, Royal Historical Society Guides and Handbooks (London, 1987), p. 59. Fisher may have used or perhaps even owned this.
71 For Lefèvre's patristic programme see E.F. Rice, 'The Humanist Idea of Christian Antiquity: Lefèvre d'Etaples and his Circle' in *French Humanism 1470–1600*, ed. W.L. Gundersheimer (London, 1969), pp. 163–80.
72 Hughes, *Lefèvre*, p. 34. His summary of Lefèvre's educational programme (*Lefèvre*, pp. 27–8) is remarkably similar to that proposed for Fisher above in chs. 1 and 3.

5 Fisher and the Catholic campaign against Luther

1 R. Morison, *Apomaxis Calumniarum* (London: Berthelet, 1537), fol. 77.v, 'ille nihil aliud quam omnem vitam rixabatur cum Luthero, Oecolampadio, gloriae cupidior quam gregis sibi commissi amantior'.
2 S. Thompson, 'The bishop in his diocese', in *HRR*, pp. 67–80, at p. 71, and app. 3, p. 250.
3 *ALC*, dedication to the reader, fol. 2.r (c. 273), 'sed ut succurrerem infirmioribus animis, quorum fides, quasi super acie novaculae, iam diu stetit anceps et ambigua, cui parti sit inclinatura magis ... Ob istos nimirum labor aliquis, a viris nostri potissimum ordinis, exanclandus fuit, ... si nostra negligentia (quod absit) depereat, sanguis illius e nostra manu requiratur.'
4 Capito to Luther, 18 Feb 1519, *WA Briefwechsel* 1, p. 336.
5 'Day-book of John Dorne', pp. 155–7. The figure for Erasmus should perhaps be higher, as many entries for patristic, classical and rhetorical works probably represent editions or compositions of his.
6 *EE* III, ep. 980, to Luther, 30 May 1519, p. 606, 'Habes in Anglia qui de tuis scriptis optime sentiant, et sunt ii maximi.'
7 *More's Correspondence*, p. 210. It hardly supports Meyer's conclusion that 'Luther was still heard respectfully in England' at the beginning of 1520. See C.S. Meyer, 'Henry VIII Burns Luther's Books', *Journal of Ecclesiastical History* 9 (1958), pp. 173–87, esp. p. 175.
8 *CSD*, fol. II.r.
9 *LP* 3. i, app. to preface, pp. ccccxxxviii–ccccxxxix, Tunstall to Wolsey, 21 Jan 1521.
10 Although the precise date is unknown, late Jan or Feb seems most likely. Dorne sold a copy of Luther's *Lipsica Disputatio* in Dec 1520, indicating a *terminus a quo* ('Day-Book of John Dorne', p. 139), which is confirmed by Tunstall's letter of 21 Jan. A letter from Leo X to Wolsey of 17 March 1521, thanking him for the ban, provides a *terminus ad quem* (*LP* 3. i. 1234). This is confirmed by an undated letter from de Medici, probably sent with Leo's (*LP* 3. i. 1210), and by interrogatories put to Humphrey Monmouth in 1528, which suggest that the ban was public knowledge by April 1521 (*LP* 4. ii. 4260, 14 May 1528). Allowing time for the news to reach Rome gives us late January or February.
11 *LP* 3. i. 1218. See also Pace to Wolsey, 7 and 16 April, *LP* 3. i. 1220 and 1233.

12 For more detail on this, and for an argument that the university theologians were also deputed to help compose, or at least to 'vet' and polish, Henry's *Assertio*, see my 'The English Campaign against Luther', *Transactions of the Royal Historical Society* 5th ser. 39 (1989), pp. 85–106.

13 For a description of the event, see *Calendar of State Papers, Venetian*, iii, nos. 210 and 213.

14 *EW*, pp. 311–48. The title page of the original edition (reproduced opposite *EW*, p. 311) testifies to Wolsey's instigation of the sermon.

15 *The sermon of Johan the bysshop of Rochester* (London: de Worde, n.d., *c.* late 1521; *STC* 10894); and *Contio quam Anglice habuit* (Cambridge: Siberch, 1522 *STC* 10898). Pace had completed his translation by 1 June 1521 when he despatched a copy to Leo X. His covering letter is reprinted by P. Balan, in *Monumenta Reformationis Germaniae* (Berlin, 1883), ep. 98, pp. 255–6. The English version had three further editions in the 1520s, and another in 1556 (*STC* 10895–7).

16 *EW*, pp. 313 and 346–7.

17 The *Assertio* lacks the insight into the question of justification that is found even in Fisher's sermon. The range of patristic citation is far more limited than is that of Fisher's works, and the style of composition is very different. If Fisher had played a major part in the composition of the *Assertio*, Henry's propagandists would probably have turned this against him later.

18 Rex, 'English Campaign', p. 89.

19 See below, pp. 96–7, 104 and 118.

20 SJC D 105.43 (undated) and 44 (1 July) transcribed by Gray in 'Letters of Bishop Fisher', pp. 136 and 142. The first letter refers to Pace's efforts in translating the sermon and is probably from around 1 June 1521, by which time Pace had finished (see above, n. 15). The second letter cannot date from 1521 because Fisher was at Halling that day while his chaplain writes from Rochester, and because he could hardly have finished *ALC* so soon. Fisher was at Rochester on 1 July 1522 (see 'Itinerary', p. 243).

21 'Itinerary', p. 243.

22 *CC*, sig. A.1.r (p. 1299). The reference to Tunstall as 'nunc suis meritis Londiniensem Electum' puts it between his nomination *c.* Jan 1522 (*LP* 3. ii. 1972 and 2032) and his consecration (Stubbs, *Registrum Sacrum Anglicanum*, p. 98). Fisher's remark that Tunstall had shown him Velenus's book several months after he had begun his refutation of Luther provides additional confirmation for the dating of *ALC*, and the use of 'nunc electus' suggests that Tunstall had done this before his nomination to London.

23 Gouda, Gemeentelijke Archiefdienst MS 959 (Letters of H. Lethmaet), Fisher to Lethmaet, unfoliated, side 7 (c. 1707), thanking Lethmaet for assisting Addison.

24 *ALC*, title page, verso.

25 *DRA*, ded. to West, 6th leaf recto (p. 101).

26 Tunstall brought it to Erasmus's attention in a letter of 5 June, in what was clearly a hint that Erasmus should refute it. Was Fisher second choice for this task? *EE* V, ep. 1367, p. 292.

27 *DRA* VI, fol. LXVI.r (c. 204), and *SSD* III, fol. XLIII.v (c. 1298). Copies of the original editions are commonly found in a single binding.

28 PRO SP2/R, fol. 192.v, 'quoniam ad instanciam illustrissimi Regis, hos psalmos ad hunc modum enarrandos aggresi [sic] sumus'.

29 *EE* V, ep. 1513, from Vives, 13 Nov 1524, p. 576, 'Quid Rex cupiat te in Psalmos annotare'; VI, ep. 1581, to Noel Beda, 15 June 1525, p. 103, 'Nuper allatae sunt

litterae a Rege Angliae, quae efflagitant impense ut aliquid scriberem in Psalmos'; VIII, ep. 2315, to Sadoleto, 14 May 1530, p. 443, 'Non semel rogatus sum, quum ab aliis, tum ab Anglorum Rege, ut in omnes Psalmos aederem commentarios.'

30 PRO SP2/R, fol. 202.r, refers to 'falsario scripturarum Pomerano'. The exposition to which Fisher objects is found in J. Bugenhagen, *In Librum Psalmorum Interpretatio* (n.p., June 1524), pp. 57–9. Surtz's observation, 'References to Luther and his doctrines, however, seem infrequent', is incorrect. There are implicit or explicit attacks on Luther and his teachings throughout. His suggestion, 'Fisher might well have worked on these [commentaries] from his ordination to the time of the seizure of his papers in April 1534', is improbable. Such a method of work would be uncharacteristic, as Fisher tended to work on his books swiftly and single-mindedly. See Surtz, *Works and Days*, p. 402, n. 5.

31 *EW*, pp. 429–76. Longland's letter to Wolsey of 5 Jan 1526, misplaced at *LP* 4. i. 995 in Jan 1525, notes Henry's desire that Fisher should preach at the recantation. See also Foxe, *Acts and Monuments*, iv, p. 608.

32 *A sermon had at Paulis* (London: Berthelet, n.d.), sig. E.1.r. remarks on the disagreements between Luther, Carlstadt and Oecolampadius. Compare *DVC* I, preface, sig. BB.5.r (p. 750). The commendation of the books of More, Catharinus, Emser, Cochlaeus, Eck 'and many other' (sig. E.1.r) is reminiscent of the list at *DVC* I, preface, sig. BB.4.r (pp. 748–9).

33 Cochlaeus to Pirckheimer, 15 Sept 1526, passes on news about Fisher's progress with his refutation. I owe this reference to Surtz, *Works and Days*, pp. 337 and 512, n. 1.

34 J. Cochlaeus, *Fasciculus Calumniarum* (Leipzig: Schuman, 1529), dedication to Fisher, 5 July 1529, 'Quod in Lutherum nihil amplius aedis aut scribere intendis, meo quidem iudicio recte facis.'

35 *SSD*, sig. a.4.r, thanks Tunstall for help with *ALC* and *SSD*. See also above, nn. 22 and 26.

36 *DVC* III, preface, fol. LXIIII.r (p. 928).

37 Surtz, *Works and Days*, p. 97.

38 *LP* 3 i. 1193, Warham to Wolsey, 8 March 1527. Brewer, following H. Ellis, *Original Letters, Illustrative of the English Reformation* (11 vols., 1825–46), 3rd ser., i, pp. 239–42, placed this letter in 1521, but its content shows that it belongs in the aftermath of the Cardinal's College affair. See Rex, 'Campaign', p. 89, n. 27.

39 Cochlaeus, *Commentaria*, p. 135.

40 Foxe, *Acts and Monuments*, iv, pp. 621–31 for the involvement of Fisher, West and Tunstall (among others) in the trial of Bilney and Arthur in Nov and Dec 1527. For the oath, see F.J. Heal, 'The bishops of Ely and their diocese during the Reformation period: ca. 1515–1600' (unpublished Cambridge Ph.D. dissertation, 1971), pp. 60–1. See below, n. 66, for Cochlaeus. For Bilney's licence, see West's register, CUL, Ely Diocesan Records, G/I/7, fol. 33.r. For a recent re-assessment of Bilney's case, see G. Walker, 'Saint or Schemer? The 1527 Heresy Trial of Thomas Bilney Reconsidered', *Journal of Ecclesiastical History* 40 (1989), pp. 219–38.

41 SJC D 105.44, Sharpe to Metcalfe, 1 July (1522), printed in Gray, 'Letters of Fisher', p. 142.

42 After long and loyal service to Fisher, which culminated in imprisonment over the affair of the Holy Maid of Kent, Addison accepted the royal supremacy, and became a client of Cromwell.

43 *Vie*, x, p. 226.
44 Gouda, Gemeentelijke Archiefdienst, MS 959, side 7, (c. 1707), proposing to insert the parenthesis 'Si Hieronymo credimus' to satisfy Lethmaet's query. See *ALC* 31, fol. 169.v (c. 613) for the insertion.
45 J. Eck, *Enchiridion Locorum Communum*, ed. P. Fraenkel, Corpus Catholicorum 34 (Münster, 1979), p. 24*.
46 *DVC* I, preface, sig. BB.4.r (p. 749).
47 For more information on their activities and those of others mentioned in this paragraph, see Rex, 'Campaign', pp. 91–5.
48 Baynes, Croke, Day and Wakefield were fellows on Fisher's private foundation at St John's. John Rudd was a fellow on the foundation of Hugh Ashton, himself an old friend and colleague of Fisher. Greenwood received a one-off payment from Fisher's foundation at Fisher's express request in 1532. SJC, accounts of Fisher's foundation, D 106.6, e.g., fol. 12.v (Midsummer 1525, Bayne, Day, Wakefield); 55.r (Greenwood); Master's Accounts, M3.5 (Croke); and accounts of Ashton's foundation D 57.92, some of them printed by Cooper, *Memoir of Margaret*, p. 256, where Rudd appears to be both fellow and administrator of Ashton's foundation.
49 Henry Gold. See act of attainder 25 Hen VIII c. 12; and *Chronicle of the Grey Friars*, ed. J.G. Nichols, Camden Soc. 53 (1852), p. 37, which refers to him as the parson of St Mary Aldermary.
50 Elton, *Policy and Police*, pp. 21–2. To be fair, Ainsworth was probably insane, as Elton observes.
51 Rex, 'Campaign', pp. 93–4.
52 Scott, 'Notes from the College Records', *The Eagle* 31 (1910), p. 332 printing a deposition by Thomas Watson of 15 Oct 1565; 'Doctor Metcalf after the aforesaid visitation … was in trooble before … Lord Crumwell, and shortly after I was present in the Colledge Chaple when he returnyng home dyd in the presence of all the fellows resygne the Maystershippe, saying that he was commaunded to do so, whych he dyd with weepyng tears.'
53 Wilson wisely refused this honour, and Day was duly installed, though he soon took the opportunity to move on to the provostship of King's. A nearly contemporary note on the inside rear cover of SJC Thin Red Book notes that within a single year the College had four masters – Metcalfe, Wilson, Day and John Taylor.
54 *EE* V, eps. 1486, to Wolsey, 2 Sept 1524; 1487, to Tunstall; 1488, to Warham; and 1489, to Fisher, all 4 Sept; and 1493, to Henry, 6 Sept, pp. 530–541.
55 *LP* 3. ii. 3373 and 3390, Morley to Wolsey, Sept and 4 Oct 1523, show that Murner travelled back with Morley's embassy to the Diet of Nuremberg, and mention Fisher's hospitality *en route*.
56 J. Fabri, *De Intercessione Sanctorum*, in his *Opuscula*, sig. d.6.r.
57 H.S. Herbrüggen, 'A Letter of Dr Johann Eck to Thomas More', *Moreana* vol. 2, no. 8 (1965), pp. 51–8, tells the story of Eck's visit. Eck himself described it in a letter to Clement VII of 17 Sept 1525, printed in Balan's *Monumenta*, pp. 538–40. For Fisher's letter to the duke, see Bridgett, *Blessed John Fisher*, pp. 114–16.
58 Eck, *Enchiridion*, p. 2. The critical edition attempts to identify Eck's sources.
59 Eck, *Enchiridion*, p. 300.
60 *Von dem hochgelehrten geistlichen bischoff Jo von Roffen uss Engelland, seines grosen nutzichen buchs zwen artikel verteutscht von Doctor Jo. Cochlaeus* (Strasbourg: Grieninger, 1523). J. Cochlaeus, *Adversus Latrocinantes et Raptorias Cohortes Rusticorum. Responsio Johannis Cochlaei Wendelstini* (Cologne: Quentell, 1525), title

page verso, which also records his wish to translate the whole of *ALC*, 'Ego quidem articulos duos XV, et XVI olim teuthonicos utrunque feci, totum forsitan opus in linguam nostram traducturus, si fidus tum et idoneus mihi Chalcographus fuisset.' See also Surtz, *Works and Days*, p. 409.

61 Rupert, *De Glorificatione Trinitatis* (Cologne: Quentell, 1526), included an edition of an early (spurious) papal letter, with a dedication to Fisher. For the despatch of volumes for Henry, Wolsey and Fisher, see BL Cottonian MS Vit. B. xxi, fol. 11, Sir John Wallop to Wolsey, 30 Sept 1526.

62 In his dedication to Henry VIII of Rupert, *In Apocalypsim*, (Cologne: Quentell, 1526), title page verso, Cochlaeus cited a letter from Fisher in which the bishop expressed eagerness to see the edition of Rupert on John's Gospel and the Apocalypse.

63 Surtz, *Works and Days*, p. 337. See above, n. 33.

64 *DVC* I, preface, sig. BB.3.v (p. 748) and V, preface, fol. CXXXVII.r (p. 1134). J. Cochlaeus, *Funff Vorrede* (n.p., prob. Dresden: Stöckel, 1528).

65 *EE* VII, ep. 1928, from Cochlaeus, 8 Jan 1528, p. 288, urging Erasmus to write against the Anabaptists, and reporting a similar request made to Fisher. Cochlaeus to More, 29 June 1531, in J.H. Pollen, 'Johannes Cochläus and König Heinrich VIII von England und Thomas Morus', *Römische Quartalschrift* 13 (1889), pp. 43–9, at p. 48, exclaims 'Utinam Rosseus vester aut R.D. Roffensis hunc rhetorem digne pro meritis excipiat.'

66 Cochlaeus dedicated twelve other works or parts of works to English patrons: West (3), Henry VIII, Tunstall, Robert Ridley and More (2 each) and Wolsey (1). See M. Spahn, *Johannes Cochläus* (Berlin, 1898), pp. 347–56.

67 J. Cochlaeus, *Defensio Ioannis Episcopi Roffensis et Thome Mori adversus Richardum Samsonem* (Leipzig: Lotther, 1536), and *Scopa Ioannis Cochlaei Germani in Araneas Ricardi Morysini* (Leipzig: Wolrab, 1538).

68 Surtz, *Works and Days*, pp. 385–9.

69 These figures derive mainly from W. Klaiber, *Katholische Kontroverstheologen und Reformer des 16. Jahrhunderts. Ein Werkverzeichnis*, Reformationsgeschichtliche Studien und Texte 116 (Münster, 1978). See J. Eck, *Tres Orationes Funebres*, ed. J. Metzler, Corpus Catholicorum 16 (Münster, 1930), pp. LXVII–CXXXII for editions of Eck's *Enchiridion*. See also T. More, *Utopia*, ed. E. Surtz and J.H. Hexter, CWTM 4 (Yale, 1965), pp. clxxxiii–cxciii (nine Latin edns. in the sixteenth century). The figure for Erasmus, *De Libero Arbitrio*, is based on various catalogues and bibliographies.

70 R. Tapper, *Explicatio Articulorum*, in *Opera Omnia* (2 vols., Cologne: Birckmann, 1582), i, p. 231, 'copiose atque catholice respondet clarissimus Christi martyr Ioan. Roffensis. Quare ea hic repetere, quae in omnium manibus sunt, operaeprecium non est.'

71 My calculation is based on the footnotes in Fraenkel's critical edition.

72 A. de Castro, *Adversus Omnes Haereses* (Leipzig: Novesianus, 1539) and A. de Vega, *De Vera Iustificatione* (Cologne: Quentell, 1572). My attention was directed towards these works by Surtz (*Works and Days*, p. 387), but the calculations, based on counting names in these works, are mine. Since sixteenth-century authors only rarely acknowledge debts to contemporaries, the numbers are small relative to the size of the works.

73 *CT* 5, pp. 877–8 (on the real presence, also noticed by Surtz, *Works and Days*, p. 348); 6. iii, pp. 258 (on purgatory), 340 (indulgences) and 403 (sacrifice of the mass); and 7. i, p. 121 (on communion in both kinds).

74 See J. Cochlaeus, e.g., *De Authoritate Ecclesiae et Scripturae* (n.p., prob. Strasbourg: Grieninger, 1524), sig. A.4.v; *Philippicae Quatuor* (Leipzig: Faber, 1534), sig. E.1.r; *De Canonice Scripturae Autoritate* (Ingolstadt: Weissenhorn, 1543), sig. I.3.r; and *Commentaria . . . de actis et scriptis Martini Lutheri* (Mainz: Behem, 1549), pp. 38, 64, 118–19 and 153.

75 G. Weidermann, 'Martin Luther versus John Fisher: some ideas concerning the debate on Lutheran theology at the university of St Andrews, 1525–30', *Records of the Scottish Church History Society* 22 (1984), p. 22, citing Alesius, 'ex Roffensi Lutheri assertiones refutavi cum applausu theologorum'.

76 Leedham-Green, *Cambridge Inventories*, ii, pp. 345–6. Surviving sixteenth-century Cambridge inventories list eight copies of *ALC*; five of *DVC*; three of *SSD*; and two each of *DRA*, *CC* and *DUM*. For Parkyn, see Leedham-Green, i, p. 692. For Bullock and Ridley, see *BRUC*. For Day (referring to *DVC* during the House of Lords debates on the eucharist in 1548) see F. Gasquet and E. Bishop, *Edward VI and the Book of Common Prayer* (London, 1890), p. 435.

77 Eck, *Enchiridion*, p. 83. P. Polman, *L'Elément historique dans la controverse religieuse du XVIe siècle* (Gembloux, 1932), p. 288. See below, ch. 6, p. 97.

78 T. More, *Responsio ad Lutherum*, ed. J.M. Headley, CWTM 5, pt 1 (Yale, 1969), pp. 88–91; J. Dietenberger, *Phimostomus Scripturariorum*, ed. E. Iserloh and P. Fabisch with J. Toussaert and E. Weichel, Corpus Catholicorum 38 (Münster, 1985), p. 67; Eck, *Enchiridion*, p. 76; Erasmus, *Hyperaspistes*, in *Opera Omnia*, x, p. 1305. See below, ch. 6, p. 98.

79 Fisher was citing 'Dionysius's' *Ecclesiastica Hierarchia* in the translation by Ambrogio Traversari. See Surtz, *Works and Days*, pp. 106 and 459, n. 18; G.H. Tavard, *Holy Writ or Holy Church* (London, 1959), pp. 202–3 and 207; and More, *Responsio*, p. 738.

80 More, *Responsio*, pp. 138–41. Castro, *Adversus Omnes Haereses*, fols. CLXXVIII.v–XXIX.r, 'scripsit . . . grande volumen Ioannes Echius . . . scripsit etiam Ioannes Faber . . . Rem eandem optime pertractat Ioannes Roffensis.' I owe this reference to Surtz, *Works and Days*, p. 370.

81 *CT* 9, p. 120, 3 Nov 1562, 'Haec non est mea responsio, sed gloriosi antistitis illius Roffensis in sua assertione contra Lutherum in titulo de primatu Petri.'

82 See *De Vera Iustificatione*, p. 621, and compare *ALC* 1, fols. 21–2 (c. 314). Surtz notices this relationship (*Works and Days*, p. 508, n. 28), but without observing that Vega is depending on Fisher for much of his information about Luther.

83 *De Vera Iustificatione*, p. 394, referring to *ALC* 6, fol. 68.v (c. 407).

84 *De Vera Iustificatione*, p. 401, 'Quod si apud Luterum, ut testis est Roffensis, Nullum esse peccatum veniale, sed omnia sunt mortalia.' *ALC* 8, fol. 78.r (c. 425), 'Adde, quod tibi visum est adversum Eckium omne peccatum veniale, cum (ut illic asseris) contra legem fiat, ex natura sua mortale esse.'

85 J. Redman, *De Iustificatione*, ed. C. Tunstall (Antwerp: Withagus, 1555), pp. 20–1, citing 2 Pet 1:10, and laying especial emphasis on the Greek word 'Belaiam', as Fisher had done at *ALC* 1, fol. 25.v (c. 319). They both follow Erasmus, *Novum Instrumentum*, p. 171, and *Annotationes*, p. 615.

86 By Lippomano (bishop of Verona) and Ioannes Fonseca, *CT* 5, pp. 699 and 730. The only other contemporary cited was John Driedo – see H. Jedin, *A History of the Council of Trent*, tr. E. Graf (2 vols., London, 1961), ii, p. 296.

87 Thus Karl Zickendraht as cited by B.A. Gerrish, *'De Libero Arbitrio*: Erasmus on piety, theology, and the Lutheran dogma', in *Essays on the Works of Erasmus*, ed. R.L. DeMolen (Yale, 1978), pp. 187–209, esp. pp. 204–5.

88 G. Chantraine, *Erasme et Luther: libre et serf arbitre* (Paris, 1981), p. 463.

89 *Explicatio, Opera I*, p. 231. On p. 210 he summarised an argument from *ALC* 36, fol. 195.r–v (cc. 664–5).

90 Cochlaeus, *De Libero Arbitrio* (n.p., 1525), sig. K.7.r–v; Eck, *Enchiridion*, pp. 313–25; Castro, *Adversus Omnes Haereses*, fol. CLVI.r; Vega, *De Vera Iustificatione*, p. 25.

91 Quentell produced edns. in folio, 4to and 8vo in 1527, and Cervicorn of Cologne produced an 8vo the same year. Cochlaeus's partial translation appeared in Leipzig in 1528, and *DVC* was included in Fleischmann's Würzburg *Opera Omnia* of 1597.

92 Ex inf. J.J. Scarisbrick, who worked from it in his own research upon Fisher. Unfortunately, this volume cannot now be located, and is unknown even to the leading authority on Cranmer's library, the Revd D.G. Selwyn. For the jibe at Gardiner, see Cranmer, *On the Lord's Supper*, ed. J.E. Cox (Parker Soc., 1844), p. 190.

93 *A reporte of Maister Doctor Redmans answeres* (London: Reynold, 1551), sig. B.2.r, 'I returned agayne to Tertullian & Ireneus, and when I hadde obserued theyr sayinges, myne opinion that there shuld be transubstantiation, Prorsus erat abolita, was quyte dasshed.'

94 W. Peryn, *Thre Sermons* (London: Herforde, n.d., c. 1546), *passim*. Compare *DVC* II, preface (pp. 839–44) with *Thre Sermons*, fols. LXXXVI.r–XCVI.r; *DVC* III, preface, (pp. 917–28) with fols. LXIX.v–LXXI.r and CXII.r–v; *DVC* IV, preface (pp. 989–98) with fols. XCVI.r–CX.v; and *DVC* V, preface (pp. 1125–34) with fols. XLV.r–XLVII.r.

95 R. Smyth, *The Assertion and Defence of the Sacramente of the Aulter* (London: Herforde, 1546), fols. 16.r–26.v. Compare *DVC* IV, preface, fols. LXXXV.r–LXXXVIII.v (pp. 991–7), in inverse order.

96 *DVC* (Cologne: Quentell, 4to, 1527), CUL Rel. d. 52. 17, facing title page: 'G.C. Lectori. Quanquam opus hoc grande tibi videri possit Lector consultum tamen tibi velim ut in perlegendo non desistas. Nam si hunc assecutus fueris satis strenuum ac armatum fore adversus impias sacramentariorum sycophantias spero. Vale et Spartam quam nactus es hanc adorna. 1545.' On the title page is the signature 'Gulielmus Cicyll'. Professor Sir Geoffrey Elton has pointed out to me that the italic hand is not at all like the secretary hand of Elizabeth's Lord Treasurer. But we do not have any Cecil autograph from the 1540s with which to compare it. Italic was taught at Cecil's college, St John's. As no other William Cecil is known to have been at Cambridge in the sixteenth century, I am inclined to ascribe the book to Cecil, but it cannot be regarded as certain.

97 A. Langdaile, *Catholica Confutatio ... N. Ridlaei* (Paris: Vascosanus, 1556), mentions Fisher only once, in passing, fol. 7.r, 'Ubi et Roffensis iste [Ridley] (bis per omnia a beato Ioanne, vero illo Roffensi Episcopo discrepans).'

98 *Catholica Confutatio*, fols. 37.v–45.r.

99 C. Tunstall, *De Veritate Corporis Domini Nostri Iesu Christi in Eucharistia* (Paris: Vascosanus, 1554).

100 Castro, *Adversus Omnes Haereses*, fol. CII.r, 'Post istos omnes hoc nostro tempore contra Oecolampadium scripsit omnibus istis longe diffusius atque acutius, Ioannes Roffensis episcopus ... qui illis antiquis scriptoribus merito comparari valet ... Si omnia ad unguem quae ad hoc negotium spectant habere vis, lege viri huius ad. finem usque librum, spero deo authore, si dubius accesseris, confirmaberis, et omni scrupulo sublato discedes in firmissima fidei petra fundatus.' Cecil's comment (above, n. 96) might almost be an echo of Castro.

101 Fabri, *De Intercessione*, sig. f.1.v, 'Equidem ita te sanctorum patrum scripta mutilasse ac sententiam invertisse, tum alii tum ... Ioannes Fischerus Rocestra in Anglia ... clare docet.'

102 Tapper, *Opera* II, pp. 167 (for Fisher) and 189 (for the others).

103 F. Mendoza, *De Naturali cum Christo Unitate*, ed. A. Piolanti, Lateranum Nova Series nos. 1–4 (Rome, 1948). Piolanti dates it to 1561–6. Compare pp. 22–32 with *DVC* II, preface (pp. 839–44) which Mendoza acknowledges on p. 22. Mendoza's references to Oecolampadius are clearly dependent on *DVC*. I owe this reference to an article by H.P.C. Lyons. 'The Sacrament of Restored Nature – St John Fisher on the Eucharist', *Clergy Review* 40 (1955), pp. 520–7.

104 Jedin, *Trent*, i, pp. 399–400, estimates that Fisher's influence at the council was greater than that of the 'Louvain school' – Latomus, Dreido, Tapper and Pighius.

105 *CT* 6. iii, pp. 3–12, 'Summarium sententiarum theologorum super articulis Lutheranorum de sacramento eucharistiae.' The editors suggest that Salmeron drafted it from Lainez's notes (p. 3).

106 Compare *CT* 6. iii, p. 5 with *DVC* V, preface, p. 1125; pp. 9–11 with III, preface, pp. 921–5; p. 11 with II, preface, pp. 839–44; and p. 9 with IV, preface, pp. 990–7.

107 *CT* 7. ii, pp. 120 and 135 (14 and 16 Sept 1551).

108 *CT* 8, pp. 539, 542 and 554 (10, 11 and 15 June 1562).

109 *CT* 7. i, p. 389 and ii, p. (29 Dec 1551); and iii, p. 563 (19 Dec 1551).

110 *CT* 7. ii, pp. 602, 614, 634 and 645 (7, 8 and 9 Jan 1552); and 8, pp. 755 and 763 (11 and 13 Aug 1562). One or two of these are noticed by Surtz (*Works and Days*, p. 388), whose paragraph on Fisher's influence at Trent inspired me to investigate it further.

111 D. Power, *The Sacrifice We Offer: the Tridentine dogma and its reinterpretation* (Edinburgh, 1987), pp. 86–8.

112 *CT* 9, p. 58 (the bishop of Ross); and 12, p. 692 (Lorenzo Mazocchio).

113 *CT* 1, p. 478; 5, p. 730; 6. i, pp. 81–2; 6. ii, p. 371; 7. i, p. 380; and 7. ii, p. 614.

6 Authority

1 Lewis, *Dr Fisher*, i, p. 207.

2 Y. Congar, *Tradition and Traditions*, tr. M. Naseby and T. Rainsborough (London, 1966), pp. 508–19.

3 For these two concepts of tradition, see H.A. Oberman, *The Harvest of Medieval Theology: Gabriel Biel and late mediaeval nominalism* (Cambridge, Mass., 1963), p. 371.

4 Tavard, *Holy Writ*, p. 41.

5 Tavard, *Holy Writ*, p. 22.

6 *Contra epistolam manichaei quam vocant Fundamenti*, *PL* 42, p. 176. 'Ego evangelio non crederem, nisi me catholicae ecclesiae commoveret auctoritas.'

7 Tavard, *Holy Writ*, p. 22.

8 J. Gerson, *De sensu litterali sacrae scripturae*, in *Oeuvres Complètes* (10 vols., Paris, 1960–73), iii, p. 334.

9 'Ecclesiae non crederem, nisi Evangelium me compelleret', cited by J. Trithemius in his *Liber Octo Quaestionum* of 1508 (edition used, Mainz, 1601, p. 45).

10 In the high Middle Ages, canon law exempted the popes from all human jurisdiction. See W. Ullmann, *Principles of Government and Politics in the Middle Ages* (London, 1961), pp. 49 and 89. Only popes who fell into heresy, and were therefore deemed *ipso facto* deposed, were capable of being brought to judgment. See Gratian, *Decretum*, pt 1, dist. 40, ch. 6, in *Corpus Iuris Canonici*, ed. E. Friedberg (2

vols., Graz, 1959), i, p. 146, and A. Catharinus, *Apologia pro Veritate Catholicae et Apostolicae Fidei*, ed. J. Schweizer, Corpus Catholicorum 27 (Münster, 1955), p. 239. And Catharinus believed in the dogmatic infallibility of the pope (see below, n. 76).

11 See M. Lienhard, *L'Evangile et l'Eglise chez Luther* (Paris, 1989), pp. 132–3.

12 Farge, *Orthodoxy and Reform*, pp. 125–8 and 165–9.

13 Bainton, *Here I Stand*, p. 89 for Prierias, and pp. 107–20 (esp. pp. 116–17) for Leipzig.

14 I have not been able to trace the first formulation of this principle, but it is certainly expressed in his *Assertio Omnium Articulorum* cited at *ALC*, proem, fol. 19.v (c. 307), 'Nolo omnium doctior iactari, sed solam scripturam regnare.' S.H. Hendrix, in an admirable study of Luther's relations with the papacy, maintains that he did not formulate this principle in 1519, *Luther and the Papacy* (Philadelphia, 1981), p. 87.

15 See its occurrence at, e.g., *WA* 1, p. 584.

16 Congar, *Tradition*, pp. 30–42.

17 Luther, *Enarrationes ... in Epistolas Petri* (Strasbourg: Hervagius, 1525), fol. 9.v, 'Inde facile discitur, epistolam, Iacobi nomine inscriptam, haudquaquam Apostolicam esse epistolam', cited by Fisher, *DRA* I, fol. II.v (c. 104).

18 *EW*, p. 331. Fisher's concern with Luther's 'artycles' offers further confirmation that he was already at work on the *ALC* when he delivered the sermon in 1521.

19 *ALC*, proem, fols. 5.v–13.v (cc. 279–96). These represent perhaps the most commonly cited passage of Fisher's Latin polemics. See, e.g., Surtz, *Works and Days*, p. 311; Wiedermann, 'Martin Luther versus John Fisher', pp. 32–3.

20 *ALC*, proem, fol. 5.v (c. 279); *EW*, p. 312.

21 I owe the Longland reference to Blench, *Preaching*, p. 248. For Fisher's citation of Origen, see *ALC*, preface, fol. 12.v (c. 293), and *EW*, p. 333. Surtz observes Tyndale's contempt for Fisher's use of a notorious heretic to support his argument (*Works and Days*, p. 457, n. 10).

22 *ALC*, proem, fol. 9.v (c. 287); *EW*, pp. 332–6.

23 *ALC*, dedication to the reader, fol. 1.r (c. 272).

24 *ALC*, proem, fol. 5.r–v (cc. 278–9). Compare citation with *Opera Q. Septimii Florentii Tertulliani*, ed. B. Rhenanus (Basel: Froben, 1521), p. 93. If Fisher had had access to Tertullian before, it is inconceivable that he should not have used him in the sermon of 1521.

25 J.F. D'Amico, 'Beatus Rhenanus, Tertullian and the Reformation', *Archiv für Reformationsgeschichte* 71 (1980), pp. 37–60, esp. pp. 40–2 and 57.

26 *Opera Tertulliani*, sig. b.8.r.

27 *ALC* proem, fol. 8.v (c. 285). Compare *EM*, sig. B.3.r. See above, ch. 4, p. 74.

28 *Tertius Tomus Epistolarum Divi Eusebii Hieronymi*, ed. Erasmus (Basel: Froben, 1516), fol. 2.r, 'Hunc igitur Helvidium refellit Hieronymus, et confirmat Mariam perpetuo fuisse virginem, etiam si hoc non est aperte scriptam in litteris divinis, sed apostolorum ac sanctorum patrum traditione, veluti per manus ad nos derivatum.'

29 See, e.g., Potter, *Zwingli*, p. 89, for Zwingli's views.

30 *ALC* 37, fol. 222.r (c. 718), 'quoniam scriptura sacra, conclave quoddam est omnium veritatum, quae Christianis scitu necessariae sunt, nemini potest ambiguum esse, quin purgatorii veritas in ipsa contineatur, et quin ex ipsa quoque probari potest'; and 'non sit credibile purgatorium non posse ex scriptura sacra probari, quum sit ea res Christianis omnibus usqueadeo scitu necessaria'.

31 *ALC* 37, fol. 221.v (c. 717), 'tametsi non possit ex scripturis probari purgatorium, veritas eius nihilominus Christianis cunctis credenda est, et maxime ... ex Ecclesiae vetustissima consuetudine'.

32 Tavard, *Holy Writ*, pp. 79, 114 and 172.

33 Congar, *Tradition*, p. 513, cites Clichtove, Driedo and Schatzgeyer on this.

34 *EW*, p. 332.

35 PRO SP6/5, fol. 46.v, referring to Hilary, probably to *Prologus in Librum Psalmorum* (*PL* 9, p. 238), 'septuaginta seniores, secundum Moysi traditionem ad custodiendam legis doctrinam in synagoga manentes, postea quam illis a rege Ptolomaeo transferendae ex hebraeo in graecum sermonem totius legis cura mandata est'. See also *Tractatus Psalmi II* (*PL* 9, p. 262), 'quaedam ex occultis legis secretiora mysteria' as distinct from 'Veteris Testamenti verba in litteris.'

36 Polman, *L'Elément Historique*, p. 316, probably based on the sixth, seventh and eighth truths, *ALC*, proem, fols. 9v–12.r (cc. 287–92).

37 *ALC*, fol. 11.v (c. 290), 'de sacris Ecclesiae doctoribus contingit, haud absque divina dispensatione, nempe ut suis ingeniis relicti, nonnunquam in errores inciderint'. See also PRO SP1/64, fol. 244.r, 'Nam qui in nullo penitus erraverit vix reperietur.'

38 PRO SP6/5, fols. 53.r–v, 'Errare forte potuit Hieronimus'; and 76.r, 'Inter autores quantumvis eruditos nemo facile reperietur qui in libris ab eo scriptis nusquam errasse creditur.'

39 See above, ch. 4, p. 74.

40 *CC*, sigg. G.1.r (c. 1330) and L.4.r (c. 1357).

41 As was suggested by Surtz, *Works and Days*, p. 33. His evidence undermines his conclusion.

42 Tavard, *Holy Writ*, p. 171.

43 *EW*, p. 336.

44 *EM*, sig. R.3.v, 'summi Pontificis decreto, revelationes eedem approbentur'. The standard edition, *Revelationes Celestes* (Nuremberg: Koberger, 1517), carried among its prefatory materials the approbatory conclusions of a committee chaired by Cardinal Turrecremata and, for good measure, bulls of canonisation by Boniface IX and Martin V (fols. III.r–VIII.v).

45 *ALC* 27, fol. 154.v (c. 583).

46 *ALC* 18, fol. 111.v (c. 497), 'partim ex revelationibus, partim ex scripturis, fuisse creditum'.

47 Rupert of Deutz, *In Apocalypsim*, ed. J. Cochlaeus (Cologne: Quentell, 1526), dedication to Henry VIII (title page verso, not printed in all copies), citing a letter from Fisher, 'Nam semper mihi visum fuit difficillimum, ut quisquam citra novam revelationem, ea mysteria, tam variis et obscuris adumbrata figuris, digne pro mente scriptoris unquam explicare.'

48 *EW*, p. 108. See also *ALC* 28, fol. 159.r (c. 592), 'Ego certe persuassimum habeo, Ecclesiam errare non posse, in iis quae ad substantiam fidei pertinent.'

49 *ALC* 28, fol. 159.v (c. 593), 'spiritu veritatis infallibiliter edocta'.

50 *ALC* 29, fol. 160.v (c. 595), 'Neque enim quisquam audire potuit unquam universalem ecclesiam hoc vel illud affirmantem. Sed nec possibile fuit, ut in uno loco tanta multitudo congregaretur; unde posset audiri.' See also *ALC* 16, fol. 101.r (c. 475), 'Nam ut omnes christiani simul una convocentur, est prorsus impossibile, congruum igitur fuit, ut quoties de credendis inter christianos lis aliqua suboriretur, Episcopi de quaqua natione christianitatis statim convenirent, litis eius dirimendae gratia. Qui us afflatum sancti spiritus haudquaquam defuturum, certo confidendum est.'

51 *ALC* 28, fol. 159.r (c. 592), 'Nam Pontificem una cum Concilio, non est dubium,

Ecclesiam universalem repraesentare' and 159.v (c. 593), 'Praeiudicatum igitur est cuique christiano ... ne dissentiat ab iis, quae summus Pontifex una cum concilio credenda decrevit.' See below, note 57, for the proviso about the Holy Spirit.

52 Surtz, *Works and Days*, p. 65, citing *EM*.

53 For a brief discussion of More's ecclesiology, see the debate in *Moreana* 64 (1980), with contributions by F. Oakley, 'Headley, Marius and the matter of Thomas More's conciliarism', pp. 82–8; J. Headley, 'The Nos Papistae of Thomas More', pp. 89–90; and R. Marius, 'More the conciliarist', pp. 91–9, and references therein. For a full-scale treatment, see Gogan, *The Common Corps of Christendom*.

54 See below, note 89. This position was a commonplace even among papal theologians like Cajetan (see B. Gogan, 'Fisher's view of the Church', in *HRR*, pp. 131–54, at p. 148; and the infallibilist Catharinus (see n. 10 above).

55 *DUM* III, fol. XLVII.v (c. 1453), 'nihil est in terris summo pontifice maius'.

56 *ALC* 29, fols. 161.v–2.r (c. 598), 'Nam semper mihi suspecta videntur, ubi vel a concilio Pontifex dissideat, vel concilium a Pontifice, nisi manifestissima Pontificis culpa factum id fuerit.'

57 *ALC* 29, fol. 161.v (c. 597), 'Neque ego penitus cuiuscunque concilii decreta probanda censeo, sed eius, quodcumque fuerit in spiritu sancto, Pontificis autoritate, cunctisque premonitis, quorum interest adesse, convocatum.'

58 Fisher outlines the distinction and gives the example at *EM*, sig. a.2.r–v (after sig. Z). *ALC* 16, fol. 101.r (c. 475), observes that explicit consensus can only be ascertained through a general council.

59 *LP* 4. ii. 3147, Wolsey to Henry VIII, 2 June 1527.

60 *DUM* I, fol. IV.v (c. 1397), 'Dicat igitur quisnam erit cui fidem, in hac re plebs christiana potissimum adhibeat. Ego nimirum id genus arbitror summos imprimis pontifices.'

61 *DUM* III, fol. XLVII.v (c. 1453), 'propter supremam eorum in ecclesia auctoritatem'; 'nihil est in terris summo pontifice maius, ad quem in omnibus controversiis recursum habere Christianos decet, atque illius decretis obedire, maxime in his quae ad fidem evangeliorum spectant'.

62 A. J. Lamping, *Ulrich Velenus and his Treatise against the Papacy*, SMRT 19 (Leiden, 1976), identifies Velenus, reprints his treatise and provides a thorough introduction to it. Fisher's *CC* also reprints Velenus's treatise verbatim.

63 *CC*, sigg. K.2.v–3.r (c. 1351), citing Bede, and referring to Lyra, Tertullian, Jerome and Eusebius.

64 *CC*, sig. G.4.r (c. 1334), 'id quod nemini scriptorum, unquam in mentem ante venerat'.

65 *CC*, sig. B.1.r (c. 1303), 'Quum enim ex tot scriptoribus nemo unquam aut scripserit, aut senserit contrarium quin Petrus Romae fuisset, sed omnes id concorditer asserant.'

66 *CC*, sig. A.4.v (c. 1302), 'Denique christum ipsum servatorem nostrum, nec mortem obiisse pro nobis credemus, si diversa scriptorum supputatio, sententiaque discors eius rei fidem nobis auferre possit.'

67 *CC*, sig. I.2.v (c. 1344).

68 *CC*, sig. G.3.v (c. 1334) refers to Lefèvre's versions of the accounts of Peter and Paul by 'Linus', printed in his *In Epistolas Pauli*, fols. 259.r–64.r.

69 *CC*, sig. A.4.r (c. 1302).

70 Lamping, *Velenus*, pp. 157–8.

71 *ALC* 25, fols. 127.v–31.v (cc. 530–8).

72 *ALC* 25, fols. 132.r–4.r, citing Hilary, Ambrose, Leo, Gregory, Cyprian, Augustine and Jerome; and Chrysostom, Eusebius, Cyril of Alexandria, Origen, Athanasius, Theophilus, Basil and 'Dionysius'.

73 *ALC* 25, fol. 134.r–v (cc. 543–4), referring to Flavio Biondo and Gian Francesco Pico della Mirandola. For the decree see Denzinger, *Enchiridion*, n. 694.

74 T. de Vio Cajetan, *De Divina Institutione Romani Pontificis*, ed. F. Lauchert, Corpus Catholicorum 10 (Münster, 1925), chs. 2–7 on Matthew, 8–12 on John and 14 on the fathers. Cajetan's book appeared in 1521.

75 See, e.g., B. Tierney, *The Origins of Papal Infallibility 1150–1350*, SHCT 6 (Leiden, 1976), pp. 2 and 278.

76 Catharinus, *Apologia*, pp. 236–43, esp. p. 242.

77 *ALC*, proem, fol. 15.r (c. 298), citing Luther's *Assertio Omnium Articulorum*, 'fabulantes Ecclesiam (id est Papam) non posse errare in fide'.

78 *ALC* 28, fol. 158.v (c. 591), 'Neque enim credibile est Christum . . . ita suam ecclesiam, absque omni duce et rectore destitutam reliquisse, ut nemo prorsus esset ad quem in rebus dubiis diffiniendis . . . accederent christiani, sed oporteret, pro levissimis quibusvis negociis congregare concilium.'

79 *ALC*, proem, fols. 6.v–7.r (cc. 281–2), 'Adest ergo . . . in ecclesia potestas iudiciaria, sufficiens ad omnem controversiam, sive quae de scripturis, seu quae de veritate quavis alia, ad catholicam Ecclesiam spectante nascitur, dissoluendam . . . ut figurae suae respondeat veritas, locus adeundus est, quem elegit dominus, qui nimirum apud nos, cathedra Petri iure censetur. Nam ut apud Moseos cathedram, Iudaeis iudices erant quaerendi, ita et nobis Christianis ad Petri cathedram, pro dirimendis controversiis confugiendum est.'

80 See, for example, Catharinus, *Apologia*, pp. 76–7 and 240–2. E. Powell, *Propugnaculum Summi Sacerdotii Evangelici* (London: Pynson, 1523), fols. 7.v–11.v, explores the OT high priesthood as a 'figure' of the papacy without specifically mentioning Deut 17:8.

81 *ALC*, proem, fol. 7.v (c. 283), 'Ecce qui Moseos cathedram occupavit, quanquam avaritia, et ambitione, ac symonia, corruptissimus fuerat, tamen quia summus erat illius anni Pontifex, Iudaeis protulit iudicii veritatem. Et qui Petri Cathedram legittime sortitus est, non potest hoc facere Christianis? Absit. Et maxime quum Petro dictum sit. Et super hanc petram.'

82 T. Aquinas, *Opuscula*, ed. A. Michael de Maria SJ (3 vols., Città di Castello, 1886), ii, p. 519.

83 *ALC* 37, fol. 227.r (c. 727).

84 *DUM* III, fols. XLVII.v–XLVIII.r (c. 1454), 'unde enim potius expetenda est eius rei certitudo, quam a summis pontificibus, qui loco praesunt, quem dominus elegit, hoc est sacrae sedi apostolicae?' The resonances of 'certitudo' are similar to those of our term 'infallibility'.

85 *ALC*, fol. 9.r (c. 286), 'Quem iudicem hic adibimus, nisi Petri cathedram? quae profecto dubiis in rebus, et ad fidem praecipue spectantibus, nunquam non erit adiuta divinitus, ut certam nobis depromat veritatem.'

86 BL Otho C. x. fol. 196.v, 'Expedit rei publicae Christianae quum propter extinguenda scismata, tum ob pacem et tranquillitatem habendam, ut potestas non solum interpretandi scripturas et concilia generalia pontificisque decreta, verumetiam dispensandi iuxta priorem modum, pontifici adsit.'

87 Gogan, 'Fisher's view of the Church', p. 145.

88 *ALC* 28, fol. 158.v (c. 591), 'Quando igitur is, qui primus est, et totius ecclesiae

princeps, cuique totius orbis cura, Christi decreto commissa fuit, hunc vel illum sensum una cum caeteris ecclesiae proceribus approbaverit: istis nimirum alios (qui reliqui sunt) nisi rationem efficacissimam in contrarium attulerint, se conformare decebit.' One must therefore add a nuance of doubt to Scarisbrick's assertion of Fisher's belief in papal infallibility ('Conservative Episcopate', p. 372). Having said this, one wonders whether any reason could have been found strong enough to convince Fisher that a pope had erred in a particular matter of faith or morals. I remain unconvinced by Gogan's attempt to recruit Fisher as an exponent of the 'magisterium theologorum' by interpreting 'proceribus' as 'theologians' by analogy with its use at *ALC* 16, fol. 103.v (c. 480). See Gogan, 'Fisher's view of the Church', p. 140).

89 BL Arundel MS 151, fol. 331.v, 'Non inficiamur certe quin pontifices errare possunt: homines enim sunt atque ideo labi possunt, nisi divinis praesidiis intime nitantur. Caeterum his freti, non est dubium quin a divino spiritu dirigantur, in iudiciis omnibus quae ad salutem animarum sibi commissarum concernunt. Quod si forsan a recto tramite nonunquam humana fragilitate declinaverunt, si modo gravis et manifestarius error fuerit, prassertim in materia fidei, non inficiamur quin per ecclesiam admoneri possunt et inde revocari.'

90 *ALC* 25, fol. 140.r (c. 555), 'Nonne cernimus christianos e sacerdotibus nasci, sacerdotes autem ex Episcopis. Episcopos quoque ab ipso Pontifice summo (quoties necesse fuerit) propagari?' This point is also made by Gogan, in 'Fisher's view of the Church', p. 138.

91 *ALC* 19, fols. 114.r–15.r (cc. 502–4).

92 *ALC*, proem, fol. 9.r (c. 286). See also *EW*, p. 313 for a similar argument in the 1521 sermon against Luther.

93 See above, ch. 4, p. 70 and below, ch. 8, p. 132.

7 Faith, grace and justification

1 Chantraine, *Erasme et Luther*, p. 463.

2 Surtz, *Works and Days*, pp. 222, 227 and 233. He summarises Fisher's teaching on justification at some length in chs. 11 and 12, pp. 194–234, but does not place it in any sort of context.

3 A.H.T. Levi, 'The Breakdown of Scholasticism and the Rise of Evangelical Humanism', in *The Philosophical Assessment of Theology: essays in honour of Frederick Copleston*, ed. G.J. Hughes (Georgetown, 1987), pp. 101–28, at p. 121. Levi's judgment may not be based on a close reading of Fisher. On the same page he suggests that Fisher dealt with free will in his *Contra Captivitatem Babylonicam* (another title for *DRA*) and also in the *Epistola ad Martinum Lutherum* of 1526. In fact, Fisher dealt with free will in *ALC* (art. 36, fols. 193.v–221.r, cc. 660–716), hardly mentioned it in *DRA*, and did not even write the *Epistola* which, though it is printed in the *Opera Omnia* (cc. 81–110) went under Henry VIII's name and was probably the work of Juan Luis Vives, for which see D. Birch, *Early Reformation English Polemics* (Salzburg, 1983), p. 27.

4 J.H. Newman, *Difficulties of Anglicans* (2 vols., London, 1901, reprint of standard edn.), i, p. 371. A. McGrath's recent synthesis, *Iustitia Dei: a history of the Christian doctrine of justification* (2 vols, Cambridge, 1986), provides an indispensable introduction to the whole subject.

5 *Ad Simplicianum, passim* (*PL* 40, pp. 101–48). Augustine remarked in his *De*

Praedestinatione Sanctorum (*PL* 44, p. 966) that his replies to Simplicianus had providentially constituted a refutation of Pelagius in advance. See also McGrath, *Iustitia Dei*, i, pp. 24–5.

6 For the controversy, see P. Brown, *Augustine of Hippo* (London, 1968), chs. 29–33, pp. 340–407.

7 McGrath, *Iustitia Dei*, i, pp. 30–1.

8 Bernard, *De Gratia et Libero Arbitrio* (*PL* 182, pp. 1001–30); Lombard, *Sententiae*, Spicilegium Bonaventurianum 4 (2 vols., Rome, 1971–81), lib. II, dist. xxv–xxvii (vol. i, pp. 461–91).

9 McGrath, *Iustitia Dei*, i, p. 74.

10 Pelagius's *Libellus Fidei ad Innocentium* was cited in Lombard's *Sententiae* as a work of Jerome's: lib. II, dist. xxviii, cap. iv (vol. i, p. 491); and dist. xxxvi, cap. vi (vol. i, p. 542). Lombard himself defused this strong assertion of free will, but not all his followers were so cautious. We shall see below that a work of the Semipelagian Gennadius of Marseilles was widely ascribed to Augustine.

11 McGrath, *Iustitia Dei*, i, pp. 86–7, 90 and 111–18.

12 The debate on late medieval Augustinianism is summarised by D.C. Steinmetz in *Misericordia Dei: the theology of J. von Staupitz in its late medieval setting*, SMRT 4 (Leiden, 1968), pp. 30–4; and by H.A. Oberman, *Masters of the Reformation* (Cambridge, 1981), ch. 6, pp. 64–110. The most judicious treatment is the appendix to D.R. Janz's *Luther and Late Medieval Thomism: a study in late medieval anthropology* (Waterloo, Ontario, 1983), pp. 158–65.

13 McGrath, *Iustitia Dei*, i, pp. 86–7. Janz, *Luther and Thomism*, pp. 57–8. J.A. Weisheipl, *Friar Thomas D'Aquino* (Oxford, 1975, p. 249.

14 Janz, *Luther and Thomism*, p. 67. McGrath, *Iustitia Dei*, ii, p. 64.

15 The 'official' theologian of the Augustinians was Giles of Rome, an exponent of 'facientibus quod in se est'.

16 Oberman, *Masters*, p. 69.

17 Steinmetz, *Misericordia Dei*, pp. 33–4. McGrath, *Iustitia Dei*, i, p. 87.

18 Oberman, *Harvest*, p. 177. F. Clark has criticised the way Oberman applied this term to Biel. See his 'A New Appraisal of Late-Medieval Theology', *Gregorianum* 46 (1965), pp. 733–65, esp. pp. 741–51. See also McGrath, *Iustitia Dei*, i, pp. 77–8.

19 Janz, *Luther and Thomism*, pp. 126–39. Cajetan held an intermediate position, affirming the possibility of morally good acts without the help of grace, but denying the possibility of preparation for justifying grace without that help.

20 Augustine, *Opera Omnia* (10 vols., Basel: Amerbach, 1490–1506).

21 For Staupitz see Steinmetz, *Misericordia Dei, passim*, esp. pp. 30, 73 and 173. For Colet see P.I. Kaufman, *Augustinian Piety and Catholic Reform: Augustine, Colet, and Erasmus* (Mercer University Press, 1982), ch. 3, esp. pp. 69–73.

22 McGrath, *Iustitia Dei*, ii, p. 11.

23 See, e.g., McGrath, *Iustitia Dei*, ii, pp. 5–9 and *Luther's Theology of the Cross* (Oxford, 1985), p. 146. Luther *WA* 54, pp. 185–6. McGrath dates this change around 1515, but warns, wisely, against equating Luther's personal development with the development of Protestant thought as a whole.

24 H. Denifle, *Die abendländischen Schriftausleger bis Luther über Justitia Dei und Justificatio* (Mainz, 1905), *passim*.

25 Luther's preface to his *Opera Omnia*, *WA* 54, pp. 185–6 is the key text for this problem. It shows that Luther regarded his insights as having been attained before his second course of lectures on the Psalms. What is less clear is whether they were

attained before, during or after his lectures on Romans, Galatians and Hebrews (1515–18). L.C. Green opts for 1518–19 on the basis of a comment of Luther's in 1539 that he had been a 'son of Hagar' for thirty-five years (i.e., 1483–1518) before becoming a 'son of Sarah' (*WA* 47, p. 682); and of a similar comment in his *Von den Konzilien und Kirchen* (*WA* 50, p. 596) that he had been teaching the truth for twenty years. See L.C. Green, *How Melanchthon Helped Luther Discover the Gospel* (Fallbrook, 1980), p. 40. But it is risky to rest an argument on 'round number' dates.

26 McGrath, *Iustitia Dei*, ii, p. 186.

27 D.R. Janz finds understandable convergences between the late Aquinas and the early Luther, but devotes only three pages to Luther's writings after 1517, considering only *De Servo Arbitrio* (1525) and *Disputatio de Homine* (1536). See *Luther and Thomism*, p. 58.

28 *WA* 54, p. 186. L.C. Green comments on this text, 'it is questionable whether Augustine really stood so close to the Reformational Luther' (*Melanchthon*, p. 180, n. 46).

29 D.B. Fenlon rightly picks this out as one of Luther's most original contributions to theology. See his *Heresy and Obedience in Tridentine Italy: Cardinal Pole and the Counter Reformation* (Cambridge, 1972), p. 13.

30 Augustine, *Contra Duas Epistolas Pelagianorum ad Bonifacium*, bk. 1, ch. 13 (*PL* 44, pp. 526–3).

31 Brown, Augustine, p. 280.

32 'In omni opere bono, iustus peccat'. See *ALC* 31, fol. 167.r (c. 608), citing Luther.

33 *ALC* 31, fol. 171.v (c. 617), cites from Luther, 'omnis persona simul peccatrix est, dum iusta est'.

34 *WA Tischreden* 1, no. 347 (p. 140), which does not identify the citation.

35 On one occasion Luther wrongly ascribed it to *De Natura et Gratia* (*WA* 2, p. 495). It is from *De Nuptiis et Concupiscentia*, bk. i, ch. 25 (*PL* 44, p. 430): 'dimitti concupiscentiam carnis in Baptismo, non ut non sit, sed ut in peccatum non imputetur'.

36 Luther ascribed this, correctly, to *Retractationes*, bk 1, ch. 19 in his *Rationis Latomianae Confutatio* of 1521 (*WA* 8, p. 93), where it reads 'Omnia ergo mandata facta deputantur, quando quicquid non fit, ignoscitur' (*PL* 32, p. 615). Augustine is arguing not that every act is to some extent a sin, nor that the just are permanently in a state of sin, nor that the commandments are each impossible, but that it is impossible for people to fulfil the law in its totality and to live in this world without sinning daily. The context is the petition 'Forgive us our trespasses' in the Lord's Prayer. He makes the same point at, e.g., *Contra Duas Epistolas*, bk 1, ch. 13 (*PL* 44, p. 563).

37 *ALC* 3, fol. 54.r (c. 378), 'Quanquam de peccato originali variae sint apud scholasticos opiniones, ego tamen libenter Augustinum sequor.' Scarisbrick ('Conservative Episcopate', pp. 355–6) and Surtz (*Works and Days*, p. 475, n. 1) are right to emphasise Fisher's Augustinianism.

38 *ALC* 36, fol. 199.r (c. 672).

39 *ALC* 36, fol. 215.r (c. 704), 'ex disputatoribus nonnulli, quorum iudiciis ipse non subscribo, sentiant eum, qui mortali peccato gravatus sit, absque speciali auxilio gratiae, posse bene moraliter agere, ac proinde se praeparare posse, non quidem ut ex merito, sed ut ex congruo, deus ei sit daturus gratiam'. Despite this, Surtz seems to regard Fisher as an exponent of 'meritum ex congruo', *Works and Days*, pp. 206 and 234.

40 *EW*, p. 327, perhaps referring obliquely to J. Hoogstraeten's *Cum Divo Augustino Colloquia* (2 vols., Cologne: Quentell 1521–2), a work contrasting Augustine and Luther. See also *ALC* 1, fol. 37.r (c. 344).

41 *ALC* 36, fol. 212.v (c. 706), 'Haec Augustinus ... Quem auctorem ob id toties produco, quod eum tuae sententiae suffragatorem facis.'

42 As in Fisher's works generally. Surtz, *Works and Days*, p. 457, n. 1.

43 *ALC*, fols. 43.v, 176.r, 197.v, 37.v, 215.v, 44.r, 48.v, 210.r and 42.r (cc. 356, 626, 668, 344, 705, 357, 367, 693 and 353), listed here in order of composition.

44 *EW*, p. 259, citing it as 'Iubes domine: & iube quod vis. Lorde graunte me to fulfyll thy commaundement, & commaunde me what thou wylte, as who sayth the wyll of god can not be kepte without his helpe.' See also McGrath, *Iustitia Dei*, i, p. 71.

45 *EW*, p. 100.

46 *EW*, p. 98.

47 *EW*, pp. 346–7.

48 Latomus, *Opera Omnia* (Louvain: Gravius, 1550), fols. 25.r–6.r.

49 Catharinus, *Apologia*, pp. 284–5 ('sola fides'); and pp. 75, 78 and 319 (free will).

50 *ALC* 1, fol. 22.v (c. 314), 'De Sacramentis, an gratiam necne conferant, quia Rex illustrissimus copiose tecum egit, nihil nunc dicam ... Sed principio convellendus est error, qui tibi nimium insedit, nempe de fide, cui cuncta tribuens, nihil operibus facis reliqui.'

51 *ALC* 36, fols. 193.v–221.r (cc. 660–716). It bulked so large in his appreciation of Luther's teaching that it is surprising that it merited no more than a passing mention in the sermon of 1521: '[Luther] taketh away the fredome of mans wyll, and affermeth that al thyng faylleth by necessyte '(*EW*, p. 336). Since Luther did not affirm the doctrine of absolute necessity until his *Assertio Omnium Articulorum*, Fisher must presumably have read this when he gave the sermon, a further indication that he was already at work on *ALC* by May 1521. His perception of the importance of the issue must have been assisted by Luther's comment 'in hoc articulo, qui omnium optimus et rerum nostratum summa est' (*ALC* 36, fol. 218.r, c. 709).

52 *ALC* 23, fols. 123.v–4.r (cc. 522–3), 'Nam error, quem de fide concepit, errores alios sibi peperit innumeros.' See also *ALC* 25, fol. 142.v (c. 560), 'Tu supra fidem solam vis Ecclesiam aedificari'.

53 *ALC* 1, fol. 23.r–v (cc. 314–16). *De Libertate Christiana* and *De Babylonica Captivitate* were published in 1520. *De Fide et Operibus* has proved impossible to identify, although the text cited from it is typical of Luther, and Fisher is generally reliable in such matters. The other three works could have been known to Fisher from a single volume, the *Lucubrationes* (Froben: Basel, 1519).

54 *ALC* 1, fols. 22.v–3.r (c. 314).

55 *WA* 54, p. 179.

56 *DRA* II, fols. XII.r–XIIII.r (cc. 119–23). *A sermon had at Paulis*, sig. C.1.r adumbrates Luther's contradictory account of faith.

57 *ALC* 1, fols. 25.v–6.r (c. 320). The passages referred to in the original edition as from *De Babylonica Captivitate* are in fact from *De Libertate Christiana* (see *WA* 7, pp. 61–2). In the *Opera Omnia* they are attributed to *De Fide Christiana*.

58 *ALC* 1, fols. 29.r–30.r (cc. 327–8). In the sermon of 1521, he had cited ten texts with the same aim. See *EW*, pp. 329–31, identified by Surtz, *Works and Days*, p. 203. Eight of these are cited in the later sixteen, as are texts adjoining the other two. This confirms the close relationship between the sermon and *ALC*.

59 Compare J. Latomus, *Opera*, fols. 5.r–6.v with *ALC* 1, fol. 28.r–9.v (cc. 325–7).

60 *ALC* 6, fol. 65.r (c. 400), 'iustificatio, sanctificatioque, duplex utraque furerit'. See Surtz, *Works and Days*, p. 205, for Robert Barnes's identification and repudiation of this view of Fisher's.

61 *ALC* 1, fol. 27.r (c. 323), 'Nam in iis omnibus locis ut satis liquet, pro spe fiduciaque Paulus fidem usurpat, magis quam pro sola credulitate.' See Kaufman, *Augustinian Piety*, p. 56, for Colet. This casts some doubt on A.G. Dickens's claim, 'the Pauline conception of faith had come to be identified with intellectual assent to credal propositions. Interpreting St. Paul, Luther is especially insistent upon the distinction between *assensus* and *fiducia*' (*The English Reformation*, p. 84). As L.C. Green has noted, emphasis on *fiducia* was common in late medieval theology (*How Melanchthon Helped*, p. 143).

62 *ALC* 1, fols. 23.v–4.r (c. 316).

63 *ALC* 1, fols. 29.r–31.r (cc. 326–30). See Augustine *De Fide et Operibus*, *PL* 40, pp. 221–12, and Augustine, *De diversis quaestionibus octoginta tribus*, q. 76 (*PL* 40, p. 89, cited at c. 330). See also *EW*, p. 328, and Surtz, *Works and Days*, p. 203.

64 *WA* 2, p. 492. Luther encapsulated his view in the phrase, 'Non iusta faciendo iustus fit, sed factus iustus facit iusta.'

65 *Nicomachean Ethics*, bk. 2, sect. 1, in *The Complete Works of Aristotle*, ed. J. Barnes (2 vols., Princeton, 1984), i, p. 1743, 'men become builders by building; lyre-players by playing the lyre; so too we become just by doing just actions'. As early as his first lectures on Romans, Luther had emphasised that the 'iustitia dei' was not to be confused with the justice of Aristotle, which derived from the practice of just actions (*WA* 56, p. 172).

66 *ALC* 1, fol. 26.r (c. 320), 'homo iustus iuste operando iustificatior evadit . . . Quarta similitudo pro nobis facit. Nam sicut faber in operis exercitio nonnullum arti suae facit incrementum, ita iustus bene operando iustitiae suae lucrum acquirit.'

67 PRO SP2/R, fol. 156.r, 'Nemo est qui non bene sibi esse cupiat quanquam non omnes ipsam beatitudinem assequantur. Quod nimirum ideo clarum est quod in rebus eam querant in quibus minime valeat inveniri. Nam alius in corporis voluptatibus alius in divitiarum copia alius in sceleribus et [illegible word] sperat eam inveniri posse.'

68 *Nicomachean Ethics*, pp. 1730–1.

69 Luther, *Operationes in Psalmos* (*WA* 5, p. 27), 'philosophi quorum nobiliores in virtute aut opere virtutis ipsam [beatitudinem] collocaverunt, quo caeteris facti infoeliciores se et huius et futurae vitae bonis pariter privarent.'

70 *ALC* 2, fol. 53.v (c. 377), 'in quantum desperationis barathrum omnes deiicias, quum sacramentis neges peccata tolli, aut quam stolidam securitatem peccatoribus suades, quum doceas fide sola, scelera quantumcunque gravissima deleri'.

71 *ALC* 1, fol. 23.r (c. 315), citing Luther, *De Fide et Operibus*, 'Fides esse nullo modo potest, nisi sit vivax quaedam et indubitata opinio, qua homo certus est super omnem certitudinem, sese placere deo.' Similar remarks from identifiable works of Luther's could be multiplied *ad nauseam*.

72 *ALC* 1, fol. 33.r (c. 335). See also *EW*, pp. 277 and 307.

73 *ALC* 10, fols. 80.v–2.v (cc. 432–7), *passim*.

74 *ALC* 1, fol. 33.r (c. 355), 'voluit immensa Christi benignitas, ut quoniam nemo per solam fidem de sua iustificatione poterit certus esse, iam per sacramenta supplerentur, quicquid fidei sufficientiae defuerit'. Compare the argument in *DVC* II, 29, fols. LII.r–III.r (cc. 905–7), which makes the sacraments compensate for the weakness of human faith.

75 *DVC* I. 6, fol. VI.r (c. 769), 'ad hoc potissimum instituta sunt [sacramenta], ut per

245

eorum usum citra ullam dubitationem, confidamus gratiam nos esse consecutos'.

76 *DVC* II. 29, fol. LIII.r (cc. 906–7), 'quum non certo constet de fide cuiusque, quandoquidem et pessimi se testantur habere fidem, profecto citra susceptionem sacramentorum, nulla potest esse gratiae certitudo'.

77 *DVC* IV. 8, fol. XCVIII.r (c. 1024), 'Adde quoque, quod nemini compertum esse potest, nisi vel per revelationem, vel per sacramentorum susceptionem, se potitum esse fide formata.'

78 Surtz draws attention to Fisher's views on certainty, and to the *DVC*'s increasing emphasis on certainty, in *Works and Days*, pp. 209–11. But he does not distinguish certainty of present grace, towards which Fisher moves, from certainty of final perseverance, which he ascribes to special revelation alone.

79 *DVC* II. 29, fol. LII.v (c. 906), 'Est igitur sacramentum nobis infallibile quoddam organum divinae efficientiae. Operatur etenim divina virtus infallibiliter gratiam in cunctis digne suscipientibus, quoties haec sacramenta (ut diximus) administrantur.' The proviso about worthy reception leaves him a way out because of possible uncertainty about one's own disposition for the sacrament.

80 PRO SP2/R, fols. 32.r 'Animat hic psalmus non mediocriter cunctos ad habendam in Christum fiduciam'; and 200.v, 'Credas primum et citra dubitationem ullam ad semen Christi te pertinere.'

81 PRO SP2/R, fol, 32.r, 'nobis tamen assentientibus et cooperantibus'.

82 Denzinger, *Enchiridion*, decree on justification, chs. 9 on certainty of grace (no. 802) and 12 on certainty of perseverance (no. 805), and canons 13–6 (nos. 823–6); *CT* 12, p. 692, sees Fisher cited in favour of certitude of grace by Lorenzo Mazzochio, a Servite friar, in a letter to Cardinal Marcello Cervino of Oct 1546. But Zanettini cited him against in a letter of 2 Aug 1546 (*CT* 10, p. 587).

83 PRO SP2/R, fol. 149.r, 'sacramenta quibus ipsi modo velint possint iustificari non sua, que nulla est, sed dei iusticia'.

84 *EW*, p. 238, 'the ryghtwysnes of god is not so gretly to be fered of wretched synners, namely of suche as hath taken vpon them the ryght way of lyuynge, that is to say after goddes lawes, & be truly repentaunt for theyr offences done & past, the sayd ryghtwysnes is vnto all those rather a grete helpe & socour, for almyghty god of his fydelyte & Iustice must nedes forgyue them that be confessed truly and with good wyll do penaunce for theyr synnes'.

85 PRO SP2/R, fol. 200.r, 'Et haec est generatio nova, quae grata erit in oculis dei, utpote quae per iustitiam Evangelii quam apostoli per orbem praedicabunt, iustificabitur. Inter hos et patrem, Christus mediator erit atque advocatus. Si quid recte gesserint, id ipse patri annunciabit, curabitque vicissim, ut iustitia patris illis per apostolos suos et eorum successores incessanter annuncietur.'

86 PRO SP2/R, fol. 196.r, 'Nam hauddubie sicut iustitiam suam nobis contulit, ut ipsa vere nostra fieret, ita nostra vicissim in se peccata suscepit, ut ea vere fierent ipsius propria, non sic tamen propria quod ab eo commissa fuissent, sed quod omnem conscientiae remorsum illis debitum, in se perferendum transtulisset.'

87 *ALC* 2, fol. 37.r (c. 343), 'quo posset evincere, vel in quovis opere bono peccare iustum. Nimirum ut ita de sua glorietur adinventione, qua simul in eodem peccare, pariter, et non peccare componat'; and fol. 52.v (c. 374), 'Nam quid per ista velis, ego certe vix intelligo.' Scarisbrick concluded from this latter text that Fisher genuinely failed to understand Luther on imputation ('Conservative Episcopate', pp. 382–7). Yet the former text suggests that he did indeed see what Luther was driving at, but simply thought it a contradiction in terms.

88 *ALC* 2, fol. 52.v (cc. 374–5).

89 *ALC* 35, fols. 190–1 (cc. 654–5), 'Quamobrem ut de fide quis certus esse potest, quod eam habeat, et quod eam certissime sentiat in corde suo, sic consequenter et certus esse potest, de gratia, quum sine gratia fides ipsa non sit. Porro gratia non secum ullo modo compatitur superbiae culpam, quum scriptum sit. Deus superbis resistit, humilibus autem dat gratiam. Quo fit, ut cui compertum fuerit, se gratiam habere, is identidem certus erit, se carere superbiae peccato.'

90 *ALC* 2, fols. 36.r–37.v (cc. 341–3).

91 Augustine, *De Nuptiis* (*PL* 44, p. 430), 'Hoc est enim, non habere peccatum, reum non esse peccati', cited at *ALC* 1, fol. 37.v (c. 344).

92 *ALC* 2, fol. 37. v (c. 345).

93 *ALC* 2, fols. 49.v–50.v (cc. 368–70), citing: *De Nuptiis et Concupiscentia; Contra Duas Epistolas Pelagianorum; Contra Iulianum Pelagianum*; and *De Peccatorum Meritis et Remissione.*

94 *ALC* 2, fol. 38.r (c. 345), e.g., *De Nuptiis et Concupiscentia*, bk. 1, ch. 23 (*PL* 44, p. 428); and the text cited in the following note.

95 *ALC* 2, fol. 51.r (cc. 371–2), citing *Contra Duas Epistolas*, bk. 1, ch. 13 (*PL* 44, pp. 562–3).

96 *ALC* 2, fol. 38.r (c. 345) for Fisher, and fol. 52.r (c. 374) for Luther.

97 *ALC* 2, fols. 44.v–5.v (cc. 358–60).

98 *ALC* 2, fol. 37.v (c. 344), 'Nusquam nisi in voluntate esse peccatum.'

99 *ALC* 36, fol. 195.r–v (cc. 664–5).

100 B. Lohse, 'Marginalien zum Streit zwischen Erasmus and Luther', *Luther* 1 (1975), pp. 5–24, esp. pp. 14–15. Surtz is wrong to associate this tripartite distinction with that of Altenstaig's *Vocabularius Theologie* (*Works and Days*, pp. 228 and 495, n. 30). Altenstaig, following Biel, talks of freedom *from*, rather than *to*, and his three freedoms are from sin, pain and necessity (namely, compulsion) – an entirely different triad, and without the Pauline foundation.

101 *PL* 182, p. 1005.

102 *ALC* 36, fols. 193.v–5.r (cc. 661–4), citing Augustine, Jerome, Ambrose, Leo, Tertullian, Chrysostom, Athanasius (that is, Theophylact), Damascene and Origen.

103 *ALC* 36, fol. 216.v (c. 707).

104 *ALC* 6, fol. 69.v (c. 410), 'Alioqui frustra peccatores, vel ad contiones audiendas accedunt, vel eleemosynas faciunt, aut preces fundunt, aut alia id genus opera faciunt, quibus ad ignoscendum flecti consuevit deus.'

105 PRO SP2/R, fol. 148.r, 'Docitur hoc psalmo libertas arbitrii nostri, et ex eo potissimum quod quis oblatam gratiam sponte reiiciat quum eam sequi possit modo voluerit'; and, paraphrasing Ps 35:1, 'Nulla necessitate, sed proprie voluntatis arbitrio respuens oblatam dei gratiam, secum constituit iniustus.'

106 *ALC* 36, fols. 210.r–12.v (cc. 693–5), citing Ambrose, Jerome, Leo, Origen, Chrysostom and Damascene, as well as the inevitable Augustine.

107 *ALC* 17, fol. 110.r (c. 494), 'Gratiam certe quae sola salus est animi, non conferunt indulgentiae.' For Surtz's conclusion, see *Works and Days*, p. 234. I cannot accept Surtz's claim of Fisher for the theory of 'meritum ex congruo' or his account of Fisher on the availability of grace, both of which, if true, would in fact tend to undermine his correct perception of Fisher's anti-Pelagianism.

108 *ALC* 36, fol. 215.r (c. 704), 'Sine auxilio dei qui foris pulsat, nemo posset ad gratiam parare sese.'

109 *ALC* 36, fols. 220.v (c. 715), 'prima gratia'; 219.v (c. 713), 'auxilium gratiae'; and 219.r (c. 712) 'gratia pulsans, et excitans, et (ut aiunt) praeveniens.'

110 *ALC* 36, fol. 219.r (c. 712), 'Caeterum quum adiutorium gratiae nemini defuerit, nisi penitus derelictis, quis ambigere potest, quin ante susceptionem gratiae, peccator agens quantum in se fuerit [equivalent to the standard tag 'faciens quod in se est'], per illud adiutorium vitare queat peccatum mortale: simulque bene moraliter agere?'

111 *ALC* 36, fol. 215.r (c. 704), 'ex disputatoribus nonnulli, quorum iudiciis ipse non subscribo, sentiant eum, qui mortali peccato gravatus sit, absque speciali auxilio gratiae, posse bene moraliter agere, ac proinde se praeparare posse, non quidem ut ex merito, sed ut ex congruo deus ei sit daturus gratiam'. Surtz's attempt to sign Fisher up in the same school as Altenstaig, Biel, Bonaventure and Richard of Middleton (*Works and Days*, p. 496, n. 35) seems a case of the 'monolithic' misconception of scholastic theology, ignoring the subtle distinctions between various schools of thought.

112 *ALC* 36, fol. 199.r (c. 672).

113 *ALC* 36, fol. 204.v (cc. 682–3), 'Hoc dixi propter patres, quorum sententiam sequi malui, quam scholasticorum, quum in hac re mutuo sibi pugnent. Patres enim asserunt, neminem posse quicquam boni velle sine speciali dei auxilio, nec sufficere generalem illum influxum. Nonnulli contra scholastici sic contendunt hunc sufficere, ut quis absque illo auxilio bene moraliter agere, et bonum facere posset.'

114 *ALC* 36, fol. 204.v (c. 683)

115 Bellarmine agreed with Fisher. See Surtz, *Works and Days*, pp. 224–5. It is hard to understand Surtz's difficulty with accepting Bellarmine's claim to Fisher's support on this, especially as he cites Fisher on Pharaoh. Tapper, to take a contrary example, cited Fisher as one of the leading exponents of this view before rejecting it himself, *Opera*, i, p. 210. Bellarmine, Tapper and I agree against Surtz about what Fisher actually thought.

116 *ALC* 36, fol. 212.r (c. 697), 'nemo potest invitus hac affici gratia, sed opus est, ut ultro et sua sponte quis in eam assentit'; and fol. 211.v (c. 696), of those who do not answer God's call, 'Ecce voluit Christus, et ipsi noluerunt. Quamobrem et sponte a voluntate, non absoluta necessitate, Christo resisterunt.'

117 *ALC* 1, fol. 33.r (c. 335), 'Potest equidem tanta fides esse cuipiam, et tam frugifera, ut vel sine baptismo laticis iustificetur, quemadmodum latroni contigit.'

118 *ALC* 1, fol. 27.v (c. 324), for Luther's argument.

119 *ALC* 1, fol. 33.r (c. 335) puts this in a more roundabout fashion.

120 *ALC* 11, fol. 83.r (c. 438), 'Si sola fides iustificat et tollit peccata, cur debeat absolutus credere, quod sacerdos ea remiserit pecccata? ... Adde, quod si fides integra causa fuerit remittendi peccata, quid opus esset haec sacramenta condidisse? quum causam integram et per se sufficientem, non potest effectus non evestigio concomitari. Ubertim enim ex fide iusticiam et pacem consequemur, ut iam non erit ullum Sacramentum necessarium, si Fides sola iustificat.'

121 *ALC* 36, fol. 219.v (cc. 712–13), 'Is quoniam in templo stans a longe, nolebat nec oculos in coelum attollere, sed percutiebat pectus suum, dicens, Deus propitius esto mihi peccatori, venia gratiaque donatus est, rediitque iustificatus in domum suam. Quis iam non videt, hac parabola, palam doceri, peccatorem orando, suaque scelera vindicando, caeteraque faciendo quantum in se fuerit, non modo non peccare mortaliter, verumetiam divinae gratiae praesentia sic adiuvari, ut posset bene moraliter agere, atque ita tandem promereri veniam.,

122 *ALC* 36, fol. 220.r (cc. 713–14), citing Augustine, *Ad Simplicianum*, lib. 1, q. 2 (*PL* 40, p. 112), 'In quibusdam est tanta gratia fidei, quanta non sufficit ad obtinendum regnum coelorum, sicut in catechuminis, sicut in ipso Cornelio, antequam sacra-

mentorum participatione incorporaretur Ecclesiae' and 'Per illam gratiam ... fit inchoatio quaedam conceptioni similis, quae conceptio non sufficit christiano, sed oportet eum etiam nasci, quod fit per secundam gratiam, qua quis dignus aeterna vita redditur.'

123 *ALC* 36, fol. 220.r (c. 714).

124 For the text see C.H. Turner, 'The *Liber Ecclesiasticorum Dogmatum* attributed to Gennadius', *Journal of Theological Studies* 7 (1906), pp. 78–99. Arguments in favour of Gennadian authorship are presented in C.H. Turner, 'The *Liber Ecclesiasticorum Dogmatum*: Supplenda to *J.T.S.* vii. 78–99', *Journal of Theological Studies* 8 (1907), pp. 103–14; and are convincingly corroborated by G. Morin, 'Le *Liber Dogmatum* de Gennade de Marseille et problèmes qui s'y rattachent', *Revue Bénédictine* 24 (1907), pp. 445–55.

125 *ALC* 36, fol. 220.r (c. 714), 'Manet ad quaerendam salutem arbitrii libertatem, id est rationalis voluntas, sed admonente prius deo, et invitante ad salutem'; glossed by Fisher, 'id quod sane per primam gratiam fit'.

126 Following from n. 125, 'Et mox subdit. Inicium ergo salutis nostrae, deo miserante, habemus: ut autem acquiescamus salutiferae inspirationi, nostrae potestatis est: ut adipiscamur, quod acquiescendo admonitioni cupimus, divini est muneris: ut non labamur in adepto salutis munere, solicitudinis nostrae est, et coelestis pariter adiutorii: ut labamur, nostrae potestatis et ignaviae est.' See *ALC* 36, fol. 220.r–v (cc. 714–15).

127 Following on from n. 126, 'Ecce quinque per ordinem adnotanda. Primum est initium salutis nostrae, per quod intelligit primam gratiam, qua stimulamur ad bene agendum. Secundum est assensus nostrae voluntatis, quo sequimur illam stimulationem et hunc asserit nostrae potestatis esse. Tertium est salus gratiae, qua grati Deo efficimur, quae solius Dei donantis est. Quartum est eiusdem salutis custodia, quae non solum nostra solicitudine sit, sed divino pariter adiutorio. Quintam est ab hac salute relapsus, qui sola nostra sponte, et a nobis ipsis fieri potest.' See *ALC* 36, fol. 220.v (c. 715) and Turner, '*Liber Ecclesiasticorum Dogmatum*', p. 93 (ch. 20).

128 Even Surtz, who correctly dissociates Fisher from Pelagians and Semipelagians, does not see the distance between him and the scholastics.

8 The eucharist

1 *ALC* 15, fol. 96.v (c. 466).

2 *ALC* 15, fol. 96.v (c. 466), 'Respondes ... ex hoc sacramento promitti remissionem peccatorum.' See also *DRA* V, fol. LI.r (c. 180).

3 Surtz, *Works and Days*, p. 323, where he summarises *DRA*.

4 Since even in *ALC* Fisher went back to the *De Babylonica Captivitate* for elucidation of Luther's views, it is easier for us to appreciate his refutation from the fuller version he provided in the *DRA*. *DRA* V, fol. LIIII.v (c. 185), 'legem novam a Christo latam, et eius obsignatam sanguine, cuius professores haeredes instituuntur coelestis regni'. Fisher observed that the elements of this definition answered to the five types of cause – material, formal, efficient, instrumental and final.

5 *DRA* V, fol. LV.r (c. 186), esp. 'adverte ... quam similibus Moses usus erat verbis in testamenti veteris confirmatione, his, quibus evangelistae referunt usum fuisse Christum in confirmatione novi'.

6 *DRA* VI, fols. LVIII.v–LXI.r (cc. 192–6). The Greeks were Clement, Dionysius,

Ignatius, Origen, Chrysostom and Damascene; the Latins, Tertullian, Cyprian, Jerome, Ambrose and Augustine.

7 *DVC* IV. 29, fol. CXVII.r (c. 1079), 'Non esset autem sacrificium, si nihil in ea praeter solum panem et vinum contineretur. Nam eiusmodi sacrificia iampridem repudiata fuere.'

8 *DRA* VI, fol. LXII.r–v (cc. 197–8).

9 *DRA* VI, fol. LXVI.r–v (cc. 204–5), 'Quaenam praecor est haec oblatio munda, nisi panis ipsius, qui de coelo descendit, hoc est corporis Christi sub specie panis in Eucharistia.'

10 *DRA* VI, fol. LXVI.r (c. 204). Reuchlin, *De Rudimentis*, fol. 289.v. Used by, e.g., Tapper, *Explicatio, Opera*, i, p. 247.

11 J.J. Hughes, *Stewards of the Lord: a reappraisal of Anglican orders* (London, 1970), pp. 123, 125 and 126.

12 See, e.g., *DRA* VI, fol. LXII.r (cc. 197–8), 'Neque duo tamen paschata sunt, aut duo sacrificia, sed unum pascha, unumque sacrificium. Quandoquidem alterum alterius est repraesentativam' – a text Hughes himself cites (*Stewards*, p. 124).

13 *DVC* V. 7, fol. CXLIIII.r (c. 1154), 'Chrysostomus docet, idem hoc sacrificium esse cum sacrificio crucis, quod hic inchoatum, ibi complebatur.' This text in fact underlay Henry VIII's comment 'nam in cruce consummavit sacrificium, quod inchoavit in coena'. See *Assertio*, sig. f.4.v (c. 27). This the last supper (*Stewards*, p. 126).

14 *DRA* VI, fol. LXIIII.v (c. 201), 'Missa est caeremonia seu functio sacerdotis, dum in altari conficitur Eucharistia, simul et Christi crucifixi sacrificium annunciatur', a text that Hughes himself cites (p. 125). Unfortunately, Hughes's translation of the technical term 'conficitur Eucharistia' as 'performs the eucharist' obscures the fact that these words refer precisely to the moment of consecration.

15 *DRA* VI, fols. LXIIII.v (c. 202), 'Eucharistiae consecratio, vere sacrificium est'; and LXIIII.r (c. 200), 'quoties panem et vinum consecramus, toties et sacra facimus, ac sacrificamus, omninoque sacrificium agimus'.

16 *DVC* V. 1, fol. CXXXVIII.r (c. 1136), 'Unum enim erat utrobique sacrificium, propter quod et verbo praesentis temporis usus est uterque Evangelista.'

17 See below, note 21.

18 PRO SP2/R fol. 192.v, 'holocaustum intelligo sacrificium altaris, quod ab omnibus Missam audientibus offerri debet, cum uberi devotionis pinguedine'.

19 *DVC* II. 17, fol. XLI.v (c. 873), 'pergit explicans quem in modum fieri potest, ut illa hostia quae pro nobis in cruce fuerat oblata, prorsus eadem sit, cum hac quam nos offerimus quotidie'.

20 *DVC* II. 17, fol. XLI.v (c. 873), 'Nonne per singulos dies offerimus? Offerimus quidem, sed ad recordationem facientes mortis eius. Et una est haec hostia, non multae. Quomodo una est et non multae? Et quia semel oblata est illa, oblata est in sancta sanctorum: hoc autem sacrificium exemplar est illius, idipsum semper offerimus. Nec nunc quidem alium Agnum, crastina alium, sed semper idipsum.' See Chrysostom, Homily 17 on Hebrews, *PG* 43, p. 131. The passage goes on still more unequivocally.

21 *DVC* III. 2, fol. LXV.v (c. 934), 'Quia non hanc sanctificant homines, sed Christus, qui ante sacrificaverat. Quemadmodum verba quae locutus est Christus cadem sunt quae sacerdotes nunc quoque pronunciant, ita et oblatio eadem est. Et paulo post. Et hoc igitur Christi corpus, et illud est. Qui autem hoc illo minus aliquid habere putat, ignorat Christus esse qui nunc etiam adest atque operatur' (Chrysostom, Homily 2 on 2 Timothy, *PG* 52, p. 612). Fisher comments, 'Ubi

vides lector Christum adesse, et oblationem hanc sacrificare, in qua et corpus eius ex pane conficitur, et offertur Deo. Sed neque plus offert in ea oblatione maximi meriti sacerdos, quam ille qui nullius meriti est.'

22 *SSD* I, fols. II.v–VI.r (cc. 1234–9), citing Augustine, Jerome, Ambrose, Hilary, Arnobius, Cyprian and Tertullian; and Damascene, Gennadius, Cyril, Chrysostom, Gregory Nazianzen, Basil, Eusebius, Origen, 'Hegesippus' (a version of Josephus), Ignatius, Polycarp, 'Dionysius', Philo Judaeus (from Eusebius) and Clement (to James, spurious). See Surtz, *Works and Days*, pp. 325–8 for a summary of *SSD*.

23 *SSD* II, ax. 1–10, fols. VIII.v–XXIII.v (cc. 1243–67).

24 Denzinger, *Enchiridion*, no. 701, pp. 258–9, Decretum pro Armenia.

25 Tapper, *Explicatio Articulorum*, in *Opera*, ii, art. 17, pp. 268–9.

26 *SSD* II, ax. 7–9, fols. XV.v–XX.v (cc. 1255–62). Jerome is cited (c. 1262) from his commentary on Isaiah describing ordination as 'non solum ad imprecationem vocis, sed ad manus impositionem impletur' (*PL* 24, p. 569).

27 Luther, *De Abroganda Missa Privata* (*WA* 8, p. 415), 'At mediator et doctor Christianorum praeter Christum nullus est.'

28 *SSD* III, fol. XXIX.v (c. 1277).

29 *SSD* III, fol. XXX.v (cc. 1278–9). Surtz, *Works and Days*, pp. 43–4.

30 *SSD* III, fols. XXX.v–XXXI.r (c. 1279), 'hanc dialecticam negativam velut imperitam et inefficacem saepius explosimus'.

31 *SSD* III, fol. XXXII.v (cc. 1281–2).

32 *SSD* III, fol. XXXIII.r (c. 1282).

33 *SSD* III, fol. XXXI.r (c. 1279); see also I, fol. VI.r–v (c. 1240). See Surtz, *Works and Days*, p. 125.

34 *SSD* III, fol. XXXII.v (c. 1281). Erasmus, *Novum Instrumentum* (1516), p. 279, follows the Vulgate, 'Ministrantibus autem illis domino et ieiunantibus.' But his second edn., *Novum Testamentum* (Basel: Froben, 1519), p. 275, which Fisher here follows, translates 'Cum autem illi sacrificarent domino, ieiunarentque.'

35 R.C. Trench, *Synonyms of the New Testament* (seventh edn., London, 1871), pp. 118–20.

36 PRO SP2/R, fol. 192.v, 'Quicquid operis boni pure propter deum fit, sacrificium est, quod si fiat in gratia, nunquam excidat e memoria dei.'

37 *CT* VI. 3, p. 430. Salmeron's Jesuit colleague, Lainez, also use it: *CT* VII. 1, p. 380.

38 Luther to the church of Strasbourg, in *Epistolarum Farrago* (Hagenau. Secci, 1525), sig. K.5.r–v.

39 B. Pirckheimer, *De Vera Christi Carne et Vero Eius Sanguine* (Nuremberg, 1526). See Surtz, *Works and Days*, pp. 337 and 512, n.1. J. Clichtove, *De Sacramento Eucharistiae contra Oecolampadium* (Paris: Colinaeus, 1527).

40 Cochlaeus, *Funff Vorrede*. Surtz summarises the prefaces only, for much the same reasons (*Works and Days*, pp. 339–43).

41 *DVC* I, preface, sig. BB.4.v–5.r (pp. 749–50).

42 *DVC* I, preface, sig. BB.5.v (p. 751). Surtz notes other cases alleged by Fisher (*Works and Days*, p. 344) but does not investigate them.

43 *DVC* II. 17, fol. XLI.v (c. 873) for Chrysostom; IV. 35, fols. CXXIX.v–CXXX.r (c. 1117) for Jerome; IV. 12, fols. C.v–CI.r (cc. 1032–3) for Cyprian; and IV. 3, fols. XCII.v–XCIII.r (c. 1009), for Ignatius.

44 *DVC* IV. 31, fol. CXXIIII.r (c. 1100) correctly notes an omission from bk 8 of *De Trinitate*. The words omitted by Oecolampadius are 'carnalibus manentem per carnem Christum habemus, victuris nobis'. In Erasmus's edition, *Divi Hilarii*

Pictavorum Episcopi Lucubrationes (Basel: Froben, 1523), i, p. 137, line 11 ends 'nobis' and the omitted words occupy almost all of line 12. The omission is clearly a copying error, and does not make the text tell any less heavily against Oecolampadius.

45 *DVC* IV. 4, fol. XCIII.r (c. 1010).

46 *DVC* IV. 37, fol. CXXX.v (cc. 1119–20). Cited from Gratian, *Decretum*, pt 2, causa 1, q. 1, ch. 94 (see Friedberg, *Corpus Iuris Canonici*, i, p. 391, which notes that the ascription to Augustine is spurious). Oecolampadius gave no reference, but Fisher is probably correct in tracing it to the *Decretum*. The text was a commonplace. See E.J.D. Douglas, *Justification in Late Medieval Preaching: a study of John Geiler of Keysersberg*, SMRT 1 (1966), pp. 86–7, where the idea is traced to Origen.

47 *DVC* II, preface, fol. XXIX.r (p. 839), 'Tametsi multis variis nominibus appelletur deus (quemadmodum in libro de divinis nominibus Dionysius tradit).' Swietlicki notes that medieval Spanish Cabbalists argued for the Trinity from the many names for God in the Old Testament (*Spanish Christian Cabbala*, p. 4). Surtz summarises this preface (*Works and Days*, p. 340) without appreciating either its originality or its influence.

48 *DVC* II, preface, fols. XXIX.r–XXXII.v (pp. 839–43).

49 *DVC* I. 4, fol. IV.v (c. 764), 'quis non videt, quantum istud omnes humani ingenii vires transcendat'.

50 Compare *Summa Theologiae*, 3a. pars, q. 73, art. 4, 'Utrum convenienter hoc sacramentum pluribus nominibus nominetur?' Blackfriars edition (60 vols., London, 1963–6), lviii, pp. 14–17.

51 J.F. McCue, 'The Doctrine of Transubstantiation from Berengar through the Council of Trent', *Harvard Theological Review* 61 (1968), pp. 385–430, at p. 430.

52 *DVC* II, preface, fol. XXXII.r (p. 843), 'Sunt enim vere exemplaria corporis exanguis, quod in cruce pependit, pariter et sanguinis qui in eadem fusus erat. Sunt et vere exemplaria colligationis Christianorum adinvicem, velut membrorum sub uno capite. Sunt demum, et examplaria futurorum: nimirum ipsius beatitudinis futurae.'

53 Tertullian, *Adversus Marcionem* IV, in *Opera*, ed. Rhenanus, p. 291 (*PL* 2, p. 492), 'acceptum panem, et distributum discipulis, corpus illum suum fecit: hoc est corpus meum, dicendo, id est, figura corporis mei'. Discussed at *DVC* II. 20–5, fols. XLIV.v–XLVIII.v (cc. 881–94).

54 As Newman observes, Tertullian's remarks 'admit of a Catholic interpretation when the Catholic doctrine is proved, but ... *prima facie* run counter to that doctrine'. See *An Essay on the Development of Christian Doctrine* (London, 1845), p. 24. Much depends on whether emphasis is placed on 'figura corporis mei', or 'corpus illum suum fecit', equally apodictic and wholly contradictory comments.

55 *DVC* II. 25, fol. XLVIII.v (c. 894).

56 *DVC* V. 18, fol. CLIII.r (c. 1180), 'Quod tandem asseris hoc sacramentum ob id institui potius, ut spectetur ex eo frangi corpus, et fundi sanguinem, quam ut in eo vere corpus et sanguis esse credantur, apertissimus error est. Nam ita, spectare tantum sufficeret.'

57 *DVC* II. 27, fol. L.v (c. 899), 'Nam agnus ille iugulatus et assus, longe maiorem habet energiam in repraesentando Christi mortem et passionem, quam panis et vini spectaculum.'

58 *DVC* IV. 27, fol. CXV.r–v (c. 1075), 'At haec nihilo magis praestat panis ille tuus et vinum, quam si quis imaginem crucifixi contempletur, atque meditetur ex illa pictura, charitatem illam eximiam, qua vel pater ille filium suum unigenitum, unice

dilectum, pro nobis miseris ad crucis mortem dedit, vel qua filius ipse corpore suo tenerrimo, pro nostris sceleribus expiandis tam horrendum pertulit supplicium. Et certe mihi multo magis conferret contuitus eiusmodi picturae, quam visibilium specierum panis et vini, si nihil aliud subesse crederem.'

59 *Ibid.*, 'Sed quum indicibilem illam Christi benignitatem consydero, qua se praesentem exhibere dignatur sub illo sacramento, qui possem adeo durus esse, ut non protinus amore incalescat animus, et ardenter affectem, hoc tam incomparabili cibo refici.'

60 *DVC* III, preface, fol. LVII.r–v (pp. 917–18).

61 *DVC* III, preface, fols. LVI.v–LVII.r (p. 917). Compare preface to bk V, see below, p. 141 and previous note.

62 *DVC* III, preface, fols. LVII.v–LVIII.r (pp. 918–19). Compare preface to bk IV, see below, next paragraph.

63 *DVC* III, preface, fols. LVIII.r–LX.v (pp. 919–23).

64 *DVC* III, preface, fols. LX.v–LXI.r (pp. 923–4).

65 *DVC* III, preface, fol. LXI.r–v (pp. 924–5), 'Et sane quis attente consyderet profectus et lapsus atque reformationes, quae saepius in ecclesia contingerunt, comperiet, lapsuum quidem causam fuisse neglectum et abusum huius sacramenti: contra vero, profectibus et reformationibus semper fidelem cultum est devotam eiusdem sacramenti frequentationem profuisse magnopere.' The remaining five corroborations are merely converses of some of the previous nine, arguing that Oecolampadius's interpretation cannot boast various kinds of support.

66 *DVC* IV, preface, fols. LXXXV.r–LXXXVI.v (pp. 991–4).

67 *DVC* IV, preface, fols. LXXXVI.v–LXXXVIII.v (pp. 994–7).

68 *DVC* IV, preface, fol. LXXXVIII.v (pp. 996–7). See Bessarion, *Oratio de Sacramento Eucharistiae* (Strasbourg: Schurer, 1513), sig. A.8.v. The argument from liturgy was taken further by Tunstall in *De Veritate*, fols. 35.v–6.r (on the liturgies of Chrysostom and Basil). He lent Greek texts of these liturgies to Fisher, see *DVC* III, preface, fol. LXIIII.r (p. 928).

69 *DVC* V. 22, fol. CLIII.v (c. 1185). Modern critics have mostly concluded that *De Sacramentis* is authentic. See H. Chadwick, 'Ego Berengarius', *Journal of Theological Studies* 40 (1989), pp. 414–45, at p. 420.

70 *DVC* IV. 1, fols. XC.r–XCI.v (cc. 1001–5).

71 *Summa Theologiae*, 3a. pars, q. 65, art. 4, resp. 2 (Blackfriars lvi, pp. 154–7), where Thomas cites Augustine for the spiritual interpretation. Cajetan agrees in his commentary. Even these writers permitted the text to be applied metaphorically to the sacrament. Ruard Tapper cited Fisher and Cajetan as the leading modern exponents of the rival interpretations, but preferred Cajetan: *Explicatio*, art. 15, in *Opera*, ii, pp. 243–7. Luther rejected the eucharistic interpretation in *De Babylonica Captivitate* (*WA* 6, p. 502).

72 *DVC* V. 27, fol. CLIX.r (c. 1199), 'Si locus is adeo manifestus est, atque tu praetexis, iam et Christus frustra suscepisset carnem.'

73 Erasmus, *Novum Instrumentum*,, p. 208. Surtz, *Works and Days*, p. 152. This variant first appears in texts of the ninth century. See *Novum Testamentum Graece*, ed. Nestle–Aland, 26th edn. (Stuttgart, 1979), p. 297.

74 This argument was first introduced in *ALC* 16, fol. 104.v (c. 482), in support of the sacrifice of the mass: 'Nec frustra geminatur hic verbum istud, dabo. Semel enim dicitur, pro datione carnis sub specie panis: ac rursum pro carnis immolatione.'

75 *DVC* V, preface, fol. CXXXII.r–v (pp. 1125–6), citing Chrysostom, Cyril, Cyprian, Origen, Hilary and Augustine.

76 *DVC* V, preface, fol. CXXXIII.r–v (pp. 1127–8).

77 For which authors see G. Macy, *The Theologies of the Eucharist in the Early Scholastic Period* (Oxford, 1984).

78 PRO SP2/R, fol. 201.v, 'At inquies, ego sacerdos non sum, ut sacram Eucharistiam cotidie sumam. Quid tum? An non credis in Eucharistia corpus et sanguis vere contineri? Istud credas, atque Missae devotus intersis, certus esto sacrae illius Mensae te factum esse participem. Sicut enim in tuo corpore, non a pede, non a manu, non ab alio quovis membro, sed ab ore solo cibus editur, qui singula corporis tui membra vegetat. Sic et in Missa, quanquam solus sacerdos edere videatur Eucharistiam, robur tamen eius commestionis ad singulos circumstantes hauddubie dirivatur. Atque hoc est quod Augustinus. Crede et manducastis.' See Augustine, *In Evangelium Ioannis*, tractatus 25, *PL* 35, p. 1602.

79 *DVC* III. 21, fol. LXXXI.v (c. 982), 'Sed statue duos, qui parem habeant fidem, quorum alter pie frequentet esum huius incomparabilis cibi, alter minime, non erit ambiguum, quin illius animus, qui frequentaverit multo delicatius, et solidius impinguabitur.'

80 *DVC* V. 17, fol. CLII.r (c. 1178), 'Verum quidem est quod fide et dilectione spiritualiter edamus, sed haec fides, nisi praeterea vero corporis esu corroboretur, statim deperit et evanescit.'

81 *DVC* IV. 29, fol. CXVIII.v (c. 1085), 'Cyrillus affirmat, eos qui rarius communicant, magnam amittere gratiam.' For Cyril on frequent communion, see E. Gebremedhin, *Life-Giving Blessing: an inquiry into the eucharistic doctrine of Cyril of Alexandria*, Studia Doctrinae Christianae Upsaliensia 17 (Uppsala, 1977), p. 95. Gebremedhin also concludes that Cyril's doctrine of real presence is an inevitable corollary of his doctrine of the Incarnation, in which Christ's *body* is seen as essential to his saving work (*Life-Giving Blessing*, ch. 5, pp. 75–85).

82 *DVC* IV. 8, fol. XCVII.v (c. 1022), 'At his verbis non prohibuit Augustinus esum sacramenti, ad quod alibi toties nos invitat.'

83 BL Arundel MS 152, fol. 279.v, printed by Van Ortroy, *Vie*, X, p. 141, 'Scripsit decem considerationes de fide, de spe et de charitate ad exhortandas hominum mentes ad eucharistiam maiori cum devotione suscipiendam.'

84 PRO SP6/9, fols. 159–64. See *LP* 8. 887 (5). Every leaf testifies to the eucharistic orientation of the piece. See, e.g., fol. 159.v, 'Nam ex coti[dia]no usu sacramenti huius, Christi sanctitatem imbibimus et ab ea sanctificamur.'

85 PRO SP6/9, fol. 164.r, 'totus animus per fidem clarius illustretur, per spem validius corroboretur, per charitatem denique magis ac magis accendatur et inflammetur atque ita tandem in seipso deficiat ac liquefiat in amorem Christi, absorbeatur quod transformetur in eundem penitus'. Sections 6, 8 and 9 are found at fols. 161.r, 160.r, and 159.v respectively.

86 PRO SP6/9, fol. 159.v, 'ex huius sacramenti [coti]dian[o usu . . .] iustificari ut Christi iusticia qua cum edimus nostra fi[at iustici]a. Nam que iusticia maior aut consummatior esse potest quam ipsius [Christ]i? Quare si comparuerimus Christi iusticia coram ipsius patre nihil ipse condempnacionis in nobis inveniet.' The poor condition of the manuscript upsets the grammar of the passage, but its gist is clear.

87 *DRA* V, fol. LI.r (c. 180), 'Nostram enim unionem cum Christo significat, et eandem cum deo patre non minus efficaciter praestat.'

88 *DVC* IV. 32, fol. CXXVI.r (c. 1106), 'si secunda communicatio sufficeret, nemo hominum est, qui non communicaret Christo'.

89 *DVC* VI. 32, fol. CXXV.v (c. 1104), 'Ipse igitur dei filius nostram in se suscipiens carnem, nostram naturam sibi communem fecit, atque carnem et sanguinem, ex

quibus et nos constamus, participavit sibi. Nos autem vicissim per carnem et sanguinem eius, quibus in eucharistia vescimur et potamur, ipsius participes efficimur atque ei communicamus.'

90 *DVC* IV. 32, fol. CXXVII.r (c. 1108).

91 Fisher expounds Hilary's view at *DVC* IV. 31, fols. CXXII.v–CXXIIII.v (cc. 1097–1101).

92 *DVC* III. 20, fol. LXXX.v (cc. 978–9).

93 *DVC* II, preface, fol. XXX.v (p. 842), 'non panis qui vadit in secessum, (ut Augustini verbis utar) sed supersubstantialis, qui nos convertit in Christum'.

94 *DVC* IV. 21, fol. CVIII.v (c. 1056).

95 *DVC* IV. 20, fol. CVIII.r (c. 1054).

96 *DVC* III. 16, fol. LXXVII.r (c. 968), 'Animae enim nunc credendo manducant, sicut angeli contemplando', citing Oecolampadius, *De Genuina Expositione* (n.p., n.d.), sig. E.4.v.

97 PRO SP2/R, fol. 200.v, 'Primum est animi cibus, nempe scripturae sacrae quibus animus aeque diligenter pascendus est atque materiale pane corpus.'

98 *DVC* III. 16, fol. LXXVII.r (c. 968), 'incarnatum verbum, quum in eucharistia sumitur'.

99 *DVC* V, preface, fol. CXXXVII.v (c. 1136).

100 *DVC* III. 20, fol. LXXX.v (c. 980), 'totus homo rapitur et transformatur in Christum. Sed et mentes piorum ex praesentia carnis huius velut adipe quodam, et pinguedine devotionis replentur, et saginantur ineffabili quadam suavitate.' See also III. 15, fol. LXXV.v (c. 964), 'ipsa [caro] potius totum hominem nostrum, ad se rapit atque transformat, et (ut diximus) incorporat ipsi Christo'.

101 In fact the works from which this theme took its origin were wrongly attributed to Bernard, but Fisher himself would have accepted their authenticity.

102 M.A. Screech, *Ecstasy and the Praise of Folly* (London, 1980), p. 125. For the Bernardine element in Erasmus's theology, see *Ecstasy*, p. 167.

103 Screech, *Ecstasy*, p. 128, 'ad aeterna, ad invisibilia, ad spiritualia rapitur'.

104 Screech, *Ecstasy*, pp. 206–10. Screech notices the connection of the translation with Fisher, but is unaware of the resonances of this motif with Fisher's eucharistic theology. Erasmus's emphasis on synaxis was not as distinctive as Screech seems to believe. His remark 'For many of his readers even the word synaxis was troublingly exotic' (p. 118) needs some qualification in view of the fact that Aquinas himself used it (*Summa Theologiae*, 3a. pars, q. 73, art.4; Blackfriars, lviii, pp. 14–5).

105 Even Screech concludes that Erasmus, while convinced of the real presence, was unhappy with the concept of transubstantiation (*Ecstasy*, p. 123). Screech cites Erasmus as saying that the Church had defined transubstantiation at a relatively late date (*Ecstasy*, p. 125). His view was thus probably that of Scotus, D'Ailly and others: he could not see any compelling arguments for the doctrine, but accepted it on the Church's authority. Fisher, following Aquinas rather than Scotus, thought transubstantiation the only rational interpretation of Christ's words.

106 H.C. Porter, 'Fisher and Erasmus', *HRR*, pp. 81–101, p. 93, says of early 1527, 'At that time Erasmus's own thinking about the Eucharist may have been closer to Oecolampadius than to Fisher.'

107 *EE* VI, ep. 1624, to Lupset, 4 Oct 1525, pp. 186–8.

108 *Divi Algerii . . . de Veritate Corporis et Sanguinis Dominici in Eucharistia*, ed. Erasmus (Freiburg im Breisgau: Faber Emmeus, 1530). In his dedication, Erasmus claimed never to have doubted the real presence: sigg. a.6.v–a.7.r, 'Equidem ante hac nunquam dubitavi de veritate corporis dominici, sed tamen nescio quo pacto ex hac

lectione mihi non parum et confirmata sententia est, et aucta reverentia.' It was published in parallel with *Guimundi Archiepiscopi Aversani de Veritate Corporis et Sanguinis Christi in Eucharistia*, ed. A. Marius (Freiburg: Emmeus, 1530).

109 As Bridgett did, *Blessed John Fisher*, p. 130, suggesting that *DVC* changed Erasmus's mind.

9 The inspiration and translation of scripture

1 *EE* VII, ep. 1932, from John Crucius, 28 January 1528, p. 296, 'Variatum est inter Roffensem et Pacaeum ob translationem Septuaginta etiam dentatis chartis, pressis tamen, vetus esse tibi non dubito, quum acciderit Augusto nuperrimo, dum adhuc pene domestica cum Pacaeo mihi esset consuetudo, apud Sionitas, ad quos a morbo divertaverat.'

2 Allen's conjecture was followed by Pace's biographer, Jervis Wegg, in *Richard Pace: Tudor diplomat* (London, 1932), p. 276; and by Virginia Murphy, 'The debate over Henry VIII's first divorce', p. 22.

3 *I diarii di Marino Sanuto*, ed. F. Stefani, G. Berchet and N. Barrozzi (58 vols., Venice, 1879–1903), 45 (1896), p. 631: 'Siamo stati a Syon a visitatione del reverendo Pazeo, qual fa una vita in quel bel luoco beata. Si sta nel suo habito clerical circumdato da tanti libri, che per me non ho veduto in una massa tanti giamai. S'e fatto optimo hebreo et caldeo; et hora con la cognition di queste lettere e intrato alla coretion del Vechio Testamento, nel qual ritrova tanti errori, et cosi nel Psalterio, ch'e cosa stupenda; ha gia coretto tutto lo Ecclesiastico, et tra pochi zorni li dara in luce. Va dietro a li profetti et secundo che sera opera dignissima, con qual si fara immortale. Come sia impresa la prima parte, daro opera che l'habiate.' See also *Calendar of State Papers, Venetian* 4, 144 (p. 78) for a less than wholly reliable paraphrase.

4 No Hebrew version of Ecclesiasticus was known until portions were discovered among the Genizah fragments in 1896.

5 It is regrettable that the corrected text of Ecclesiastes prepared by Pace does not survive.

6 *Praefatio*, sig. A.4.r, 'opinor non defuturos qui me maxima temeritate condemnabunt: quod audeam vel hiscere adversus eos, nedum errasse ostendere: quos tam multi, tanto consensu nihil preter veritatem a spiritu sancto traditam in ore habuisse contenderunt'.

7 PRO SP6/5, fols. 45–83, noted at *LP* 8. 887 (8). I owe the point about Cromwell to Professor Sir Geoffrey Elton.

8 PRO SP6/5, fol. 45.r. See fols. 46–52 for frequent use of 'rex' and 'pontifex'.

9 Axiom 24 (fols. 72–3) is in Fisher's hand. Axiom 17 survives in Fisher's hand (fol. 61) and a later scribal copy (fol. 60). Axioms 9, 10 and 11 survive in two scribal drafts, first with amendments in Fisher's hand (fols. 68–70), and then incorporating those amendments (fols. 54–6), There are heavy amendments in Fisher's hand on the sole surviving version of axiom 13 (fol. 83).

10 PRO SP6/5 fol. 53. v, 'sunt nunc complures qui postquam unam aut alteram hebdomadam literis hebraicis operam navaverint se vel ipso Hieronimo doctiores esse putant'. Compare Pace, *Praefatio*, sig. B.3.r, 'dixerit quispiam, unde hoc, quod tu, qui tribus dumtaxat diebus linguae hebraicae vacasti, constituis te omnium iudicem'.

11 Irenaeus is cited on fols. 57.v and 59.v, each time in manuscript amendments by Fisher to the scribal draft. These citations follow Erasmus's edition (*Adversus*

Haereses, Basel: Froben, 1526, p. 188), and are not found among the extracts from Irenaeus given in Eusebius's *Historia Ecclesiastica*. That the citations are added to the scribal draft increases the probability that Fisher had only just obtained a copy. See below, appendix, under Irenaeus.

12 In Axiom 19 (fols. 62–3) Fisher cites six alternative versions of the title of Ps. 9. It is inconceivable that he would have omitted Pagninus's version had he possessed it when he wrote the 'Pro Assertione.' He expressed a very high opinion of it in a memorandum for the legatine tribunal on Henry VIII's marriage in 1529. See Lambeth Palace Library MS 2342, fols. 29–30, where his version of the Hebrew Deut. 25:5 follows S. Pagninus, *Sacra Biblia*, (Lyons: du Ry, 1528), fol. 72.r, and describes it as rendered 'fideliter ad verbum'.

13 PRO SP6/5 fol. 70.r–v. Sauli's translation was published as Euthymius Zigabenus, *Commentationes in Omnes Psalmos* (Verona: Nicolinus, 1530), and is reprinted in *PG* 128. C. Eubel, *Hierarchia Catholica Medii Aevi* (8 vols., Münster and Padua, 1913–78), iii, p. 156, records the filling of Sauli's diocese of Brugnato (vacant by death) on 25 Sept. 1528. A. Oldoinus, *Athenaeum Ligusticum* (Perugia, 1680), pp. 473–5, puts his death in 1531, but must be wrong, as the preface of *Commentationes* (dated Jan. 1530) refers to Sauli as dead. However, Oldoinus notes that Sauli donated 300 Greek manuscripts to the Ospedale degli Incurabili (*Athenaeum*, p. 474). His MS of Euthymius was presumably among them, as it was still among the remnants of Sauli's collection held by the Bibliotheca della Missione Urbana of Genoa early this century. See A. Rahlfs, *Verzeichnis der griech Handschriften des Alten Testaments* (Göttlingen Nachschriften, Berlin, 1915), p. 71.

14 *Lettre d' Aristée à Philocrate*, ed. A. Pelletier (Paris, 1962), pp. 57–8, for date.

15 *Lettre d' Aristée*, pp. 72–6 for this and the LXX's Alexandrian context.

16 *Lettre d' Aristée*, pp. 78–80, for Philo, and pp. 81–95 for patristic testimonies.

17 J.N.D. Kelly, *Jerome* (London, 1975), pp. 169–70, 196 and 227 for Rufinus and the LXX; pp. 227–58 for Jerome's other quarrels with Rufinus; and pp. 217–18, 264, 266 and 271–2 for Augustine and the LXX.

18 See Jerome, e.g., 'Praefatio in Pentateuchum', in *Biblia Sacra iuxta Vulgatam Versionem*, ed. B. Fischer, I, Gribomont, H. Sparks, W. Thiele and R. Weber (2 vols., Stuttgart, 1975) i, pp. 3–4; and Augustine, *De Civitate Dei*, bks 18, ch. 42; and 15, chs. 11–13.

19 Erasmus, *Opera Omnia Hieronymi*, ii, fol. 191.r, 'Sed odiosum est, inquiunt, tot iam saeculis recepta labefactare. At quid olim septuaginta receptius. Nec tamen veritus est Hieronymus, frustra reclamantibus cum Augustino quibusdam episcopis, sua interpretatione corrigere.' According to John Caius, Erasmus lectured at Cambridge on Jerome's *Apologia adversum Rufinum* (Leader, *Cambridge*, p. 295).

20 Reuchlin, *De Rudimentis Hebraicis*, p. 548, appealed to Jerome's example, and to his explicit criticism of the LXX. Vives expressed doubt about the whole LXX legend in his notes on Augustine's *De Civitate Dei* (Basel: Froben, 1522), p. 620. Wakefield was critical in his *Oratio*, sig. M.3.r.

21 The translator was Matteo Palmerio. See *Lettre d'Aristée*, p. 42.

22 G. Pico, *Opuscula* (Venice: Bernardinus Venetus, 1498), sigs. A.1.r and I.4.v.

23 Galatinus, *De Arcanis*, lib. I, ca. 3, fol. XIII.v.

24 P. Sutor, *De Tralatione Bibliae et Novarum Reprobatione Interpretationum* (Paris: Petit, 1525), chs. 3–5.

25 *De Tralatione*, fol. XI. His only other authorities on the LXX were Platina (fol. V.v), Eusebius (VI.r), Bede (VIII.v), Peter Comestor (IX.r), Josephus (X.r) and Gregory (XII.r).

26 *De Tralatione*, ch. 5, fols. XII–XVII.
27 *De Tralatione*, fols. XVI–XVII.
28 *Adversus Petri Sutoris . . . Debacchationem Apologia* (Basel: Froben, 1525). Erasmus roundly rejected Sutor's view of the LXX: 'Non semel impudens est quod illic pronunciat Sutor, interpretationem Septuaginta fuisse ex afflatu spiritus, et stultissimis argumentis probat quod asserit' (sig. C.4.r). Sutor replied to Erasmus with an even longer *Antapologia*. (Paris: Petit, 1526).
29 *Praefatio*, sig. A.4.v, 'Dico igitur neminem unquam potuisse recte iudicare de. lxx. translatione, nisi trium linguarum hebraicae, graecae, et latinae bene esset peritus.'
30 *Praefatio*, sig. B.1.r.
31 *Praefatio*, sigg. B.1.v–2.r.
32 *Praefatio*, sig. B.2.v, 'Admisit etiam ecclesia divi Hieronymi translationem, quam cum magna nostra iactura desideramus. Nam quod haec quae eius nomine circumfertur ipsius non sit, multis evidentissimis argumentis probari potest.'
33 The analysis of these four themes is drawn from P. Benoit, 'L'inspiration des Septante après les Pères', in *L'Homme devant Dieu: mélanges offerts au Pére Henri de Lubac* I, *Theologie* 56 (1963), pp. 169–87.
34 PRO SP6/5 ax. 1, fol. 46.
35 PRO SP6/5 ax. 2, fol. 47.
36 PRO SP6/5 ax. 3, fol. 48.
37 PRO SP6/5 ax. 4–5, fols. 49–50.
38 PRO SP6/5 ax. 7, fol. 52.
39 PRO SP6/5 ax. 8, fol. 53.
40 PRO SP6/5 ax. 9, fol. 54.
41 PRO SP6/5 ax. 10, fol. 55.
42 PRO SP6/5 ax. 11–12, fols. 56 and 82. Compare fol. 82.r, 'constantem illam incolarum fidem, que et vera lex historiae est' with *EM*, sig. L.4.r, 'Si vulgi opinionem, veram gistoriae [*sic*, for historiae] legem esse putamus'. The account of this local tradition is derived from the *Cohortatio ad Graecos*, the earliest Christian writing to treat explicitly of the LXX. Its attribution to Justin Martyr is now rejected. It is unlikely that Fisher knew this work directly, as his reference to it is plainly based on Vives's notes to Augustine's *De Civitate Dei* (see above, n. 20).
43 PRO SP6/5 ax. 13, fol. 83.
44 PRO SP6/5 ax. 14, fol. 57.
45 PRO SP6/5 ax. 15, fol. 58.
46 PRO SP6/5 ax. 16, fol. 59.
47 PRO SP6/5, sol. 59.v, 'quum Iudei non ignorarint in manibus Christianorum versari editionem 70 interpretum quibus abunde statuere possent cuncta que de Christo credenda forent et nihilominus ausi sint proprias ad hunc modum viciare scripturas, quid non presumpsissent modo nulla talis editio potuisset ostendi?'
48 PRO SP6/5 ax. 17, fol. 60.
49 PRO SP6/5, ax. 20, fol. 64.
50 PRO SP6/5 ax. 21, fols. 65.r–68.v. Fisher does not acknowledge the obvious fact that since the apostles were writing in Greek there is a simple human explanation for their frequent use of the LXX.
51 PRO SP6/5 ax. 23, fols. 70–1.
52 PRO SP6/5 ax. 24, fols. 72–3.
53 PRO SP6/5 ax. 25, fols. 74–5.
54 PRO SP6/5 ax. 26, fols. 76–7, recapitulated the case.
55 *Adversus Debacchationem*, sig. K.2.

56 The anonymous translator has baffled my attempts at identification. The same version – 'Vincenti super morte filio' – is cited by Cajetan in his *Psalmi Davidici ad Hebraicam Veritatem Castigati* (Paris: Bade, 1532, orig. edn. in 1527), fol. XX.r. Fisher is unlikely to have obtained a copy of Cajetan's work, which was only completed on Easter Sunday 1527. He would probably have mentioned Cajetan by name had he already obtained it. Since Cajetan's work was derived from the Vulgate, Jerome's version and four unspecified 'recent' versions (fol. 1.r), he and Fisher were doubtless drawing on the same source.

57 PRO SP6/5 ax. 19, fol. 62. Fisher might have met Giustiniani (the exiled bishop of Nebbio), who came to England in autumn 1518 with the French embassy led by Stephen Poncher and in Oct received a donation of £20 from Henry VIII (*LP* 2 i. p. 1479). See *EE* III, p. 278 for Giustiniani's career.

58 PRO SP6/5 ax. 8, fol. 53.v.

59 PRO SP6/5 ax. 21, fols. 65–8. After the first few citations, the scribe gives up and leaves blank spaces instead. See Origen, *Commentaria in Epistolam ad Romanos*, *PG* 14, 1264; and H.B. Swete, *An Introduction to the Old Testament in Greek* (Cambridge, 1902), p. 392.

60 Surz, *Works and Days* p. 153.

61 See below, ch. 10, pp. 173–4.

62 Compare Lambeth Palace Library, MS 2342, fol. 25.r, 'Nam certum est latina nostra non minoris auctoritatis esse quam gracca vel hebraica' (see also fol. 6.r), with *DCM*, fol. 8.r–v, 'Nam latinus codex qui per ecclesiam receptus est minoris autoritatis habendus est quam aut hebraicus aut graecus.'

63 See below, ch. 10, p. 166, for his detection of an interpolation in the accepted text of Lev 18:16.

64 Erasmus, *Novum Instrumentum*, p. 7.

65 PRO SP6/5, fol. 64.r, 'Christus in evangelio Ioannis clamat Scrutamini scripturas ille sunt qui testimonium perhibeant de me. Et qui scrutarentur scripturas si non in aliqua lingua scriptas haberent quam intelligerent?'

66 PRO SP6/5 fol. 64.r, 'At male pasceretur grex cui nullus esset gustus eius pabuli quod ei porrigeretur edendum.'

67 PRO SP6/5, fol. 64.v, 'tam ex populo quam ex presidibus rarissimi essent qui linguam nossent hebraeam'.

68 PRO SP6/5, fol. 64.r, 'si nulla talis tunc fuisset translatio frustra Paulus Colossenses admonuisset ut dei verbum in ore semper haberent'.

69 PRO SP6/5, fol. 64.v, 'et presides et populum excerceri necesse fuit nimirum ut scripturas legerent et in earum lectione cotidie magis ac magis proficerent'.

70 Foxe, *Acts and Monuments*, vii, pp. 449–50. Buckenham was especially concerned by such texts as 'If thine eye offend thee, pluck it out '.

71 *EW*, p. 70, for Fisher's encouragement of reading the Psalms.

72 *DRA* XI, fols. LXXXIII.r–XCV.v (cc. 232–54), arguing, 'Diiudicationem dogmatum ad patres potius quam ad plebem spectare.'

73 T. Starkey, *A Dialogue between Pole and Lupset*, ed. T.F. Mayer, Camden Soc., 4th ser., 37 (1989), pp. 90–1. Starkey has Pole criticising the 'tyrannical' abuses of papal power on pp. 82 and 132, so perhaps his account must be read with caution. Yet the criticism smacks more of conciliarism and Catholic reformism than of Protestant or Anglican polemic, and does not attack the papacy in theory. This is not inconsistent with what we know of Pole.

74 Henry VIII, 'Epistola regia ad illustrissimos Saxonie duces', 20 Jan 1523, in *Assertio Septem Sacramentorum* (London: Pynson, 1523; *STC* 13083). See sig. b.2.v for his

advice to prevent completion of Luther's translation of the Bible, including the remark 'Nam ut bonum esse non negem, in quavis lingua legi Scripturam sacram, ita certe periculosum est ex versione legi, cuius mala fides fidem facit omnibus.' I owe the precise date for this letter to a marginal annotation by Thomas Baker, claiming the authority of the original ('Ex Autographo, in Bibliotheca Gothana'), in SJC Library, A.2.21. See also *LP* 4. i. 40, which misdates it to 20 Jan 1524.

75 T. More, *A Dialogue Concerning Heresies*, ed. T.M.C. Lawler, G. Marc'hadour and R.C. Marius (CWTM 6), pt 1, pp. 317 and 337–8, and pt. 2, pp. 690–2.

76 *Bishop Barlowe's Dialogue on the Lutheran Factions*, ed. A.M. McLean, Courtenay Library of Reformation Classics 15 (Sutton Courtenay, 1983), pp. 114–23.

77 *LP* 4. iii. 6367 (Henry's summons, 4 May 1503) and 6487 (the proclamation). See *Tudor Royal Proclamations*, ed. P.L. Hughes and J.F. Larkin (3 vols., New Haven and London, 1964–9), i, no. 129, p. 196.

78 PRO, Prerogative Court of Canterbury, Probate, Alenger, fol. 106.v (consulted on microfilm), 'I bequeith to Sir John Bothe my cousyn the text of the bibill in a great volume and the newe Testament in Englishe and the bishops boke callyd the Institution of a Christen Man.' He also owned another 'great byble' (probably English) as well as 'the bible in foure volumes' (probably an edition of Lyra's commentary).

79 See A. Fox, 'Interpreting English Humanism', in A. Fox and J. Guy, *Reassessing the Henrician Age* (Oxford, 1986), pp. 9–33.

80 *Adversus Debacchatione*, sig. K.2.v.

81 Elyot's copy is Bodleian Library 4to. W. 1. Th (2). Elyot's signature is found on the flyleaf at the front of the volume, which consists of several books of around 1530, in an original binding. The conclusion that he owned the volume is reasonable. Other evidence of a connection between Elyot and Pace is presented by C.W. Bouck in 'On the Identity of Papyrius Geminus Eleates', *Transactions of the Cambridge Bibliographical Society* 2 (1958), pp. 325–8, where she argues convincingly that Elyot was the 'Eleates' whose *Hermathena* (Cambridge: Siberch, 1522) is dedicated to Pace.

10 The controversy over Henry VIII's first marriage

1 *LP* 8. 859, question 8. His vagueness may be a result of failing memory, uncertainty about what constituted a book or, as he was under interrogation at the time, a reluctance to incriminate himself or others. See also PRO SP1/42, fol. 165.r, letter to Paul, 'Sed in hoc negocio tantum operis insumpsi pro dinoscenda veritate, ut alias nunquam insudaverim magis.'

2 Murphy, 'Debate', pp. 100–4. The first was a 'Liber' on the divorce, of which various summaries and excerpts survive in fragmentary refutations by Robert Wakefield. His second treatise, 'Licitum fuisse', compiled for the legatine tribunal in 1529, survives almost complete, and we also have excerpts from a revised version in refutations by Henry's advisers. His third work, a brief memorandum beginning 'Ne qua fiat', drawn up for that same tribunal, survives in two copies. The only published work was *DCM*, which contains a summary of an argument from a previous but now lost work. Besides these we have all but the closing section of 'Brevis Apologia', a refutation of the *Gravissimae Censurae* published by the king in 1531. This too summarises an argument from a lost work, We know also that Fisher compiled a last word on the divorce which he entrusted to a member of the Rochester Cathedral priory shortly before his arrest in 1534 (*Vie*, xii, p. 213). Even counting the versions of 'Licitum' as a single work, this gives eight books.

3 See below, pp. 175–6.
4 J. Dewhurst, 'The alleged miscarriages of Catherine of Aragon and Anne Boleyn', *Medical History* 28 (1984), pp. 49–56.
5 This account follows the chronology of E.W. Ives, *Anne Boleyn* (Oxford, 1986), pp. 108–9.
6 See, e.g., Aquinas, *Summa Theologiae*, 1a. 2ae. q. 97, art. 4, ad. 3 (Blackfriars, xxviii, p. 154).
7 *PL* 34, p. 705.
8 E.g., Ralph of Flaix, *In Leviticum* (Cologne: Cervicorn, 1536), lib. XIII, c. 4, p. 193.
9 E.g., Hugh of Saint Victor, *De Sacramentis*, lib. II, pt. xi, c. 4 (*PL* 176, p. 483).
10 G.H. Joyce, *Christian Marriage* (London, 1933), pp. 523–4, referring to Aquinas's early view, as expressed in his commentary on the Sentences. In his later *Summa* he seems to have been moving towards the view of Scotus, although he died before his *Summa* reached the subject of matrimony.
11 Joyce, *Christian Marriage*, p. 524.
12 For Peter of Paluda, see Scarisbrick, *Henry VIII*, p. 172.
13 Joyce, *Christian Marriage*, pp. 522–3 and 542.
14 Scarisbrick, *Henry VIII*, pp. 179–80.
15 Scarisbrick, *Henry VIII*, pp. 184–97, argues that Henry might have had more chance of success if he had chosen to impugn his marriage to Catherine on the grounds of an impediment of 'public honesty' (which had not been explicitly dispensed in the original bull) rather than of natural or divine law. H.A. Kelly has made much of this in his *The Matrimonial Trials of Henry VIII* (Stanford, 1976), *passim*, describing arguments based on the 'public honesty' issue as 'Henry's theology', though without demonstrating that Henry adopted them. Dr Murphy has in contrast shown that the natural law argument was crucial in Henry's mind from the start, 'Debate'. pp. 33–4.
16 Fisher to Wolsey, May 1527, in *Records of the Reformation*, i. 9 10.
17 *Vie*, x, pp. 296–7. The narrative implicitly suggests a later date for this interview, but is not in any case reliable on the chronology of the divorce. The purpose of an interview of this sort is more likely to have been to put pressure on Fisher before he had committed himself rather than to change his mind after he had done so.
18 PRO SP1/42, fol. 166.v, 'Mihi persuadeo Regem nihil velle quod legibus dei repugnet. Quod si propter illas prohibitiones leviticas conscienciae scrupulum admiserit, quis negabit illum recte facturum, si quod vere christianum et orthodoxum principem facere decet, se submiserit pontificis interpretationi.'
19 PRO SP1/42, fol. 166.v, 'Reges enim, ut plurimum propter suae potestatis amplitudinem sibi licere putant quicquid libet. Quare bene cum illis Regibus agitur, meo iudicio, qui decretis Ecclesiae se submiserint. Et hoc in eis proculdubio collaudandum est, ne alioqui ruptis habenis, faciant quod sibi libitum fuerit, modo speciem et colorem praetexere queant liciti.' This is reminiscent of Thomas More's reported remark to Cromwell, comparing the king to a lion, which would be difficult to control if it knew its own strength. See W. Roper, *The Lyfe of Sir Thomas Moore, knighte*, ed. E.V. Hitchcock, EETS, orig. ser. 197 (1935), pp. 56–7.
20 Pace to Henry VIII, *Kotser Codicis*, sigs. P.3.r–4.r. In fact Wakefield also assisted Pace in a book he compiled about this time in favour of the Queen. But this can hardly have been the book already presented to Henry, as Pace reported that Wakefield was prepared to defend that as 'a thing trewe infallibly' – whereas on the subject of the divorce Wakefield was initially reluctant to meddle.

21 Wakefield to Fisher, *Kotser Codicis*, sig. P.2.r.

22 Wakefield to Fisher, *Kotser Codicis*, sig. P.2.v.

23 BL Cottonian Otho C. x. fol. 185.v, 'An matrimonium, in quo dispensavit pontifex ut frater fratris uxorem duceret, firmum sit et indissolubilem?' For the identification and analysis of this MS, see Murphy, 'Debate,' pp. 23–38; and nn. 39–40 below. See also R. Wakefield, *Syntagma de Incorruptione Hebraeorum Codicum* (London, n.d., *c.* 1534), sig. A.1.v, which gives the question in full. The manuscript version is damaged in the first and last words.

24 BL Otho C. x. fol. 186.r. See *Textus Biblie* (Prima pars, Basel, 1506), fol. 245.v (second occurrence of this folio number), 'Et uxorem fratris sui nullus accipiat.' Lyra's commentary at note m observes the absence of this phrase in the Hebrew and in emended Vulgates. Fisher may have noticed Lyra's remark, but presumably checked the Greek himself. The phrase was omitted from the Sixtine edition of the Vulgate.

25 BL Otho C. x. fol. 187.v.

26 CUL, MS Ff. v. 25, fol. 177.v.

27 BL Otho C. x. fol. 191.r. The fragmentary condition of 'Responsio' leaves the precise bearing of this obscure.

28 BL Otho C. x. fol. 192.r.

29 BL Otho C. x. fol. 192.v.

30 BL Otho C. x. fol. 193.r–v.

31 BL Otho C. x. fols. 193.v–4.r.

32 BL Otho C. x. fol. 195.r.

33 BL Otho C. x. fol. 196.r.

34 BL Otho C. x. fol. 197.r. But see Scarisbrick, *Henry VIII*, p. 177.

35 BL Otho C. x. fol. 198.r.

36 BL Otho C. x. fol. 198.r. Wakefield's final remark in the 'Eruditi cuiusdam responsio' suggests strongly that the summary he is refuting encapsulates the whole of Fisher's original 'Liber': 'Et hec ut opinor pro parergis [...] tuis diluendis abunde sufficiunt et satis sunt et super [fluunt]' carries a distinct air of finality.

37 The letter is among those printed at the back of Robert Wakefield's *Kotser Codicis* in 1534, at sigg. P.1.v–3.r. Though his references to his recruitment in 1527 as 'seven years ago' seem to place the letter, and certainly place the book, in 1534, we should note that he habitually introduced such 'updating' clauses into his writings when he published them. The content of the letter is inconsistent with 1534 (to which year it is assigned by Kelly, *Matrimonial Trials*, p. 37, n. 31) for several reasons. Wakefield's offer to recant his opinion if Fisher can prove him wrong, his promise in that eventuality to tell Henry that his intentions were immoral, and his reference to Catherine as queen, are unlikely to have been made when the divorce was a *fait accompli*, and when denying its validity was tantamount to treason. The omission of Oxford from the list of places where he had taught suggests that the letter predates 1532 when he became king's reader in Hebrew there. The polite address to Fisher and the description of Metcalfe as a mutual friend suggest that the letter predated 1528, after which his attitude to Fisher became markedly offensive. This dating is supported by his description of his treatise as a 'Codex' rather than as a 'Kotser Codicis' ('fragment of a codex', the title of the book published in 1534), and by his reference to a rumour that Fisher had written 'alterum librum' on the divorce. Fisher's second treatise on the divorce was presented to the Legatine tribunal in June 1529. After that date, it can hardly have been a rumour.

38 Underwood, 'John Fisher and the promotion of learning', p. 45, n. 56.

39 British Library Cottonian MS Otho C. x. fols. 184.r–98.r. The attribution to

Wakefield was initially proposed by Edward Surtz in *Works and Days*, p. 371, though Murphy has shown that he confused this treatise with the one that precedes it in the MS ('Debate', p. 227). In further corroboration I can add that the handwriting bears a striking resemblance to the only known samples of his hand, two receipts for his fellowship stipend found among the muniments of St John's College, Cambridge. But the brevity of these samples forbids certainty on this point.

40 Murphy, 'Debate', pp. 23–4, demonstrates the textual resemblances between the 'Responsio' and the two published books, and proves Wakefield's authorship of the 'Responsio'.

41 BL Otho C. x. fol. 184.r, 'Ingentes tibi fratias habemus Reverende pater quod librum tuum adeo belle docteque resectis par[titionibus] (non multum enim mea sententia expaciatum) in compendium redegeris, adeoque folii[s paucis libri] Regii [replacing 'nostri'] summam perstrinxeris.'

42 Murphy, 'Debate', p. 24.

43 BL Otho C. x. fol. 184.r, 'nonnulla nobis videntur superflua [et ni]mis scolastica parumque firma ac valida'.

44 BL Otho C. x. fol. 198.r.

45 BL Otho C. x. fol. 195.r, 'cum quod sacras literas non vulgariter allet, tum etiam quoniam regni ipsius ned[um totius] orbis Christiani ornamentum est non parvum, utpote universis hebraeis [. . .] eximiam linguae sanctae peritiam opponens possit'.

46 Scholars of Hebrew today are in total agreement that this usage does *not* imply marriage.

47 BL Otho C. x. fol. 186.r–v; *Syntagma*, sig. A.4.r–v; *Kotser*, sigs. A.2.r–4.v.

48 Scarisbrick, *Henry VIII*, pp. 213–16.

49 Murphy, 'Debate', p. 50. *Vie*, x, pp. 311–12, names all except Veysey, de Athequa and Dr Cliff. Cliff and de Athequa voted against the divorce in April 1533, but Veysey voted for. See Pocock, *Records*, ii, pp. 457–9.

50 H.A. Kelly, *Matrimonial Trials*, pp. 77–87. Catherine's appeal was dated 16 June.

51 Campeggio's secretary, Floriano Montini, reported the dramatic scene in a letter to the secretary of the duke of Ferrara, 29 June 1529. See *Römische Dokumente zur Geschichte der Ehescheidung Heinrichs VIII von England. 1527–1534*, ed. S. Ehses (Paderborn, 1893), no. 53, pp. 116–17. See also *LP* 4. iii. 5734. Standish of St Asaph's and Peter Ligham (dean of Arches) also spoke in support of Catherine.

52 'Licitum fuisse' survives in a later and slightly defective copy, CUL MS Ff. v. 25, fols. 154.r–197.v. The incipit, 'Constat inclytissimum', was recorded in the proceedings of the legatine trubunal as the incipit of a treatise submitted by Fisher. See Murphy, 'Debate', pp. 60–1.

53 CUL MS Ff. v. 25, fol. 155.r.

54 CUL MS Ff. v. 25, fol. 155.v (prima ratio); 157.v (secunda); 159.r (tertia). They boil down to the same thing.

55 CUL MS Ff. v. 25, fol. 155.v.

56 CUL MS Ff. v. 25, fols. 155–6.v.

57 As Fisher was to point out later. See *DCM*, fol. 16.r.

58 CUL MS Ff. v. 25, fol. 157.r. Fisher deployed the latter argument at greater length in a later treatise, 'Ne qua fiat', and we shall explore it in more detail when we examine that work.

59 CUL MS Ff. v. 25, fols. 157.v–8.r, citing Jerome, Augustine, Hesychius, Chrysostom, Ambrose, Theophylact, Tertullian, Thomas Aquinas, Hugh of Vienne and Nicholas of Lyra.

60 CUL MS Ff. v. 25, fol. 158.r–v.

61 CUL MS Ff. v. 25, fol. 159.r.

62 CUL MS Ff. v. 25, fol. 161.r –v.

63 CUL MS Ff. v. 25, fols. 161.v–2.r.

64 CUL MS Ff. v. 25, fols. 164.r–7.v.

65 CUL MS Ff. v. 25, fol. 167.v.

66 This question is highly complex, as Matthew (with Mark) and Josephus disagree as to the identity of Herodias's first husband. See H.W. Hoehner, *Herod Antipas*, Soc. for NT Studies, Monograph Ser., 17 (Cambridge, 1972), ch. 7, pp. 110–71, esp. pp. 131–6.

67 CUL MS Ff. v. 25, fols. 173.v–4.v. He was on weak ground with this second point. Since the purpose of Deut 25:5 was to retain property within a family, it is likely that the levirate was practised where a man died without *sons* rather than without *children*.

68 CUL MS Ff. v. 25, fols. 174.v–5.v.

69 CUL MS Ff. v. 25, fols. 177.r–v.

70 CUL MS Ff. v. 25, fols. 177.v–81.r.

71 PRO SP 1/42, fols. 165.r–6.v, esp. fol. 165.r, which notes Paul's two concerns, 'Alterum, quod Wakefeldus repperit, nescio quid, in hebraicis literis quod instituto Regis conducit non mediocriter. Alterum, quod omnes Episcopi qui pridem a Regis voto dissidebant, iam in eius sententiam pedibus inerunt, cantantes palinodiam.' The letter is undated. Dr Murphy concludes that it was written in mid-to-late Nov 1527 ('Debate', pp. 51–2). The identity of Paul is a mystery.

72 PRO SP1/42, fol. 166.r, 'Iam perspicis opinor, et dilucide quidem, frustraneum esse, quicquid aut Wakefeldus, aut alius quisque in illis prohibicionibus repperit.'

73 The treatise, which begins (after its undistinctive address, 'Reverendissimis in Christo patribus', to the legates) 'Ne qua fiat', survives in two copies in Lambeth Place Library, MS 2342, fols. 2.r–21.v and 23.r–32.v. The second is the superior text and has Fisher's signature at the end. The first is a later copy, defective at several points, e.g., on fol. 10.r., where a line is omitted from a passage of Iuvencus cited properly at fol. 27.r. Fisher describes his triumph over Wakefield at fol. 23.r, dating it 'superiori die'. Wakefield also questioned the meaning of 'stranger' in Deut 25:5, but Fisher did not take this up.

74 Lambeth MS 2342, fol. 23.r–v.

75 Lambeth MS 2342, fols. 24.v–5.r.

76 For Cajetan's argument, see G.B. Skelly, 'Cardinal Cajetan' in *Le 'Divorce' du Roi Henry VIII: études et documents* ed. G. Bedouelle and P. Le Gal (Travaux d'Humanisme et Renaissance 221, Geneva, 1987), pp. 205–28, at pp. 211–13. Skelly seems not entirely to have understood Cajetan's argument, apparently labouring under the misapprehension that 'levir' (the Latin for the brother of a woman's husband) is Hebrew. Cajetan composed his votum on Henry's marriage in 1530 at the personal request of Clement VII, who gave him several treatises on the matter for comment. It seems that Cajetan had somehow come across Wakefield's argument.

77 This reply is wide of the mark, for as neither Boaz nor the unnamed cousin were Mahlon's brothers, they do not damage Wakefield's case. But Fisher missed a trick here. After Mahlon's death, Naomi, his mother, told Ruth that there was no point in her staying since she (Naomi) was too old to bear any further sons for her (Ruth) to marry. This is a clear reference to the levirate. However, he made this point later in his *DCM*, fol. 14.v.

78 Lambeth MS 2342, fols. 25.r–6.r.
79 Lambeth MS 2342, fols. 26.r–8.v. His list comprised Hesychius, Damascene, Chrysostom and Eusebius among the Greeks; Tertullian, Iuvencus, Ambrose, 'Augustine' and Ralph of Flaix among the Latins; Josephus, Moses Maimonides and the Targum (from the Complutensian Polyglot, sig. zz.4.r) among the Hebrews; and Lyra, Alphonsus and Jerome among the Christian Hebraists.
80 Lambeth MS 2342, fol. 28.v.
81 Lambeth MS 2342, fols. 28.v–9.r.
82 Lambeth MS 2342, fols. 29.r–30.r. The rendering of the Hebrew is taken from Pagninus, *Sacra Biblia*, fol. 72.r, and that of the Greek from the Complutensian Polyglot, *Vetus testamentum multiplici lingua nunc primo impressum*, (6 vols., Alcala: A.G. de Brocario, 1514–17), i, sig. zz.4.r.
83 Lambeth MS 2342, fols. 30.v–1.r.
84 Lambeth MS 2342, fol. 31.r, 'Tales enim leges quasi Cabalisticas patres velut per manus tradebant.'
85 Lambeth MS 2342, fols. 31.r–2.v (end).
86 This account is based on Gardiner's report to Henry VIII, printed in G. Burnet, *History of the Reformation of the Church of England*, ed. N. Pocock (7 vols., Oxford, 1865), iv, pp. 130–3. See also G.B. Skelly, 'Henry VIII consults the Universities of Oxford and Cambridge', in Bedouelle and Le Gal, *Le 'Divorce'*, pp. 59–75.
87 *LP* 4. iii. 6162, Foxe to Buckmaster, 24 Jan 1530; and 6176, Buckmaster's sentence ordering all concerned to avoid contentious preaching.
88 See Murphy, 'Debate', p. 266, for Watson and Shirwood, and next note for Baynes.
89 *LP* 8. 859, questions and answers 23–25 and 37.
90 *LP* 4. 6325, 11 April 1530; printed in Burnet's *History*, ed. Pocock, vi, pp. 32–5.
91 J.J. Scarisbrick, 'Fisher, Henry VIII and the Reformation Crisis', in *HRR*, pp. 159, 162 and 164.
92 This treatise (PRO SP1/54, fols. 130–229) is discussed by Dr Murphy, 'Debate', pp. 127–40.
93 Murphy, 'Debate', pp. 140–58.
94 *DCM*, fols. 37.r–8.v.
95 *LP* 8. 859, questions and answers 39–40.
96 In fact, the second section begins with a reprise of the five 'collectiones' of 'Ne qua fiat' (*DCM*, fols. 7.r–8.v). The chief interest here is Fisher's description of that treatise as his third on the divorce, which enables us to be reasonably confident that the initial 'Liber', 'Licitum fuisse', and 'Ne qua fiat' represent the sum total of his work on the divorce up to the end of the legatine tribunal. Murphy, 'Debate', pp. 100–1.
97 *DCM*, fols. 9.r–12.v, citing in addition Gregory Nazianzen, Jerome, Ambrose and Damascene (all, like Fisher, following Eusebius). The confusions in this convoluted theory are exacerbated by the resemblance of the names Matthan, Mathat and Nathan, as well as by Julius's statement that Heli was the son of Melchi – whom Luke makes Heli's great-grandfather. The typesetter of *DCM*, doubtless entirely baffled, makes several errors. I have tried to sort out Fisher's real argument.
98 *DCM*, fol. 13.r–v.
99 *DCM*, fols. 19.v–22.r, citing Alexander of Hales, Bonaventure, Scotus, Francis Maro and Gabriel Biel (as continued by Steinbach).
100 *DCM*, fols. 23.r–5.v, citing Chrysostom, Peter Comestor, Vincent of Beauvais, Innocent III, Antonius de Rosellis, Aquinas, Nicholas of Lyra and Turrecremata.

As for the reading concerning a living brother's divorced wife, he observed that apart from Hugh of Vienne, Robert Grosseteste and James of Lausanne, nobody so much as considered it (fols. 25.v–6.r).

101 *DCM*, fol. 26.v, following Jerome, prologue to Hosee.

102 *DCM*, fols. 29.v–34.r. Authorities were Augustine, Hugh of St Victor, Alexander of Hales, Bonaventure, Thomas Aquinas, Richard of Middleton, Paulus Burgensis and Thomas of Strasbourg. See Joyce, *Christian Marriage*, pp. 521–6. From Scotus onwards, scholastics often added brother–sister marriages to parent–child marriages as contrary to natural law.

103 Gen 20:12. But see also Gen 11:27–31; 12:11–19; and 20:2–16. Abraham's motive for calling Sarah his sister was to protect himself against powerful men who might, knowing her to be his wife, kill him to take her. For similar reasons Isaac described his wife Rebecca as his sister (Gen 26:7), though she was in fact only a cousin, granddaughter of his uncle Nahor. Fisher gave Jerome, Eucherius of Lyons, Peter Comestor and Francis Maro as authorities for the literal reading.

104 *DCM*, fol. 38.v.

105 *DCM*, fols. 38.v–9.r. This was another commonplace.

106 *DCM*, fols. 39.r–42.v.

107 Dr Murphy has explored the genesis of this work in her introduction to *Divorce Tracts of Henry VIII*, ed. E. Surtz and V. Murphy (Angers, 1987), pp. i–xliv.

108 *LP* 8. 859, question 15.

109 *LP* 8. 859, question 13. The recent conjecture that it was written by François van der Dilft (Bedouelle and Le Gal, *Le 'Divorce'*, pp. 306–7) has nothing to commend it.

110 The author remarks that he is not a theologian, and that he has not enjoyed a university education. He appears to be on good terms with Chapuys, to whom the treatise is dedicated, and he is clearly a talented humanist. As a lay humanist scholar who had not attended university, a prolific author, an occasional diplomat with clandestine connections with Chapuys, and a known opponent of the divorce, Elyot looks a prime candidate for authorship of *Non esse*.

111 G.R. Elton rightly calls Chapuys 'the centre of intrigue', in 'Sir Thomas More and the Opposition to Henry VIII', in his *Studies in Tudor and Stuart Politics and Government*, (3 vols., Cambridge, 1974–83), i, pp. 155–72, at p. 166; while Scarisbrick equally rightly notes that we cannot put Fisher 'at the centre of a web of dissidence' ('Fisher and the Reformation crisis', p. 159).

112 *LP* 8. 859, questions 1–7. Chapuys is not named, but is indubitably intended.

113 Chapuys to Charles V, 6 Feb 1530, cited at length in W. Bradford, *Correspondence of the Emperor Charles V and his Ambassadors at the Courts of England and France* (London, 1850), pp. 298–300. See also *LP* 4. iii. 6199.

114 27 Nov and 4 Dec 1530, Bradford, *Correspondence*, pp. 322 and 331. See also *LP* 4. iii. 6738 and 6757. There is no evidence that the books mentioned in Nov were those despatched in Dec, but unless Fisher's productivity was truly astounding, they probably were. Since Chapuys did not say in Nov that he had already sent them, I suspect that he was planning ahead.

115 *LP* 8. 859, question 33.

116 H.C. Agrippa, *Opera* (2 vols., Lyons: Beringi, 1600), ii, pp. 297–8 (Chapuys to Agrippa, 26 June 1531); pp. 298–301 (Agrippa to Chapuys, 21 July); pp. 312–19 (to Agrippa, 10 Sept); and p. 322 (to Agrippa, 25 Nov). See also *LP* 5, app. 11, 13, 14 and 17.

117 M.E. Kronenberg, 'Forged Addresses in Low Country Books in the Period of the

Reformation', *The Library*, 5th ser., 2 (1947–8), pp. 81–94, at p. 88. Kronenberg misses the third book, *Parasceve*.

118 *LP* 5. 39, Mai to Charles V, 10 Jan 1531.

119 Since many of the opponents of the divorce were from the north of England and had studied at Paris (e.g., Robert Ridley and Nicholas Wilson) we are unlikely to be able to identify the author.

120 *LP* 6. 726 and 900, John Coke to Cromwell, 30 June and 26 July; 889, W. Lok to Cromwell, 26 July; and 934, Vaughan to Cromwell, 3 Aug 1533.

121 *Parasceve*, sig. B.2.v, 'Parisiensi Academiae, cui ego huius eruditiunculae bonam partem libenter debeo'; 'mihi literae adferuntur e Lutetia Parisiorum, ab amico perquem [*sic*, for perquam] erudito: habeo in ea schola amicos et plusculos, pro veteri consuetudine'.

122 Brooke *et al.*, 'Fisher's itinerary', *HRR*, pp. 247–8. Since he was back at Rochester from early June, it is just possible that he was involved.

123 It survives in an almost complete but often defective copy in BL Arundel MS 151, fols. 202.r–339.v, which breaks off in the final chapter. A far superior copy of chs. 3 and 4 is in PRO SP1/64, fols. 244.r–90.v. I owe the identification of the latter as part of the former to Dr Murphy, 'Debate', pp. 232–3.

124 BL Arundel MS 151, fol. 281.v, 'cum opusculo quodam ad hoc ditato [*sic* for dictato?], authores illos qui a nobis stant, una cum testimoniis in sex classibus digesserim haud parvo numero'. The description does not correspond to a part or the whole of any surviving work by Fisher.

125 BL Arundel MS 151, fol. 295.r, 'Prohibitiones vicesimi capitis dilucide commonstrant omnia debere intelligi viventibus maritis.'

126 BL Arundel MS 151, fol. 242.v, 'Bone Iesu, qualem conscientiam habent ii doctissimi qui in re tanti momenti tam gravem authorem adeo foede lacerarunt et arroserunt, qui suum (ut ne quid acerbius dicam) errorem utcunque tueantur.'

127 *LP* 5. 112, Chapuys to Charles V, 21 Feb 1531.

128 BL Arundel MS 151, fol. 330.v, 'Videntur ii doctissimi parum curare quam angusta reddita fuerit pontificis authoritas modo possunt in hoc negotio divortium obtinere.'

129 BL Arundel MS 151, fol. 334.r, 'Ex his facile coniicies, lector, hos doctissimos parturire monstrum aliquod insigne, cum ita cunctos exacuunt contra pontificem. Et sane nostrum [*sic*, for 'monstrum'!] est et quidem pestilentissimum, nempe quod rex illustrissimus non expectato pontificis decreto, sed sua ipsius authoritate rescindat hoc sacrum matrimonium.'

130 BL Arundel MS 151, fol. 329.r, 'Hic saniorem in his doctissimis desiderem spiritum: quid enim interesset inter pontificem et quemvis simplicem sacerdotem, si nulla maior potestas illi commissa fuisset a Christo, quam ut peccata solveret.'

131 Scarisbrick, *Henry VIII*, p. 309. For Lee's involvement (and the less plausible alternative of George Brown), see Ives, *Anne Boleyn*, p. 211.

132 Pocock, *Records*, ii, pp. 447–8 and 457–9.

133 *LP* 6. 324, Chapuys to Charles V, 10 April 1533.

11 Conclusion

1 A.G. Dickens, *The English Reformation* (2nd edn., London, 1989). See also his 'The Early Expansion of Protestantism in England 1520–1558', *Archiv für Reformationsgeschichte* 88 (1987), pp. 187–222. Representative works of the 'revisionist' school

are J.J. Scarisbrick, *The Reformation and the English People* (Oxford, 1984), C. Haigh, *Reformation and Resistance in Tudor Lancashire* (Cambridge, 1975) and C. Haigh (ed), *The English Reformation Revised* (Cambridge, 1987).

2 Rex, 'English Campaign', *passim*.

3 Dickens, *English Reformation*, p. 123. See also p. 15, for 'conservative Tudor churchmen, led by Bishop John Fisher'.

4 See, e.g., *The Psalmes or, Prayers Taken out of the Holy Scripture: commonly called, The Kings Psalmes* (London, 1606), *STC* 3012.7. *STC* 3001.7–3013.5 lists twenty-three editions between 1544 and 1613.

Appendix

1 *EM* sig. X.2.r.

2 *Vie*, xii, p. 168.

3 References are given only to one occurrence of each work in Fisher's writings, usually to the first. For convenience, references are given as far as possible only to the *Opera Omnia* of Fisher rather than to the separate first editions of his works. Items marked with an asterisk are spurious attributions which Fisher, in common with most of his contemporaries, regarded as genuine. Items given in square brackets reflect cases where Fisher referred to an author without naming a particular work, but where the context suggests strongly that he has a particular work in mind.

4 Fisher cited the sermons 'de Maria Magdalena' (*DUM* 1407), 'de poenitentia Petri' (*ALC* 539), 'de fide Petri' (*ALC* 553), 'de natali Petri et Pauli' (*CC* 1432) and 'de morte fratris Satyri' (*DVC* 921).

5 The work of 'Ambrosiaster', a late fourth-century commentator. It was always included in early modern editions of Ambrose's works. Fisher cited it on Corinthians (*ALC* 460) and Timothy (*SSD* 1234).

6 PRO SP1/64, fol. 258.v.

7 Arnobius's *Commentarii in Omnes Psalmos* was first edited by Erasmus (Basel: Froben, 1522), and Fisher was probably using this edition.

8 As Fisher was mentioned in the dedication of Erasmus's edn. of Augustine's works, it is likely that he received a presentation copy. See *EE* VIII, ep. 2157, to A. de Fonseca, *c*. May 1529, p. 160.

9 This work is now generally ascribed to 'Ambrosiaster'.

10 Cited as 'Contra Pelagianum'.

11 A later compilation from various of Augustine's writings.

12 Fisher received a presentation copy of the 1530 complete edition of Chrysostom by Erasmus. See *EE* IX, eps. 2359, to C. von Stadion, 5 Aug 1530, p. 6; and 2413, from E. Schets, 18 Dec 1530, p. 95. But he plainly had most of Chrysostom's works already.

13 Copied for him from CUL, around 1520. See Gray, 'Letters of Fisher', p. 134.

14 This reference is to Hebrews. Fisher also cited Corinthians, in versions by both Aretino and Donato (*DVC* 1173), and Timothy (*DVC* 875).

15 BL Arundel MS 151, fol. 208.v.

16 Fisher cites variously from genuine letters and the 'Pseudo-Clementines'.

17 Cited as 'De Simplicitate'. Apart from the Epistolae, the other works cited here were all among Cyprian's Sermones.

18 These works were edited by Clichtove and published at Paris by Petit, 1508 and 1514.

19 First printed by Chevallon in Paris, n. d., but probably between 1525 and 1530. Its use by Fisher here suggests that it was *c.* 1525.
20 PRO SP6/5, fol. 83.r. Translation by Trapezuntius.
21 Cited as Augustine. See discussion above, ch. 7, p. 127.
22 There were various edns of the *De Trinitate* before 1522. In his later citations of Hilary, Fisher is probably using Erasmus's edn of Hilary's *Lucubrationes* (Basel: Froben, 1523).
23 PRO SP6/5, fol. 46.v, refers to Hilary's testimony in favour of the LXX. Such testimonies are found only in his commentary on the psalms.
24 Fisher makes use in his writings both of the medieval 'long recension' of Ignatius, and elsewhere of a more accurate Renaissance version. See J. Fisher, *The Defence of the Sacred Priesthood*, ed. P.E. Hallett (London, 1935), pp. 14 and 140 (n. 38). Ignatius's epistles were available in Lefèvre's edn. of 'Dionysius', which was frequently reprinted.
25 PRO SP6/5, fol. 73.r. Almost certainly the Erasmus edition (Basel: Froben, 1526). In 1526 Fisher had lamented not possessing a copy of Irenaeus. See *DVC* IV. 3. fol. CVIII.v (c. 1056), 'si nihil [*sic* – emended in *OO* to 'mihi'] fuisset ipsius libri copia'. He had clearly obtained one by summer 1527.
26 Fisher certainly possessed Jerome's works in Erasmus's edn. (9 vols., Basel: Froben, 1516). See *EE* II, ep. 474, to More, 2 Oct 1516, p. 353, mentioning that a copy is on its way to Fisher.
27 Ad Damasum. He also cited: ad Hedibiam (*EM* D.2.v); ad Augustinum (*EM* E.1.r); ad Principiam Virginem (*EM* H.3.v); ad Marcellam (*EM* H.4.r); ad Domnionem (*ALC* 311); ad Oceanum (*ALC* 358); ad Evagrium (*ALC* 570); and ad Rusticum (*DVC* 815).
28 This was not an uncommon work, but Fisher's several citations seem to follow closely the 1515 Paris edn. by Jean Petit.
29 All these works are found in Jacques Merlin's edn. of Origen's works (4 vols., Paris: Bade and Petit, 1512), which Fisher's citations seem to follow.
30 Referring to Matteo Palmerio as translator.
31 Rhenanus's edn. (Basel: Froben, 1521) was the first. Fisher's citations follow it very closely and begin in *ALC* which was being composed in 1521–2 just after the appearance of Rhenanus's edn.
32 Cited as Vulgarius (as Erasmus had mistakenly named him in his *Novum Instrumentum*). Fisher's text follows the fifteenth-century translation by C. Porsena. Compare Theophylact, *In Omnes D. Pauli Epistolas Enarrationes* (Cologne: Cervicorn, 1528), p. 664. The version had been printed before, e.g. Rome: Han, 1477.
33 Fisher cites him on Luke and Mark as 'Theophilus', on Matthew as 'Theophilactus'. All three are clearly 'Theophylact', though not from Oecolampadius's recent version. I have been unable to identify Fisher's source.
34 BL Arundel MS 151, fol. 296.v.
35 PRO SP6/5, fol. 83.r Translation by Matteo Palmerio. Several edns. by 1527.
36 CUL MS Ff.5.25, fol. 172.v.
37 Fisher donated this to Christ's College, Cambridge, according to the college library's donation book (MS 22).
38 PRO SP6/5, fol. 46.r.
39 BL Arundel MS 151, fol. 204.r.
40 Many of those who are named but not cited in Fisher's *DVC* III, preface, cc. 990–1, are identified more fully by Surtz in *Works and Days*, pp. 476–7.

41 BL Arundel MS 151, fol. 279.r.
42 Surtz suggests that this is Aelfric, abbot of Eynsham, *Works and Days*, pp. 167–8.
43 BL Arundel MS 151, fol. 298.r. This must have been from a manuscript.
44 Fisher cited this from his MS because it was so rare. The *editio princeps* was 1530.
45 'in eo opere quo potestati Pontificis pro virili detrahat'.
46 This is presumably an allusion to Ratramnus of Corbie. Unfortunately Fisher gives no citation.
47 In addition, Fisher occasionally cited from Bernardine devotional writings of doubtful authenticity.
48 See above, ch. 7, p. 124.
49 Probably *Revelationes Celestes* (Nuremberg: Koberger, 1517).
50 I owe this identification to Surtz, *Works and Days*, p. 474, n. 5.
51 Properly, Christian de Stavelot (see Surtz, *Works and Days*, p. 474, n. 4). Fisher almost certainly used the *editio princeps* (Strasbourg: Grieninger, 1514).
52 BL Arundel MS 151, fol. 332.v.
53 Probably cited from Lefèvre's edn, *Liber trium spiritualium virginum*.
54 PRO SP6/5, fol. 70.r. See discussion above, ch. 9, p. 151.
55 Cited in Fisher's letter to Lethmaet, *OO* c. 1707.
56 BL Arundel MS 151, fol. 335.v.
57 Cited from MS. The first edn. was Erasmus's in 1530.
58 BL Arundel MS 151, fol. 280.r.
59 BL Arundel MS 151, fol. 223.v.
60 BL Arundel MS 151, fol. 331.v.
61 BL Arundel MS 151, fol. 208.v.
62 PRO SP1/64, fol. 277.v.
63 BL Arundel MS 151, fol. 266.r.
64 Identified Surtz as John Baconthorpe (*Works and Days*, p. 164).
65 BL Arundel MS 151, fol. 266.r.
66 BL Arundel MS 151, fol. 263.v.
67 According to P.E. Hallett, this is probably taken from Ivo's *Liber Decretorum* (Basel, 1499). See J. Fisher, *The Defence of the Priesthood*, tr. and ed. P.E. Hallett (London, 1935), pp. 136 and 149, n. 50.
68 Fisher noted here that Warham had lent him an early MS from Canterbury.
69 BL Arundel MS 151, fol. 216.v. This was not available in print.
70 Fisher will almost certainly have owned an edn. of the Bible with the 'Glosa Ordinaria' and the commentaries and glosses of Lyra, Paulus Burgensis and Mattheus Doring.
71 BL Arundel MS 151, fol. 262.r cites Paluda's later recantation of views on the levirate that he had expressed in his commentary on the Sentences. The text comes from the commentary on Leviticus, but as this was extremely rare, and Fisher gives no reference, he may have been citing at second-hand.
72 Not available in print until 1536.
73 Fisher received a dedication in Cochlaeus's edn. of Rupert's works. He probably bought or was given the whole edn., but this cannot be known for certain.
74 Almost certainly from the *editio princeps* (Paris: Estienne, 1513).
75 I owe this identification to Surtz, *Works and Days*, p. 158.
76 BL Arundel MS 151, fol. 297.r.
77 BL Arundel MS 151, fol. 233.v.
78 BL Arundel MS 151, fol. 296.r.
79 BL Arundel MS 151, fol. 233.r.
80 I owe the identification of author and work to Surtz, *Works and Days*, p. 474, n. 5.

81 *EE* II, ep. 336, from Fisher, *c.* May 1515, p. 90. Fisher reported his pleasure in this recently purchased book.
82 BL Arundel MS 151, fol. 327.r.
83 BL Arundel MS 151, fol. 299.r.
84 BL Arundel MS 151, fol. 297.r.
85 PRO SP2/R, fol. 202.r. Work identified from citation.
86 Cologne: Quentell, 1525, ded. to Fisher.
87 Leipzig: Schuman, 1529, ded. to Fisher.
88 *EE* II, ep. 336, from Fisher, *c.* May 1515, p. 90. Surtz conclusively demonstrates Fisher's familiarity with the *Adagia, Works and Days*, pp. 508, n. 26 and 514, nn. 36–8.
89 *EE* III, ep. 653, to Fisher, 8 Sept 1517, p. 75.
90 Presentation copy. *EE* V, ep. 1489, to Fisher, 4 Sept 1524, p. 538.
91 Presentation copy. See *EE* III, ep. 784, to Fisher, 5 March 1518, p. 237.
92 Presentation copy. See *EE* III, ep. 432, from Fisher, *c.* June 1516, p. 268. Fisher's copy was sold at Sotheby's, London, in 1961. See *Sotheby's Sale Catalogue* for Mon. 23 Feb 1959, p. 42, lot 212 and plate. This is the only volume known for certain to have survived from Fisher's collection. For this and another volume wrongly ascribed to Fisher's library, see my 'A Note on St John Fisher and Erasmus', *Journal of Ecclesiastical History* 40 (1989), pp. 582–5.
93 For these last five edns., see above under the name of the relevant author.
94 PRO SP6/5, fol. 62.r.
95 This unacknowledged citation was spotted by Secret, *Les Kabbalistes*, pp. 228–9.
96 PRO SP6/5, fol. 59.r.
97 Fisher presumably received a presentation copy of the first edn., London: Pynson, 1521.
98 BL Arundel MS 151, fols. 202–339 refutes this work.
99 All the works by Luther mentioned so far were in the *Lucubrationum pars una* (Basel: Petri, 1520).
100 It has not yet proved possible to identify this work from which Fisher, however, confidently cites a typically Lutheran text.
101 Fisher cites Luther's letter to the Christians of Strasbourg in this Latin translation (the other edns. were all in German).
102 Ded. to Fisher.
103 Gray, 'Letters of Fisher', p. 143.
104 Ded. to Fisher.
105 Deduced from Fisher's refutation. See above, ch. 9, *passim.*
106 Fisher donated this to Christ's College, Cambridge, according to the college library's donation book, MS 22.
107 Cited without acknowledgment in Lambeth Palace Library MS 2342, fols. 29.v–30.r.
108 Cited without acknowledgment at PRO SP2/R, fol. 166.r. I owe this to Surtz, *Works and Days*, p. 141.
109 *EE* II, ep. 324, to Reuchlin, 1 March 1515, p. 50.
110 *EE* II, ep. 300, to Reuchlin, *c.* Aug 1514, p. 4, expresses an intention to send Fisher a copy.
111 See *EE* II, ep. 592, from Fisher, *c.* June 1517, p. 598.
112 Ded. to Fisher.
113 Fisher donated this to Christ's College, Cambridge, according to the college library's donation book, MS 22. He cited from it without acknowledgment in Lambeth Palace Library MS 2342, fols. 29.v–30.r.

Bibliography

Manuscripts

LONDON

1 Public Record Office
SP1/42, fols. 165–6. Letter from Fisher to Paul.
SP1/64, fols. 244–70. Two chapters of Fisher's 'Brevis Apologia' against Henry VIII's *Gravissimae Censurae*. Written in 1532.
SP2/R, fols. 28–274. Commentary and paraphrase on the first 51 psalms. Probably written around 1525.
SP6/5, fols. 45–83. Fisher's defence of the inspiration of the Septuagint. Written in 1527.
SP6/9, fols. 159–64. Fragments of Fisher's 'Decem Considerationes', a devotional work advocating frequent communion. Probably written after 1526.

2 British Library
Arundel MS 151, fols. 202–339. 'Brevis Apologia seu Confutatio'. Fisher's refutation of Henry VIII's *Gravissimae Censurae*. Breaks off in final chapter. Written in 1532.
Cottonian MS Otho C. x. fols. 184–98. Robert Wakefield's 'Eruditi cuiusdam responsio.'
Cottonian MS Vit. B. xxi, fol. 11. Letter of Sir John Wallop to Cardinal Wolsey.
Lansdowne MS 978. Kennett's Collections, vol. 44.
Royal MS 3. D. i. 'Tabula super Genesim'.

3 Lambeth Palace Library.
MS 2342, fols. 2–32. 'Ne qua fiat', Fisher's short treatise on levirate marriage submitted to the legatine tribunal in 1529. Two copies.
MS DC1. Register of Doctors Commons.

CAMBRIDGE

1 University Library
University Archives Lett. 1. 'Epistolae Academicae I'.
University Archives LIC. A. 1 (1). Licences for preachers.
MS Ff. v. 25, fols. 154–197. 'Licitum fuisse'. Fisher's treatise for the legatine tribunal on Henry VIII's marriage, 1529.
MS Kk. 1. 18. Declaratio Doctoris William Chubys Magistri Coligii Ihesu Cantabrigie super Scotum in Secundo.
Ely Diocesan Records, G/I/7. Register of Nicholas West, bishop of Ely.

2 St John's College, Muniments.
Thin Red Book. Contemporary transcripts of letters and papers relating to college.
D 5.14. Foundation deed of Lady Margaret Beaufort readership in divinity.
D 56.1–. Letters and papers of Dr Metcalfe.

D 57.92. Accounts of Hugh Ashton's foundation.
D 57.156. Inventory of early gifts to college.
D 58.4. Foundation deed of Constable scholarships.
D 105.38–. Letters and papers of Dr Metcalfe.
D 106.6. Master's accounts.
M 3.5. Early accounts.

3 Christ's College
MS 22. Early catalogue of donations to the library.

GOUDA

Gemeentelijke Archiefdienst
MS 959. Letters of Hermann Lethmaet. Consulted on microfiche.

Fisher's printed works

A sermon had at Paulis. London: Berthelet, n.d.
Assertionis Lutheranae Confutatio. Antwerp: Hillenius, 1523.
Contio quam Anglice habuit. Cambridge: Siberch, 1522. *STC* 10898.
Confutatio Secundae Disceptationis per Iacobum Fabrum habitae. Paris: Bade, 1519.
Convulsio Calumniarum U. Veleni, quibus Petrum nunquam Romae fuisse cavillatur. Antwerp: Vorstermann, 1522.
De Causa Matrimonii serenissimi regis Angliae liber. Alcala: Eguia, 1530.
Defensio Regiae Assertionis contra Babylonicam Captivitatem. Cologne: Quentell, June 1525.
De Unica Magdalena, libri tres. Paris: Bade, 1519.
De Veritate Corporis et Sanguinis Christi in Eucharistia. Cologne: Quentell, Feb 1527.
Erasmus and Fisher: their correspondence 1511–1524, ed. J. Rouschausse. De Pétrarque à Descartes 16. Paris, 1968.
Eversio Munitionis quam I. Clichtoveus erigere moliebatur adversus unicam Magdalenam. Louvain: Maartens, 1519.
Opera, quae hactenus inveniri potuerunt omnia. Würzburg: Fleischmann, 1597.
Sacri Sacerdotii Defensio contra Lutherum. Cologne: Quentell, June 1525.
Sacri Sacerdotii Defensio, ed. H.K. Schmeink. Corpus Catholicorum 9. Münster, 1925.
Saint John Fisher: discours, traité de la prière, écrits de prison, ed. J. Rouschausse. Namur, 1964.
The Defence of the Priesthood, tr. P.E. Hallett. London, 1835.
The English Works of John Fisher, Part I, ed. J.E.B. Mayor. EETS extra ser. 27. London, 1876.
The Funeral Sermon of Margaret Countess of Richmond and Derby, ed. J. Hymers. Cambridge, 1840.
The sermon of Johan the bysshop of Rochester. London: de Worde, n.d. *STC* 10894.
Two fruytfull sermons, ed. M.D. Sullivan. Ann Arbor, 1965.

Printed sources

Agrippa, H.C., *Opera Omnia.* 2 vols. Lyons: Beringi fratres, 1600.
Alger of Liège, *De Veritate Corporis et Sanguinis Dominici in Eucharistia,* ed. D. Erasmus. Freiburg im Breisgau: Faber Emmeus, 1530.

Aquinas, T., *Opuscula*, ed. A. Michael de Maria SJ, 3 vols. Città di Castello, 1886.
Summa Theologiae. Blackfriars edn. 60 vols. London, 1963–6.
Aristeas, *Lettre d'Aristée à Philocrate*, ed. A Pelletier. Paris, 1962.
Aristotle, *Complete Works*, ed. J. Barnes. 2 vols. Princeton, 1984.
Ascham, R., *English Works*, ed. W.A. Wright. Cambridge, 1904.
Augustine of Hippo, *De Civitate Dei*, ed. J.L. Vives. Basel: Froben, 1522.
Baldwin of Canterbury, *De Sacramento Altaris*. Cambridge: Siberch, 1521. *STC* 1242.
Balan, P., ed. *Monumenta Reformationis Germaniae*. Berlin, 1883.
Bale, J., *Index Britanniae Scriptorum*, ed. R.L. Poole and M. Bateson. Anecdota Oxoniensia, Medieval and Modern Series 9. Oxford, 1902.
Barlow, W., *Bishop Barlowe's Dialogue on the Lutheran Factions*, ed. A.M. McLean. Courtenay Library of Reformation Classics 15. Sutton Courtenay Press, 1983.
Baron, S., *Sermones declamati coram alma universitate Cantibrigiensi*. London: de Worde, n.d. *STC* 1497.
Bateson, M., ed. *Catalogue of the Library of Syon Monastery*. Cambridge, 1898.
ed. *Grace Book B, Part I*. Cambridge, 1903.
ed. *Grace Book B, Part II*. Cambridge, 1905.
Bede, *Secundi Tomi Operum Veneb. Bedae*, ed. J. Bade. Paris: Bade, 1521.
Bessarion, *Oratio de Sacramento Eucharistiae*. Strasbourg: Schurer, 1513.
Bible, *Textus Biblie*. Basel, 1506.
Vetus testamentum multiplici lingua nunc primo impressum (Complutensian Polyglot). 6 vols. Alcala: de Brocario, 1514–17.
Novum Testamentum Graece, ed. Nestle-Aland. 26th edn. Stuttgart, 1979.
Biblia Sacra iuxta Vulgatam Versionem, eds. B. Fischer, I. Gribomont, H. Sparks, W. Thiele and R. Weber. 2 vols. Stuttgart, 1975.
See also Erasmus, D; Pagninus, S.
Bridget of Sweden, St., *Revelationes Celestes*. Nuremberg: Koberger, 1517.
Bugenhagen, J., *In Librum Psalmorum Interpretatio*. N.p., 1524.
Cajetan, T. de Vio, *Psalmi Davidici ad Hebraicam Veritatem Castigati*. Paris: Bade, 1532.
De Divina Institutione Romani Pontificis, ed. F. Lauchert. Corpus Catholicorum 10. Münster, 1925.
Calendar of Entries in the Papal Registers relating to Great Britain and Ireland: Papal Letters. ed. W.H. Bliss *et al.* London 1893–1960. Dublin, 1978–
Calendar of State Papers and Manuscripts, relating to English affairs, existing in the archives and collections of Venice, ed. R. Brown *et al.* London, 1864–
Castro, A. de, *Adversus Omnes Haereses*. Leipzig: Novesianus, 1539.
Catharinus, A., *Apologia pro Veritate Catholicae et Apostolicae Fidei*, ed. J. Schweizer. Corpus Catholicorum 27. Münster, 1955.
Chambers, R.W. See Harpsfield, N.
Chrysostom, J., *Tomus Quartus Divi Ioannis Chrysostomi*. Basel: Cratander, 1525.
Clark, A., ed. *Lincoln Diocese Documents 1450–1544*. EETS orig. ser. 149 (1914).
Clarorum Virorum Epistolae. Tübingen: Anshelm, 1514.
Clichtove, J., ed. *Opus Insigne Beati Patris Cyrilli Patriarchae Alexandrini in Evangelium Ioannis*. Paris: Hopilius, 1508.
Disceptationis de Magdalena Defensio. Paris: Estienne, 1519.
Cochlaeus, J., *De Authoritate Ecclesiae et Scripturae*. N.p. (probably Strasbourg: Grieninger, 1524).
De Libero Arbitrio. N.p. 1525.
Adversus Latrocinantes et Raptorias Cohortes Rusticorum. Responsio Johannis Cochlaei Wendelstini. Cologne: Quentell, 1525.

Fasciculus Calumniarum. Leipzig: Schuman, 1529.

Philippicae Quatuor. Leipzig: Faber, 1534.

De Canonice Scripturae Autoritate. Ingolstadt: Weissenhorn, 1543.

Commentaria . . . de Actis et Scriptis Martini Lutheri. Mainz: Behem, 1549.

tr. *Von dem hochgelehrten geistlichen bischoff Jo. von Roffen uss Engelland, seines grosen nutzichen buchs zwen artikel verteutscht von Doctor Jo. Cochlaeus.* Strasbourg: Grieninger, 1523.

tr. *Funff Vorrede.* N.p. (probably Dresden: Stöckel), 1528.

ed. Rupert of Deutz, *De Glorificatione Trinitatis.* Cologne: Quentell, 1526.

ed. Rupert of Deutz, *In Apocalypsim.* Cologne: Quentell, 1526.

Colet, J., *Letters on the Mosaic Account of Creation,* ed. J.H. Lupton. London, 1876.

Concilium Tridentinum: diariorum, actorum, epistularum, tractatuum nova collectio. Societas Gorresiana. Freiburg im Breisgau, 1901–

Corpus Iuris Canonici, ed. E. Friedberg. 2 vols. Graz, 1959.

Cranmer, T., *On the Lord's Supper,* ed. J.E. Cox. Parker Soc. 1844.

Cranmer's Remains. Parker Soc. 1846.

Croke, R., *Orationes Ricardi Croci Duae.* Paris: Colinaeus, 1520.

Cyril of Alexandria. See Clichtove, J.

Denzinger, H., *Enchiridion Symbolorum,* ed. K. Rahner. 30th edn. Freiburg im Breisgau, 1955.

Dietenberger, J., *Phimostomus Scripturariorum,* eds. E. Iserloh and P. Fabisch with J. Toussaert and E. Weichel. Corpus Catholicorum 38. Münster, 1985.

Eck, J., *Tres Orationes Funebres,* ed. J. Metzler. Corpus Catholicorum 16. Münster, 1930.

Enchiridion Locorum Communum, ed. P. Fraenkel. Corpus Catholicorum 34. Münster, 1979.

Ehses, S., *Römische Dokumente zur Geschichte der Ehescheidung Heinrichs VIII. von England, 1527–1534.* Paderborn, 1893.

Ellis, H., ed. *Original Letters, Illustrative of the English Reformation.* 11 vols. London, 1825–46.

Epistolae Aliquot Eruditorum Virorum. Basel: Froben, 1520.

Erasmus, D., *Novum Instrumentum.* 2 parts. Basel: Froben, 1516.

Novum Testamentum with *Annotationes* (2nd. edn. of above). Basel: Froben, 1519.

Apologia . . . qua respondet invectivis Eduardi Lei. Antwerp: Hillenius, 1520.

Responsio ad annotationes Eduardi Lei. Antwerp: Hillenius, 1520.

De Conscribendis Epistolis. Cambridge: Siberch, 1521. *STC* 10496.

Adversus Petri Sutoris . . . Debacchationem Apologia. Basel: Froben, 1525.

Opera Omnia. 10 vols. Leiden, 1703–6.

Opus Epistolarum Des. Erasmi Roterodami, ed. P.S. Allen. 12 vols. Oxford, 1906–47.

Paraphrases on Romans and Galatians, ed. R.D. Sider. CWE 42. Toronto, 1984.

The Correspondence of Erasmus 1519–1520, tr. R.B. Mynors, annotated P.G. Bietenholz. CWE 7. Toronto, 1987.

Enchiridion Militis Christiani, tr. C. Fantazzi. CWE 66. Toronto, 1988.

Erasmus, D., ed. See Alger, Hilary, Irenaeus, Jerome and Seneca.

Fabri, J., *Opuscula.* Leipzig: Wolrab, 1538.

Fox, R., *Letters of Richard Fox 1486–1527,* ed. P.S. Allen and H.M. Allen. Oxford, 1920.

Foxe, J., *Acts and Monuments,* ed. G. Townsend. 8 vols. London, 1843–9.

Galatinus, P., *De Arcanis Catholicae Fidei.* Ortona: Suncinus, 1518.

Garin, E., ed. *Prosatori Latini del Quattrocento.* Milano e Napoli, 1952.

Gerson, J., *Oeuvres Complètes.* 10 vols. Paris, 1960–73.

Grandval, M. de, *Apologia seu Defensorium*. Paris: Bade, 1518.

Tutamentum et Anchora. Paris: Bade, 1519.

Gray, G.J., 'Letters of Bishop Fisher, 1521–3'. *The Library*, 3rd. ser., 4 (1913), pp. 133–45.

Harpsfield, N., *The Life and Death of Sir Thomas Moore, Knight*, ed. E.V. Hitchcock and R.W. Chambers. EETS orig. ser. 186 (1932).

Henry VIII, *Assertio Septem Sacramentorum*. London: Pynson, 1523. *STC* 13083.

Divorce Tracts of Henry VIII, ed. E. Surtz and V. Murphy. Angers, 1987.

Hermelink, H., ed. *Die Matrikeln der Universitat Tübingen*. Tübingen, 1906.

Hilary of Poitiers, *Lucubrationes*, ed. D. Erasmus. Basel: Froben, 1523.

Hitchcock, E.V. See Harpsfield, N.

Hughes, P., ed. *Saint John Fisher: the earliest English life*. London, 1935.

Hughes, P.L. and Larkin, J.F., eds. *Tudor Royal Proclamations*. 3 vols. New Haven and London, 1964–9.

Hymers, J. See Fisher's works.

Illustrium Virorum Epistolae. N.p., 1519.

Irenaeus, *Adversus Haereses*, ed. D. Erasmus. Basel: Froben, 1526.

Jerome, *Opera Omnia*, ed. D. Erasmus. 9 vols. Basel: Froben, 1516.

Langdaile, A., *Catholica Confutatio . . . N. Ridlaei*. Paris: Vascosanus, 1556.

Larkin, J.F. See Hughes, P.L.

Latimer, H., *Sermons*, ed. G.E. Corrie. Parker Soc. Cambridge, 1844.

Latomus, J., *Opera Omnia*. Louvain: Gravius, 1550.

Leathes, S.M., ed. *Grace Book A*. Cambridge, 1897.

Lee, E., *Apologia Edoardi Leei contra quorundam calumnias*. Paris: Gourmont, n.d.

Leedham-Green, E.M., *Books in Cambridge Inventories*. 2 vols. Cambridge, 1986.

Lefèvre d'Etaples, J., *In Epistolas Pauli*. 2nd edn. Paris: Estienne, 1516.

De Maria Magdalena, et triduo Christi disceptatio. Paris: Estienne, 1517.

De Maria Magdalena, triduo Christi, et ex tribus una Maria, disceptatio. Paris: Estienne, 1518.

Letters and Papers, Foreign and Domestic, of the Reign of Henry VIII, 1509–47. eds. J.S. Brewer, J. Gairdner and R.H. Brodie. 21 vols. London, 1862–1910.

Luther, M., *D. Martin Luthers Werke*. Kritische Gesammtausgabe. Weimar, 1883–

Enarrationes . . . in Epistolas Petri. Strasbourg: Hervagius, 1525.

Epistolarum Farrago. Hagenau: Secer, 1525.

Madan, F., ed. 'The Day-Book of John Dorne', in *Collectanea I*. ed. C.R.L. Fletcher. Oxford Historical Soc. 1885.

Mayor, J.E.B., *Early Statutes of St John's College, Cambridge*. Cambridge, 1858.

Melton, W., *Sermo exhortatorius*. London: de Worde, n.d., *c.* 1510. *STC* 17806.

Mendoza, F., *De Naturali cum Christo Unitate*, ed. A. Piolanti. Lateranum Nova Series 1–4. Rome, 1948.

Migne, J.P. *Patrologiae Cursus Completus*. Paris.

More, T., *The Correspondence of Sir Thomas More*, ed. E.F. Rogers. Princeton, 1947.

Utopia, eds. E. Surtz and J.H. Hexter. CWTM 4. Yale, 1965.

Responsio ad Lutherum, ed. J.M. Headley. CWTM 5. Yale, 1969.

A Dialogue Concerning Heresies, eds. T.M.C. Lawler, G. Marc'hadour and R.C. Marius. CWTM 6. Yale, 1981.

Morison, R., *Apomaxis Calumniarum*. London: Berthelet, 1537.

Murphy, V. See Henry VIII.

Nichols, J.G., ed. *Chronicle of the Grey Friars*. Camden Soc. 53, 1852.

North Country Wills. Surtees Soc. 106 (1908).

Oecolampadius, J., *De Genuina Verborum Domini, Hoc Est Corpus Meum, Expositione Liber*. Hagenau: Secer, *c*. 1525.

Oldoinus, A., *Athenaeum Ligusticum*. Perugia, 1680.

Pace, R., *De fructu qui ex doctrina percipitur liber*. Basel: Froben, 1517.
  Praefatio in Ecclesiasten Recognitum ad Hebraicam Veritatem. London: Pynson, n.d., but certainly 1527. *STC* 19082.

Pagninus, S., *Sacra Biblia*. Lyons: du Ry, 1528.

Parker, R.E., ed. *The Middle English Stanzaic Versions of the Life of Saint Anne*. EETS orig. ser. 174. London, 1928.

Peryn, W., *Thre Sermons*. London: Herforde, n.d., *c*. 1546. *STC* 19785.5.

Peter Lombard, *Sententiae*. Spicilegium Bonaventurianum 4. 2 vols. Roma, 1971–81.

Philalethes Hyperboreus (pseud.), *Parasceve*. 'Luneberg: Golsen' [namely, Antwerp: Keyser], 1533.

Pico della Mirandola, G., *Opuscula*. Venice: Bernardinus Venetus, 1498.
  De Dignitate Hominis, ed. E. Garin. Respublica Literaria I. Berlin, 1968.

Pocock, N., *Records of the Reformation: the divorce 1527–1533*. 2 vols. Oxford, 1870.

Powell, E., *Propugnaculum Summi Sacerdotii Evangelici*. London: Pynson, 1523. *STC* 20140.

Raines, J., *The Historians of the Church of York and its Archbishops*. Rolls Series. 3 vols. London, 1886–94.

Ralph of Flaix, *In Mysticum Illum Moysi Leviticum Libri XX* (Cologne: Cervicorn, 1536).

Redman, J., *De Iustificatione*, ed. C. Tunstall. Antwerp: Withagus, 1555.
  A reporte of Maister Doctor Redmans answers. London: Reynold, 1551. *STC* 20827.

The Register of Thomas Rotherham, Archbishop of York 1480–1500. Part I, ed. E.E. Barker. Canterbury and York Soc. 69 (1976).

Reuchlin, J., *De Rudimentis Hebraicis*. Pforzheim: Anshelm, 1506.
  De Arte Cabbalistica. Hagenau: Anshelm, 1517.

Reusens, E. See Schillings, A.

Rhenanus, B., ed. *Opera Q. Septimii Florentii Tertulliani*. Basel: Froben, 1521.

Roper, W., *The Lyfe of Sir Thomas Moore, knighte*, ed. E.V. Hitchcock. EETS orig. ser. 197. London, 1935.

Rouschausse, J. See Fisher's works.

Sanuto, M., *I Diarii di Marino Sanuto*, ed F. Stefani, G. Berchet and N. Barrozzi. 58 vols. Venice, 1879–1903.

Schillings, A., with E. Reusens and J. Wils, eds. *Matricule de l'Université de Louvain*. 10 vols. 1903–67.

Scott, R.F., ed. 'Notes from the College Records'. *The Eagle* (privately printed magazine of St John's College, Cambridge) 16 (1891), pp. 341–57; 17 (1893), pp. 465–81; 31 (1910), pp. 323–58; 35 (1914) pp. 2–35.
  ed. *Records of St John's College, Cambridge*, 4th ser. (Cambridge, privately printed, 1934, p. 281.

Searle, W.G., *Grace Book Γ*. Cambridge, 1908.

Seneca, L.A., *Lucubrationes Omnes*, ed. D. Erasmus. Basel: Froben, 1515.

Smyth, R., *The Assertion and Defence of the Sacramente of the Aulter*. London: Herforde, 1546. *STC* 22815.

Starkey, T., *A Dialogue between Pole and Lupset*, ed. T.F. Mayer. Camden Soc. 4th ser. 37 (1989).

Stow, J. *Annales, or a Generall Chronicle of England*. London, 1631. *STC* 23340.

Surtz, E. See Henry VIII.

Sutor, P., *De Tralatione Bibliae et Novarum Reprobatione Interpretationum*. Paris: Petit, 1525.

Tapper, R., *Opera Omnia*. 2 vols. Cologne: Birckmann, 1582.

Tertullian. See Rhenanus, B.

Testamenta Eboracensia III, IV and V. Surtees Soc. 45 (1864), 53 (1869) and 79 (1884).

Third Report of the Deputy Keeper of the Public Records. London, 1842.

Traversagni di Savona, L.G., *Margarita Eloquentie Castigate*. St Alban's, 1480. *STC* 24190.

Trithemius, J., *Liber Octo Quaestionum*. Mainz, 1601.

Tunstall, C., *De Veritate Corporis Domini Nostri Iesu Christi In Eucharistia*. Paris: Vascosanus, 1554.

Van Ortroy, F., ed. 'Vie du Bienheureux Martyr Jean Fisher'. *Analecta Bollandiana* 10 (1891), pp. 121–365, and 12 (1893), pp. 97–287.

Vega, A. de, *De Vera Iustificatione*. Cologne: Quentell, 1572.

Vives, J.L. See Augustine of Hippo.

Wakefield, R., *Oratio de laudibus et utilitate trium linguarum*. London: de Worde, n.d., c. 1528. *STC* 24944.

Kotser Codicis. London: de Worde, n.d., c. 1534. *STC* 24943.

Syntagma de hebraeorum codicum incorruptione. London: Berthelet, n.d., c. 1534. *STC* 24946.

Wharton, H., *Anglia Sacra*. 2 vols. London, 1691.

Wils, J. See Schillings, A.

Wimpina, K., *Farrago Miscellaneorum*. Cologne: Soter, 1531.

Secondary literature

Albert, G., Parent, J.M., and Guillemette, A., 'La légende des trois mariages de Sainte-Anne'. *Etudes d'histoire littéraire et doctrinale du XIIIe siècle*. Publications de l'institut d'études médiévales d'Ottawa 1, 1932.

Bailey, T., *The Life and Death of that Renowned John Fisher Bishop of Rochester*. London, 1655.

Bainton, R.H., *Here I Stand: a life of Martin Luther*. London, 1951.

Erasmus of Christendom. New York, 1969.

Baker, T., *History of the College of St John the Evangelist, Cambridge*, ed. J.E.B. Mayor, 2 vols. Cambridge, 1869.

Bedouelle, G. and Le Gal, P., eds. *Le 'Divorce' du Roi Henry VIII: études et documents*. Travaux d'Humanisme et Renaisance 221. Geneva, 1987.

Benoit, P., 'L'inspiration des Septante après les Pères.' In *L'Homme devant Dieu: mélanges offerts au Père Henri de Lubac I, Theologie* 56 (1963), pp. 169–87.

Bietenholz, P.G. with Deutscher, T.B., eds. *Contemporaries of Erasmus*. 3 vols. Toronto, 1985–7.

Birch, D., *Early English Reformation Polemics*. Salzburg, 1983.

Bishop, E. See Gasquet, F.A.

Blench, J.W., *Preaching in England in the late Fifteenth and Sixteenth Centuries*. Oxford, 1964.

Bossy, J., *Christianity in the West*. Oxford, 1985.

Bouck, C.M., 'On the Identity of Papyrius Geminus Eleates'. *Transactions of the Cambridge Bibliographical Soc.* 2 (1958), pp. 352–8.

Bowker, M., *Secular Clergy in the Diocese of Lincoln*. Cambridge, 1968.
The Henrician Reformation: the diocese of Lincoln under John Longland 1521–1547. Cambridge, 1981.
Bradford, W., *Correspondence of the Emperor Charles V and his Ambassadors at the Courts of England and France*. London, 1850.
Bradshaw, B., 'The Christian Humanism of Erasmus'. *Journal of Theological Studies* 33 (1982), pp. 411–47.
Bradshaw, B. and Duffy, E., *Humanism, Reform and Reformation: the career of bishop John Fisher*. Cambridge, 1989.
Bridgett, T.E., *Life of Blessed John Fisher*. London, 1888.
Brown, P., *Augustine of Hippo*. London, 1968.
Bruce, J., 'Observations on the circumstances which occasioned the death of Fisher, bishop of Rochester'. *Archaeologia* 25 (1834), pp. 61–99.
Burnet, G., *History of the Reformation of the Church of England*, ed. N. Pocock. 7 vols. Oxford, 1865.
Chadwick, H., 'Ego Berengarius'. *Journal of Theological Studies* 40 (1989), pp. 414–45.
Chantraine, G., *Erasme et Luther: libre et serf arbitre*. Paris, 1981.
Clark, F., 'A new appraisal of late medieval theology'. *Gregorianum* 46 (1965), pp. 733–65.
Congar, Y., *Tradition and Traditions*, tr. M. Naseby and T. Rainsborough. London, 1966.
Cooper, C.H., *Annals of Cambridge*. 5 vols. Cambridge, 1842–1908.
Memoir of Margaret, Countess of Richmond and Derby. Cambridge, 1874.
Cooper, C.H. and T., *Athenae Cantabrigienses*. 2 vols. Cambridge, 1838–61.
D'Amico, J.F., 'Beatus Rhenanus, Tertullian and the Reformation'. *Archiv für Reformationsgeschichte* 71 (1980), pp. 37–60.
DeMolen, R.L., ed. *Essays on the Works of Erasmus*. Yale, 1978.
Denifle, H., *Die abendländischen Schriftausleger bis Luther über Justitia Dei und Justificatio*. Mainz, 1905.
Dewhurst, J., 'The alleged miscarriages of Catherine of Aragon and Anne Boleyn'. *Medical History* 28 (1984), pp. 49–54.
Deutscher, T.B. See Bietenholz, P.G.
Dickens, A.G., *Lollards and Protestants in the Diocese of York 1509–1558*. Oxford, 1959.
The English Reformation 2nd. edn. London, 1989.
Douglas, E.J.D., *Justification in Late Medieval Preaching: a study of John Geiler of Keysersberg*. SMRT 1. Leiden, 1966.
Duffy, E. See Bradshaw, B.
Elton, G.R., *Policy and Police: the enforcement of the Reformation in the age of Thomas Cromwell*. Cambridge, 1972.
Studies in Tudor and Stuart Politics and Government. 3 vols. Cambridge, 1974–83.
Reform and Reformation: England, 1509–1558. London, 1977.
Emden, A.B., *Biographical Register of the University of Oxford to 1500*. 3 vols. Oxford, 1957–9.
Biographical Register of the University of Cambridge to 1500. Cambridge, 1963.
Biographical Register of the University of Oxford, 1500–1540. Oxford, 1974.
Eubel, C., *Hierarchia Catholica Medii Aevi*. 8 vols. Münster and Padua, 1913–78.
Farge, J.K., *Orthodoxy and Reform in Early Reformation France*. SMRT 32. Leiden, 1985.
Farris, G., *Umanesimo e Religione in Lorenzo Guglielmo Traversagni di Savona*. Milan, 1972.

Fenlon, D.B., *Heresy and Obedience in Tridentine Italy: Cardinal Pole and the Counter Reformation*. Cambridge, 1972.

Fox, A. and Guy, J.A., *Reassessing the Henrician Age*. Oxford, 1986.

Friedman, J., *The Most Ancient Testimony*. Ohio, 1983.

Friedmann, P., *Anne Boleyn*. 2 vols. London, 1884.

Gasquet, F.A., and Bishop, E., *Edward VI and the Book of Common Prayer*. London, 1890.

Gebremedhin, E., *Life-Giving Blessing: an inquiry into the eucharistic doctrine of Cyril of Alexandria*. Studia Doctrinae Christianae Upsaliensia 17. Uppsala, 1977.

Gilson, J.P. See Warner, G.F.

Gleason, J.B., *John Colet*. Berkeley, 1989.

Godfrey, W.R., 'John Colet of Cambridge'. *Archiv für Reformationsgeschichte* 65 (1975), pp. 6–17.

Gogan, B., *The Common Corps of Christendom: ecclesiological themes in the writings of Sir Thomas More*. SHCT 26. Leiden, 1982.

Green, L.C., *How Melanchthon Helped Luther Discover the Gospel*. Fallbrook, 1980.

Guillemette, A. See Albert, G.

Gundersheimer, W.L., ed. *French Humanism 1470–1600*. London, 1969.

Harrison, W.J., *Notes on the Masters, Fellows, Scholars and Exhibitioners of Clare College, Cambridge*. Cambridge, 1953.

Headley, J.M., 'The Nos Papistae of Thomas More'. *Moreana* 64 (1980), pp. 89–90.

Heath, P., *The English Parish Clergy on the Eve of the Reformation*. London, 1969.

Hendrix, S.H., *Luther and the Papacy*. Philadelphia, 1981.

Herbrüggen, H.S., 'A Letter of John Eck to Thomas More'. *Moreana* 2, no. 8 (1965), pp. 51–8.

Hoehner, H.W., *Herod Antipas*. Soc. for New Testament Studies, Monograph Ser. 17. Cambridge 1972.

Hufstader, A., 'Lefèvre d'Etaples and the Magdalen'. *Studies in the Renaissance* 16 (1969), pp. 31–60.

Hughes, G.J., ed. *The Philosophical Assessment of Theology: essays in honour of Frederick Copleston*. Georgetown, 1987.

Hughes, J.J., *Stewards of the Lord: a reappraisal of Anglican orders*. London, 1970.

Hughes, P.E., *Lefèvre: Pioneer of Ecclesiastical Reform in France*. Grand Rapids, 1984.

Ives, E.W., *Anne Boleyn*. London, 1986.

James, M.R., *A Descriptive Catalogue of the Manuscripts other than Oriental in the Library of King's College, Cambridge*. Cambridge, 1895.

Janz, D.R., *Luther and Late Medieval Thomism: a study in late medieval anthropology*. Waterloo, Ontario, 1983.

Jedin, H., *A History of the Council of Trent*, tr. E. Graf. 2 vols. London, 1961.

Joyce, G. H., *Christian Marriage: an historical and doctrinal study*. London, 1933.

Kaufman, P.I., *Augustinian Piety and Catholic Reform: Augustine, Colet, and Erasmus*. Mercer University Press, 1982.

Kelly, H.A., *The Matrimonial Trials of Henry VIII*. Stanford, 1976.

Kelly, J.N.D., *Jerome*. London, 1975.

Klaiber, W., *Katholische Kontroverstheologen und Reformer des 16. Jahrhunderts. Ein Werkverzeichnis*. Reformationsgeschichtliche Studien und Texte 116. Münster, 1978.

Knowles, D., *The Religious Orders in England*. 3 vols. Cambridge, 1948–59.

Kristeller, P.O., *Iter Italicum*. 3 vols. London, 1963–

Kronenberg, M.E., 'Forged Addresses in Low Country Books in the Period of the Reformation'. *The Library* 5th ser. 2 (1947–8), pp. 81–94.

Lamping, A.J., *Ulrich Velenus and his Treatise against the Papacy*. SMRT 19. Leiden, 1979.

Leader, D.R., 'Professorships and Academic Reform at Cambridge: 1488–1520'. *Sixteenth Century Journal* 14 (1983), pp. 215–27.

'Teaching in Tudor Cambridge'. *History of Education* 13 (1984), pp. 105–19.

A History of the University of Cambridge. Cambridge, 1988.

Lewis, J., *The Life of Dr. John Fisher*, ed. T.H. Turner. 2 vols. London, 1855.

Lienhard, M., *L'Evangile et l'Eglise chez Luther*. Paris, 1989.

Lloyd Jones, G., *The Discovery of Hebrew in Tudor England: a third language*. Manchester, 1983.

Lohse, B., 'Marginalien zum Streit zwischen Erasmus und Luther'. *Luther* 1 (1975), pp. 5–24.

Lupton, J.H., *Life of John Colet*. New edn. London, 1909.

Lyons, H.P.C., 'The Sacrament of Restored Nature – St John Fisher on the Eucharist'. *Clergy Review* 40 (1955), pp. 520–7.

Macklem, M., *God Have Mercy: the life of John Fisher of Rochester*. Oberon Press, 1967.

Macy, G., *The Theologies of the Eucharist in the Early Scholastic Period*. Oxford, 1984.

Marius, R., 'More the conciliarist'. *Moreana* 64 (1980), pp. 91–9.

McConica, J., *English Humanists and Reformation Politics*. Oxford, 1965.

McCue, J.F., 'The Doctrine of Transubstantiation from Berengar through the Council of Trent'. *Harvard Theological Review* 61 (1968), pp. 385–430.

McGrath, A., *Luther's Theology of the Cross*. Oxford, 1985.

Iustitia Dei: a history of the Christian doctrine of justification. 2 vols. Cambridge, 1986.

Meyer, C.S., 'Henry VIII Burns Luther's Books'. *Journal of Ecclesiastical History* 9 (1958), pp. 173–87.

Moran, J.A.H., *The Growth of English Schooling: learning, literacy, and laicization in pre-Reformation York diocese*. Princeton, 1985.

Morin, G., 'Le Liber Dogmatum de Gennade de Marseille et problèmes qui s'y rattachent'. *Revue Bénédictine* 24 (1907), pp. 445–55.

New Catholic Encyclopedia. McGraw-Hill, Maidenhead, Berks., 1967.

Newman, J.H., *An Essay on the Development of Christian Doctrine*. London, 1845.

Difficulties of Anglicans. 2 vols. Reprint. London, 1909.

Nichols, J.G., ed. 'Inventories of the Wardrobes, Plate, Chapel Stuff, etc. of Henry Fitzroy'. *Camden Miscellany III*. Camden Soc., 1855.

Oakley, F., 'Headley, Marius and the matter of Thomas More's conciliarism'. *Moreana* 64 (1980), pp. 82–8.

Oberman, H.A., *The Harvest of Medieval Theology: Gabriel Biel and late medieval nominalism*. Cambridge, Mass., 1963.

Masters of the Reformation. Cambridge, 1981.

Owst, G.R., *Preaching in Medieval England: an introduction to the sermon manuscripts of the period c. 1350–1450*. Cambridge, 1926.

Parent, J.M. See Albert, G.

Pfaff, R.W., *New Liturgical Feasts in Later Medieval England*. Oxford, 1970.

Pico della Mirandola, G., *L'Opera e il Pensiero di Giovanni Pico della Mirandola nella Storia dell'Umanesimo*. 2 vols. Florence, 1965.

Pollen, J.H., 'Johannes Cochläus an König Heinrich VIII von England und Thomas More'. *Römische Quartalschrift* 13 (1889), pp. 43–9.

Polman, P., *L'Elément Historique dans la controverse religieuse du XVIe Siècle*. Gembloux, 1932.

Potter, G.R., *Zwingli*. Cambridge, 1972.

Power, D., *The Sacrifice We Offer: the Tridentine dogma and its reinterpretation*. Edinburgh, 1987.

Rahlfs, A., *Verzeichnis der griech Handschriften des Alten Testaments*. Göttlingen Nachschriften. Berlin, 1915.

Renouard, P., *Bibliographie des Imprimeurs et des Oeuvres de Josse Badius Ascensius*. 3 vols. Paris, 1908.

Rex, R.A.W., 'The English Campaign against Luther in the 1520s'. *Transactions of the Royal Historical Soc.* 5th ser. 39 (1989), pp. 85–106.

Reynolds, E.E., *Saint John Fisher*. London, 1955 (2nd. revd. edn., London, 1972).

Rose, P.L., 'Erasmians and Mathematicians at Cambridge in the early sixteenth century'. *Sixteenth Century Journal* 8 (1977), pp. 47–59.

Rouschausse, J., *La Vie et l'Oeuvre de John Fisher Evêque de Rochester*. Nieuwkoop, 1973.

Ruysschaert, J., 'Lorenzo Guglielmo Traversagni di Savona (1425–1503): un humaniste franciscain oublié'. *Archivum Franciscanum Historicum* 46 (1953), pp. 195–210.

Scarisbrick, J.J., *Henry VIII*. London, 1968.

The Reformation and the English People. Oxford, 1984.

Schofield, B., ed. *Muchelney Memoranda*. Somerset Record Soc. 42 (1927).

Screech, M.A., *Ecstasy and the Praise of Folly*. London, 1980.

Searle, W.G., *The History of the Queens' College of St Margaret and St Bernard*. Cambridge Antiquarian Soc. Publications 9, 1867.

Secret, F., *Les Kabbalistes Chrétiens de la Renaissance*. Paris, 1964.

Seebohm, F.H., *The Oxford Reformers*. 3rd edn. London, 1887.

A Short-Title Catalogue of books printed in England, Scotland and Ireland and of English books printed abroad 1475–1600. Eds. A.W. Pollard and G.R. Redgrave. 2nd edn. revised by W.A. Jackson, F.S. Ferguson and K.F. Pantzer. 2 vols. London, 1976–86.

Spahn, M., *Johannes Cochläus*. Berlin, 1898.

Stafford, W.S., 'Repentance on the Eve of the Reformation: John Fisher's sermons of 1508 and 1509'. *Historical Magazine of the Protestant Episcopal Church* 54 (1985), pp. 297–338.

Steinmetz, D.C., *Misericordia Dei: the theology of J. von Staupitz in its late medieval setting*. SMRT 4. Leiden, 1968.

Stubbs, W., *Registrum Sacrum Anglicanum*. 2nd edn. Oxford, 1897.

Surtz, E., *The Works and Days of John Fisher*. Cambridge Mass., 1967.

Swete, H.B., *An Introduction to the Old Testament in Greek*. Cambridge, 1902.

Swietlicki, C., *Spanish Christian Cabala*. Columbia, Miss., 1986.

Tavard, G.H., *Holy Writ or Holy Church*. London, 1959.

Thomas, M., 'Tunstall – Trimmer or Martyr?' *Journal of Ecclesiastical History* 24 (1983), pp. 337–55.

Tierney, B., *The Origins of Papal Infallibility 1150–1350*. SHCT 6. Leiden, 1976.

Trench, R.C., *Synonyms of the New Testament*. 7th edn. London, 1871.

Turner, C.H., 'The *Liber Ecclesiasticorum Dogmatum* attributed to Gennadius'. *Journal of Theological Studies* 7 (1906), pp. 78–99.

'The *Liber Ecclesiasticorum Dogmatum*: supplenda to *J.T.S.* vii. 78–99'. *Journal of Theological Studies* 8 (1907), pp. 103–14.

Ullmann, W., *Principles of Government and Politics in the Middle Ages*. London, 1961.

Underwood, M., 'The Lady Margaret and her Cambridge Connections'. *Sixteenth Century Journal* 13 (1982), pp. 67–81.

Vocht, H. de, *History of the Collegium Trilingue Lovaniense, part I*. Université de Louvain Recueil de Travaux d'Histoire et de Philologie, 3rd. ser., 42. Louvain, 1951.

Walker, G., 'Saint or Schemer? The 1527 Heresy Trial of Thomas Bilney Reconsidered'. *Journal of Ecclesiastical History* 40 (1989), pp. 219–38.

Warner, G.F., and Gilson, J.P., *A Catalogue of the Manuscripts in the Royal Library*. 4 vols. London, 1921.

Watson, A.G., *Medieval Libraries of Great Britain: a list of surviving books; supplement to the second edition*. Royal Historical Soc. Guides and Handbooks. London, 1987.

Wegg, J., *Richard Pace: Tudor diplomat*. London, 1932.

Weisheipl, J.A., *Friar Thomas d'Aquino*. Oxford, 1975.

Weiss, R., *Humanism in Fifteenth-Century England*. 3rd edn. Oxford, 1965.

Wiedermann, G., 'Martin Luther versus John Fisher: some ideas concerning the debate on Lutheran theology at the university of St Andrews, 1525–1530'. *Records of the Scottish Church History Soc.* 22 (1984), pp. 13–34.

Wilkie, W.E., *The Cardinal Protectors of England*. Cambridge, 1974.

Unpublished dissertations

Heal, F.J., 'The bishops of Ely and their diocese during the Reformation period: ca. 1510–1600'. Cambridge, Ph.D., 1971.

Murphy, V., 'The debate over Henry VIII's first divorce: an analysis of the contemporary treatises'. Cambridge, Ph.D., 1984.

Scarisbrick, J.J., 'The conservative episcopate in England 1529–1535.' Cambridge, Ph.D., 1955.

Index